Shot/Countershot

British Film Institute Cinema Series
Edited by Ed Buscombe

The British Film Institute Cinema Series opens up a new area of cinema publishing with books that will appeal to people who are already interested in the cinema but want to know more, written in an accessible style by authors who have some authority in their field. The authors write about areas of the cinema where there is substantial popular interest, but as yet little serious writing, or they bring together for a wider audience some of the important ideas which have been developed in film studies in recent years.

Richard Dyer: **Heavenly Bodies: Film Stars and Society**
Thomas Elsaesser: **New German Cinema: A History**
Lucy Fischer: **Shot/Countershot: Film Tradition and Women's Cinema**
Jane Feuer: **The Hollywood Musical**
Douglas Gomery: **The Hollywood Studio System**
Colin MacCabe: **Godard: Images, Sounds, Politics**
Steve Neale: **Cinema and Technology**

Series Standing Order

If you would like to receive future titles in this series as they are published, you can make use of our standing order facility. To place a standing order please contact your bookseller or, in case of difficulty, write to us at the address below with your name and address and the name of the series. Please state with which title you wish to begin your standing order. (If you live outside the United Kingdom we may not have the rights for your area, in which case we will forward your order to the publisher concerned.)

Customer Services Department, Macmillan Distribution Ltd
Houndsmills, Basingstoke, Hampshire, RG21 2XS, England.

Shot/Countershot

Film Tradition and Women's Cinema

Lucy Fischer

First published 1989

Published by
MACMILLAN EDUCATION LTD
Houndsmills, Basingstoke, Hampshire, RG21 2XS and London
Companies and representatives
throughout the world

Printed in the United States of America

British Library Cataloguing in Publication Data
Fischer, Lucy
Shot/countershot: Film tradition and women's cinema
    1. Cinema films. Women directors   2. Cinema films—Feminist viewpoints
I. Title
791.43′0233
ISBN 0-333-48060-0
ISBN 0-333-48061-9 pbk

For my aunt, Frances Levine

Contents

Illustrations

ILLUSTRATIONS

Acknowledgments

This book takes an intertextual approach to the issue of women and cinema—seeing each individual film as part of a network of those that preceded and followed it. I would be less than honest if I did not bring a similar perspective to my own work, which builds on that of others.

I would like to thank several people who read drafts of the manuscript-in-progress and offered me their helpful comments and suggestions. I am fortunate to have two extraordinary colleagues at the University of Pittsburgh who gave magnanimously of their time and insights: Marcia Landy and Dana Polan. Each was supportive of my work, in a manner that combined the best of professionalism and friendship. I am also grateful to Colin MacCabe for his encouragement concerning the publication of the book. The secretarial staff of the Department of English assisted in the preparation of the text: Pat Renkiewicz, Susan Berovik, and Gerri England.

Several scholars of women and film generously read the manuscript and contributed ideas toward its revision: Mary Ann Doane, Judith Mayne, Tania Modleski, Patricia Erens, and Linda Williams. Scott MacDonald shared with me several interviews with experimental filmmakers and made useful suggestions concerning films to consider. Channa Newman was good enough to translate sections of Gérard Genette's *Palimpsestes*.

I am also appreciative of the support of my former chairperson, Mary Louise Briscoe (now Dean of the College), for awarding me released time for this task. Robert Hinman, Director of Graduate Studies, kindly assigned me several capable graduate research assistants: Sean Monagle, Tanya Kotys, Mary Hall, Annie Ruefle, Mary Savanick and Steve Parks. Several grants from the Office of Research helped bring this project to fruition by paying for materials or a summer stipend. I am also indebted to the many students participating in my Women and Film classes over the years, who allowed me a context in which to test my ideas and offered their valuable observations.

I received much assistance from the staff of the Film and Video Section of the Carnegie Museum of Art. I benefited from the programming skills of Curator William Judson and of Assistant Curators Geralyn Huxley and Carol O'Sullivan. It was through the Carnegie that I first saw Yvonne Rainer's *The Man Who Envied Women*, Stephanie Beroes's *Recital*, Kathy Rose's performance pieces, and Doris Dörrie's *Straight through the Heart*. The staff was also exceedingly patient when I asked them for some bibliographic reference or photocopy.

For photographic stills, I thank Mary Corliss of the Museum of Modern Art/Film Stills Archive and Jenny Sussex of the British Film Institute. New Line Cinema kindly provided me with a still for *Straight through the Heart*, and RCA/Columbia Pictures Home Video provided me with one for *Sotto, Sotto*. I would also like to thank World Artists for giving me access to a tape of *The Eighties*. I am grateful to the filmmakers who loaned me frame enlargements: Yvonne Rainer, Kathy Rose, and Gunvor Nelson. Ms. Rainer also sent a script of her work to facilitate my transcription of direct quotations. Ms. Rose agreed to participate in an interview with me in the spring of 1986.

Parts of the book were previously published. A section of Chapter 5 appeared in *Film Quarterly* 30, no. 1 (Fall 1976): 2–11, and a segment of Chapter 6 was published in *Cinema Journal* 23, no. 1 (Fall 1983): 24–43. A part of Chapter 3 will appear in *Making Visible the Invisible* (Scarecrow Press). I would like to thank the editors who assisted in clearing the rights for those pieces: Chick Callenbach, Virginia Wexman, Dana Polan, and Carole Zucker. Most of all I am indebted to the editor of this volume, Joanna Hitchcock. From my first contact with her she has been personable, reliable, supportive, and extraordinarily capable—qualities that rarely coincide in the publishing (or any other) world. I would also like to thank Jay Wilson for his work on the British coproduction of this volume.

Several people within my family provided a "life-support system" for this project. My sister, Madeleine, convinced me that even humanists should use computers. I value the time she spent "retooling" me; this book would not be done without that process. I treasure my five-and-a-half-year-old son, David, for his patience with an author/mother—and for learning how to "exit" a program and turn the computer off. He also taught me (through the joy of his very existence) to "exit" and "turn off" in a more profound sense of the term—by insuring that work would be placed in a larger and richer context. I am beholden to my husband, Mark, for his help with this and all other endeavors—for his sanity, his strength, his generosity, and his faith in me.

Pittsburgh
July 1988

Shot/Countershot

Films are a way through which
we can re-imagine. —Yvonne Rainer

1 Pre/Texts: An Introduction

> *I believe that feminine artistic production takes place by means of a complicated process involving conquering and reclaiming, appropriating and formulating, as well as forgetting and subverting. In the works of . . . female artists . . . one finds artistic tradition as well as the break with it.*
> *—Silvia Bovenschen*[1]

Talking Back

Over the past decade, feminist criticism in the arts has followed two major paths. One route has examined works in the male canon, rereading them for patriarchal presuppositions masked by traditional scholarship. In literature, this perspective characterizes Simone de Beauvoir's pioneering analyses of Montherlant, Lawrence, Claudel, Breton, and Stendhal in *The Second Sex* and Kate Millett's methodology in *Sexual Politics*.[2] In the field of cinema, this approach forms the basis of such studies as Molly Haskell's *From Reverence to Rape*, Marjorie Rosen's *Popcorn Venus*, Sumiko Higashi's *Virgins, Vamps and Flappers*, E. Ann Kaplan's *Women in Film Noir*, and Mary Ann Doane's *The Desire to Desire*.[3] Other critics have found it equally fruitful to address the male-authored classics from a radically different vantage point, reading them (in a deconstructionist spirit) "against the grain" for their feminist moments or for textual "weak spots" where contradictions are revealed. Such an approach informs Tania Modleski's essay on *Letter from an Unknown Woman* (1948), Lucie Arbuthnot and Gail Seneca's discussion of *Gentlemen Prefer Blondes* (1953), and Lea Jacobs's piece on *Now, Voyager* (1942).[4]

[1] Silvia Bovenschen, "Is There a Feminine Aesthetic?" *New German Critique*, no. 10 (Winter 1977): 134.

[2] Simone de Beauvoir, *Le Deuxième Sexe* (Paris: Librairie Gallimard), 1949; Kate Millett, *Sexual Politics* (Garden City, N.Y.: Doubleday, 1970).

[3] Molly Haskell, *From Reverence to Rape: The Treatment of Women in the Movies* (Baltimore: Penguin, 1974); Marjorie Rosen, *Popcorn Venus: Women, Movies and the American Dream* (New York: Avon, 1973); Sumiko Higashi, *Virgins, Vamps and Flappers: The American Silent Movie Heroine* (St. Albans, Vt.: Eden Press Women's Publications, 1978); Mary Ann Doane, *The Desire to Desire: The Woman's Film of the 1940s* (Bloomington and Indianapolis: Indiana University Press, 1987).

[4] Tania Modleski, "Time and Desire in the Woman's Film," *Cinema Journal* 23, no. 3 (Spring 1984): 19–30; Lucie Arbuthnot and Gail Seneca, "Pretext and Text in *Gentle-*

The other broad path traversed by feminist critics has entailed the study of female artists in an attempt to underscore their existence or to establish consciousness of a woman's tradition. In the field of art history, Germaine Greer has adopted this stance in *The Obstacle Race*, as have Linda Nochlin and Ann Sutherland Harris in *Women Artists: 1550–1950*.[5] In literary studies, this perspective informs Patricia Meyer Spacks's *The Female Imagination*, Ellen Moers's *Literary Women: The Great Writers*, Sandra Gilbert and Susan Gubar's *The Madwoman in the Attic*, and Elaine Showalter's *A Literature of Their Own*.[6] In the area of cinema, Claire Johnston has drawn critical attention to Dorothy Arzner, one of the few female directors to work in Hollywood during the classical era.[7]

Even when one concentrates on the artwork of women, however, the male canon does not simply disappear. Contemporary criticism has reformulated the notion of literary history as a dynamic interplay of texts, and the feminist critic who focuses on the creations of female artists must yet decide how to position them, what intertextual network to assume. Again, the theorist confronts a fork in the road, a critical choice. Shall the work of women artists be situated within the preexistent male discourse? Or should it be constituted as a separate province, an alternate heritage?

Taking the first path are those theorists who claim that women's art should be integrated within the male canon, since female authorship is not a significant organizing principle. This position seeks to minimize the role of sexual difference, asserting that the art of women and of men are, fundamentally, the same. Minda Rae Amiran, for example, calls the current interest in women's writing "degrading" and its teach-

---

men Prefer Blondes," *Film Reader*, no. 5 (1982): 13–23; Lea Jacobs, "*Now Voyager*: Some Problems in Enunciation and Sexual Difference," *Camera Obscura*, no. 7 (1981): 89–109.

[5] Germaine Greer, *The Obstacle Race: The Fortune of Women Painters and Their Work* (New York: Farrar, Straus & Giroux, 1979); Ann Sutherland Harris and Linda Nochlin, *Women Artists: 1550–1950* (Los Angeles: Museum Associates of the Los Angeles Museum of Art, 1978).

[6] Patricia Meyer Spacks, *The Female Imagination* (New York: Knopf, 1975); Ellen Moers, *Literary Women: The Great Writers* (New York: Doubleday, 1976); Sandra Gilbert and Susan Gubar, *The Madwoman in the Attic: The Woman Writer and the Nineteenth-Century Literary Imagination* (New Haven, Conn.: Yale University Press, 1979); Elaine Showalter, *A Literature of Their Own: British Women Novelists from Brontë to Lessing* (Princeton, N.J.: Princeton University Press, 1977).

[7] Claire Johnston, ed., *Dorothy Arzner: Towards a Feminist Cinema* (London: British Film Institute, 1975).

4

ing "a subversion of women's liberation." "The whole point of leaving the doll's house," she continues, "was to become a person among people."[8]

Choosing the other broad critical road are those who argue that women's artwork can be bracketed from patriarchal culture—who embrace the notion of sexual difference and stress the "special" features of women's creative production. Annis Pratt, for example, speaks of her desire to investigate novels by women as "a self contained entity following its own organic principles."[9] Ultimately, she finds the works evincing a "core of feminine self-expression" and attributes the repeated patterns she detects to women's oppressed political standing.[10] Patricia Meyer Spacks also examines women's work as a separate enclave and finds "evidence of sharing . . . persistent ways of feeling," "patterns of self-depiction that survive the vagaries of change"[11]: "Women writing directly about their own lives in letters, journals, autobiographies, or indirectly in . . . fiction, demonstrate that the experience of women has long been the same, that female likenesses are more fundamental than female differences."[12] Like Pratt, she sees this woman's perspective as arising from social conditioning but finds it "an outlook sufficiently distinct to be recognizable through the centuries."[13]

French feminist critics have recently offered a more radical rationale for configuring women's artwork as a separate field. They see shared properties as arising not simply from common social influences or lived experiences but from inherent psychological and biological factors. Thus French psychoanalyst Luce Irigaray argues for the existence of a feminine mode of discourse, based on woman's unique sexual/anatomical make-up:

> *Woman has sex organs more or less everywhere.* She finds pleasure almost anywhere. . . . The geography of her pleasure is much more diversified, more multiple in its differences, more complex, more subtle, than is commonly imagined—in an imaginary rather too narrowly focused on sameness.
>
> "She" is definitely other in herself. This is doubtless why she is said to be whimsical, incomprehensible, agitated, capricious—not to mention her language in which "she" sets off in all direc-

---

[8] Minda Rae Amiran, "What Women's Literature?" *College English* 39 (1978): 653.

[9] Annis Pratt, *Archetypal Patterns in Women's Fiction* (Bloomington: Indiana University Press, 1981), x.

[10] Ibid.   [11] Spacks, 3.   [12] Ibid., 5.   [13] Ibid.

tions leaving "him" unable to discern the coherence of any meaning.[14]

In a similar vein, Hélène Cixous sees women's writing as evincing the mark of the feminine unconscious: "Things are starting to be written ... that will constitute a feminine Imaginary, the site, that is, of identifications of an ego no longer given over to an image defined by the masculine."[15]

There is, clearly, no single approach to the study of women's art; it is the critic's choice to assume the context germane to the reading proposed. Women's art has relevance to work created by males *and* females; each frame will provide its own fruitful insights. While asserting the worth of various perspectives, it is also crucial to see their limitations. To deny sexual difference and integrate women's work into the established tradition may prevent its marginalization, but it may ignore its noteworthy features—be they culturally, psychologically, or biologically determined. On the other hand, to emphasize sexual difference may highlight what is unique in women's art, but it can encourage essentialist thinking and the false impression that female artists operate outside of broader cultural history.

Perhaps there is a way to bridge the gap between these two opposing critical stances, to find a crossroads at which they intersect, allowing us to extract what is most valuable in each. Myra Jehlen argues for this perspective in "Archimedes and the Paradox of Feminist Criticism" and offers a possible trail. Using a geographical metaphor, she suggests that rather than view women's artwork as a separate "territory," we see it as "one long border" and concentrate on its fluid "interacting juxtaposition" with the patriarchal domain.[16] This translates into a methodology of "radical comparativism," whereby the work of female artists is related to that of men:

> Comparison reverses the territorial image along with its contained methodology and projects instead, as the world of women, something like a long border. The confrontation along that border between, say, *Portrait of a Lady* and *House of Mirth*, two literary worlds created by two gods out of one the-

[14] Luce Irigaray, *This Sex Which Is Not One*, trans. Catherine Porter (Ithaca, N.Y.: Cornell University Press), 28–29.

[15] Hélène Cixous, "Castration or Decapitation?" trans. Annette Kuhn, *Signs* 7, no. 1 (Autumn 1981): 52.

[16] Myra Jehlen, "Archimedes and the Paradox of Feminist Criticism," *Signs* 6, no. 4 (Summer 1981): 582.

matic clay, can light up the outer and most encompassing parameters (perimeters) of both worlds.[17]

But to say that feminist studies should take a comparative approach is not to indicate what the precise nature of that comparison might be. Other theorists have offered leads in that direction—critics who differ greatly in their ideological positions. Art historian Linda Nochlin rejects the notion of an essential feminine mode but sees women's art as unified by a shared subversion of the established order:

> I often see woman's style as being partly conditioned by opposition, as having meaning in the context of being opposed to existing styles—I find analogies in how [women artists] invent in opposition to what's prevailing, but I don't find a common thread and I don't think that's necessary.[18]

French critic Julia Kristeva has called woman "a perpetual dissident" who is "here to shake up, to disturb, to deflate masculine values and not to espouse them."[19] For her, "a feminist practice can only be negative, at odds with what already exists."[20]

What critics as diverse as Nochlin and Kristeva are arguing is not only to view women's artwork diacritically (its meaning seen as difference from the male standard) but to regard it as aggressively establishing a *counter-heritage*. This perspective allows the theorist to note common features in women's artwork while still asserting its relation to the dominant mode. There is no need, then, to look for static, innate patterns in women's creations or for a universal feminine style. Yet one need not abandon the idea of a female artistic tradition. Rather, a unity may be found in women's collective dissension from the mainstream culture—a revolt that arises from historical rather than archetypal exigencies.

The elaboration of a feminist counter-heritage contains certain assumptions. In much criticism, an equation is made between *dominant* and *patriarchal* culture, with a further implication that the practitioners of that mode are *male*. Not all works by men will replicate conven-

[17] Ibid., 585.

[18] Linda Nochlin, quoted in Lucy Lippard, *From the Center: Feminist Essays on Women's Art* (New York: Dutton, 1976), 84–85.

[19] Julia Kristeva, quoted in Josette Feral, "The Powers of Difference," in Hester Eisenstein and Alice Jardine, eds., *The Future of Difference* (New Brunswick, N.J.: Rutgers University Press, 1985), 92.

[20] Julia Kristeva, in *About Chinese Women*, quoted in Gayatri Spivak, "French Feminism in an International Frame," *Yale French Studies*, no. 62 (1981): 169.

tional structures; there are always some artists who gravitate toward the avant-garde. And the work of all male artists need not be patriarchal; being a man does not necessarily commit one to that position. But what literary and film criticism of the past decade has revealed is the regrettable likelihood of that equation's being sustained—the sheer magnitude of cases in which the established male canon has reflected masculine values. Feminist theorists can thus be excused for taking on the terminology as a kind of "shorthand," assuming that feminist artists will be women countering sexist works by men. Though the terms are not synonymous, they have all too frequently coincided. In truth, it would be more precise to use the label "patriarchal" for the mode against which women artists have rebelled, for that epithet is devoid of any association with a particular sex or creative practice.

In raising the notion of rebellion in artistic creation, the work of Harold Bloom immediately comes to mind. In such books as *The Anxiety of Influence*, *A Map of Misreading*, and *Kaballah and Criticism*, he articulates a theory of poetic influence that posits the artist as engaged in a struggle against some prior creator[21]: "A poet . . . is not so much a man speaking to men as a man rebelling against being spoken to by a dead man (the precursor) outrageously more alive than himself."[22] According to Bloom, the artist achieves his personal style only by "misreading" the work of his central predecessor: "To live, the poet must *misinterpret* the father, by the crucial act of misprision, which is the re-writing of the father."[23] Because of Bloom's view of the psychodynamics of authorship, his theory emphasizes the intertextual aspects of literary history. "Influence," as he conceives it, "means there are *no* texts, but only relationships *between* texts."[24]

While some of Bloom's insights are quite relevant to our discussion, his position poses serious problems for feminists.[25] The authors he examines are exclusively male, thus implying that female writers have never been part of true literary history. Even the language he uses to describe the psychology of creation has a decidedly masculine strain. He talks of poets as "men speaking to men" and of their process of

[21] Harold Bloom, *The Anxiety of Influence: A Theory of Poetry* (New York: Oxford University Press, 1973); *A Map of Misreading* (New York: Oxford University Press, 1975); *Kaballah and Criticism* (New York: Seabury, 1975).
[22] Bloom, *Map*, 19.   [23] Ibid.   [24] Ibid., 3.
[25] See Annette Kolodny, "A Map for Rereading: or, Gender and the Interpretation of Literary Texts," *New Literary History* 11, no. 3 (Spring 1980): 451–67; Joanne Fait Diehl, "Come Slowly Eden: An Exploration of Woman Poets and Their Muse," *Signs* 3, no. 3 (1978): 572–87.

rebellion as an Oedipal act of "re-writing the father." Finally, his notion of the struggle between artistic generations exudes a tone of machismo. He envisions poets "war[ring] against one another in the strife
of Eternity" and conceives of "poetic strength" as arising from "a
triumphant wrestling with the greatest of the dead."[26]

What Bloom fails to confront is the possibility that the writer may
be female. As Joanne Fait Diehl notes:

> Although Bloom keeps alluding to the sexual aspects of the
> poet's dilemma, he repeatedly avoids the question raised by his
> own speculations, "What if the poet be a woman?" But how
> might the process of influence differ for women poets, and how
> do women poets perceive their relation to a male-dominated
> tradition?[27]

When Bloom does concede the notion of female writers, he sees their
presence as establishing a radical *dis*continuity, thus ignoring the possibility of their interacting with the canon itself:

> I prophesy . . . that the first true break with literary continuity
> will be brought about in generations to come, if the burgeoning
> religion of Liberated Woman spreads from its clusters of enthu-
> siasts to dominate the West. Homer will cease to be the inevi-
> table precursor, and the rhetoric and forms of our literature
> then may break at last from tradition.[28]

While it is perhaps forward-thinking of Bloom to imagine an exclusively female tradition (where Homer could no longer function as primal progenitor), it is retrograde to assume that such an occasion would
fracture historical lineage—that women writers could never engage in
an intertextual dialogue with their male counterparts.

I will assert that they do. But I do not suggest that we simply invert
Bloom's model—seeing women writers as creative "daughters" mired
in Romantic, symbolic battle with their artistic "parents." Such a paradigm carries with it all the drawbacks of an individualistic and Freudian approach to creation. Rather, I argue that we envision women's art
as engaged in an oppositional struggle with the patriarchal tradition—
not out of some personalized Oedipal or Electral desire to replace the
parent but, rather, out of a wish simply to speak *at all*. For the canon/
cannon has functioned aggressively to intimidate and silence women.

In *The Madwoman in the Attic: The Woman Writer and the Nine-*

[26] Bloom, *Map*, 5, 9.   [27] Fait Diehl, 572–73.   [28] Bloom, *Map*, 33.

9

teenth-Century Literary Imagination, Sandra Gilbert and Susan Gubar address Bloom's theories of influence. After analyzing the link between authorship and paternity, they note how the creative impulse is thwarted in women. They ask: "If the pen is a metaphorical penis, with what organ can females generate texts?"[29] While male authors feel free to address tradition, women can only circulate as images in those canonical texts:

> Implicit in the metaphor of literary paternity is the idea that each man ... has the ability, even perhaps the obligation, to *talk back* to other men by generating alternative fictions of his own. Lacking the pen/penis which would enable them similarly to refute one fiction by another, women in patriarchal societies have historically been reduced to *mere* properties, to characters and images imprisoned in male texts.[30]

Thus Gubar and Gilbert reject Bloom's "anxiety of influence" as inapplicable to the female author. They envision her instead, as experiencing "an even more primary 'anxiety of authorship'—a radical fear that she cannot create, that because she can never become a 'precursor' the act of writing will isolate or destroy her."[31]

Contemporary French feminists agree that patriarchal discourse renders woman mute. Hélène Cixous remarks how

> the complete set of symbolic systems—everything said, everything organized as discourse—art, religion, family, language—everything that seizes us, everything that forms us—everything is organized on the basis of hierarchal oppositions which come back to the opposition man/woman.[32]

Because language serves the male, feminists must "grab culture by the word, as it seizes us in its word." Cixous maintains "that political thought cannot do without ... work on language."[33] If discourse is tainted with sexism, it follows that female artists must refuse the dominant tradition—must "destroy in order to create." [34]

This notion necessitates a revamping of Bloom's view of influence as a highly personal, psychological dynamic. Whereas he sees the young male poet as rebelling against a specific literary antecedent in order to fashion his individual style, we can envision the woman artist as op-

---

[29] Gilbert and Gubar, 7.   [30] Ibid., 12 (my italics).   [31] Ibid., 48–49.
[32] Cixous, quoted in Donna Stanton, "Language and Revolution: The Franco-American Disconnection," in Eisenstein and Jardine, 73.
[33] Ibid.   [34] Jehlen, 583.

posed to patriarchal tradition as a whole—without the need to focus on some particular figure whom she seeks to annihilate or succeed. The necessity for woman's discursive rebellion (as a precondition of her speaking) also radically revises Bloom's notion of artists as willfully "misreading" the work of their predecessor. In the case of female writers, no such *mis*interpretation is required to sow the seeds of opposition. Where there is blatant misogyny, misprision is not at issue in the act of revolt. As Judith Fetterley has noted, a feminist's first act "must be to become a resisting rather than assenting reader."[35] In a similar vein, Gubar and Gilbert stress that the woman writer must reject her male precursor's "reading of *her*."[36]

Gubar and Gilbert also posit a *dialectical* stance in woman's artistic production. They see women writers as having conceived of "fictional worlds in which patriarchal images and conventions [are] severely, radically revised"[37]: "Such writers, therefore, both participated in and . . . 'swerved' from the central sequences of male literary history, enacting a uniquely female process of . . . redefinition."[38]

This view has also informed the writing on feminist film. Claire Johnston has spoken of a "counter-cinema" that creates new meanings by "disrupting the fabric of male bourgeois cinema within the text of the film."[39] She has urged women's cinema "to interrogate" the dominant mode.[40] Laura Mulvey has also argued that a feminist avant-garde cinema "can . . . only exist as a counterpoint" to the dominant tradition.[41] More recently, Mary Ann Doane, Linda Williams, and Patricia Mellencamp have asserted that a "feminist discourse on film can only be written as a . . . re-vision, of the more orthodox canon."[42] And Annette Kuhn has spoken of a feminist "deconstructive" cinema whose "character at any moment is always shaped, in an inverse manner by dominant cinema."[43]

[35] Judith Fetterley, *The Resisting Reader: A Feminist Approach to American Fiction* (Bloomington: Indiana University Press, 1978), xxii.

[36] Gilbert and Gubar, 49.   [37] Ibid., 44.   [38] Ibid., 73.

[39] Claire Johnston, "Woman's Cinema as Counter-Cinema," in Patricia Erens, ed., *Sexual Stratagems: The World of Women in Film* (New York: Horizon, 1979), 140.

[40] Ibid.

[41] Laura Mulvey, "Visual Pleasure and Narrative Cinema," in Gerald Mast and Marshall Cohen, *Film Theory and Criticism*, 3rd ed. (New York and Oxford: Oxford University Press, 1985), 805.

[42] Mary Ann Doane, Patricia Mellencamp, and Linda Williams, eds., *Re-Vision: Essays in Feminist Film Criticism* (Frederick, Md.: American Film Institute and University Publications of America, 1984), 2.

[43] Annette Kuhn, *Women's Pictures* (London: Routledge & Kegan Paul, 1982), 161.

What I will suggest is that we extend and *literalize* this metaphor of a confrontational cinema and conceive of women's artwork as engaged in an argumentative discourse with patriarchal culture—in an ongoing critical "debate." In *The Female Imagination*, Patricia Meyer Spacks sees women as traditionally entrapped by male society and deterred from creating their own discursive forms.

> Women serve as guardians of culture, upholders of society. They go to the symphony on Friday afternoon, they act as volunteer guides in the art museums, they campaign . . . against dirty movies.
> *They talk about the culture men create.*[44]

But to "talk about" male culture should not be viewed as an entirely passive enterprise, for such an act contains the possibility of critique and reevaluation.

What I propose is that we examine women's art within the context of works by men—not in order to factor it into some hallowed tradition, or to hierarchize it within a canon, but rather to envision it as engaged in an ongoing *intertextual debate*. Myra Jehlen points out that "women cannot write monologues; there must be two in the world for one woman to exist, and one of them has to be a man."[45] It is this concept of women's art in *dialogue* with male culture that I wish to advance. If, as Spacks would have it, women have been in the habit of talking "about" patriarchy, they have also been known to talk "*back*."

To facilitate this imaginary "argument of texts," I will organize each chapter around films on similar topics: some made by men, some by women. My analysis will demonstrate how the latter works critique, "rewrite," and even "exorcise" the former—films that have been chosen to represent the cinematic "norm," be it the classical or art-cinema mode. Unlike Bloom, I will not postulate any real historical influence between works, although this is always possible. (Norwegian director Anja Breien, for example, made *Wives* [1975] as a direct response to John Cassavetes's *Husbands* [1970]; avant-garde filmmaker Carolee Schneeman made *Fuses* [1964–67] as a reaction to Stan Brakhage's *Loving* [1956]; Marjorie Keller made *Misconception* [1977] with Brakhage's birth films in mind.)[46] The debate I envision, however, is

---

[44] Spacks, 227 (my italics).   [45] Jehlen, 584.

[46] See Gorham Kindem, "Norway's New Generation: Anja Breien, Vibeke Lokkeberg, and Laila Mikkelsen," paper presented at the meeting of the Society for Cinema Studies, New York City, June 1985; and David James, "Interventions by Women in Three Phases of the Pre Feminist Avant-Garde," paper presented at the meeting of the Society for Cinema Studies, New Orleans, April 1986.

primarily *fictional*, yet one that illuminates the nature of feminist creation. Thus, when I pose *Riddles of the Sphinx* (1977) as "addressing" *The Lady from Shanghai* (1948), I am not claiming that Laura Mulvey and Peter Wollen had the Welles film in mind. Rather, I am using the comparative framework as a rhetorical device to emphasize how feminist work must counter the artifacts of the dominant culture. In *Pursuits of Happiness* (a treatise on screwball comedy), Stanley Cavell asserts that Ibsen's *A Doll's House* posed a *"problematic* to which the genre of remarriage constitutes a . . . response."[47] It is this sense of artworks as establishing a "problematic" that subtends my construction of an imaginary intertextual debate—a quandary to which other works must react.

There is a particular advantage to arranging the book in this fashion. In *Gender and Reading*, Patrocinio P. Schweickart asserts that feminist criticism involves a dual dynamic. The story "will have *at least* two chapters," she notes, "one concerned with feminist readings of male texts, and another with feminist readings of female texts."[48] My model solicits *both* approaches in each chapter. This structure allows us to envision two opposing positions for the female viewer. In confronting the patriarchal cinema, she will find limited room for modes of progressive identification. In addressing the feminist film, however, she will find that a greater space opens up. Hence, this methodology facilitates a step away from cynicism. As Schweickart notes, the move to women's writing "brings with it a shift in emphasis from the negative hermeneutic of ideological unmasking to a positive hermeneutic whose aim is the recovery and cultivation of women's culture."[49]

Other productive insights arise from considering the feminist reader. It is possible to see women artists who fashion a counter-cinema as, first and foremost, *readers* of dominant film. As Jonathan Culler has noted, writing is only "the historical praxis of reading made visible."[50] Thus there is a match between feminist filmmaking and my own critical task—two parallel modes of analysis. While I read both male- and female-authored texts, the latter will already incorporate interpreta-

---

[47] Stanley Cavell, *Pursuits of Happiness* (Cambridge, Mass., and London: Harvard University Press, 1981), 23 (my italics).

[48] Patrocinio P. Schweickart, "Reading Ourselves: Toward a Feminist Theory of Reading," in Elizabeth A. Flynn and Patrocinio P. Schweickart, eds., *Gender and Reading: Essays on Readers, Texts, and Contexts* (Baltimore and London: Johns Hopkins University Press, 1986), 39.

[49] Ibid., 51.

[50] Jonathan Culler, "Presupposition and Intertextuality," *Modern Language Notes* 19, no. 6 (1976): 1382–83.

tions of the former. Over the past two decades, scholars have noted this interplay between film theory and production. As Johnston has stated: "If film criticism . . . is to have any use, . . . it should provide a greater understanding of how film operates which will ultimately feed back into filmmaking itself."[51]

In juxtaposing works, I have aimed at a wide range of texts, allowing them to intermix through "artificial insemination." Thus I might compare a mainstream film like Busby Berkeley's *Dames* (1934) with an avant-garde musical like Chantal Akerman's *The Eighties* (1985), without respecting rigid generic boundaries. Similarly, for works of the patriarchal cinema I have chosen not only classical texts (like *Letter from an Unknown Woman* [1948]) but art films (like *Persona* [1966]). While certain theorists (like Laura Mulvey) have favored experimental work as the ideal counter-cinema (since it opposes not only the content but the language of traditional film), other critics (like Annette Kuhn and E. Ann Kaplan) have suggested that conventional texts can make feminist statements as well.[52] I endorse the broader view, and my selection of women's films ranges from the anti-illusionism of *Riddles of the Sphinx* through the modernism of *The Girls* (1969) to the realism of *Girlfriends* (1978). Significantly, most of the traditional works I consider have been made in the independent sector; hence, despite their orthodox style, they resist the ethos of the dominant cinema.

In collocating men's and women's films, I draw on contemporary theories of intertextuality. In "The Limits of Pluralism," J. Hillis Miller characterizes the literary work as "inhabited . . . by a long chain of parasitical presences, echoes, allusions, guests, ghosts of previous texts."[53] Similarly, in "The Death of the Author," Roland Barthes talks of the text as "a multi-dimensional space in which a variety of writings, none of them original, blend and clash." He sees the artwork as "a tissue of quotations drawn from the innumerable centres of culture."[54] The author "can only imitate a gesture that is always anterior, never original. His only power is to mix writings, to counter the ones with

---

[51] Claire Johnston, ed., *Notes on Women's Cinema*, Screen Pamphlet 2 (London: SEFT, 1973 [repr. 1975]), 3.

[52] See Annette Kuhn's discussion of the "new women's film" in *Women's Pictures*, 136–40; see E. Ann Kaplan's discussion of "The Realist Debeate in the Feminist Film" in *Women and Film: Both Sides of the Camera* (New York: Methuen, 1983), 125–41.

[53] J. Hillis Miller, "The Limits of Pluralism III: The Critic As Host," *Critical Inquiry* 3, no. 3 (Spring 1977), 446.

[54] Roland Barthes, *Image Music Text*, trans. Stephen Heath (New York: Hill and Wang, 1977), 146.

the others."⁵⁵ Though Barthes finds each work "woven entirely with citations," he does not endorse a search for "origins": "To try to find the 'sources,' the 'influences' of a work, is to fall in with the myth of filiation; the citations which go to make up a text are anonymous, untraceable, and yet *already read*: they are quotations without inverted commas."⁵⁶

It is this sense of intertextuality that I wish to suggest in my critical model. Of necessity, women's artwork must confront the male canon—must constitute a web of citations from it. By offering a critical model that literally counterposes feminist and patriarchal films, I hope to illuminate this discursive process. In so doing, I will not suggest that the latter are in any way "sources" for the former. Rather, I see women's films as addressing texts that are "anonymous, untraceable . . . *already read*." I also find feminist films *revising* works from the dominant canon, or, to borrow a phrase from Geoffrey Hartman, rewriting "words already uttered, texts . . . already written."⁵⁷

Literary critics have often tried to categorize modes of intertextuality, and I will periodically invoke these schemata. Most useful is the taxonomy proposed by Michael Riffaterre in "Syllepsis":

> So far as I can make out, there are *three types of intertextuality*: first, the *complementary* type (every sign has a reverse and an obverse; the reader is forced to interpret the text as the negative, in the photographic sense, of its intertext); second, the *mediated* type (where the reference of text to intertext is effected through the intercession of a third text functioning as interpretant that mediates between sign and object. . . .); and third, the *intratextual* type (where the intertext is partly encoded within the text and conflicts with it because of stylistic or semantic incompatibilities).⁵⁸

Also relevant are the theories of Gérard Genette, who, in *Palimpsestes*, explicates various modes of textual "transcendence."⁵⁹ For Genette, *hypertextuality* signifies a relation "uniting Text B . . . to an anterior Text A . . . upon which it [Text B] grafts itself." He calls the latter work a text "in the second degree"—one derived from another

⁵⁵ Ibid.   ⁵⁶ Ibid., 160.
⁵⁷ Geoffrey H. Hartman, "The Culture of Criticism," *PMLA* 99, no. 3 (May 1984): 382.
⁵⁸ Michael Riffaterre, "Syllepsis," *Critical Inquiry* 6, no. 4 (1980): 627.
⁵⁹ Gérard Genette, *Palimpsestes: La Littérature au Second Degré* (Paris: Seuil, 1982), 10, trans. Channa Newman.

15

preexistent artifact.[60] For Genette, hypertextuality is a universal aspect of literature, but certain works evince this quality more overtly than others. "The less massively and explicitly asserted the hypertextuality of a work," he notes, "the more its analysis depends on . . . an interpretive decision of the reader." Thus Genette boasts that he can decide that the *Confessions* of Rousseau are a "remake" of those of Saint Augustine: such matters are ultimately affairs of "critical ingenuity."[61] I find support for my model in Genette's theories. If all women's films are entwined in a hypertextual network with those of the dominant tradition, I can make the "interpretive decision" to throw that relationship into relief.

Genette uses the word "remake" to describe the relationship between hyper- and hypo-text. The same terminology arises (in a different context) in Teresa de Lauretis's book *Alice Doesn't*. While discussing feminist films, she writes:

> *Rebecca* . . . could be remade in several ways, some of which may actually be already available as films: *Les Rendez-Vous d'Anna*, or *Jeanne Dielman* (Chantal Akerman), *Thriller* (Sally Potter), probably many others. *Marnie* could be interestingly remade as *Sigmund Freud's Dora* . . . and *Vertigo* definitely should be remade as *Bad Timing*.[62]

It is this sense of feminist films as "remakes" of the canon that I will pursue in my model by juxtaposing works that share certain thematic and stylistic features. For example, on the issue of woman and myth, I will see *Riddles of the Sphinx* as a "remake" of *The Lady from Shanghai*, while on the topic of female friendship I will compare George Cukor's *Rich and Famous* (1981) with Claudia Weill's *Girlfriends*. On the subject of the actress, I will juxtapose Ingmar Bergman's *Persona* with Mai Zetterling's *The Girls*; and on the question of romance— Max Ophuls's *Letter from an Unknown Woman* with two films by women: Stephanie Beroes's *Recital* (1978) and Doris Dörrie's *Straight through the Heart* (1983). On the theme of the femme fatale, I will compare Claude Chabrol's *Violette* (1978) with Marleen Gorris's *A Question of Silence* (1981), and on the topic of the female double, certain 1940s melodramas (*A Stolen Life* [1946], *Cobra Woman* [1944], *The Dark Mirror* [1946]) with several women's films (Mulvey/Wollen's *The Bad Sister* [1983] and Margarethe von Trotta's *Sisters, or*

---

[60] Ibid., 11–12.   [61] Ibid., 16.

[62] Teresa de Lauretis, *Alice Doesn't: Feminism, Semiotics, Cinema* (Bloomington: Indiana University Press, 1984), 157.

The Balance of Happiness [1979]). In a chapter that focuses on genre, I will compare a mainstream musical like *Dames* with several feminist works: Dorothy Arzner's *Dance, Girl, Dance* (1940), Akerman's *The Eighties*, and the performance pieces of Kathy Rose (1983). In *Women's Pictures*, Annette Kuhn has remarked that "deconstructive cinema is always . . . casting a sideways look at dominant cinema."[63] By placing films in a diptych or triptych frame, I imagine them stealing an oblique glance at one another, articulating a critical/historical "eyeline match."

Given my assertion of an intertextual network, I find it interesting that many recent women's films incorporate quotations within their discourse. Ulriche Ottinger invokes the figure of Dr. Mabuse in *The Mirror-Image of Dorian Gray in the Yellow Press* (1984). In *Sigmund Freud's Dora* (1979), the filmmakers include a series of pornographic excerpts and television advertisements. In Lina Wertmuller's *Sotto, Sotto* (1984), characters discuss *Notorious* (1946), *Divorce Italian Style* (1962), and *The Red Desert* (1964). In Ellen Hovde and Mirra Bank's *Enormous Changes at the Last Minute* (1983), lovers go to the movies and watch *Intermezzo* (1939). In Connie Fields's *The Life and Times of Rosie the Riveter* (1980), sequences from 1940s documentaries are intercut with contemporary interviews. Since the structure of these films replicates, on a formal level, the intertextual dialogue that I create within the book, I devote a final chapter to one of them— Yvonne Rainer's *The Man Who Envied Women* (1985).

I must issue certain caveats for my approach. The process of defining feminist cinema is a monumental project and not the task of this book, which focuses on criticism. My use of the term draws on Kuhn's formulation of feminism as entailing an analysis of "the social/historical position of women as subordinated, oppressed or exploited either within dominant modes of production . . . and/or by the social relations of patriarchy."[64] I have tended to apply the label in a broad rather than a narrow sense, overcoming the fear of reserving the appellation for works assured of garnering the seal of approval from all critics. While the oppositional films I consider highlight women's subaltern social or cinematic placement, they do not necessarily offer solutions to those problems or advance entirely positive female screen images. I have nonetheless included them in a discussion of feminist film to the extent that they surface crucial questions concerning sexual difference.

The question of locating wherein the feminism of a particular work resides is also a tricky one. Can it be said to exist in the author's inten-

[63] Kuhn, 161.   [64] Ibid., 4.

tions? Within the "content" of the text? Or within the reader's response to the work? While I reject the first formulation, my view of the issue falls somewhere between the second and the third. I agree with recent theory that has stressed the reader's power to create meaning in a dynamic interplay with the text, but I also believe that the semantic construction of certain works predisposes us to respond in a particular way. For this reason, some may ask whether I have allowed adequate "space" for the female viewer (who may locate in a work of apparent sexism some empathic strain). While I respect the viewer's ability partially to transcend and transform a text, I am also concerned that such a skill may lull her into complacency, may dull her sense of the dangers of the discourse: "What? Me worry?"

I should also state that, in focusing on a counter-cinema, I do not mean to imply that *all* woman's creations will be oppositional. Even those who speak of a "feminine" discourse acknowledge that the writer's sex is no guarantee of this mode. Cixous remarks: "Most women . . . do someone else's—man's—writing, and in their innocence, sustain it and give it voice, and end up producing writing that's in effect masculine."[65] Elaine Showalter also speaks of an "imitative" stage in the history of women's writing, marked by "*internalization* of [male] standards of art and views on social roles."[66] Thus there will always be female artists (like Ida Lupino) whose work conforms to the patriarchal standard.[67] In arguing for a woman's counter-cinema, I am obviously making a conscious selection—though it is one that reveals an important trend. The works that I consider are also limited to the Western, middle-class tradition, and I have not attempted to generalize my conclusions to other cultural terrains.

It must also be said that women have no monopoly on feminist art. As filmmaker Nelly Kaplan has written: "Men can . . . make non-misogynic films, once in a million, or twice, when they touch the androgynic state of grace required."[68] In Chapter 8, I will openly confront this issue by *reversing* the paradigm I establish, looking at a male-authored film (John Sayles's *Lianna* [1983]) that is more enlightened than its female-authored counterpart (Lina Wertmuller's *Sotto, Sotto*). Here the feminist film is created by a man, and the patriarchal one by a woman.

Though I will stress the links between female- and male-authored

[65] Cixous, 52.   [66] Showalter, 13.

[67] See Wendy Dozoretz, "The Mother's Lost Voice in *Hard, Fast, and Beautiful,*" *Wide Angle* 6, no. 3 (1984): 50–57.

[68] Nelly Kaplan, in Claire Johnston, ed., *Notes*, 23.

18

works, I do not mean to deny the existence of influence between women. While I do not spotlight this relationship, the point does arise in my discussion of certain films (e.g., Stephanie Beroes's quotation of Carolee Schneeman and Billie Holiday in *Recital*, Yvonne Rainer's allusion to Babette Mangolte, Martha Rosler, and Trisha Brown in *The Man Who Envied Women*). I will also examine how women filmmakers recoup (as "precursors") certain female mythic figures (like the Sphinx in *Riddles of the Sphinx* or the Witch in *The Bad Sister*).

The contrast I invoke between the politics of patriarchal and feminist works is not altogether a clear one, since the former may display progressive elements. In my discussion of *Dames*, for example, I will read the film "against the grain" and find in it a virtual treatise on voyeurism—a fact that almost "redeems" its misogyny. Although I establish feminist and patriarchal cinema as contra-dictions—discourses opposed to each other—I admit the contradictions *within* each mode that deny their status as monolithic or coherent systems. I am reminded of Judith Mayne's observation that the most challenging work on women and film addresses that very paradox.[69] But to see these inconsistencies in patriarchal texts, it is necessary to approach them in an open fashion. As Elizabeth Flynn writes, all too often a feminist reader either "resists the text and so deprives it of its force, or the text overpowers the reader and so eliminates the reader's powers of discernment." She imagines a third possibility in which "reader and text interact with a degree of mutuality . . . and so create a kind of dialogue."[70] It is this dynamic that I will seek to maintain.

Another important question is whether the notion of a women's counter-cinema locks us into a posture of negation or traps us in the role of the Other, solidifying the male/female dichotomy of which Cixous speaks. As Irigaray has shown, however, patriarchal notions of woman's sexual *difference* are often based more profoundly on the assumption of *sameness*, on the "old dream of symmetry." Thus she emphasizes how Freud conceptualized female sexuality "on the basis of 'masculine' parameters."[71] Hence, perhaps, we can conclude that for women it is not *true* difference that is problematic but the *misread-*

[69] Judith Mayne, "Review Essay: Feminist Film Theory and Criticism," *Signs* 11, no. 1 (Autumn 1985): 83.

[70] Elizabeth Flynn, "Gender and Reading," in Flynn and Schweickart, *Gender and Reading*, 268.

[71] Irigaray, *This Sex*, 68; and *Speculum of the Other Woman*, trans. Gillian G. Gill (Ithaca, N.Y.: Cornell University Press, 1985). See the section of *Speculum* entitled "The Blind Spot of an Old Dream of Symmetry," 11–129.

19

ing of that term. In film studies, the notion of difference takes on another layer of complexity. While critics have repeatedly shown how the dominant cinema assumes a binary sexual division, cinema's illusion of movement, in fact, depends on the *denial* of difference between frames.[72] Thus, within the very technical mechanism of the cinematic medium, a paradox of difference is sustained.

Feminist thinkers have recently found new value in the notion of difference. Carolyn Burke argues that we attempt "to see woman not as man's 'other,' as in the negative sense of 'difference,' but as a plurality of meanings, . . . recharg[ing] the concept with a new, more positive valence."[73] It is this revamped sense of difference that I invoke in my discussion of women artists, who are not simply man's other but other than *that*.

In configuring an imaginary dialogue between texts, I risk creating fantasies that rival those of the films I consider: Hartman has duly noted the critic's "debt to fiction."[74] My method also privileges the theorist's imagination as the site of intertextual juncture. Riffaterre admits that intertextuality is "a modality of perception" and conceives of the intertext as the corpus of works "the reader may legitimately connect with the one before his eyes." This *oeuvre* "can go on developing forever in accordance with the reader's cultural level; it will expand as his readings expand and as more texts are published that can be linked up to the original point whence these associated memories took their departure."[75]

The intertextual approach also assumes a highly active role for the spectator/reader, who must simultaneously configure several works. Carmela Perri lays out a five-stage process by which the perceiver assimilates the "allusion markers" within the derivative text:

1. The audience *comprehends* the literal, un-allusive significance of the allusion-marker.
2. The audience *recognizes* the allusion-marker to be an echo of a past source text.
3. The audience does not fully understand the alluding text

[72] For a discussion of how the cinema "masks" the difference between film frames, see Jean-Louis Baudry, "Ideological Effects of the Cinematographic Apparatus," *Film Quarterly* 28, no. 2 (Winter 1974–75): 42.

[73] Carolyn Burke and Jane Gallop, "Rethinking the Maternal," in Eisenstein and Jardine, 107.

[74] Geoffrey H. Hartman, *The Fate of Reading and Other Essays* (Chicago and London: University of Chicago Press, 1975), x.

[75] Riffaterre, 625, 626–27.

upon recognition of source text and *realizes* that construal is required.

4. The audience *remembers* aspects of the source text's intension.

5. The audience *connects* one or more of these aspects with the alluding text to complete the allusion-marker's meaning.[76]

Thus the intertextual approach presumes the cognitive curiosity, patience, and agility of its audience.

My method circumvents the framework of traditional history, permitting films to interact within a synthetic time/space. Thus I allow myself certain critical leaps—as artificial as those of the dancer in Maya Deren's *A Study in Choreography for Camera* (1945). Johnston's views on historical method are relevant here; in discussing Dorothy Arzner, she argues against a traditional approach to the filmmaker's work:

> Merely to introduce women into the dominant notion of film history, as yet another series of "facts" to be assimilated into the existing notions of chronology, would quite clearly be sterile and regressive. . . . Only an attempt to situate [women's] work in a theoretical way would allow us to comprehend [their] real contribution to film history.[77]

It is such a context that I wish to establish—one that evades more conventional notions of fact and chronology.

In writing about women's studies, Peggy Kamuf recognizes the need for the discipline to "locate itself on the map of the known world's division—either in a canonical mainstream . . . or in an outlying and unexplored region."[78] Ultimately, Kamuf has doubts about this dichotomy and finds it merely a convenient intellectual conceit. She questions "the capacity of any map to represent more than a fiction of the world's contours." Given this uncertainty, she claims that "feminist practice can have its greatest force if, at the same time as it shifts the sands of historical sedimentation, it leaves its own undecidable margins of indeterminacy visible, readable on the surface of the newly countoured landscape."[79] In creating the framework that I do, I endorse the spirit of Kamuf's words. If I configure a new "map" of the critical terrain, I aspire to leave the "margins of indeterminacy visible."

[76] Carmela Perri, "On Alluding," *Poetics* 7, no. 3 (September 1978): 301.

[77] Johnston, *Dorothy Arzner*, 2.

[78] Peggy Kamuf, "Replacing Feminist Criticism," *Diacritics* 12 (Summer 1982): 46.

[79] Ibid., 46–47.

21

My critical stance draws upon many strains of feminist and film theory. Perhaps the strongest influence is psychoanalytic criticism—an orientation that informs my discussions of *The Lady from Shanghai*, *Riddles of the Sphinx*, *Letter from an Unknown Woman*, *The Bad Sister*, *Dames*, and *Violette*. Many of the chapters return to the question of Oedipal structures in film—an issue that has recently received much scholarly attention. Throughout the book, however, I invoke other sources: literary hermeneutics (in my discussion of the figure of the double); sociological perspectives (in my examination of female friendship, the woman criminal, and heterosexual romance); formal analysis (in discussions of *Recital* or *The Eighties*); genre study (in my analysis of the musical); and poststructuralism (in my reading of the textual "instabilities" of *Dames, Violette*, or *Sotto, Sotto*). Rather than impose a predetermined methodology upon each film, I have tried to allow the nature of the work to suggest an approach. Rather than align myself with one particular critical "camp," I have tried to extract productive strategies from various theoretical models. Just as I have resisted any narrow focus in filmic material (delimiting my discussion to experimental or modernist or traditional texts), so I have drawn on a broad spectrum of critical stances. In avoiding a monolithic approach, I am reminded of a statement by Mary Gentile, who, in *Film Feminisms: Theory and Practice*, says:

> Let us not define feminist film theory . . . by its opposition to or its exclusion of other film theories—the semiotic, psychoanalytic, structuralist, auteurist, or avant-garde. Rather let feminist film theory be that which exists in the spaces between all these theories.[80]

It is within that intertextual "space" that my critical position resides.

Finally, I would like to offer a series of metaphors for my approach, taken from film and photographic terminology, each of which casts my project in a slightly different light. Among early photographic viewing devices was the stereopticon—an instrument used to impart a three-dimensional effect to two images of the same scene taken at slightly different angles and viewed through binocular eyepieces. I see the works that I pair, thematically, in this book as extensions of those stereoscopic prints and hope that the framework I provide will add critical "depth" to the manner in which they are perceived. Extending the fig-

---

[80] Mary Gentile, *Film Feminisms: Theory and Practice* (Westport, Conn.: Greenwood Press, 1985), 5.

ure even further, one can also see the stereopticon as quintessentially an intertextual device, requiring, as it does, the viewer to apprehend two works simultaneously.

I also find a parallel for my approach in the cinematic sense of montage, which entails a connection between diverse celluloid materials brought together by the editor's sleight of hand. Implicit in this concept is the potential for artificial relations—the conjunction of filmic artifacts that bear only imaginary links. Lev Kuleshov hailed cinema's ability to create a "synthetic geography" that could attach the stairs of one building to the door of another, the face of one woman to the body of a second.[81] I like to think that my linkage of filmic texts is in the spirit of the medium, which gives both artists (and critics) the urge to juxtapose. I also find in the Eisensteinian formulation of montage another crucial lesson. It is hoped that through the "collision" of films arranged in this book, certain new meanings are created that might have remained submerged without the act of collocation.[82]

In classical film language, there is a pattern called *shot/countershot* that is frequently used to edit an encounter between two individuals. In the first shot of this trope, the spectator might see a character (Ms. A), and it is understood that the camera frames her from a second character's point of view (Mr. B, who is offscreen). As Ms. A looks at the camera, the audience imagines that she looks at them, and they are temporarily "sewn into" the filmic enunciation. With the next cut, the structure is reversed—and the spectator sees Mr. B from Ms. A's visual stance. If we imagine the history of cinema in terms of this model, we come to a rather disturbing conclusion: although we have watched countless images of women, as seen from a male perspective—and (as viewers) have been "stitched into" the filmic discourse—women have rarely been accorded the privilege of the reverse-angle view. If, according to the old saw, children should be seen, not heard, then we might say that women should be seen, not *see*. As Linda Williams has shown, even when woman looks in the classical cinema, she is likely to view only a distorted, masculine vision of herself.[83]

---

[81] Lev Kuleshov, discussed in V. I. Pudovkin, *Film Technique and Film Acting*, trans. Ivor Montagu (New York: Grove Press, 1970).

[82] Gentile mentions the concept of montage in Chapter Four of *Film Feminisms*, which concerns Eisenstein, 25–45. For Eisenstein's discussion of the term, see *Film Form*, trans. and ed. Jay Leyda (New York: Harcourt, Brace & World, 1949).

[83] Linda Williams, "When The Woman Looks . . ." in Mary Ann Doane et al., *Re-Vision*, 83–99.

Perhaps this is why many women filmmakers have disrupted the shot/countershot structure in their creations, as though to underscore its traditional containment of the female.[84] By juxtaposing male- and female-authored films, I am trying to "restore" this trope on another level—to advance woman's suppressed reverse-angle vision, her submerged countershot. In so doing, I aspire to recoup not only woman's vision but her discourse—to provide a cinematic "*voice-over*" for the canonical track. As Judith Fetterley writes: "Feminist criticism represents the discovery/recovery of a voice . . . a uniquely powerful voice, capable of canceling out those other voices."[85]

Test Case: Fatima's Revenge

> *A nude . . . is a picture for men to look at, in which Woman is constructed as an object of somebody else's desire.*
> —*T. J. Clark*[86]

I would like to rehearse and demonstrate my methodology on two short works. In a reel of American "Films of the 1890s," circulated by the Museum of Modern Art, there are two texts of special interest to the feminist critic. The first, *Morning Bath* (1896), shows a woman standing at a table with a basin of water. She holds an infant in the tub and washes him with soap. Like most children, he cries, but, unlike others, he does so in perpetuity. The second film, *Fatima* (1897), depicts the routine of a famous belly dancer who had achieved notoriety at the Chicago Columbian Exposition of 1893. The film is shown in two versions, censored and uncensored.

Here, neatly registered on this reel of primitive film, are the two polar roles of woman's existence (the madonna and the whore) and the two favored spheres of her operation (the domestic and the theatrical). For the moment, however, my interests lie in the latter realm: in woman's cinematic figuration as "showgirl"—a privileged representation of the female from the very birth of the cinema.

[84] Mary Gentile sees a denial of this trope in *A Question of Silence*; Annette Kuhn finds a refusal of it in *Jeanne Dielman* (1975); E. Ann Kaplan finds a subversion of it in *Sigmund Freud's Dora*. See Gentile, 158–59; Kuhn, 175; Kaplan, 146.

[85] Fetterley, xxiii.

[86] T. J. Clark, *The Painting of Modern Life: Paris in the Art of Manet and His Followers* (New York: Knopf, 1985), 131. Although I will be focusing on the work of John Berger in this section, the work of T. J. Clark on the representation of the nude and of the prostitute is also very useful and insightful.

In *Ways of Seeing*, John Berger has examined this image of woman—one that he finds exemplary of her status in patriarchal culture:

> *Men act* and *women appear*. Men look at women. . . . Thus [woman is] . . . an object—and most particularly an object of vision: a sight.[87]

Berger applies the term "surveyor" to the male voyeuristic stance, but he notes that woman incorporates this process of scrutiny into her own behavior:

> A woman must continually watch herself. She is almost continually accompanied by her own image of herself. Whilst she is walking across a room, or whilst she is weeping at the death of her father, she can scarcely avoid envisaging herself walking or weeping.[88]

Berger also discusses the competition that surrounds woman's physical appearance and finds the "beauty contest" a paradigm of this economy:

> Those who are not judged beautiful are *not beautiful*. Those who are, are given the prize. The prize is to be *owned* by a judge—that is to say, to be available for him.[89]

Though Berger does not examine woman's representation in the cinema, he does deal with the female nude in European oil painting, and many of his insights are relevant to woman's semiotic placement in film. He notes, for example, the importance of the absent subject in the dynamics of the genre—the man who apprehends the nude from outside the picture frame:

> In the average European oil painting of the nude the principal protagonist is never painted. He is the spectator, in front of the picture and he is presumed to be a man. Everything is addressed to him. . . . It is for him that the figures have assumed their nudity. But he, by definition, is a stranger—with his clothes still on.[90]

Berger also asserts that the portrayal of the female nude is a highly stylized one, at odds with her figuration as "natural." She is consistently represented as languid and passive, denoting that "women are

[87] John Berger, *Ways of Seeing* (London: British Broadcasting Corporation and Penguin, 1978), 47.
[88] Ibid., 46.   [89] Ibid., 52, (final italics mine).   [90] Ibid., 54.

25

there to feed an appetite, not to have any of their own."[91] Her face is arranged with a "come-on" look, which is "the expression of a woman responding with calculated charm to the man whom she imagines looking at her."[92] Because of this conventionalized demeanor, Berger claims that the nude is not really naked:

> To be naked is to be oneself. To be nude is to be seen naked by others and yet not recognized for oneself. . . . To be on display is to have the surface of one's own skin . . . turned into a disguise. . . . Nudity is a form of dress.[93]

Finally, Berger claims that within the iconographic system of the nude painting, the woman is frequently "blamed" for her eroticism:

> You painted a naked woman because you enjoyed looking at her, you put a mirror in her hand and you called the painting "Vanity," thus morally condemning the woman whose nakedness you had depicted for your own pleasure.[94]

Fatima demonstrates Berger's conception of the showgirl as an object for man's specular consumption (see fig. 1). The belly dancer is positioned at center stage, with the camera watching her from an ideal theater viewer's seat. She is framed frontally, in long shot, her body fully figured and contained. Her scant costume jangles with coins— icons of the prize she garners for being judged beautiful, for embodying male expectations.

Typical of cinematography in this era, the camera is static, staring at her for the duration of the film. She dances before it, undulating left and right across the screen; and it seems possible that the camera has been overcranked to emphasize the sensual quality of her movements. If she has desires of her own, we cannot read them, for she is fashioned to fulfill the fantasies of the male voyeur, who (like the spectator of a painted nude) remains invisible, outside the frame. Comparable to women in European painting, Fatima is symbolically "blamed" for the sensuality she exudes, this time by the stroke of the censor's brush, which obliterates her erogenous zones (see fig. 2).

Almost eighty years after Fatima's famous dance, Gunvor Nelson, an American experimental filmmaker, produced *Take Off* (1973). Though no apparent link exists between the two disparate works, they form an intertextual network—with the latter film critiquing and rewriting the earlier documentary.

[91] Ibid., 55.   [92] Ibid.   [93] Ibid., 54.   [94] Ibid., 51.

Take Off begins with an abstract, white line drawing set against a black background. At first the animation is difficult to decipher, but it soon forms the figure of a woman. The graphic lines gradually coalesce into a photographic image of a showgirl (Ellion Ness) dancing against a black void. To the accompaniment of raunchy jazz music, she executes a striptease, sequentially divesting herself of furs, dress, hose, bra, pasties, panties, and G-string. As we watch her performance, however, various cinematic techniques *interfere* with our voyeuristic pleasure. Her image is frequently doubled or tripled in superimposition, obscuring our erotic view. A similar effect is achieved by the blending of images through dissolves. Other shots (of her fishnet stockings or sequined costume) are rendered in extreme close-up, segmenting her body and removing it from our full apprehension. Certain shots (like those of her fan dropping) are presented in sluggish slow motion, while others (her bumps and grinds) are accelerated, thus lessening their sensuous spell. This visual static (or "ungrammaticality") is reminiscent of the "scrambling" process that Riffaterre finds indicative of derivative works:

> Where the text contains words, phrases or sentences also found in a hypogram [intertext] but with their order changed; and where, further, the links in the sequence they form in the hypogram have been perhaps completely destroyed, or at least bypassed or made implicit—that is scrambling.[95]

When Nelson's dancer is completely "nude," a strobe light begins to pulsate. As though to continue her striptease, she reaches for her head and removes a wig, tossing it to the spectator like one more garment. She then "unscrews" her legs, ears, breasts, arms, nose, and head, and hurls them toward the camera. Finally, her bare torso is launched into outer space, where it orbits like a vagrant asteroid.

The message of the film is clear. As the showgirl *takes off* her clothes, Nelson *takes off* the stag film—a genre that *takes* woman *off* to nowhere. In its status as parody, *Take Off* illustrates the intertextual mode that Riffaterre deems "complementary," in which "the reader is forced to interpret [a] text as the negative, in the photographic sense, of its intertext."[96] Through this inversion, Nelson reveals the corporeal violence at the stag genre's core/corps. For the showgirl dismembers herself as though she were an object, an automaton designed for male sight. Her actions also emphasize the fragmentation of the female body

[95] Riffaterre, "Intertextual Scrambling," *Romanic Review* 68 (1977): 199.
[96] Riffaterre, "Syllepsis," 627.

27

1. *Fatima* (uncensored/1897). *Fatima* demonstrates John Berger's conception of the showgirl as an object for man's specular consumption.

that obtains in patriarchal culture—that is manifest in an obsession with big breasts, shapely legs, or blonde hair. As Rosalind Coward notes, even *women* "think about their bodies in terms of parts, separate areas ... the foundation for an entirely masochistic or punitive relationship with one's own body."[97]

Unlike the typical showgirl, Nelson's subject is not "attractive" by traditional male standards. She is overweight and well beyond the "first blush of youth." Neither does she sport a provocative look. Instead, she bears a smug and cynical grin—an expression that mocks the viewer's sense of superiority and control (see fig. 3). Rather than submit to self-blame, she tosses guilt back at the spectator, who recoils from the unexpected scenes of disfigurement. "Is this what you *really* want?" she seems to inquire. In this respect, Nelson's *Take Off* bears a similarity to Manet's *Olympia* (1865)—a painting that T. J. Clark claims renders the nude "embarrassing."[98]

In Freud's essay "Medusa's Head" (1922), he advances the theory

[97] Rosalind Coward, *Female Desire* (London: Paladin Granada Publishing, 1984), 43–44.
[98] Clark, 131.

28

2. *Fatima* (censored/1897). Fatima is symbolically "blamed" for the sensuality she exudes.

that the image of decapitation signifies the fear of castration. "To decapitate = to castrate," he writes.[99] The fact that a mythic *woman* suffers this fate makes clear the anxiety that men feel toward the female body as a site devoid of any comforting phallic presence.

By aggressively confronting the spectator of *Take Off* with images of dismemberment and decapitation, Nelson not only reveals the violence to women at the heart of pornography but also alludes to the psychological dynamics that subtend its discourse: man's fear of the female body and his attendant need to master it through voyeuristic possession. Perhaps even the notion of the striptease itself enacts this dread of castration, of things being "taken off," as it were.[100] As though to articulate this tension of presence and absence, the stripper plays peek-a-boo with the spectator, hiding parts of her body, then making them reappear.[101]

[99] Sigmund Freud, "Medusa's Head," in Philip Rieff, ed., *Sexuality and the Psychology of Love* (New York: Collier, 1963), 212.

[100] For a discussion of dismemberment in the trick film, see Linda Williams, "Film Body: An Implantation of Perversions," *Ciné-Tracts* 3, no. 4 (Winter 1981): 19–35.

[101] Clark, 135. He points out, in his discussion of the nineteenth-century nude, that

29

3. *Take Off* (1973). Nelson's showgirl (Ellion Ness) bears a smug and cynical grin, mocking the viewer's superiority and control.

Freud reads the snakes on the Medusa's head as phallic substitutes that compensate for the missing organ. He also discusses the horror that men feel at the sight of her, which "makes the spectator *stiff with terror*."[102] Freud links this final image to the process of excitation/erection. Nelson's showgirl also fills the viewer with horror and, in this way, reveals that the striptease is a *dance macabre*—for the woman who performs and for the man who fuels his needless fear of women.

If Fatima assumes a rather languorous pose in her turn-of-the-century film, Nelson's contemporary exotic dancer takes an aggressive stance—in this sense, she "talks back" to the earlier text and to the viewers who have watched it. But it is in a modern poem that she truly "recoups" her voice. In "Belly Dancer," Diane Wakoski challenges the treasured male view that the showgirl performs for *him*—"offering up her femininity as the surveyed."[103] Instead, Wakoski conceives the dancer as addressing other women to apprise them of their repressed, sensual bodies:

> While the men simper and leer
> Glad for the vicarious experience and exercise
> They do not realize how I scorn them
> Or how I dance for their frightened,
> unawakened, sweet women.[104]

---

often the hand placed at the model's crotch reveals that "*nothing*" is precisely "what has to be hidden."

[102] Freud, 212 (my italics).   [103] Berger, 55.

[104] Diane Wakoski, "Belly Dancer," in Mary Anne Ferguson, ed., *Images of Women in Literature*, 2nd ed. (Boston: Houghton Mifflin, 1977), 321.

It is this interior monologue that I imagine I hear (as a "voice-over") in Nelson's *Take Off*—one that not only speaks for woman but (to paraphrase Fetterley) seems capable of canceling out those other voices. Hence, while Nelson's stripper seems to have the last laugh, Fatima may have the last word.

2 Mythic Discourse

The myth of womanhood flourishes not in the carefully wrought prescriptions of sages, but in the vibrant half-life of popular literature and art, forms which may distill the essence of a culture though they are rarely granted culture's weighty imprimatur. —Nina Auerbach[1]

Nina Auerbach has claimed that in order to comprehend the mythos of an era we must investigate its mass culture rather than its canonical forms of art: there we will unearth the epoch's vision of woman. Earlier, Claire Johnston applied a similar insight to film, finding myth "the major means in which women have been used in the cinema."[2] While the screen image of woman may appear entirely "natural," it is frequently imbued with tendentious stereotypes: the madonna, the vamp, the Amazon. As she notes, "Myth transmits and transforms the ideology of sexism and renders it invisible."[3]

For this reason, Johnston opposes a purely sociological analysis of cinema—one that accepts realism and denies the existence of symbolic discourse. Rather, she believes that "it is in the nature of myth to drain the sign (the image of woman/the function of woman in the narrative) of its meaning and superimpose another."[4]

In this chapter we will examine "myth in operation" by establishing an intertextual dialogue between two works: *The Lady from Shanghai* (1948) and *Riddles of the Sphinx* (1977). On a superficial level, no more disparate films could be found. The former is an American commercial narrative made in the late 1940s and the latter an independent, avant-garde British feature of the 1970s. Yet the two can be seen as constituting a curiously matched pair, an engaging (if seemingly incompatible) couple. If *The Lady from Shanghai* proposes a masked mythology on the subject of woman, *Riddles* actively interrogates that system, reformulating it from a feminist perspective.

[1] Nina Auerbach, *Woman and the Demon: The Life of a Victorian Myth* (Cambridge, Mass., and London: Harvard University Press, 1982), 10.

[2] Claire Johnston, "Myths of Women in the Cinema," in Karyn Kay and Gerald Peary, eds., *Women and the Cinema: A Critical Anthology* (New York: Dutton, 1977), 409.

[3] Ibid.   [4] Ibid., 410.

The Lady from Shanghai: Myths Embraced

> To say that woman is mystery is to say, not that she is silent,
> but that her language is not understood; she is there but
> hidden behind veils. . . . What is she? Angel, demon, one
> inspired, an actress? . . . perhaps in her heart she is even for
> herself quite indefinable: a sphinx. —Simone de Beauvoir[5]

The Lady from Shanghai was made in 1946, a difficult period
in Orson Welles's personal and professional life. After bursting on the
Hollywood scene as a wunderkind in 1940, he had suffered many de-
feats. Though a critical success, *Citizen Kane* (1941) was a box-office
failure, as was his next film, *The Magnificent Ambersons* (1942). A
third work, *It's All True* (1941–1942), was never completed; and
Welles assigned another director, Norman Foster, to finish his final film
for RKO, *Journey into Fear* (1942). *The Stranger*, in 1946, did nothing
to redeem his reputation as poison with the Hollywood financiers.
Welles's private life was also in shambles. His marriage to actress Rita
Hayworth was troubled, and the couple had already separated.[6]

About this time, Welles secured the rights to a Sherwood King novel,
If I Die before I Wake, and tapped it as the source of the screenplay
for *The Lady*. Producer Harry Cohn decided to reunite Welles and
Hayworth for the film's production—a fact that would ensure it ample
publicity.[7]

In its shooting stage, *The Lady* created quite a stir when it became
known that Hayworth would play the role of a femme fatale, diverging
from her benign status as "All-American hooker."[8] As Maurice Bessy
recollects, columnists were invited to a public-relations session that he
deemed "the execution of Rita Hayworth":

> The press was convened for the birth of the new Rita, which
> had been announced by Orson with great flurry and fuss. Before
> the eyes of a startled, not to say sarcastic, public, the long red-
> gold tresses of the Goddess of Hollywood fell under the scissors
> of a master hairdresser specially called for the occasion. Coiffed
> now like a little boy, Rita no longer bore any resemblance to

[5] Simone de Beauvoir, *The Second Sex*, trans. H. M. Parshley (New York: Vintage, 1974), 290 (my italics).

[6] Maurice Bessy, *Orson Welles*, trans. Ciba Vaughan (New York: Crown, 1971), 19–21.

[7] Barbara Leaming, *Orson Welles: A Biography* (New York: Viking, 1985), 332.

[8] Marjorie Rosen, *Popcorn Venus* (New York: Avon, 1973), 26.

that idealized figure who, during the war, had haunted the dreams of so many American GIs.[9]

Barbara Leaming reports that publicity stills for the film showed Welles himself "clipping her trademark" locks.[10]

When the film was previewed by Columbia executives, they were horrified by the transformation of Hayworth's image. As Bessy notes:

> Welles had taken the "ideal woman" ... Hollywood had created—and denounced her as a man-eater, a praying mantis. For the first time, woman, who had always served as man's saving angel, is as criminal as man, if not more so.[11]

In response to this radical metamorphosis, Columbia delayed release of *The Lady* for two years, meanwhile casting Hayworth in several more conventional roles.[12]

On a narrative level, *The Lady* is a murder mystery in the *film noir* mode. A young sailor, Michael O'Hara (Orson Welles), encounters the beautiful and elusive Elsa Bannister (Rita Hayworth) one evening in the park and is immediately smitten with her. Through a series of co-incidences, he is hired by her lawyer/husband, Arthur Bannister (Everett Sloane), as a mate on their yacht, *The Circe*, which is setting out on a pleasure cruise.

Once on board, O'Hara senses that the Bannisters' world is rife with intrigue. Elsa makes mysterious appeals to him, implying that she is in imminent danger. "You've got to stay," she pleads one afternoon on the ship. Elsa's maid refrs to her mistress as a "poor child" and tells O'Hara that "she needs you bad." Since Arthur Bannister is a sardonic, malevolent man, O'Hara believes that Elsa is her husband's helpless victim.

Strange things begin to occur. Bannister's colleague, George Grisby (Glenn Anders), attempts to enlist O'Hara in a bizarre scheme. He confesses that he wants to "disappear" from his current life and proposes that O'Hara pretend to kill him for a $5,000 fee. Grisby assures him that, with no corpse to be found, O'Hara will escape conviction and emerge a free and rich man. Because he wants the money to elope with Elsa, O'Hara becomes enmeshed in Grisby's macabre caper.

Somehow Elsa learns of O'Hara's plans and warns him that it is a frame-up—one of Arthur Bannister's "tricks." In a chain of confusing events, Grisby shoots the ship steward, Broome (who is really a divorce

---

[9] Bessy, 60.   [10] Leaming, 335.   [11] Bessy, 69.
[12] Joseph McBride, *Orson Welles* (London: Secker and Warburg, 1972), 97.

detective hired by Elsa's husband). Just before he expires, Broome tells O'Hara that he has been framed and that Elsa and Grisby are plotting to kill Bannister and to let O'Hara take the fall. O'Hara rushes to Bannister's office in order to prevent the crime but finds the police there carrying out Grisby's corpse. O'Hara is mistakenly arrested for murder, and Bannister is assigned as his legal counsel.

During the trial, Elsa encourages O'Hara to swallow a bottle of pills, and, in the ensuing mayhem, both escape to a nearby Chinese theater. When O'Hara discovers a gun in Elsa's purse, he realizes that she is the mastermind behind all the murderous schemes.

When he confronts her with this knowledge, she orders her thugs to beat him, and he awakens from a state of unconsciousness in the fun house of a nearby amusement park. In a room of paneled, distorted mirrors, a shoot-out occurs in which the Bannisters kill each other. O'Hara emerges from the bloodbath hoping to forget his love for Elsa but suspecting that he will "die trying."

This cursory plot summary reveals how *The Lady* is steeped in *mystery*—a staple of mythic discourse—and as spectators of the drama, we are as perplexed as Michael O'Hara within the diegesis. Harry Cohn was, in fact, so dazed and irate following a screening of the film that he is reputed to have said, "I'll give a thousand dollars to anyone who can explain the story to me."[13]

The narrative conundrums of the film center around the persona of Elsa Bannister, who is conceived as an archetypal enigma. In this portrayal, her character participates in a broader stereotype of woman discussed by Simone de Beauvoir: "Of all . . . myths, none is more firmly anchored in masculine hearts than that of the feminine 'mystery' . . . it permits an easy explanation of all that appears inexplicable."[14]

In both the film's plot and iconography, Elsa is invested with a sense of paradox. Many of her actions are contradictory, generating the image of an unfathomable creature. Much of her behavior is inconsistent—a fact that is clear from O'Hara's first encounter with her in the park. She says that she does not smoke but accepts one of his cigarettes; she claims that she cannot shoot a gun but carries a pistol; she discards her weapon-laden purse just when some muggers attack her.

Ambiguous comments about her background continually circulate, as though she has something to hide. Arthur Bannister snidely tells O'Hara, "You ought to hear how Elsa became my wife," and Elsa asks Michael if he wants to know what Bannister has on her. Significantly,

[13] Ibid., 99.   [14] De Beauvoir, 289.

35

none of this tantalizing information is ever revealed, leaving O'Hara and the viewer in limbo. Elsa's enigmatic qualities are at times brought directly to the surface. When she alerts Michael that her husband "knows about [them]," he responds sarcastically, "I wish *I* did." On another occasion, she boldly warns him: "I'm not what you think I am."

The visual style of the film also constructs Elsa as a fabulous being. Hayworth is forever bathed in glowing light, as though she were some luminous creature. Exemplary are the scenes of her in the hansom carriage, on shipboard at night, and at the Mexican picnic. Hayworth's facial expression is consistently opaque; hence, she projects an enigmatic demeanor, wryly gloating over the secrets that she keeps.

Given this characterization, *The Lady* cannot be read as a simple murder thriller, a naive who-dunit. The quest on which O'Hara embarks aims not merely at the solution of some criminal scheme or the resolution of a domestic drama. Rather, his encounter with Elsa initiates a search to comprehend her, a goal equivalent to fathoming the cosmic "mystery" of woman.[15]

Definitions of myth stress its explanatory function, which helps people understand the apparent mysteries of life. Thus it "bring[s] the unknown into relation with the known."[16] In some respects, *The Lady* can be seen as a cinematic fable that "explains" the enigma of woman—and, in so doing, draws upon established mythic structures.

The narrative has a cyclical form—an aspect of myth described by Jurij Lotman.[17] Since *The Lady* unfolds in flashback, O'Hara's narration starts after the conclusion of the events we witness, thus connecting beginning to end. Even O'Hara's words underscore the plot's circularity: "If I'd known how it would end, I'd never have started."

From the opening moments, Welles creates a fairy-tale atmosphere, as O'Hara tells his story in a "once upon a time" mode. He refers to Elsa as the "Princess Rosalie" and asks "from whence she has come." Later he promises to take her away to a "far place," and Elsa deems him her "knight-errant." Elsa's exoticism is further advanced by her obscure, oriental background (the lady from Shanghai) and her com-

---

[15] As a general rule, women are portrayed as "mystery" within the *film noir* genre. *The Lady from Shanghai* shares that feature with other such films. See E. Ann Kaplan, ed., *Women in Film Noir* (London: British Film Institute, 1978).

[16] William Morris, ed., *American Heritage Dictionary* (Boston: Houghton Mifflin, 1978), 868–69.

[17] Jurij Lotman, in Teresa de Lauretis, *Alice Doesn't: Feminism, Semiotics, Cinema* (Bloomington: Indiana University Press, 1984), 117.

mand of the Chinese tongue. As de Beauvoir points out, when woman is conceived as enigmatic, "her language is not understood."[18] Elsa frequently speaks in riddles. "Human nature is eternal," she tells Michael. "One who follows his nature keeps his original nature in the end."

The bizarre formal style of the film contributes to its mythical atmosphere. On a visual level, Welles employs disorienting camera setups: extreme high-angle shots of Elsa lying on the boat and extreme low-angle shots of O'Hara looking at her. Similarly, Welles exaggerates his use of the close-up, particularly as it frames the repugnant face of George Grisby. Welles also shifts abruptly between static and peripatetic camera shots, creating a disquieting pictorial effect—as when Elsa runs away from O'Hara in Mexico. Sets in the film are often highly artificial: the opening park scene reeks of theatrical mise-en-scène. Even sound violates the codes of realism. Sometimes it is considerably louder than expected (when Grisby appears on the Bannister yacht). Other times it is radically diminished (when Elsa and Michael talk in the aquarium). The acting style seems deliberately false: one thinks of Anders's grotesque facial expressions, Hayworth's comatose demeanor, and Welles's phony Irish accent.

Through these hyperbolic formal and narrative strategies, Welles creates a sense of mystery and mythos. In particular, this aura adheres to the figure of woman, who is seen as both enigmatic and dangerous. Thus the dramatic structure of *The Lady* conforms to the paradigm for mythic discourse that positions women as an "obstacl[e] man encounters on the path of life, on his way to manhood, wisdom, and power."[19] This view seems to have paralleled Welles's real-life attitude, for Maurice Bessy quotes him as stating that he "hate[s] women" but "need[s] them."[20]

In *The Lady*, woman is loathed for her guile and dissembling, for her predatory nature. Posing as a helpless victim, Elsa is really a malevolent femme fatale, a shark in the waters, lusting for blood. The words of Hélène Cixous seem relevant here, for she claims that men "need femininity to be associated with death," because "it's the jitters" that turn them on.[21]

Elsa's portrayal as an evil woman transcends the borders of realism and enters a mythic domain. The narrative of *The Lady* can be reformulated as a version of the Greek epic the *Odyssey* (a text Welles also

[18] De Beauvoir, 290.   [19] De Lauretis, 110.   [20] Orson Welles, in Bessy, 71, 74.

[21] Hélène Cixous quoted in De Lauretis, 135. From "The Laugh of the Medusa," trans. Keith Cohen and Paula Cohen, in Elaine Marks and Isabelle de Courtivron, eds., *New French Feminisms* (Amherst: University of Massachusetts Press, 1980), 255.

wanted to film), with O'Hara cast as a modern-day Ulysses.[22] Both Ulysses and O'Hara are sailors whose stories involve crucial ocean voyages. Moreover, both heroes are returning from battle: O'Hara from the Spanish Civil War and Ulysses from the Trojan conflict. Both stories contain crucial water imagery. *The Lady* opens with a shot of the ocean's surface, and a major scene is played out against the backdrop of an aquarium.

Within this context, the figure of Elsa achieves a certain resonance and bears comparison to characters in the *Odyssey*. The Bannisters' yacht is called *The Circe*, a reference to the island enchantress empowered to change men into animals. Clearly, Elsa has had the same effect upon her lovers. But she does more than encourage men to fight for her like savages: while O'Hara is continually associated with idealism, Elsa is linked to cynicism, to "making terms" with evil. She tries to transform O'Hara into a man without morals, into a beast.

Animal imagery abounds in *The Lady*, giving credence to the parallel between Elsa and the mythic sorceress. Michael compares both of the Bannisters to rattlesnakes and bloodthirsty sharks. In the Mexican picnic scene, alligators and snakes abound; on shipboard, a dog viciously barks; the final fun-house set is decorated with expressionistic spiderwebs and shark jaws. When Michael and Elsa tryst at the Steinhardt Aquarium, the couple stand in silhouette against a background of sea creatures magnified to monstrous proportions. The scene literalizes O'Hara's statement that in working for the Bannister household, he is "living on a hook."

Elsa also evokes the Sirens, sea maidens whose song drives sailors mad, luring them to destruction on the rocks. From the first moment Michael encounters her, she casts a quasi-hypnotic spell on him. The night they meet in the park, he speaks of not having his "head about [him]," of not being "in [his] right mind." By the final trial scene, just her glance orders him to down a bottle of pills. Interestingly, this sequence (rendered in shot/countershot) figures *woman* as the bearer of the look—a situation that imperils man. As O'Hara tells Elsa later, "I saw you begging me with your eyes."

Elsa's song, like that of a Siren, is especially enticing. One evening, as she sings "Please Don't Kiss Me," Michael is drawn mesmerically to her from the ship's hold (like Lucy Harker to Nosferatu). Elsa is also frequently seen posed on the rocks like a sea nymph or Lorelei.

---

[22] Leaming, 456. James Naremore, *The Magic World of Orson Welles* (New York: Oxford University Press, 1978), 160. He is quoting William Johnson.

On one occasion, Grisby watches her through his binoculars as she sunbathes, and he is held in a lascivious, voyeuristic spell.

Although the parallels between *The Lady* and the *Odyssey* are most obvious, there are other mythic references that circulate in the film. Primary among these is the legend of Oedipus—one that (as Raymond Bellour has noted) subtends much of the American narrative cinema.[23] The two sources of the film present intriguing oppositions: if the *Odyssey* is a tale of homecoming, of a father's restoration of the family circle, the legend of Oedipus is a story of domestic derangement, of a son's annihilation of kinship structures. It is the latter ambience that pervades *The Lady* and provides its sinister tone.[24]

It is not difficult to see the mysterious Elsa Bannister as reminiscent of the Sphinx—the creature whose puzzle Oedipus must eventually solve. Elsa's face is masklike and inscrutable and bears a sly grin. She speaks and acts in paradoxical riddles, either giving false leads or contradictory information. In her portrayal as a malevolent predator, she is also frequently likened to a beast, thus reflecting the Sphinx's status as half-human, half-animal. It is interesting that O'Hara refers to her both as a princess and as a rattlesnake because, as Teresa de Lauretis has noted, the Sphinx "is an 'assimilation' [from earlier myths] of the princess who poses a difficult task or enigma (to the hero), and the serpent, who exacts a human tribute."[25]

Like the story of Oedipus, the narrative of *The Lady* involves the solution of a puzzle. From the beginning, O'Hara attempts to navigate the Bannister labyrinth and, in so doing, to answer a series of questions. He must decide whether Elsa is her husband's victim or oppressor, and whether Grisby's lunatic plot is in earnest or a ruse. He must also determine who killed Broome and Grisby, and whether Elsa is in love with him or playing him for a sucker. Parallel to the tale of Oedipus, when the mystery is solved, the creature meets its death. In the Greek myth, when Oedipus correctly solves the riddle, the Sphinx plunges down the mountainside; and in *The Lady*, when O'Hara perceives Elsa as the murderer, she is shot in the Magic Mirror Maze.

Like the tale of Oedipus, *The Lady* transcends the boundaries of mere story and is invested with psychosocial meaning. The case for the

[23] Janet Bergstrom, "Alternation, Segmentation, Hypnosis: Interview with Raymond Bellour," *Camera Obscura* 3–4 (Summer 1979): 90.

[24] See excellent analyses of the film by E. Ann Kaplan, *Women and Film: Both Sides of the Camera* (New York: Methuen, 1983), 60–73; Ann West, "A Textual Analysis of *The Lady from Shanghai*," *enclitic*, no. 10–11 (Fall 1981/Spring 1982): 90–97.

[25] De Lauretis, 114–115.

Oedipal drama is clear. For Freud, it enacts a basic psychic and familial conflict, as expressed from the male child's point of view. Oedipus allegedly lives out every boy's fears and fantasies: to have his mother as a lover, to kill his rival father, and to be punished for his loathsome acts. In this sense, the Oedipal tale is about an individual who has not made the proper life adjustments from infantile to adult stage, transferring love for a parent to a more suitable sexual partner. For Freud, the spectator at *Oedipus Rex* is warned and chastened by this domestic drama:

> Each member of the audience was once, in germ and phantasy, just such an Oedipus, and each one recoils in horror from the dream-fulfillment here transplanted into reality, with the whole quota of repression which separates his infantile state from his present one.[26]

The riddle of the Sphinx evokes the stages of human life, since its solution involves recognition of a passage from infancy to youth and old age. Scholars have also read the puzzle for psychological and sexual meaning concerning the difficulties in human relationships. Anthropologist Weston La Barre writes:

> Everyone knows the Riddle of the Sphinx asked Oedipus as he traveled along a road alone. "What is it that walks on four legs, then on two legs, and then on three?" Many men . . . lost their lives in not being able to answer it. But all of us now know the answer. It is man. As a baby he creeps on all fours; when he learns to walk, he stands erect; and when he is old, he walks with a cane. But the Riddle and its answer are deceptively simple. When studied and thought about, the meaning becomes deeper and deeper. For man is also the mammal whose inner essence lies in his extra-ordinary ability to love others of his own kind, varyingly with age and circumstance.
>
> The fact is complicated too, since man has a number of ways of loving, several of which he must learn in order to become human. As a child he must love in one way, but as an adult in others. Thus the Riddle that the Sphinx puts to the animal that lives in families is much more complex. Each individual is asked it at some point on his road through life. And if he cannot answer it, he dies, in so far as his full potential as a man is con-

[26] Sigmund Freud, quoted in Juliet Mitchell, *Pychoanalysis and Feminism: Freud, Reich, Lang and Women* (New York: Vintage, 1975): 61.

40

cerned. In this form the Riddle is more baffling: *"Who may love, but not love the one whom he loves?"*

Elsewhere, La Barre offers a response to the enigma, which touches on the subject of incest:

> The answer is human beings: of whatever kind and condition, primitive or civilized, male or female, old or young. . . . For the child the solution is this: "He may love (dependently), but not love (sexually) the one whom he loves (mother)." For the adult man there is a different solution: "He may love (women, sexually), but not love (sexually) the one whom he loves (dependently once, mother)."[27]

Reading the Oedipal challenge in a similar vein, psychiatrist Martin Grotjahn identifies the infamous smile of the Sphinx with the mother's recognition of her son's illicit fantasies:

> The son's most secret desire is known to the mother. She betrays her knowledge through the smile shown in Mona Lisa and the Sphinx. Their smile is different from any other smile. It is the smile of mystery and secrecy; with this smile the mother gives recognition to the secret of her son. I know what you want; I feel it myself, and you will get it. Perhaps you must wait for the final embrace—which will be the embrace of death.[28]

But how does the Oedipal conflict relate to *The Lady*—a film not obviously about mothers and sons?[29] Of primary import is the fact that it is told from a masculine point of view—with Michael O'Hara (the mythic subject) as first-person narrator. Although not any character's progeny, he is represented as a wide-eyed, naive youth—a "fool" in

[27] Weston La Barre, *The Human Animal* (Chicago: University of Chicago Press, 1955), 208–9 (my italics), 214.

[28] Martin Grotjahn, *Beyond Laughter: Humor and the Subconscious* (New York, Toronto, and London: McGraw-Hill, 1966), 106. Dana Polan has also offered to me a reading of the Sphinx's riddle as self-discovery: "There's actually another completely workable answer, beyond 'Man' to the riddle: 'Oedipus,' for if any man will be on crutches by the end of his life it will be the blinded Oedipus, forced to hobble around with Antigone's help (and as a child with a cut tendon, Oedipus is also definitely on all fours at the beginning of his life). All this is to suggest that the Riddle of the Sphinx is a riddle to Oedipus not only about the human condition but about his own specific relation to that condition. The riddle is not about some abstract knowledge but about self-knowledge—a self-knowledge that hubristic men like Oedipus and Michael O'Hara try to disavow (until they admit that they are 'somebody's fool')."

[29] Ann West speaks of the film's "Oedipal patterning" in West, 90.

41

the hands of the Bannister woman. This term comes up repeatedly in the film. In the opening sequence, he tells us: "When I start out to make a fool of myself, there's little can stop me." And later on, when he learns that Elsa is married, he says: "I figure if she fools [her husband] she'll fool me." When they return to San Francisco from their ocean cruise, he remarks, "It's amazing how much a fool like me can swallow." At the end of the film when Elsa is dead, he muses cynically that "everybody's somebody's fool." Thus O'Hara is seen as a childlike innocent, duped by a sophisticated and experienced woman—a situation that replays the male child's "misinterpretation" of maternal love.

Like a mother, Elsa seems fundamentally taboo. She is Arthur Bannister's wife, which marks any liaison with her as adulterous. But it is Bannister's particular status that grants Elsa a heightened prohibition. Throughout the film, he is shown to be considerably older than O'Hara; and the fact that he is crippled gives him a rather aged, infirm aura. It is easy to see him in a paternalistic position, which is underscored when he takes over O'Hara's legal defense. Ann West has noted the particular significance of Bannister's role as an attorney, since, in Lacanian terms, the Oedipal stage represents the son's entrance into the realm of the symbolic—into the domain of the Law.[30]

The primal struggle between youth and age (between father and son) is also apparent in the Sherwood King novel. At one point, Bannister eyes the younger man's physique and exclaims: "Do you know what I'd give to be twenty-six again, with a build like yours?" At another, Grisby says that Bannister has a "quirk in his brain about youth shuffling along."[31] When Bannister realizes that his wife and O'Hara are mutually attracted, he says: "He's young; she's young; he's strong; she's beautiful." Bannister's portrayal as a patriarchal figure augments the sense of Elsa's unavailability, giving O'Hara's love for her an incestuous taint. Significantly, the theme song of the film (which she sings on shipboard) is entitled "Please Don't Kiss Me." As though to literalize the trajectory of thwarted desire, the camera tracks into Hayworth as the lyrics caution to stay away. Thus, in coming to work for the Bannister couple, O'Hara enters a perverse kind of "family," in which he stands as the desirous son. The film's final shoot-out occurs in an amusement-park fun house—perhaps a grand metaphor for the demented Bannister menage.

[30] West, 91 (she is referring to the theories of French psychoanalyst Jacques Lacan); Kaplan, 69–71.
[31] Sherwood King, *If I Die before I Wake* (New York: Simon & Schuster, 1938).

If O'Hara is represented as childlike and Bannister as parental, in what sense might Elsa represent a "mother"? She does not fit that description in any literal sense; she has no children and is anything but nurturing. Rather, she functions "maternally" on a more submerged textual plane that is mediated by O'Hara's fears and wishes.

On the most obvious level, Elsa is positioned maternally in her characterization as a worldly woman who sees O'Hara as a charming "fool." She is forever lecturing him on the sordidness of the "real world" and mocking his idealism—much as a parent might condescendingly instruct a child. When he proposes that they run off together, she tells him: "You can't take care of yourself; how would you take care of me?" When they kiss in the aquarium, a group of schoolchildren follows them and giggles, as though recognizing O'Hara as an equal. But the implications of the film's maternal discourse run deeper than that.

In his essay "On Narcissism: An Introduction," Freud theorizes that men and women experience love in profoundly different ways. Females, he finds, are rather "narcissistic" and consumed with themselves. Males, on the other hand, experience maternal love more deeply as children and transfer that affection more readily to an adult sexual partner:

> Complete object-love of the anaclitic type is, properly speaking, characteristic of the man. It displays the marked sexual over-estimation which is doubtless derived from the original narcissism of the child, now transferred to the sexual object.[32]

It is this sense of the masculine, infantile "overestimation" of the love object (originally the mother) that characterizes O'Hara's unbalanced infatuation with Elsa Bannister and justifies his Oedipal blindness to her blatant faults. This excess explains the representation of Elsa as an idealized icon—an untouchable goddess, sculpted in light, privileged within the frame. Obviously, O'Hara's obsession with Elsa is not an expression of mature love. Rather, as E. Ann Kaplan has noted, it belies a need for "refusion," for reentry into the Lacanian imaginary.[33]

Elsa also represents archetypal mother in a more perverse sense—in her figuration as a dangerous woman. As Susan Lurie has noted,

---

[32] Sigmund Freud, "On Narcissism: An Introduction," in *Collected Papers, Volume IV*, trans. Joan Riviere (London: The Hogarth Press and The Institute of Psycho-Analysis, 1949), 45.

[33] Kaplan, *Both Sides*, 63.

though the son longs for his mother, he also fears her greater (potentially castrating) sexual powers:

> [The male child] fantasizes that *union with Mother is to be what she is, not what he is.* That is, he fantasizes that this union is one in which Mother's superior will presides to so great an extent that he is formed in her likeness. And while this seems to have been a satisfactory . . . arrangement during infancy, his present individual/sexual self, symbolized in his penis, clearly could not survive such an arrangement.[34]

Elsa's status as a castrating woman surfaces at various moments in the film, attached to diverse phallic objects. In the first scene, Michael offers Elsa a cigarette, and though she claims not to smoke, she folds it into a handkerchief and hides it in her purse. Later, on shipboard, she tells him she is learning to smoke. Finally, when she lies on the deck, singing her seductive song, the camera scans her body as she passes a cigarette to Grisby. Other scenes center on her possession (or dispossession) of a revolver. In the beginning of the film, she has a nonthreatening relation to her gun. In the park scene, she throws it down and tells O'Hara that she does not know how to shoot. By the end of the narrative (when we sense her as pernicious and taboo), her relation to the pistol is entirely different. When she and O'Hara escape the trial and meet in a Chinese theater, she tells him to hug her in order to dodge the police. At this moment of embrace, he reaches into her dark (womblike) purse and pulls out a gun. It is then (when she possesses the phallus) that he acknowledges her treachery and evil. "I was right," he tells us. "She was gonna kill me. [I was] safe from the cops but not from her." While Elsa's characterization as femme fatale has been read by some critics as a demystification of woman's traditional idealization, it can be seen as the flip side of the coin—with dread standing in for overvaluation.[35] It is intriguing to reconsider a scene that preceded the making of the film: "the execution of Rita Hayworth." For what better metaphor for annulling the threat of woman could there be than that of the actress shorn of her Medusa's coiffure?

As O'Hara and Elsa kiss in the Chinese theater, his Oedipal vision blurs—ostensibly from an overdose of pills. "I came to in the Crazy House," he tells us. This final sequence bears comparison to the Oedipal legend, and to the Sphinx's riddle concerning the proper passage

[34] Susan Lurie, "Pornography and the Dread of Woman: The Male Sexual Dilemma," in Laura Lederer, ed., *Take Back the Night* (New York: Morrow, 1980), 159.
[35] Kaplan, *Both Sides*, 71.

44

through the stages of life. When O'Hara awakens, he falls down a trapdoor, passes through a dragon's jaw, and slides into a black void. Landing prone on the floor, he is surrounded by signs that urge him to "Stand up, or give up."

In this dreamlike sequence, we can read a symbolic return to the womb via the *vagina dentata* and the Fallopian tubes. In fact, Jurij Lotman has seen *all* narratives as entailing "a hero's entry into and emergence from a closed space . . . that can be variously interpreted as 'a cave,' 'the grave,' a 'house,' or '*woman*.' " When O'Hara leaves the Magic Mirror Maze, he occupies the triumphant position of the male mythic protagonist who has conquered an obstacle that is "morphologically female and indeed, simply, the womb."[36] E. Ann Kaplan gives the sequence an alternate, but related, reading, viewing the fun house as a symbol for the imaginary and for the mirror phase.[37]

The episode details a dangerous reversal of the stages of life—one associated with woman—and the signs that decorate the room seem to warn us to *grow* up or give up. Echoed in this scene (by O'Hara's prone position) are the Sphinx's words concerning an infant that "creeps on all fours." When Arthur Bannister (who uses canes) enters the maze with his three- (or four-) legged crippled gait, he seems an incarnation of the Sphinx's figure of age.

At the scene's conclusion, Bannister lies dead on the floor, and the wounded Elsa leans, Sphinx-like, on her elbows (see fig. 4). As though to literalize woman's role in narrative denouement, a sign on the fun-

[36] Discussed in de Lauretis, 118–19.   [37] Kaplan, *Both Sides*, 69.

4. *The Lady from Shanghai* (1948). The wounded Elsa Bannister (Rita Hayworth) leans Sphinx-like on her elbows.

house door reads "closed."[38] Elsa pleads for Michael's support, as though to seduce him into the final death embrace that Grotjahn imagines. O'Hara, however, exits coolly on two feet, vowing to forget her or to "die trying." He predicts that he will be found blameless of Grisby's murder but admits that "innocence" is "a big word." Hence, we surmise that O'Hara is guilty of other things.

The Lady enacts a traditional *myth of male passage*, in which the hero overcomes obstacles identified with the female. As de Lauretis has written: "In its making sense of the world, narrative endlessly reconstructs it as a two-character drama in which the human person creates and recreates *himself* out of an abstract or purely symbolic other—the womb, the earth, the grave, the woman."[39] Kaplan has argued that O'Hara's heroism is somewhat qualified by his characterization as a "fool."[40] But that subversion is itself recouped. Much is made of his nickname, "Black Irish," and of the fact that he has killed a man in the Spanish Civil War. Despite his self-mockery, we feel that he is truly heroic, and that his emasculation by Elsa Bannister is all the more tragic. Finally, O'Hara's characterization as a childlike "boob" does not so much undercut his heroic stance as render it infantile, anchoring him to the Oedipal desire that subtends the male mythic stance.

If, within the plot space, Elsa impedes O'Hara's journey into manhood, she also functions as an obstacle to the narrative flow—with each iconic, mesmerizing shot of her literally freezing both time and story line.[41] But it is her specific positioning as *mother* that fulfills the impedimentary function of woman in myth. It is her lurid maternal advances that must be rebuffed if phallic potency is to be attained (if one is to "stand up" rather than "give up"). It is her Sphinx-like mysteries that must be penetrated if man is to escape her riddled maze.[42] When Michael O'Hara emerges from the fun house, he is at a pivotal moment; having relinquished maternal desire, he is ready to enter the adult sexual world. He tells us that he will avoid trouble and concentrate on "grow[ing] old." As spectators of *The Lady*, we have been warned of the dangers of transgression, like Freud's audience at *Oedipus Rex*.

What is significant about *The Lady* (and other male myths) is the *distortion* they accomplish in dramatizing the Oedipal psychody-

[38] De Lauretis, 118–19.   [39] Ibid., 121.   [40] Kaplan, *Both Sides*, 71.
[41] Laura Mulvey, "Visual Pleasure and Narrative Cinema," in Gerald Mast and Marshall Cohen, eds., *Film Theory and Criticism*, 3rd ed. (New York and Oxford: Oxford University Press, 1985), 809.
[42] West, 91, 94.

namic.[43] If mother must be rejected, she must also be blamed; if she must be discounted, she must also be seen as unfathomable. Thus *The Lady* enacts a discourse of perverse *wish fulfillment*. If mother *were* evil, it would be easy to cease loving her; if she *were* mysterious, there would be no need to comprehend her. If father *were* crippled, one could easily succeed him. When Arthur Bannister taunts O'Hara about "how Elsa got to be [his] wife," his words address a universal childhood longing to know the titillating details of one's parents' premarital lives. What Welles has regrettably not realized is that woman's "enigma" resists decoding because it is a male fabrication: "If man fails to discover the secret essence of femininity, it is simply because it does not exist."[44] While Welles allows his protagonist to emerge from the conundrums of the Magic Mirror Maze, his film remains trapped within its ideological refractions.

The notion that Welles ended the film with an unsatisfactory conclusion brings to mind a provocative article by the French feminist philosopher Sarah Kofman. In "The Narcissistic Woman: Freud and Girard," she discusses her view of the former's "false solution" to the problem of woman.[45] She points to Freud's treatise "On Narcissism," in which he tentatively configures woman as inherently independent because of her great capacity for self-love. Kofman quotes a section of Freud's article in which he compares woman to the assured beast or criminal:

> the charm . . . of a child is to a large extent based on his narcissism, his self-sufficiency . . . his inaccessibility . . . likewise the charm . . . of certain animals who seem unconcerned with us, such as cats and large beasts of prey. Even the great criminal and the humorist . . . compel our interest by the narcissistic consistency they display while keeping away from their ego all that would depreciate it.[46]

If one follows Freud's reasoning to its logical conclusion, Kofman finds that

> what renders woman enigmatic would no longer be some "natural deficiency," a lack of some kind or other, but on the con-

[43] Ibid.   [44] De Beauvoir, 292.

[45] Sarah Kofman, "The Narcissistic Woman: Freud and Girard," *Diacritics* (Fall/September 1980): 36–45. There is also a good discussion of this topic in Mary Jacobus, *Reading Women: Essays in Feminist Criticism* (New York: Columbia University Press, 1986).

[46] Ibid., 37.

trary her affirmative narcissistic self-sufficiency and her indifference. It would no longer be she who envies man for his penis, but he who envies her for her inaccessible libidinal position.[47]

Kofman wonders what threat might have caused Freud to reject this conception of woman as the strong, narcissistic "criminal" and to replace it with the model of the weak and pliant "hysteric": "Everything takes place . . . as if Freud had *covered over* . . . a certain knowledge or a certain solution [of the enigma of woman] by a *false solution*, one more pleasing for men if it is not so for women."[48]

It is this process of "covering over"—of supplanting the image of woman as "criminal" or "beast" with that of the "hysteric"—that we see at work in *The Lady*, for there is almost no female character in the history of cinema who so warrants the epithet of "narcissistic" as Elsa Bannister. Although on one level, she represents a sexual vision for the male spectator, on another, she is self-contained and unassailable, exuding a sense of autoeroticism over exhibitionism.[49] Like Narcissus of Greek legend, she dies looking at her own reflection in the Magic Mirror Maze. Elsa is also, quite literally, a criminal and is frequently compared to a beast. Significantly, however, within the narrative she *plays* at being the vulnerable "hysteric" in order to seduce men—as though she realizes that this is woman's preferred role. Thus she feigns being the victim of Arthur Bannister and tells O'Hara that she has "considered suicide." Curiously, her pretense of weakness has been misunderstood by certain male critics. Joseph McBride describes Elsa as involved in "self-indulgent hysteria" and claims she needs "security so desperately that she has succumbed to Bannister's economic blackmail."[50]

Although for most of the film Elsa is in control of the hysterical discourse (using it as a clever subterfuge), by the end, Welles establishes his dominance and situates her in a fun house/madhouse—ostensibly an objective correlative for her state of mind. We leave Elsa frantic and expiring, groveling on the floor for O'Hara's aid, the blood draining out of her, like meaning from one of Claire Johnston's "signs."

Welles, like Freud, ends *The Lady* with a classic "false solution." Having queried the riddle of woman's "mystery," he resolves it in a manner consonant with sexist preconceptions. (As André Bazin has written, "The misogyny of the American cinema has become a com-

[47] Ibid.   [48] Ibid., 45 (my italics).   [49] Kaplan, *Both Sides*, 66.
[50] McBride, 103.

48

monplace of intellectual criticism. Rita Hayworth was undoubtedly one of its first victims, and remains . . . its most glorious martyr."[51])

The tendentious conclusion of *The Lady* makes us wonder (with Kofman) what "vital exigency" requires "both that man attempt to solve . . . an enigma and at the same time . . . 'really' be unable to solve it."[52] Kofman imagines that men, subliminally, perceive that their vision of woman is wrong. "If it is true . . . that a riddle . . . always has a solution," then it follows that "he who asks the riddle knows the answer to it even if some deep-seated interest commits him not to give it away."[53]

Riddles of the Sphinx: Myths Replaced

> *The alternative cinema provides a space . . . that is radical in both a political and an aesthetic sense that challenges the basic assumptions of the mainstream film. —Laura Mulvey*[54]

In bracketing *Riddles of the Sphinx* with *The Lady*, it is useful to reconsider Annette Kuhn's notion of "deconstructive cinema," for *Riddles* opposes the dominant mode on the levels of both ideology and style.[55] Moreover, its thematic concerns make it a resonant intertextual match for the Welles film, since it addresses and "revises" the discursive system of that work.

One of the primary ways in which *Riddles* challenges *The Lady* is on the level of production. It is not an expensive commercial feature, but a low-budget, independent work, sponsored by the nonprofit British Film Institute. Furthermore, it results from a collaboration between a man and a woman (Peter Wollen and Laura Mulvey) who were husband and wife at the time. Thus its making parallels, but diverges from, that of *The Lady*, where a male director controlled and manipulated the career and performance of his actress/wife.

Riddles also differs from *The Lady* in its openly theoretical orientation. While one suspects that Welles did not set out to query the myth of woman (but did so unconsciously), Mulvey and Wollen clearly intend to. Both are noted film scholars. In *Signs and Meaning in the Cinema*, Wollen has examined the semiotics of the medium, and in "Visual

[51] André Bazin, *Orson Welles*, trans. Jonathan Rosenbaum (New York, Hagerstown, Md., San Francisco, and London: Harper Colophon Books, 1972), 94.
[52] Kofman, 45. [53] Ibid. [54] Laura Mulvey, in Kay and Peary, 414.
[55] Annette Kuhn, *Women's Pictures* (London: Routledge & Kegan Paul, 1982), 161.

Pleasure and Narrative Cinema," Mulvey has considered feminism and film.[56] *Riddles* is an extension of their theoretical work—in filmic rather than written form.

Riddles differs from *The Lady* on the level of genre as well. It is an experimental film, not a conventional drama. While it has many abstract qualities, it is not entirely devoid of a story element. Rather than shun narrative, it redefines it and thereby gains relevance to the Welles film.

Riddles also counters the spectator address of *The Lady*, which is fashioned to draw the male viewer into a nostalgic identification with O'Hara's Oedipal journey. Although *Riddles* concerns similar issues, it takes a more distanced Brechtian stance, discouraging emotional response and encouraging intellectual engagement.

But what in particular makes *Riddles* an appropriate intertext to pair with *The Lady*? To pursue this, we must analyze the complex structure of the Mulvey/Wollen work and consider its thematic concerns.[57] In its overall plan, *Riddles* might be conceived as a Godardian "essay film"—a piece that not only recounts a narrative but articulates an expository thesis as well. The filmmakers are interested in this cinematic mode, and Wollen has written on the work of the French filmmaker.[58] Like *Vivre Sa Vie* (1963), *Riddles* is divided into sections, reminiscent of book chapters. In the opening moments, these segments are laid out (in superimposed titles) like a table of contents: (1) Opening pages, (2) Laura speaking, (3) Stones, (4) Louise's story, told in thirteen shots, (5) Acrobats, (6) Laura listening, (7) Puzzle ending. The literary quality of the film is underscored by the script's eventual publication in *Screen* magazine as a text in and of itself.[59]

But a list of the film's segments gives us very little sense of the conceptual issues it raises and their relevance to *The Lady*. "Opening pages" provides a clue. In it we peruse a French horror-film journal

[56] Mulvey, "Visual Pleasure"; Peter Wollen, *Signs and Meaning in the Cinema* (London and Bloomington: Indiana University Press, 1969).

[57] For analyses of the film, see E. Ann Kaplan, *Both Sides*, 171–81; and Keith Kelly, "*Riddles of the Sphinx*: One or Two Things about Her," *Millennium Film Journal* 1, no. 2 (Spring/Summer 1978): 95–100.

[58] Peter Wollen specifically mentions the work of Jean-Luc Godard in relation to *Riddles* in the British Film Institute (London) Production Board catalogue in which *Riddles* is listed: 52. He has also written on Godard's film *Wind from the East* (see Wollen's *Readings and Writings: Semiotic Counter-Strategies* [London: Verso Editions and NLB, 1982]).

[59] My quotes here and following are taken from the published script of the film in *Screen* 18, no. 2 (Summer 1977): 61–77.

(*Midi-Minuit Fantastique*) and read the words: *Le mythe de la femme.*
We also view a photomontage of Greta Garbo depicted as the Sphinx.

What this introduction announces is that the subject of *Riddles* will
be the legends of womanhood, and that its focus will be on the figure
of the Sphinx. Furthermore, it associates that mythology with the cinema and the female star. The parallels to *The Lady* are already apparent—in the notion of woman as archetype and in the invocation of the
Oedipal fable so central to the Welles film.

In identifying three forms of intertextuality, Michael Riffaterre discusses the "mediated" mode, "where reference of text to intertext is
effected through the intercession of a third text functioning as the in-
terpretant that mediates between sign and object."[60] In a sense, the
Oedipal story constitutes such a "third text" in relation to the Welles
and Mulvey/Wollen films, uniting them in an oblique fashion. But
while the myths of femininity are accepted and embraced in *The Lady*,
they are questioned and replaced in *Riddles*.

This critique is launched on various levels of the film and articulated
on diverse registers. In section two ("Laura speaking"), Mulvey directly addresses the viewer about the theoretical issues animating the
film. Her image is periodically intercut with shots that evoke the Oedipal tale: a Greek vase, a detail from Gustave Moreau's *Oedipus and
the Sphinx*, footage of the Egyptian monument. Mulvey explains that
the film is about motherhood—a subject that will be rendered in the
central segment ("Louise's story"). To enact this drama, the filmmakers will use the voice of the Sphinx as an "imaginary narrator." She has
been chosen because of her ties to the notion of "motherhood as mystery"—an association (one infers) that exists for several reasons. First,
the Sphinx is a character in a tale about maternal incest, and her riddle
concerns the life cycle with which woman is traditionally linked.
Moreover, in her function of devouring baffled men, she is seen as an
awesome, "cannibalistic mother."

The submerged connections between *Riddles* and *The Lady* are
clear: Welles associates Elsa Bannister with a mythic, Sphinx-like figure, and her characterization belies a decidedly maternal configuration. But while Welles accepts the Oedipal scenario at face value
(seeing the Sphinx, and Elsa, as dissembling, malevolent forces), Mul-
vey/Wollen seek to reinterpret the tale, divesting it of its masculine
bias. In this respect, *Riddles* partakes of a broader trend in feminist art
which seeks to reclaim patriarchal mythos. As Auerbach writes:

[60] Michael Riffaterre, "Syllepsis," *Critical Inquiry* 6, no. 4 (1980): 627.

It may be time ... to circle back to those "images" of angels and demons, nuns and whores, whom it seemed so liberating to kill, in order to retrieve a less tangible, but also less restricting, facet of woman's history than the social sciences can encompass.[61]

Through an act of displacement, the filmmakers give the Sphinx a more important role in the drama than previously assigned. As Mulvey states:

In some ways the Sphinx is the forgotten character in the story of Oedipus. Everybody knows that Oedipus killed his father and married his mother, but the part played by the Sphinx is often overlooked.

Secondly, by noting her position outside the city gates, they make her a symbol of woman's exclusion from male culture. Their use of her imaginary voice-off underscores this sense of woman's alienation. Moreover, Mulvey/Wollen present the Sphinx as a figure of "resistance to patriarchy" through her ceaseless and aggressive interrogation of men. Mulvey states that "she challenges the culture of the city, with its order of kinship and its order of knowledge, a culture and a political system which assign women a subordinate place." Finally, the filmmakers reject the notion of her riddled discourse as a pernicious snare and see it as a valid expression of woman's confusion within male society. Mulvey notes:

To the patriarchy, the Sphinx as woman is a threat and a riddle, but women within patriarchy are faced with a never-ending series of threats and riddles—dilemmas which are hard for women to solve, because the culture within which they must think is not theirs.

Segment three ("Stones") also conjures up the Oedipal myth. In a montage (lasting some seven minutes), we view found footage of the Egyptian Sphinx, refilmed with the aid of a motion-analyst projector. The footage is decelerated, reversed, step-printed, and frozen. The camera frequently zooms into extreme close-ups of the Sphinx's lips—simultaneously an emblem of her silence and of her alternate discourse. This sequence gives us a visual equivalent for Mulvey/Wollen's ideological analysis of the Oedipal tale. In rephotographing several "gen-

[61] Auerbach, 3.

erations" of the print, the filmmakers also technically literalize the sense of a myth as passed down from one epoch to another.

By framing a modern-day narrative with an ancient legend, the filmmakers highlight the crucial role played by mythic discourse in contemporary culture and its power to "transmit and transform the ideology of sexism and render it invisible." Through their invocation of the image of Garbo as Sphinx, they also emphasize the cinema's special attraction to myth, particularly in its configuration of the female. For the picture of Garbo, we could just as well substitute one of Hayworth, illustrating Johnston's point that "Myth ... represents the major means in which women have been used" in film.[62]

While many filmmakers (like Welles) employ myths unconsciously, Mulvey/Wollen do so knowingly to reevaluate (not reproduce) them. Furthermore, their specific choice (the Oedipal tale) is decidedly central. In dramatizing it, they restructure it. Whereas the Oedipal story is told from the male point of view, *Riddles* aligns its perspective with woman: the Sphinx is the imaginary narrator, and the film's dramatic protagonist is Louise. While the Oedipal fable concerns the question of sonhood, *Riddles* focuses on the maternal dimension. The film's orientation thereby opposes not only the Oedipal myth but its resurrection in *The Lady*. In revamping the perspective, *Riddles* partakes of a structure typical of women's art. As Patricia Meyer Spacks notes:

> To read books by women answers few questions, raises many. The books do not destroy or even seriously challenge the old, man-created myths about women. *But they shift the point of view.*[63]

The most dramatic result of this transformation is to alter our attitude toward the Sphinx as a symbolic image. Mulvey/Wollen defuse her threat (as a dangerous, castrating agent) and liberate her (as a figure of female strength and resistance). In so doing, they redeem her as a heroine for contemporary women.

The movement from ancient myth to modern reality is marked by the passage from segment three to four—and the beginning of Louise's story—which is told in thirteen, 360-degree pan shots. The filmmakers intend that this drama be seen within the context of the Oedipal myth:

[62] Johnston, 409.

[63] Patricia Meyer Spacks, *The Female Imagination* (New York: Knopf, 1975), 315 (my italics).

53

> By juxtaposing a fable of everyday life, dealing with real and urgent personal and political problems, with the story of Oedipus and the Sphinx, we want to provide a framework within which we can begin to see new connections and ask new questions.[64]

But what is important about Louise's narrative? What kind of questions does it raise? Furthermore, how can it be seen to cast a "sideways glance" at *The Lady*? First, it is told from a woman's point of view. Rather than the interiorized male voice-over of O'Hara, we have the stream-of-consciousness monologue of the Sphinx/Louise.[65] In shot one, for instance, she muses:

> Time to get ready. Time to come in. Things to forget. Things to lose. Meal time. Story time.

Louise is also a mother, so her drama reorients the narrative perspective of the Oedipal cinema (as typified by *The Lady*). Moreover, Louise's child is female, so the issue here is mothers and daughters, not mothers and sons.

Where the film engages the latter relationship, it does so self-consciously and from a female perspective. The eleventh pan shot of Louise's story occurs in a film-editing room, where she watches Mary Kelly's *Post-Partum Document* (1976). In this work, Kelly recounts her experience as mother of a boy—and her thoughts on the dynamics of their mutual separation:

> The diaries in this document are based on recorded conversations between mother and child (that is, myself and my son) at the crucial moment of his entry into nursery school. . . . There also occurs at this moment a kind of "splitting" of the dyadic mother/child unit.

This analytical discourse on the part of a mother (about the question of separation) is a far cry from the Oedipal yearnings of Michael O'Hara, who longs for the maternal imaginary.

Beyond motherhood, *Riddles* also portrays woman as far more independent than she is in *The Lady*. In the Welles film, Elsa feigns reliance on Bannister and O'Hara despite her superior survival skills and ruthless intelligence. In *Riddles*, Louise separates from her husband in

[64] British Film Institute catalogue, 49.

[65] Although the voice-off in the film is formally identified as that of the Sphinx, it frequently seems to be identified with Louise.

shot three, and their reconciliation is never at issue. Instead, the film stresses her growing friendship with her black friend, Maxine, and endorses female bonding. The only woman (besides Elsa) who appears in *The Lady* is her mulatto maid, and their relationship is hierarchal and exploitative.

Aside from plot parallels, there are more profound comparisons between *Riddles* and *The Lady*. While the latter film veers toward hysteria (Elsa's final stance in the fun house/asylum), *Riddles* charts a movement from confusion to clarity, from depression to health. In the first segments, we hear Louise's disturbed, muddled, stream-of-consciousness discourse, reminiscent of that of the heroine in Jean-Luc Godard's *The Married Woman* (1965). It is a montage of disconnected impressions of marriage, family, and motherhood. At one point, she thinks:

> Keeping in the background. Fish-slice. Domestic labour.
>
> Disheartened, Burdened. Keeping calm. Keeping clean. Fitting like a glove. Remorse. Things to mend.

By the middle of Louise's story (shot nine), her interior monologue takes the form of rational, political speculation—a series of questions on parenthood and society. Thus, she has bridged "th[e] hypothetical spaces . . . between private and public realms"—a theme Judith Mayne finds in women's films and novels.[66] Louise asks:

> Should women demand special working conditions for mothers? Can a child-care campaign attack anything fundamental to woman's oppression? Should women's struggle be concentrated on economic issues?

Significantly, this shot (marking Louise's emerging consciousness) occurs at a children's playground—a site reminiscent of (but opposed to) the macabre amusement park (the scene of Elsa's hysterical descent) in *The Lady*. By the end of *Riddles*, Mulvey/Wollen will reject a purely social discourse for one inflected by the language of the feminine unconscious, but this never implies a move toward dementia. *Riddles* also avoids imbuing woman with mythic glamour by situating her within the quotidian world of work, child care, motherhood, and friendship.

[66] Judith Mayne, "The Woman at the Keyhole," in Mary Ann Doane, Patricia Mellencamp, and Linda Williams, *Re-Vision: Essays in Feminist Film Criticism* (Frederick, Md.: American Film Institute and University Publications of America, 1984), 53.

This is not the stuff of the Hollywood cinema, unless overlaid with themes of melodramatic martyrdom.

Finally, the Mulvey/Wollen film redefines the notion of woman's "riddles," seeing them not as ensnaring devices (the weapon of Elsa or the Sphinx) but as a series of political questions that woman is forced to ask within patriarchy. As the voice-off states in segment eight: "Questions arose which seemed to form a linked ring, each raising the next until they led the argument back to its original point of departure." Thus woman is not (like Elsa) an archetypal enigma, and her queries are not devious, rhetorical conundrums. If she speaks in riddles, it is because her life is marked by the contradictions of being female in a male culture.

This sense of paradox and circularity is further advanced by various formal tropes. Louise's story concerns the dissolution of the family "circle" and is recorded in a series of 360-degree pans; the design of her dishware is that of concentric rings; the nursery van that Louise rides during shot seven traverses a roundabout.

The cinematic style of *Riddles* also interrogates the dominant tradition. Though convoluted, Welles's narrative still proposes a continuous story that we should struggle to comprehend. In *Riddles*, any hope of coherence is gone entirely, with Louise's drama announced as thirteen fragments and introduced by intertitles that begin or end in midsentence. Shot two, for instance, is initiated with the words: "Bedtime, she likes to stay in Anna's room, waiting for her to fall asleep and tidying away traces of the day. She still seems to need——" According to Riffaterre, it is precisely these stylistic "ungrammaticalities" that spark associations to an intertext: "Connection takes place when the reader's attention is triggered by . . . clues . . . by intratextual anomalies—obscure wordings, phrasings that the context alone will not suffice to explain."[67]

Beyond the shattered narrative, the viewer's apprehension of *Riddles* is thwarted by the evasive camerawork, which (through much of the dramatic section) shows us only the torsos of characters. This style refuses to accommodate itself to a voyeuristic stare—and withholds the female (and male) body from possession. Finally, although Louise's story is the material of melodrama (a tale of the single mother, like *Mildred Pierce* [1945] or *Imitation of Life* [1934/1959]), it is treated ascetically, in a manner that frustrates emotional release.

[67] Riffaterre, 627.

Though none would contest *Riddles'* opposition to the mainstream cinema, some have rejected its political approach.[68] In focusing on the Sphinx as imaginary narrator, Mulvey/Wollen not only pursue the implications of an ancient myth but the possibilities of the female psyche. Mulvey's opening remarks even refer to Oedipus as standing for the conscious mind, and the Sphinx "for the unconscious." In taking this perspective, Mulvey/Wollen draw on other writers' conceptions of the female. In her diaries, Anaïs Nin speaks of woman as "the mermaid with her fish-tail dipped in the unconscious," whose task is "to make articulate this obscure world which dominates man, which he denies being dominated by."[69]

The filmmakers are also influenced by French feminist theorists who see woman as psychologically distinct from men. They valorize the female "non-linear," "non-logocentric" mind. Luce Irigaray, for example, speaks of this issue in a passage that links woman's consciousness with ancient culture—a theme important in *Riddles*:

> One would have to dig down very deep indeed to discover beneath the traces of this civilization, of this history, the vestiges of a more archaic civilization that might give some clue to woman's sexuality. That extremely ancient civilization would undoubtedly have a different alphabet, a different language ... woman's desire would not be expected to speak the same language as man's; woman's desire has doubtless been submerged by the logic that has dominated the West since the time of the Greeks.[70]

In investigating the potential of the female psyche to transform woman's life, *Riddles* swerves from more social/historical solutions, for which it has been challenged. Keith Kelly writes:

> In the twelfth episode, Louise reads from Maxine's dream diary ... as Maxine preens before one of a dozen Sirk/Lacan mirrors. ... The retreat from political involvement is completed when catharsis for Louise comes in a setting distantly removed from contemporary struggle: the Egyptology collection at the British Museum.

[68] Kelly, 96; and Kaplan, *Both Sides*, 180.

[69] Anaïs Nin, *The Diary of Anaïs Nin, Volume Two 1934–1939*, ed. Gunther Stuhlman (New York: Swallow and Harcourt, Brace & World, 1967), 235–36.

[70] Luce Irigaray, *This Sex Which Is Not One*, trans. Catherine Porter with Carolyn Burke (Ithaca, N.Y.: Cornell University Press, 1985), 25.

He also refers to the film as evincing a "post-1968 disillusionment."[71]

Mulvey and Wollen, however, argue that social and psychological solutions to women's issues are not mutually exclusive: "The film is committed to a feminist politics which relates problems of day-care etc., subject to conscious political action, to problems of desire and self-construction, which inflect and disturb the whole course and nature of our social practice." Mulvey also notes that although the film suggests feminine "regression," that process is only a "poetic moment which women must retraverse imaginatively on their way forward."[72]

While *Riddles* is fascinated by the female unconscious, it represents a very different notion of the psyche from that advanced in the mainstream cinema. In *The Desire to Desire*, Mary Ann Doane has noted that Hollywood's favorite characterization of the female mind involves insanity, and she finds scenarios of masochism, paranoia, and hysteria in the 1940s "woman's film."[73] In *Riddles*, the context of psychic exploration is radically revised.

The question of the female unconscious is raised most dramatically in section twelve, when Louise recites a transcript of Maxine's dream. The two women sit in a mirrored room with blood-red curtains, as the camera executes a circular pan, capturing disorienting multiple reflections (see fig. 5). Significantly, this segment follows episode ten, in which Louise visits her mother, and episode eleven, in which Mary Kelly discusses the infantile mirror stage and the separation of the child from the maternal dyad. As Kelly states:

> For both the mother and the child, the crucial moment of "weaning" is constituted by the intervention of a "third term" (that is, the father), thus consolidating the Oedipal triad and undermining the Imaginary dyad which determined the intersubjectivity of the pre-Oedipal instance. This intervention situates the imaginary "third term" of the primordial triangle ... and the paternal "image" of the mirror phase within the dominance of the Symbolic structure through the Word of the father.

The juxtaposition of sections ten through twelve implies that the room in which Maxine and Louise sit is a physical equivalent of the mirror phase. It even offers us (in its reflective *mise-en-abyme*) an infinite spatial regression. The recitation of Maxine's dream signals a

[71] Kelly, 99, 100.

[72] Mulvey and Wollen, British Film Institute catalogue, 49, 52.

[73] Mary Ann Doane, *The Desire to Desire: The Woman's Film of the 1940s* (Bloomington and Indianapolis: Indiana University Press, 1987), 1–37.

58

5. *Riddles of the Sphinx* (1977). The room in which Maxine (Merdelle Jordine) sits is a physical equivalent of the mirror phase.

move to the female unconscious which allegedly contains the remnants of a maternal discourse—a language that existed prior to the mediation of the paternal third term. As though to match this retreat on a formal level, segments eleven through thirteen are rendered in *reverse* pan shots.

Welles's Magic Mirror Maze has also been configured as the Lacanian imaginary.[74] But while, in *The Lady*, this site marks O'Hara's rejection and blame of the mother (Elsa) at the moment of paternal intervention (the appearance of Bannister), in *Riddles*, the mirrored room is a place for female bonding, for sharing recollections of a benign parent. Maxine recounts the following story:

> Yes. I remember now—it's about how she went out with her mother and her little brother and how her mother laughed at them when they said they weren't going home.

This meditation on motherhood is extended into section thirteen, which takes place in the Egyptian Room of the British Museum, establishing a parallel between psychological and archaeological "digging." As Louise tours the exhibits with her daughter, she recalls a childhood experience:

[74] Kaplan, *Both Sides*, 69.

59

She remembers how, when she had been very small, her mother had lifted her up to carry her on her hip and how she had hovered around her cot while she fell asleep. She remembered her feeling of triumph when her father left the house and the sudden presentiment of separation which followed.[75]

Here there are no thoughts of the son's awesome, seductive parent— mother *qua* Elsa Bannister. Rather, there is the sense of mother as a nurturing force whom woman has no need to reject.

For Mulvey/Wollen, the unconscious can help women to retrieve their pre-Oedipal language and renew a sense of maternal plenitude. Louise discovers this voice in the British Museum, where it is identified with the Sphinx:

Suddenly, she heard a voice, very quiet, coming from the box, the voice of the Sphinx, growing louder, until she could hear it clearly, compellingly, and she knew that it had never ever been entirely silent and that she had heard it before, all her life, since she first understood that she was a girl!

The film concludes with three non-narrative segments. "Acrobats" depicts superimposed, video-enhanced images of women doing gymnastics and juggling. On one level, these images suggest the plight of the working mother who must balance multiple roles. But other, more subtle interpretations are possible. In the British Museum, Louise had recalled the inscription on a box: "Anatomy Is No Longer Destiny." The sequence of graceful, gravity-free acrobats seems to prophesy woman's liberation from the limitations of her body (configured within patriarchy) and her escape from the weighty burdens of the material world. At one point, the voice-off also makes specific reference to acrobatic figures:

She had been drawing acrobats, trajectories of the body and displays of skill and balance. . . . She was fascinated by the gap between the feeling of bodily exertion and the task of drawing and writing.

Here the Sphinx's words seem to engage the French feminist notion of "writing" the female body, of discourse as tied to woman's corporeal existence.[76] This notion revises Freud's linkage of anatomy with destiny. In an alternate reading, Kaplan has seen the acrobatic sequence

75 Kaplan sees this passage as representing Anna's (Louise's daughter's) thoughts.
76 Cixous, "Castration or Decapitation?" *Signs* (Autumn 1981): 50–55.

as standing for the "release of energy in women once they connect with the world of the Sphinx."[77]

In segment six ("Laura listening"), Mulvey attends to a tape recording of her own voice (rehearsing the introduction she had delivered in section two). She also recites (what seems to be) a dream about the state of pre-Oedipal maternal fusion—and its eventual shattering—a theme suggested by images of blood, milk, water, islands, and the act of splitting:

> I was looking at an island in the glass. It was an island of comfort in a sea of blood. It was lonely on the island. I held tight. It was night and, in the night, I felt the past. Each drop was red. Blood flows thicker than milk, doesn't it? Blood shows on silk, doesn't it? It goes quicker. Split. No use trying. No use replying. Split. It goes stickier. The wind blew along the surface of the sea. It bled and bled. The island was an echo of the past. It was an island of comfort, which faded as it glinted in the glass.

The dream is not only suggestive of the imaginary but also reminiscent of a reverie experienced by the character of Giuliana (Monica Vitti) in *The Red Desert*—a woman who (like Louise) is an alienated mother and housewife. *Riddles* concludes with segment seven, "Puzzle ending," in which hands shift a plastic maze until two balls of mercury reach the center. When they coalesce, the maze is violently shaken. This puzzle image is curiously suggestive of *The Lady* and its Magic Mirror Maze—a trope that recurs in other Welles films and is central to his world view. He once told Andrew Sarris, "If we are looking for something, the labyrinth is the most favorable location for the search."[78]

On one level, the maze in *Riddles* (with its "nested" boxes) seems a reference to woman's domestic placement. In shot two of Louise's story, she had specifically used this imagery in her voice-over monologue: "Nesting. In the nest. Comfort. Effort ... Nesting. Acquiesced." On another level, the journey of the mercury balls back to the center, and their eventual merging, parallels the return to the maternal dyad that is referred to elsewhere in the film. Early on in Louise's story, for example, one of her stream-of-consciousness monologues talks of how "the warmth was far within. Hidden within ... in the center." Furthermore, the mirrored room is a kind of maze, and it is

---

[77] Kaplan, *Both Sides*, 79.

[78] Welles, quoted in Andrew Sarris, *Interviews with Film Directors* (New York: Avon, 1967), 532.

the site of discussions of maternal bonding. The shaking of the puzzle implies the brutal, but inevitable, end to the dyadic state—a termination that is most traumatic for women, who must enter the male symbolic world.

On a third level, the maze (with its cul-de-sacs and rimmed boxes) seems to represent the entrapping social world in which woman must operate—a terrain that presents her with only dead ends and false starts. It seems intriguing that in this film about woman's entrance into the work world the balls in the maze are made of mercury—perhaps a reference to the ancient god of commerce. According to this interpretation, the jarring of the puzzle suggests a necessary (if violent) reordering of the social structure, which would allow woman a freer and more navigable cultural space. Thus the maze in *Riddles* is not a romantic symbol of the universe or a static and pessimistic configuration for social or psychological existence. Rather, it is viewed as a barrier that must be destroyed if productive life is to be achieved.

By placing *The Lady from Shanghai* and *Riddles of the Sphinx* in an intertextual frame, we have induced a dialogue between the two around the issue of woman. The Welles film amply illustrates Mary Daly's point that "patriarchy perpetuates its deception through myth."[79] It also demonstrates Johnston's notion that contemporary cinema is imbued with an aura of mythos, which contains the female in problematic roles. Whether the "leading lady" is Elsa Bannister or Mildred Pierce, she may well be a stand-in for Jocasta, the Sphinx, or Earth Mother. In contrast, the Mulvey/Wollen work brings this subterranean process to the fore, reorienting myth for feminist purposes.

In *Riddles* the filmmakers juxtapose historically diverse material (a modern-day story and an ancient fable) to produce what they term "new connections."[80] I have sought to do this on a critical level by simulating their cinematic montage in my analytical placement of films.

[79] Mary Daly, *Gyn/Ecology: The Metaethics of Radical Feminism* (Boston: Beacon, 1978), 44.
[80] Mulvey and Wollen, British Film Institute catalogue, 49.

3 The Lives of Performers: The Actress as Signifier

Of all the arts that mankind has invented to clothe its concept of reality and to ornament its leisure moments, none is more suited to the genius of the female of the species than that of theatre. —Rosamond Gilder[1]

Even reactionary theories of art always credited women with ability in the performing arts. —Silvia Bovenschen[2]

Introduction

Over the past decade, feminist film critics have analyzed the persona of notable actresses. They have discussed the screen character of Mae West, arguing for or against her liberating aspects; they have examined the image of Bette Davis, noting her incarnation of a strong woman model; they have investigated the figure of Marlene Dietrich, citing her highly ambiguous sexuality. During this same period, scholars have studied the fictional roles assigned to women in film, be they positive or negative—prostitute, lawyer, or mother.[3]

What we have not seen, however, is these two concerns coming together: the question of the actress who performs in film and the role she embodies. Where these issues quite naturally collide is in the work depicting the life of the fictional actress, raising the question of woman and performance simultaneously on two levels. In *Stage Fright* (1950), for example, the entertainer Charlotte Inwood is played by the actress Marlene Dietrich, while in *Sunset Boulevard* (1950), the movie queen Norma Desmond is played by the star Gloria Swanson. One of the few film critics to underscore the import of this genre has been Molly Haskell, although she notes it only in passing. In *From Reverence to Rape*, she writes:

---

[1] Rosamond Gilder, *Enter the Actress* (Boston and New York: Houghton Mifflin, 1931), xv.

[2] Silvia Bovenschen, "Is There a Feminine Aesthetic?" *New German Critique*, no. 10 (Winter 1977): 129.

[3] See the discussions of female stars in Molly Haskell, *From Reverence to Rape* (Baltimore: Penguin, 1974) and in Karyn Kay and Gerald Peary, eds., *Women and the Cinema: A Critical Anthology* (New York: Dutton, 1977), especially the chapter on "Actresses," 75–136.

> The actress—whether as literal thespian . . . or as a symbol for the role-playing woman—is a key female figure throughout film history. . . .
>
> In one sense, the actress merely extends the role-playing dimension of women, emphasizing what she already is.[4]

Haskell's observation is certainly confirmed by a brief listing of films that portray fictional female performers. In the American cinema alone, one thinks of *Dangerous* (1935), *The Velvet Touch* (1948), *Indiscreet* (1958), *Torch Song* (1953), *All About Eve* (1950), *The Barefoot Contessa* (1954), *The Goddess* (1958), and *Inside Daisy Clover* (1965), to name but a few.

If the actress has appeared as dramatic character so frequently, what does her ubiquity signify? Why has she proved to be a "key figure" in film history? What might her privileged role tell us about the positioning of woman in traditional culture? How does the actress emphasize what woman "already is"? To pursue these questions, we will examine the issue of female "theatricality," then trace its manifestation in two contemporary Swedish works: Ingmar Bergman's *Persona* (1966) and Mai Zetterling's *The Girls* (*Flickorna*/1969).

Two-Faced Woman

In *Spectacle et Société*, Jean Duvignaud indicates how the lives of *all* human beings participate in the dramatic:

> Our own existence, that of the culture, is a played-out representation of instincts and drives. Sexuality, death, economic or aesthetic exchanges, work, all is manifest, all is acted out. Man is the sole dramatic species.[5]

But feminist criticism has argued that women, especially, have been forced to role-play in society. Cast as the "Other" to the male norm, they have been urged to embody a wide range of dramatis personae: from earth mother to temptress, from madonna to whore. (Simone de Beauvoir, in characterizing woman as mystery, noted that she is alternately seen as "angel, demon" or "*actress*.") These roles are frequently incompatible, placing the woman who seeks to fulfill them in a hope-

---

[4] Haskell, 242–43.

[5] Jean Duvignaud, *Spectacle et Société* (Paris: Editions Denoël, 1970), 17. This passage was translated by Channa Newman.

less double bind.[6] In particular, women have been encouraged to dissemble for their man: to appear submissive (though they may be strong), to seem dumb (though they may be smart)—all to create a safe and appealing veneer. Magazines like *Cosmopolitan* offer women scenarios for catching or keeping a lover; movies like *How to Marry a Millionaire* (1953) picture woman's role in romance as a mode of theatrical deception. Luce Irigaray characterizes the female stance as a "masquerade of femininity," in which woman ultimately "loses herself." She has also claimed that the primary "path . . . historically assigned to the feminine: [is] that of *mimicry.*"[7]

Two-Faced Woman (1941)—though not a film about an actress—highlights the pressure placed on women to "act" for their man. Starring Greta Garbo, it tells the story of a ski instructor, Karin Borg, who meets a vacationing magazine editor, Lawrence Blake (Melvyn Douglas), when he hires her for lessons. Blake is attracted to her wholesome appearance and way of life, and when stranded together overnight because of a snowstorm, they fall in love and elope. Blake promises Karin to renounce his workaholic way of life. When he does not appear in his New York office, two assistants come to find him and convince him to return to the magazine world. He orders Karin to go to the city with him, but she refuses, being a highly independent woman. He leaves and keeps postponing his return to the ski lodge, taking up with an old flame. Karin decides to fight for her man and, abandoning her earthy looks, gets dolled up for a trip to New York. When she arrives at a theater (where Blake's secretary has said he will be), she finds him with his old lover and slinks off, depressed and unnoticed, determined to return home. As she exits, she encounters one of Blake's assistants whom she had met at the lodge. He addresses her as Karin, but to cover herself, she pretends to be Katrin, Karin's phony "twin sister." She behaves in a highly sophisticated, vampish manner to convince him that she is someone else, but this only attracts him, and he invites her to dinner. At the restaurant, she encounters Blake and continues the deception. Although he suspects some ruse, he falls in love with this second Karin—the one who is consonant with the traditional male ideal.

---

[6] Simone de Beauvoir, *The Second Sex,* trans. H. M. Parshley (New York: Random House, 1974), 223, 290. In the former passage, she speaks of woman as having a "double and deceptive visage" for man, as incarnating "all moral values, from good to evil, and their opposites."

[7] Luce Irigaray, *This Sex Which Is Not One,* trans. Catherine Porter (Ithaca, N.Y.: Cornell University Press, 1985), 84, 76–77.

The film ends with Blake confronting his wife with her duplicity, but her "split personality" is never resolved. He calls her "Karin/Katrin."

This film reveals the need for all women to be "two-faced"—to cover their identities with a mask. The real Karin is never as appealing to Blake as the role of Katrin that she plays—a persona molded for male desire. Significantly, her transformation takes place near a stage.

If notions of female "theatricality" surface in films that have nothing to do with the drama, it will be even more intriguing to trace their appearance in those that do. In *The Velvet Touch*, Rosalind Russell plays a musical-comedy star who has worked throughout her career with a domineering male impresario/lover. In the opening scene, she terminates their association in order to appear in a serious drama. She also reveals her involvement with another man. The producer is enraged and threatens to sully her reputation. In the heat of the moment, she strikes him with a statuette and accidentally kills him. Rather than report the crime, she flees. During the rest of the film, she "acts" the role of an innocent bystander to both her suitor and a policeman. When blame for the crime is to be placed on another woman, the actress is tortured with guilt. In the film's final sequence, she plays the last scene of *Hedda Gabler*, and we fear that she, like the drama's heroine, will commit suicide. When the curtain rises for the actors' bows, she is still alive and sends a confessional note to the police investigator.

The Velvet Touch emphasizes the actress's need to role-play *off* the stage. Typically, the heroine's career has been at the mercy of a powerful man who has exacted a sexual, as well as a professional, price for his support. When she vows to end that relationship, he threatens to ruin her with some unstated innuendo. Though she has killed him unwittingly, she feels unable to reveal her situation. Here her role as Hedda Gabler seems significant, as both women are independent and incapable of fulfilling the prescribed societal norm.

Other films about the actress display a similar fascination with extratheatrical role-playing. In *Stage Fright*, Marlene Dietrich is a performer who feigns romantic interest in a man to dupe him into murdering her husband. When the man commits the crime, he tries to pin the blame on her, then asks for help from another actress, Eve Gill (Jane Wyman). Since Eve is in love with the man, she assists him and, in order to discern the truth, enacts many roles offstage, including those of a reporter and a maid. Similarly, *Indiscreet* casts Ingrid Bergman as an actress who has fallen in love with a married businessman (Cary Grant). As an unconventional woman, she accepts the situation and is content with their affair. When she learns, however, that the man is a bachelor (who has lied to avoid marital pressure), she is furious. In retaliation, she enacts a scenario to make him jealous. *Indiscreet* also portrays the actress role-playing offstage, and her need to dissemble is tied to her relationship with a man. Ironically, in *Indiscreet* the actress's urge to deceive is caused by her lover's mistaken assumption that she will demand to play the conventional role of wife—a part she would just as soon avoid.

Although woman's need to dissemble in society may partially explain the popularity of the actress figure in the cinema, it does not address the entire issue. There would seem to be deeper reasons for her favored position, and these lead back to the history of western theater. In *Enter the Actress*, Rosamond Gilder discusses the common belief that the first performers were religious leaders enacting sacred rituals. In most cultures, such figures were originally women:

> In Phrygia she was called Cybele, Great Mother of the Gods; in Babylonia and Phoenicia, Ishtar and Ashtoreth; in Egypt, they hailed her as Isis, Queen of Heaven; but wherever she appeared, she was the prototype of that first actress-priest of the primitive grove, and her attributes remained the same—the symbols of fertility—the child who dies to be reborn and the band of attendant women dancing the drama of birth and death and resurrection.[8]

As Gilder notes, eventually the cult of the mother was replaced by that of the son, and with it came the banishment of women from primary roles in religious services. Gilder sees the same process at work in the exclusion of women from ancient drama, an exile that lasts some two thousand years. During this period, some of the greatest theatrical roles depicted women, but they were enacted by men. She writes:

> From the technical point of view the fact that women were not allowed to act on the Athenian stage would present little difficulty to the poet or choregus superintending the production of a play. All the actors wore masks and flowing robes which entirely covered them. . . . The voice alone could betray the fact that Antigone, Electra or Clytemnestra was being portrayed by a man, and this particular difficulty was overcome by the great care given to the training of the actors, for in the Greek theatre

[8] Gilder, 2.

the flexibility, power and beauty of a voice was the actor's greatest glory.[9]

When women eventually returned to performance, their position was far below that of sacred priestess. "When . . . the nobler aspects of the theatre were closed to her, [the actress] came in . . . by the Devil's way."[10] During the Roman era, female mimes performed during the interludes of the drama or in the street or marketplace. Such actresses were officially classed as prostitutes and were legally prohibited from marrying Roman citizens. Beyond that, the audience had "the right on certain days, to force the actress to strip . . . naked on the stage."[11]

This review of theatrical history reveals that: (1) woman originally had a sacred position in the drama; (2) this status was debased through exclusion or association with prostitution; and (3) the absence of women in the theater (from the classical period until the Renaissance) was compensated for by female impersonation. At the center of this issue would seem to be female sexuality: woman's early role of actress/priestess was dependent on her powers of fertility; her fallen position of actress/harlot was tied to her alleged promiscuity. Thus, within the history of the drama, female sexuality has either been celebrated, banished, or degraded.

The modern fascination with woman as actress may thus reveal ancient attitudes and ambivalences toward that role. Consider the fact that many female stars of the Hollywood classical cinema have been noted for their androgyny: Marlene Dietrich, Katharine Hepburn, Greta Garbo, and Joan Crawford, to name a few. Certain feminist critics see their masculinity as fetishistic, making the female body less awesome to the male spectator.[12] But none, to my knowledge, have linked this aura to the ancient practice of male cross-dressing in the theater, yet another technique for dispelling the threat of the female. Thus the male discomfort with the actress figure may yet live on in a more subtle fashion. Here I am reminded of Kenneth Tynan's remarks on Greta Garbo:

> I half-believed, until I met her, the old hilarious slander which whispered that she was a brilliant Swedish female impersonator who had kept up the pretense too long; behind the dark glasses, it was hinted, beneath the wild brown hair, there lurked the

[9] Ibid., 6.   [10] Ibid., 9.   [11] Ibid., 16.

[12] See Laura Mulvey, "Visual Pleasure and Narrative Cinema," in Gerald Mast and Marshall Cohen, eds., *Film Theory and Criticism* (New York: Oxford University Press, 1985), 803–16.

features of a proud Scandinavian diplomat, now proclaiming their masculinity so stridently that exposure to cameras was out of the question.[13]

Tynan assures us that, upon meeting Garbo, "this idle fabrication was demolished," for "This was a girl, all right." He asserts that it is "an indication of the mystery which surrounds [Garbo] that [he] felt pleased even to have ascertained her sex."

This mode of Hollywood androgyny differs from that of the ancient theater, for it involves women who seem manly rather than men aspiring to the feminine. But, on another level, these differences overlap—like the sexuality of the performer in *Victor/Victoria* (1982), who is both a woman and a woman playing a man playing a woman.

In *The World in a Frame*, Leo Braudy sees the contemporary obsession with the lurid sex lives of Hollywood stars as linked to the ancient association between drama and prostitution. But he fails to indicate that this connection has obtained only for women:

> Gossip about the fact that film actors and actresses may have been prostitutes or may have performed some kind of sexual acts to get their jobs has often been used as a way of minimizing them. . . . But such charges show an ignorance of stage history. Many great stage *actresses* in the Restoration, when *women* were first allowed onto the English stage, often kept up their practice as prostitutes. . . . There is an aesthetic continuity between all the professions that display the body.[14]

Why, if *all* acting emphasizes the body, was it only the *female* body that was traditionally associated with prostitution? This is a question that Braudy does not confront.

Perhaps there are more deep-seated connections between women and acting that explain the confusion of the actress with her sexuality. Gilder points to one when she traces the actress's appearance back to Genesis: "Ever since Eve invented costume, and, coached by the Serpent, enacted that little comedy by which she persuaded Adam that the bitter apple of knowledge was sweet and comforting, there has been something satanic in the very nature of the theatre."[15] In her charac-

[13] Kenneth Tynan, "Garbo," in Mast and Cohen, 722–23. For a more recent discussion of the issue of androgyny in the Hollywood cinema, see Rebecca Bell-Metereau, *Hollywood Androgyny* (New York: Columbia University Press, 1985).

[14] Leo Braudy, *The World in a Frame* (Garden City, N.Y.: Doubleday, 1976), 214 (my italics).

[15] Gilder, 8.

69

terization of Eve as actress, and her linkage of Eve's "performance" to original sin, Gilder reiterates ancient notions of woman as dangerous dissembler. As we well know, Eve's punishment will be a biological one—the menstrual cycle and the pangs of childbirth—demonstrating once more the ties between acting and the feminine.

Beyond this biblical association of woman and theatricality, there may be other, more psychological reasons for this characterization—and here I am offering pure speculation. In the previous chapter we have shown that the root of classical narrative resides in the male Oedipal situation, and we have seen that drama replayed in *The Lady from Shanghai.* At the heart of the Oedipal conflict is both the infant boy's desire to cast the mother as his sexual partner and his misprision that she will accept the role. After all, doesn't she shower him with love and affection, tend to all his bodily needs, and create for him a world of sensual pleasure linked to her very own body? When this fantasy is denied (at the symbolic stage), is it not possible that the son misconstrues his mother's prior behavior as a deceptive *act*? Could this explain some of the traditional male hostility to women? Could this explain man's tendency to see woman as archetypal performer?

Persona: Mommie Dearest

No film confirms this conjecture more clearly than Ingmar Bergman's experimental drama *Persona.* On a narrative level (to the extent that term applies), it is the story of an encounter between Elisabeth Vogler (Liv Ullmann), a performer experiencing a nervous breakdown, and Sister Alma (Bibi Andersson), a nurse who has been assigned to care for her at a seaside home. Since Elisabeth's primary "symptom" is her refusal to speak, Alma passes time by talking to her in lengthy monologues, confessing private details of her life. Elisabeth responds with mute but supportive silence, and Alma imagines them friends. One day, while taking Elisabeth's mail to the post office, Alma notices an unsealed letter and succumbs to the temptation to read it. She is crushed to find that Elisabeth has been corresponding with her husband about Alma's secrets, boasting that it has been fun to "study" her. Alma returns home enraged and, without telling Elisabeth why, becomes extremely hostile. At this point, the realistic story breaks down. What transpires is a series of confrontations between the women that seem to exist at a purely psychic level, that may or may not have "happened."

But to analyze *Persona*, one must begin with the work's abstract prologue, before the emergence of the narrative. A group of images depict an arc lamp illuminated and a film projector set in motion. We then see a montage of imagery that alludes to Bergman's earlier films: a spider, a bloody sheep's head, a crucified hand, a winter forest, a primitive silent film. Our attention is eventually directed to the figure of a young boy lying on a morgue slab or hospital bed. He sits up and then, facing us, touches what seems to be the anterior surface of the screen. In a reverse-angle shot (from behind him), we find that he is caressing huge projected photographic slides of women's faces that dissolve into one another. It is here that we first see the title of the film: *Persona.*

Bergman has stated that, in conceiving the work, he "made believe [he] was a little boy who'd died, yet who wasn't allowed to be really dead."[16] This is apparently the child we encounter in the prologue. One would have to look far and wide in the history of cinema to find a better symbol of the Oedipal perspective than this little boy (identified with the male director), who quizzically caresses the image of women on the movie/mind screen. But the Oedipal thrust of *Persona* goes far beyond the prologue and works its way into the narrative itself.

On one level, the story told in *Persona* can be viewed as a universal human drama. For Susan Sontag, it enacts a primal struggle of existence:

> If the maintenance of personality requires the safeguarding of the integrity of masks, and the truth about a person is always the cracking of the mask, then the truth about life as a whole is the shattering of the total facade behind which lies an absolute cruelty.[17]

Although this theme of the duplicity of all human life is certainly extant in *Persona*, it must be remembered that Bergman has chosen to dramatize it in a film exclusively about *women*—a fact that is generally ignored. Critic Robert Boyers, for instance, says that "[i]t never occurred to [him] to take seriously the suggestion that Bergman was interested specifically in *women*" when he made *Persona*.[18] We, however, *will* in order to wrest from the film those elements that stress the inauthenticity of the female.

[16] Ingmar Bergman, quoted in Bruce Kawin, *Mindscreen* (Princeton, N.J.: Princeton University Press, 1978), 107.

[17] Susan Sontag, "*Persona*: The Film in Depth," in Leo Braudy and Morris Dickstein, eds., *Great Film Directors* (New York: Oxford University Press, 1978), 83.

[18] Robert Boyers, "Bergman and Women," *Salmagundi*, no. 40 (Winter 1978): 132.

Central to this issue is the characterization of Elisabeth Vogler, who is the professional actress and the one ostensibly disturbed. Because *Persona* is not a conventional narrative, we are denied the usual exposition of her problems, but over the course of the film, a pattern nonetheless emerges. We are told that she first fell silent during a performance of the Greek tragedy *Electra* (see fig. 6). While she is still in the hospital, we see her reject a letter from her husband and destroy a photograph of her son. Already, the matricidal theme of *Electra*, the torn image of her child, her anxiety about her husband make us suspect that she is uncomfortable with her maternal and marital roles.

The primary revelation about Elisabeth however, comes later in the film after her relationship with Nurse Alma has entirely deteriorated. Alma finds (or imagines that she finds) Elisabeth hiding the snapshot of her son in her hand. She asks Elisabeth what she is concealing, then asks to talk about it. What follows is a speech by Alma about Elisabeth. It is rendered in a voice-over monologue as the camera focuses on images of the actress.[19]

Alma begins by describing how Elisabeth made the decision to have a child, making clear that it was tied to her profession as an actress:

[19] The text below is quoted from the English-subtitled version of the film. It may not represent a word-for-word translation. A variation on this text appears in the published screenplay for the film: Ingmar Bergman, "*Persona* and *Shame*," trans. Keith Bradfield (New York: Grossman, 1972). Some passages are quoted from it.

6. *Persona* (1966). The actress (Liv Ullmann) fell silent during a performance of *Electra*.

> It was one evening at a party, wasn't it? . . . In the small hours
> someone said: "Elisabeth, you have everything as a woman and
> an artist; but you lack motherliness." You laughed; you thought
> it was silly. But you couldn't help thinking of what he said. You
> grew more and more worried; and you let your husband make
> you pregnant. You wanted to be a mother.

Alma then recounts how Elisabeth grew severely apprehensive about
her pregnancy, though she continued to play the role of radiant madonna:

> When you were certain, you grew afraid . . . afraid of respon-
> sibility, of being tied down, afraid of pain, afraid of dying,
> afraid of your swelling body. But all the time you acted . . . the
> part of a happy, expectant mother. And everyone said: "How
> lovely she is; never has she been so beautiful."

Finally, Alma relates how Elisabeth's doubts about pregnancy grew
into loathing and violence, unleashing murderous impulses:

> You tried to get rid of the fetus, but you failed. When there was
> no going back, you began to hate the child, and hope it would
> be stillborn. You wanted a dead child. It was a long and difficult
> delivery. . . . You looked with disgust and horror at your de-
> formed baby and whispered: "Can't you die?"

Alma concludes her monologue by describing Elisabeth's hostile rejection of her son:

> it survived . . . and you hated him. You were afraid, you had a
> bad conscience. At last the boy was taken in by relatives and
> you could leave your sickbed and go back to the theater. But
> your suffering was not over. The boy was seized by a strange
> and violent love for his mother. . . . Your meetings with him are
> cruel and clumsy. You are cold and indifferent.

This text makes clear an association between Elisabeth's breakdown
and her failure to fulfill the maternal role—to be a "natural" woman.
Beyond that, it seems to mark as the site of female authenticity her
reproductive function. Surely, if the crisis had occurred to a man, it
would have been about something *different*: we think of the Knight's
existential doubts in *The Seventh Seal* (1958), or of the pastor's religious agony in *Winter Light* (1962), or of the artist's struggle in *The
Magician* (1959).

This confrontation also makes clear the association of woman/ac-

73

tress with the maternal role. Alma accuses Elisabeth of playing the part of the glowing pregnant woman, even though she hates her fetus. The monologue also voices the Oedipal complaint of the unloved son, who continues to adore his mother despite her brutality toward him, who is seized by an "incredible violent love." This emphasis urges us to recast retroactively the prologue boy (already a surrogate for Bergman) as a stand-in for Elisabeth's child. It would seem to be *he* who caresses the images of his mother, trying to possess or fathom them. As Alma intones her monologue, we see ever-larger close-ups of Elisabeth's face until they reach the size assumed in the prologue when the boy tries to grasp them. The similar size of the facial images not only links the two sequences but ties them to the perspective of an infant, for whom the maternal visage is grand, awesome, and grotesque. The fact that the boy caresses *photographs* of the actress's face reinforces the sense of her duplicitous distance, for this mode of mechanical reproduction negates (what Walter Benjamin would term) her "aura" and alienates her from her filial audience.[20]

Elisabeth not only has to fake her maternal role but must feign the conjugal duties of a wife—further evidence of her need to perform off-stage. Earlier in the film, Alma imagines herself surprised by a visit from Mr. Vogler, who (apparently blind, like an aged Oedipus) approaches the nurse as though she were his wife. Alma enacts the role of Elisabeth, as the actress voyeuristically looks on. When the couple retreats to the bedroom to make love, Mr. Vogler asks: "Do you like being with me? Is it good with me?" At first, Alma says he is a "wonderful lover" but then calls for "something to stupefy [her] senses." Finally, she cries: "I can't do it any longer. . . . You mustn't touch me, it's shame, a dishonour, [a] counterfeit, a lie."[21] Thus Alma's dramatization casts the actress's sex life as a sham, merely a prostitute's "trick." This sense of Elisabeth's romantic disingenuousness is furthered by the homoerotic themes of the film, which interrogate the status of Elisabeth's heterosexuality itself as a theatrical routine.

We cannot regard *Persona* as a realistic drama that creates fully rounded characters. Nonetheless, it is significant that the sketchy "motivations" Bergman provides for his abstract personae so completely conform to the stereotype of woman as archetypal actress. Again, in *Persona* the actress/woman must role-play in life. As ever, her status as

[20] Walter Benjamin, "The Work of Art in the Age of Mechanical Reproduction," in *Illuminations*, ed. Hannah Arendt, trans. Harry Zohn (New York: Harcourt, Brace & World, 1968), 217–51.

[21] This quote is from the screenplay for *Persona*, 88–89.

performer is tied to her fecundity and her sexual relations with men. In the prologue's image of a half-dead boy, we even have a reiteration of the "child who dies to be reborn," which Gilder cites as a staple of fertility rites. In the figure of Alma, we have a representation of one of the goddess's "attendant women."

That Bergman means this picture of woman/actress to hold for *all* females is clear from his portrayal of the other character in the film, Nurse Alma. Although, on a diegetic level, she is not a performer, she is shown to dissemble. (She even confesses to Elisabeth that once, after seeing her in a film, she felt that she could be "just like her.") Again, Alma's theatricality will center on her maternal function and her sexual encounters with men.

In the beginning of the film, Alma views herself as a well-adjusted woman who knows what she wants, personally and professionally. As she goes to sleep one night in the hospital, she muses:

> I'll marry Karl-Henrik and we'll have a couple of kids that I'll bring up. That's all decided, it's in me somewhere. I don't have to work things out at all, how they're going to be. That makes you feel very safe. And I'm doing a job I like. That's a good thing too—only in a different way. I wonder what's really wrong with Mrs. Vogler.[22]

She sees herself as opposed to the actress—and, for the time being, so do we.

As the narrative progresses, however, and Alma confesses more about herself, her life begins to seem less coherent. She reveals that she was involved with a married man and that, although she will wed Karl-Henrik, "you only love once." She also tells Elisabeth about an orgy that she experienced with a girl friend and some young boys. Though she never admitted it to her fiancé, sex with him on the night of the debauch was never again so good. Finally, she confesses that she became pregnant from the orgy and had an abortion. She is tortured with guilt and, in recounting the incident, breaks down in sobs.

Alma's maternal function is questioned in yet another way. At the start of the film, she defines herself as a nurse—a nurturing medical professional. By the end of the narrative, however, she has shed that role and is as hostile and hysterical as her patient. At the outset Alma seems the Good Mother to Elisabeth's Bad, but by the end of the work, the polarities have collapsed into a single composite image of maternal

---

[22] Ibid., 32.

malevolence—a concept symbolized in the women's blended, bisected faces.

Alma has evidently been as much of an actress as Elisabeth. Although she imagines her life in order, she has severe doubts. Significantly, her concerns are identical to those of Elisabeth: she questions her maternal impulse and her ability to love a man. This sense of the two women as coequal is made most explicit when Alma describes Elisabeth's experience of maternity. In the original screenplay, Alma keeps interchanging the pronouns "you" and "I" in addressing Elisabeth, making it clear that she confuses herself with the actress. In the English-subtitled version, that verbal slippage is eliminated, but Alma's monologue about Elisabeth is repeated, the second time presenting images of her onscreen. Furthermore, we might wonder how Alma knows Elisabeth's most secret feelings if they are not, on some level, her own. Bergman obviously sees the taint of inauthenticity as applicable to both figures—a theme he extends through a web of doubling imagery in the film. The women are often dressed identically in black turtlenecks or straw hats. Often their blocking transforms them into a composite being: in one scene of the women at the kitchen table, Alma's head seems superimposed on Elisabeth's body. But the charge of inauthenticity extends beyond Alma and Elisabeth to all women who are envisioned as actresses in their maternal and sexual roles.

Although Alma and Elisabeth play out a drama of Good Mother versus Bad, they also enact the relationship of mother and child—a theme that Birgitta Steene has found prevalent in Bergman's work.[23] As Alma relinquishes her maternal, medical functions, she slips into a juvenile relationship with Elisabeth, confessing things to her like a daughter and imagining herself the apple of her confidante's eye. This illusion is shattered by Elisabeth's letter, which reveals a parental attitude of bemused, concerned condescension. After this epiphany, Alma behaves like a hurt, rejected child who feels her parent has not loved her enough. With her short-cropped hair, she even looks like the prologue boy, which links her view of Elisabeth to his Oedipal complaint.

There are even scenes in *Persona* where the women symbolically enact the Lacanian "mirror phase," in which the mother holds the child up to a reflecting surface, whereupon the latter first recognizes itself as a separate being. As E. Ann Kaplan explains:

[23] Birgitta Steene, "Bergman's Portrait of Women: Sexism or Suggestive Metaphor?" in Patricia Erens, ed., *Sexual Stratagems: The World of Women in Film* (New York: Horizon, 1979), 91–107.

> The illusory unity with the Mother is broken ... with the
> child's recognition of the Mother as a separate image/entity and
> of himself as an image (ego-ideal), creating the structure of the
> divided subject. ... Although the child now lives in the sym-
> bolic, he still longs for the world of the imaginary.[24]

The most evocative scenes, in this respect, are those in which Elisabeth brings Alma to (what seems to be) a mirror and brushes the latter's hair away from her face, making the women look more alike.
Here Elisabeth again functions as the mother who shows the child that
she is distinct but (in some ways) "just like her." Later in the film, when
the women's relationship has ruptured, Alma looks into another mirror alone and repeats the gesture, whereupon an image of Elisabeth's
visage is superimposed on her face. Once more, this Lacanian discourse articulates the theme of mothering and the child's difficulties in
separation. Retroactively, the character doubling in *Persona* can be
read as expressing an infantile longing for symbiosis, "for the world of
the imaginary."

The film ends with an abstract epilogue that matches the opening
sequence. Just before the arc lamp is extinguished, the boy is seen
touching the huge facial images of Alma/Elisabeth projected on a
screen. The implications of this boy go beyond his identification with
Bergman or his connection to Elisabeth's son. Rather, he seems the
implied *protagonist* of the narrative, the central consciousness through
which the drama is formulated. It is his Oedipal view of women that
we must witness, his complaints that we must hear. In this sense, Alma
and Elisabeth (as women) are only the "pseudocenters" of the filmic
discourse, despite their omnipresence on camera.[25]

But the boy in supplication before the screen is suggestive of something else. In his essay "The Apparatus," Jean-Louis Baudry examines
the ideological implications of the cinema setup: the darkened room,
the projected light, the shadows on the screen, the spectator in the audience. Baudry sees a parallel between this situation and Plato's myth
of the cave, in which prisoners (chained there since birth) watch shadows projected on the cave wall and mistake them for the real world.
Baudry links both Plato's cave and the cinema to yet another text—
Freud's theories of dream and the unconscious. Like the prisoners in

---

[24] E. Ann Kaplan, *Women and Film: Both Sides of the Camera* (New York and London: Methuen, 1983), 19.

[25] Claire Johnston, "Myths of Women in the Cinema," in Karyn Kay and Gerald
Peary, *Women and the Cinema: A Critical Anthology* (New York: Dutton, 1977), 411.

Plato's womblike cave, Baudry configures the cinema spectator as engaged in a regression toward an infantile state that reestablishes an illusory dyad with the mother.

On one level, Baudry sees this state as almost prenatal. He tells us that cinema replicates the dream, and that, according to Freud, "Sleep . . . is *a reviviscence of one's stay in the body of the mother*."[26] But on another level, the cinema (and dream) also harks back to the oral stage. Here Baudry draws on Bertram Lewin's notion of the dream screen— a phenomenon that presents "itself in all dreams as the indispensable support for the projection of images."[27] Ultimately, Lewin sees this dream screen as an "hallucinatory representation of the mother's breast on which the child used to fall asleep after nursing."[28] Thus the cinema apparatus may be likened to the mother not only in its replication of a dream/womb state but in its presentation of a surface for imagery—like the maternal breast on which the dozing infant once projected its fantasies (the work of reproduction in the age of mechanical art).

For Baudry, the presuppositions of the cinema—the conditions of spectatorship, the film equipment itself—solicit and answer the viewer's need for regression toward maternal union—and, in this sense, constitute a device of wish fulfillment. We can suppose that the wish might have a stronger pull on the male, who has experienced a more traumatic separation from the mother than the female. But Baudry's conception also would seem to literalize Gilles Deleuze and Félix Guattari's notion of desire as a "machine"—a concept discussed in *Anti-Oedipus*. Here is how they describe the relation between desire and creation:

> The artist is the master of objects; he puts before us shattered, burned, broken-down objects, converting them to the regime of desiring machines, breaking down is part of the very functioning of desiring-machines. . . . Even more important, the work of art is itself a desiring-machine.[29]

[26] Sigmund Freud, quoted in Jean-Louis Baudry, "The Apparatus," *Camera Obscura*, no. 1 (1976): 114.

[27] Bertram Lewin, quoted in ibid., 116. Baudry is referring to Bertram Lewin, "Sleep, The Mouth and the Dream Screen," *Psychoanalytic Quarterly* 15 (1946): 419–43, and "Inferences from the Dream Screen," *International Journal of Psychoanalysis* 29 (1948): 224–431.

[28] Ibid., 117.

[29] Gilles Deleuze and Félix Guattari, *Anti-Oedipus: Capitalism and Schizophrenia*,

If, for Baudry, the cinema apparatus is an elaborate desiring machine, so is the particular film that Bergman has crafted—one that literally "breaks down," "shatters," and "burns" during the course of its unwinding. For Baudry, the cinema apparatus itself injects an Oedipal dimension into the art. On the one hand, such a view might help feminist critics explain the prevalence of this scenario within the mainstream film; on the other hand, acceptance of Baudry's formulation leaves women no way out, since the cinema's very technology is thereby damned.

In *Persona*, Bergman literalizes Baudry's notion of the filmic apparatus, stumbling upon it himself. And the reason that he does so may be tied to the film's production. Like one of Baudry or Plato's cave dwellers, Bergman himself was an immobile "prisoner" prior to the making of the film, confined to a hospital bed. He has stated:

> Before making [*Persona*] I was ill, having twice had pneumonia and antibiotic poisoning. I lost my balance for three months. . . . I remember sitting in my hospital bed looking directly in front of me at a black spot—because if I turned my head at all, the whole room began to spin.[30]

As Baudry has noted, motionless states encourage regression, since they replay, on a somatic level, our infantile physical constraints.

It is also useful to recall Bergman's "surrogate" in *Persona*—the boy who sits at the screen. What better emblem could there be for Baudry's archetypal spectator than this child who caresses a screen on which is reflected the maternal visage? (One critic even described the boy as lying in a "fetal position," as appearing to be in "the womb.")[31]

Throughout *Persona* there are countless ways that the text (through a hyperbolic use of shot/countershot) sutures the audience into the narrative, urging acceptance of the film's point of view. Characters often look right at the camera and, by extension, at the viewers who watch them. When Elisabeth takes Alma to the "mirror," the women look at us, and we become the implied reflective surface. At another point, Elisabeth is shown taking a photograph, and she aims her lens at the

trans. Robert Hurley, Mark Seem, and Helen R. Lane (Minneapolis: University of Minnesota Press, 1983), 32.

[30] Bergman, quoted in Kawin, 104–5.

[31] Marilyn Johns Blackwell, *Persona: The Transcendent Image* (Urbana and Chicago: University of Illinois Press, 1986): 26–27.

audience. In other scenes, characters talk directly to us, although we "represent" other figures in the drama. Early on, when Elisabeth is still in the hospital, Alma is summoned by a psychiatrist. During their session, the doctor remains offscreen, and Alma responds to her voice while addressing us. But it is the boy at the screen with whom we most identify. As Robert Eberwein has pointed out:

> It is as if the boy's glance and movement toward us initially connect us as mirror images. Now, as he watches, we also (the beings implied by his first glance) duplicate his perceptual activity.[32]

Thus *Persona* is not only a film that, on a dramatic level, sees woman as mother, and mother as quintessential actress, but one that creates an image to literalize the Oedipal perspective on narrative and associate woman's body with the cinema apparatus. Curiously, it is not Bergman but Federico Fellini who best articulates this view of film:

> I think the cinema is a woman. . . . This uterus which is the theater, the fetal darkness, the apparition—all create a projected relationship, we project ourselves onto it . . . just as we do with women.[33]

The Girls: The Actress as Activist

> As an actress, singer, dancer, showing my legs and my
> cleavage, I had been no threat at all: men could fantasize
> about me. . . . But now that I have managed to take that
> decisive step and become a director of films, I am considered
> unusual: I am not the same any more in the eyes of men.
> —Mai Zetterling[34]

Having analyzed *Persona*, we turn to another film about the actress: Mai Zetterling's *The Girls*. Beyond a shared subject, the films can be intertextually paired for other reasons. Both were made in Sweden in the late 1960s and display a modernist aesthetic, dispensing with realistic narrative to present an interior world where fantasy and reality clash. Both cast Bibi Andersson in leading roles, lending them

---

[32] Robert Eberwein, *Film and the Dream Screen* (Princeton, N.J.: Princeton University Press, 1984): 124.

[33] Federico Fellini, in Gideon Bachmann, "Federico Fellini: The Cinema Seen as a Woman . . . ," *Film Quarterly* 34, no. 2 (Winter 1980–81): 8.

[34] Mai Zetterling, *All Those Tomorrows: An Autobiography* (New York: Grove Press, 1985), 2.

an even greater symmetry. Furthermore, Zetterling once acted in a Bergman film, *Music in the Dark* (1947), and seems to have felt ambivalence toward the director. In her autobiography she writes: "Whenever I am asked what I think of Ingmar Bergman, I always say the same thing: 'You don't necessarily need to like genius, but you can . . . admire it.' "[35] Although Zetterling does not directly criticize Bergman's work, she does so obliquely through an anecdote she relates about her lover, Tyrone Power: "[He] found it hard to believe that Ingmar preferred women to men, as he felt that the women in Ingmar's movies were bitchy and hard, castrating ladies, and that men were always shown in a more interesting and positive light. . . . It was interesting to hear that from Tyrone, as it was not the accepted view."[36]

On a dramatic level, *The Girls* concerns a troupe of touring actors appearing in a production of Aristophanes' *Lysistrata*. Although the film presents the group as a whole, it concentrates on three actresses; the male director and other performers are decidedly minor characters. Rather than follow the external action of the company's trip across Sweden, the narrative focuses on the consciousness of the women, constantly shifting from exterior to interior views. Real occurrences merge with the women's thoughts, memories, and fantasies, and the status of screen events is highly ambiguous. Unlike *Persona*, this move into woman's mind is not read as a descent into madness but rather as a route to a sane perspective on a sexist world.

While *Persona* takes a mythic stance—identifying the actress with woman as "duplicitous" mother or lover—*The Girls* presents a far more materialist picture of the female performer, despite its fantastic aura. Though motherhood is a central issue in the film, it is not treated with the Oedipal overlay of *Persona*. Instead, it is seen within the context of the working woman and the problems associated with her stressful, fractured life. In the film's opening sequence, Marianne (Harriet Andersson) runs onto the stage, late for a rehearsal. The play's director curtly asks her where she has been, then criticizes her delivery of certain lines. "An actress who wasn't late," he says, "could make [the dialogue] sound urgent." We then see a flashback, from Marianne's point of view, in which she wrests her son from a man. A child's scream is heard in the reverie, then merges with the sound of her son crying in the theater wings. The director snaps: "I hope you're not taking *him* on tour!" The sequence demonstrates the tensions faced by the actress as a working parent and the insensitivity displayed by her

[35] Ibid., 77.   [36] Ibid., 135–36.

male employer. Zetterling herself recalls the tribulations of a stage career conjoined with motherhood:

> [My] child was brought to the theater and fed in the wings at rehearsal. I was playing Electra in *The Flies*. . . . It was a wild role that took all the energy I had left, only two months after the birth. On the first night, when the author was there, I fainted between two long speeches and yet again when I ran into the wings.[37]

Several other sequences of *The Girls* concentrate on maternity, approaching the topic from a concrete perspective. Early in the film, Marianne leaves a store and hears a child screaming on the street. As she runs home, the noise continues on the soundtrack. When she opens her apartment door, she is relieved to find her son perfectly content. Clearly, the child on the street has made her anxious about her own son at home. Here, and throughout the film, the free-associational logic of Zetterling's audiovisual editing immerses us in the minds of the actresses and allows us to empathize with their psychological plight. It also gives us access to the female voice—a perspective we are denied with the mute Elisabeth Vogler.

The theme of motherhood is extended in *The Girls* by following a second actress, played by Gunnel Lindblom. In one sequence, she stands in a travel agency, recalling or fantasizing a scene of her children draping toilet paper around the house as their helpless father watches. Much to Zetterling's credit (as coscenarist of the film), one of the performers she considers, Liz (Bibi Andersson), is apparently not a parent, so there is no attempt to impose motherhood as a favored role. Liz's lack of maternity is not portrayed as a problem, as it was for Elisabeth Vogler; rather, it seems to liberate her for feminist/political action.

Other women's issues are raised in *The Girls* through its focus on the figure of the actress, who is seen as the archetypal female living in a paternalistic world. The women are clearly devalued by their male director and coperformers. As the men watch them being interviewed on television, they chuckle and ask: "Have you ever met women who could take things seriously?" The men's position is all the more outrageous because they are appearing in *Lysistrata*, which details women's crucial role in stopping war. Like the men in *Lysistrata*, they are really the ones who fail to see what is serious in life.

The actresses are also shown to face sexism from their male audi-

[37] Ibid., 80.

ence, who are trained to see them as "showgirls." Zetterling experienced this phenomenon in her own career. "To be admired for your beauty, your sexiness . . ." she writes, "is both dangerous and disconcerting." She recalls feeling "ill-suited to playing the cutie-pie, the piece of ass."[38]

In *The Girls*, when Liz has dinner with a couple in a town on the tour, the man thinks that she is "beginning to look old" and wonders whether she "could be fun." These thoughts would not surface about an actor, whose age, beauty, or sexual availability are less tied to his role. Later in the film, during a fantasy sequence, Liz disrobes for a group of male reporters. We are again reminded of the historic root of the actress's profession in prostitution and of the Roman crowd's right to demand that she undress. In aggressively casting herself in a striptease, Liz attempts to subvert her social roles by "play[ing] with mimesis." As Irigaray notes, this requires that women "make visible" by an effect of playful repetition what was supposed to remain invisible.[39] Liz's imagined striptease also characterizes femininity as a "masquerade"—a concept elaborated by Mary Ann Doane. Thus Liz can be seen to "flaunt her femininity, produce herself as an excess of femininity . . . foreground the masquerade . . . acknowledg[ing] that it is femininity itself which is constructed as mask—as the decorative layer which conceals a non-identity."[40]

The actresses in *The Girls* face sexual innuendo in nontheatrical areas of their lives. When one (Gunnel Lindblom) goes to a market, the cheese salesman comments lasciviously that she can have "anything [she] wants." When the actresses dine one evening at a restaurant, some men try to pick them up and are insulted when the women do not respond. The men claim that they should be "grateful" for not being left alone. Zetterling follows this encounter with a whimsical scene of the women back in their hotel room, dancing together and having fun.

The actresses face other problems that riddle women's lives: for example, how their careers affect male mates. In a flashback, the husband of one actress inquires sarcastically how long the tour will last, indicating that he resents being left alone. The husband of another implies that he is uncomfortable earning less than his wife. One actress complains that her husband does not take her work seriously.

[38] Ibid., 99, 103.   [39] Irigaray, 76.
[40] Mary Ann Doane, "Film and the Masquerade—Theorising the Female Spectator," *Screen* 23, no. 3–4 (September–October 1982): 81.

Still other questions are raised about the double standard that applies to men's and women's erotic lives. Liz's husband, Carl, is having affairs with at least two women. Ironically, his wife's career as a touring performer enables him to conduct these liaisons quite effortlessly. Although Carl thinks he is being discreet, Liz knows about these trysts and finds them rather ridiculous. In one of her fantasies, she imagines Carl arriving to visit her, unpacking his mistresses from his suitcase, using them as hangars on which to drape his clothes. He implores his wife to be cheerful and understanding and to welcome his friends. In the final scene, Liz fantasizes that she publicly announces their divorce.

Throughout the film, Zetterling rejects Bergman's formulation of the actress as mythic screen for male fears and desires—and instead envisions her as incarnating *socialized* woman, confronting myriad untenable roles in masculine culture. Many of the differences between the films surface around (what Riffaterre would call) the "third text" that "mediates" them: Greek drama. While Bergman's actress performs in *Electra*—a narrative of matricide and a daughter's revenge—Zetterling's actresses appear in *Lysistrata*—a comedy in which women assume a role in opposing war. Significantly, the heroines of both works would originally have been played by men, in keeping with ancient theatrical tradition.

Within *Lysistrata*, women are mocked for their attempt to confront affairs of state, but it is clear that they (and not the men) have the humane and rational perspective on politics. If male expertise is associated with death, then female power will be aligned with life. As she embodies Lysistrata, Liz becomes convinced that in order to prevent massive global destruction, women must take action. Here *The Girls* not only traces Liz's attempts to grow as an actress but to forge a political role for herself. As she enacts the play in various cities on tour, she becomes angry at the audience's inattention. During one performance, she breaks character and directly addresses the spectators, asking them if it is possible to change themselves and the world. The director shouts, "What? Another revolt among women?" and takes her off the stage. The events of *Lysistrata* are doubled in the story of Liz, who becomes progressively more interested in a social role (see fig. 7). Furthermore, the male world portrayed in *The Girls* is not only sexist but violent and necrophilic—a manifestation of Mary Daly's vision of patriarchy as a "state of war."[41]

[41] Mary Daly, *Gyn/Ecology: The Metaethics of Radical Feminism* (Boston: Beacon Press, 1978), 31, 61.

84

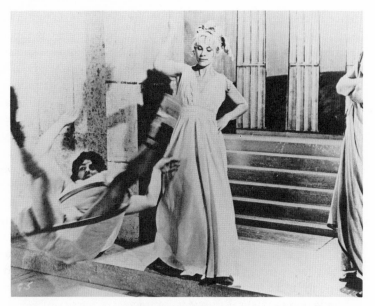

7. *The Girls* (1969). The events of *Lysistrata* are doubled in the story of the actress, Liz (Bibi Andersson).

This theme of masculine destruction is advanced by a fantasy sequence depicting the women sitting in a movie theater, jeering at newsreels of Lyndon Johnson, Benito Mussolini, and Adolph Hitler. They throw pies at the screen as their spouses and lovers appear on stage before the images of goose-stepping armies. These women are not the numbed, infantile film spectators envisioned by Baudry (and Bergman) but aggressive participants (and opponents) in the cinematic spectacle.

In the next scene, the actresses tour a bomb shelter, as a male guide proudly shows them the youth club, bar, and theater. In a later fantasy, the husband of one actress complacently sits in an armchair in a war-ravaged forest, ignoring the detonating bombs around him. On the soundtrack we hear a line from *Lysistrata* in which a man tells the women: "You haven't the least idea what war means." The actress's satirical critique of war in *The Girls* contrasts sharply with Elisabeth Vogler's stunned response to world violence in *Persona*, as she stands mesmerized by scenes of Vietnam brutality on her television screen or paralyzed by a photograph of Jews rounded up in the Warsaw ghetto.

This points up a larger difference between the two works, based again on the texts that "mediate" them. While *Persona* draws upon the model of tragedy (alluding to *Electra*), *The Girls* incorporates the stance of comedy—not only in its homage to *Lysistrata* but in its stylistic mode. Significantly, at one point, Liz (in her role as the Greek heroine) comments that women are a "helpless lot" and exclaims: "No wonder tragedies are written about us." Zetterling intends to revise literary and cinematic history by drawing on a satirical paradigm.

Throughout *The Girls*, Zetterling utilizes the play-within-a-play motif to demonstrate parallels between the world of Aristophanes' ancient drama and that of her three contemporary women. Early in the film, Marianne recalls a sexual romp with her lover that ends in tears. Intercut with this flashback are scenes from the play, in which women discuss the strategy of withholding sex from men in order to force them to cease warfare. One woman shouts: "I won't lift my legs to the sky" or "crouch on all fours"; another promises that she will "stiffen and reject" her lover. We have the sense that Marianne, too, should adopt this posture as a way of terminating her unhappy affair. This parallel between the actress and the world of *Lysistrata* is underscored at a later point in the film when, during a performance, Marianne's lover suddenly and fantastically appears onstage.

Like Aristophanes, Zetterling sees hope for the world in women's political action—aimed simultaneously at countering male sexism and militarism. Within the play, Lysistrata cries: "Now it's up to the women folk to do something about the world." Thus Liz shares the ideology of her stage persona. After noticing the men asleep in the audience, she suggests a staging for women alone. Moreover, she dares to break out of her dramatic role and admonish the audience to attend to the message of the play. "I know," she says, "I shouldn't say something apart from the play," but she proceeds to speak in her own voice, discarding the lines of the printed text.

Although Zetterling can be applauded for having her female protagonist call for political action, she must be criticized for leaving the solutions entirely vague. If men have failed to lead the world, how will women succeed? What kind of positions must they take? Zetterling also seems to undercut her call for a feminist movement when, in one fantasy sequence, a group of demonstrating women begin to fight with one another. Finally, even her choice of *Lysistrata* as a literary text is problematic. We might ask, first of all, whether an ancient drama can really stand as a model for action today. Furthermore, while it advances the notion of woman's political role, it is only her sexual powers that give her clout. The play does, however, make clear the stance of femininity as a masquerade, and the regrettable fact that only by "flaunting" her theatrical role does woman traditionally achieve any power.

Despite its limitations, *The Girls* contrasts sharply with Bergman's *Persona* in its presentation of the actress as feminist and activist. Unlike Bergman, Zetterling does not mythify the female performer or burden her with male ideals or stereotypes. Rather, she sees her as a woman in the world—destined to play a role not only in the household or theater but on the political "stage."

Curtain Call: All About Eve

It was the time of the sweater-girls with prominent tits. . . . I remember standing in the Champs-Elysées gaping in wonder and surprise at the great tits that had suddenly grown [on me] on the poster of Frieda. *My breasts are of normal size, nothing outstanding, or should I say, upstanding, but on the poster they certainly were, quite out of proportion to the rest of my body. If I had had such ornaments in reality, I would have been quite dangerous, as they were pointed like needles.*
—Mai Zetterling[42]

The actress role has, indeed, been a "key female figure throughout film history," and there are many reasons for her privileged position in fictional screen narrative. We have noted woman's societal "role-playing dimension," finding that many films about the actress focus on her need for deception both on and off the stage. These works have also stressed the actress's need to perform for men—to enact the feminine Other.

In addition to this sociological notion, we have found deeper, more concealed reasons for woman's association with theatricality. We have traced the historical trajectory of the actress's fate: from her original sacred position to her exile from the stage to her demotion to prostitute. Throughout, the female performer has been associated with her sexuality—be it the fertility of the actress/priestess or the contamination of the actress/harlot.

Going beyond theater, we have located certain psychological causes for the male formulation of woman as actress, finding the Oedipal perspective of son confronting mother central in this regard. Also important is the male fear of woman performing disingenuously in sex—feigning pleasure, enacting the prostitute's "trick."

[42] Zetterling, 102–3.

87

We have also unearthed the biblical characterization of woman as actress, and theatricality as original sin. This notion finds its way into a contemporary film like Alfred Hitchcock's *Stage Fright*, where one actress is named Eve and the second (Charlotte Inwood) is implicated in murder by a blood-stained skirt. One evening, while Charlotte is performing, Eve's father tries to force a confession from her by bringing a doll into the theater costumed in a bloodied dress. What better symbols could there be of Eve's biblical punishment than the sullied dress and childlike doll—icons of the "curse" of menstruation/maternity?

In Ingmar Bergman's *Persona*, we have found a confirmation of the male stereotype of woman as dissembler—especially in her primal roles of mother and lover. Mai Zetterling's *The Girls* rebuts this view—in part, through the mediation of Greek theater. Zetterling does not mythify the actress but treats her as a working woman juggling maternal and career goals in a hostile, male-oriented world. For Zetterling, the actress's role is not inherently perverse but potentially redemptive, giving woman a platform and a voice. Instead of being passive (like the catatonic Elisabeth Vogler), Zetterling's actress is a vital figure. She does not simply perform; she *acts*—she makes an imp*act* on the world. Perhaps, in this aggressive stance, Eve finally gets the right part after being "miscast" in the long-running patriarchal drama.

In the Bergman film, the actress personifies what woman is in *nature* (an alleged figure of duplicity), whereas within the Zetterling work, she epitomizes what woman is in *culture* (an inveterate masquerader). But just as Liz momentarily explodes the social charade with her ironic striptease, so Irigaray envisions women attempting to subvert theatricality through a shift in emphasis: "One must assume the feminine role deliberately. Which means already to convert a form of subordination into an affirmation, and thus to begin to thwart it."[43] It is this tone of ironic rebellion that we sense in Zetterling's thoughts on the Champs-Elysées and that resurfaces in *The Girls*.[44]

[43] Irigaray, 76.

[44] I presented this chapter in the form of a paper at the Columbia University Film Seminar in September 1986 and received many useful comments from Joan Copjec, Miriam Hansen, Janet Staiger, E. Ann Kaplan, John Belton, Liz Weis, Charles Affron, Charles Musser, and Tom Gunning.

4 Kiss Me Deadly: Heterosexual Romance

Foreword

Man's love is of man's life a thing apart; 'Tis woman's whole existence. —Lord Byron[1]

One gets an impression that a man's love and a woman's are a phase apart psychologically. —Sigmund Freud[2]

It is a truism of the commercial cinema that the subject of love is central to the standard plot mechanism. Whether the genre is western, musical, crime film, or comedy, the fulcrum of the drama typically rests on a heterosexual romance. In this respect, films partake of a broader feature of the storied world which (contemporary critical theory has shown) relentlessly enacts the erotic quest.[3] Roland Barthes writes: "At the origin of Narrative, desire."[4] And Teresa de Lauretis applies that notion to the cinema: "The very work of [film] narrativity is the engagement of the subject in certain positionalities of meaning and desire."[5]

In their portrayal of love, however, diegetic forms have not been neutral; they have plotted the romantic quest along the lines of sexual difference, for desire does not exist in the abstract but attaches to a subject, either male or female. Here it is important that the clichéd summary of a love story is the phrase "boy meets girl," revealing the male bias at its core. As de Lauretis points out, storytelling involves the "mapping . . . of sexual difference into each text."[6]

This chapter will consider the portrayal of heterosexual romance in the cinema through an examination of several representative works, positioned for comparative analysis. The first film is Max Ophuls's

---

[1] Lord Byron, quoted in Simone de Beauvoir, *The Second Sex*, trans. H. M. Parshley (New York: Vintage, 1974), 712.

[2] Sigmund Freud, "Femininity," in James Strachey, ed., *The Standard Edition of the Complete Psychological Works of Sigmund Freud* (London: Hogarth Press, 1955), 22:134. Quoted in Teresa de Lauretis, *Alice Doesn't: Feminism, Semiotics, Cinema* (Bloomington: Indiana University Press, 1984), 133.

[3] Roland Barthes, *S/Z*, trans. Richard Miller (New York: Hill and Wang, 1974); Roland Barthes, *The Pleasures of the Text*, trans. Richard Miller (New York: Hill and Wang, 1975); René Girard, *Deceit, Desire and the Novel: Self and Other in Literary Structure*, trans. Yvonne Freccero (Baltimore: Johns Hopkins, 1966); Edward Branigan, *Point of View in the Cinema: A Theory of Narration and Subjectivity in Classical Film* (New York: Mouton, 1984).

[4] Barthes, *S/Z*, 88.   [5] De Lauretis, 106.   [6] Ibid., 121.

Letter from an Unknown Woman (1948), a text from the Hollywood cinema that advances rather conventional attitudes toward the woman in love. The second group of films were made by women directors and launch a challenge to the traditional depiction of heterosexual love. Doris Dörrie's *Straight through the Heart* (*Mitten ins Herz*), made in West Germany in 1983, is a drama that offers a cynical twist on the sentimental screen romance. Stephanie Beroes's *Recital* (1978) is an experimental work that assaults not only the love story's premises but its cinematic style. In considering these films, I will pay attention to the notion of fiction as structured by desire, as "mapping" sexual difference into the text.

Seduced and Abandoned

> *The service of women (as well as the military service of the State) demands that nothing relating to that service be subject to forgetting.* —Sigmund Freud[7]

As critic Michael Walker has noted, the "woman's film" has always stressed "love as the most crucial determining factor in women's actions."[8] By this standard, *Letter from an Unknown Woman* emerges as an exemplary work. It recounts the story of the lifelong passion of Lisa Berndle (Joan Fontaine) for a renowned musician, Stefan Brand (Louis Jourdan), who has seduced and abandoned her as a young woman.[9] Given this emphasis, we will want to evaluate the

[7] Freud, *The Psychopathology of Everyday Life*, trans. A. A. Brill (New York: New American Library), 79.

[8] Michael Walker, "Ophuls in Hollywood," *Movie*, nos. 29–30 (Summer 1982). The section on *Letter* is on 43–48.

[9] *Letter* is set in Vienna in about 1900. Pianist Stefan Brand returns to his apartment in the early hours of the morning, having been challenged to a duel; he intends to flee from that engagement. His servant hands him a letter, which he begins to read. It is from Lisa Berndle, a woman who has loved him since her childhood, whom he can barely remember. In flashbacks, narrated by Lisa's voice-over monologue, the events of the past are recalled for Stefan: the day he moved into the apartment house where the adolescent Lisa lived, her crush on him, her refusal to marry a young officer because of her desire for Stefan. In addition to informing Stefan of events in which he did not participate, Lisa's letter reminds him of their encounters. After Lisa's parents move to Linz, she returns to Vienna, working as a model and stalking the street on which Stefan lives. One night he notices her, and they share a romantic evening. He dates her once again, then informs her that he must leave on tour; he promises to return in two weeks but never does. We learn that Lisa has become pregnant by Stefan and bears his child without ever contacting him. She later marries Johann Stauffer, a wealthy officer, and settles into a comfortable bourgeois existence with him and Stefan's son. One night (some ten years later) at the opera, she recognizes Stefan in the audience, and he reveals that he senses they have met before. The next day, Lisa sends her son back to boarding school without

film's stylistic and thematic assumptions, locating them as either endorsing or resisting traditional romantic views. We will be asking whether *Letter* conforms to the ideology of the dominant cinema or whether it invites a reading "against the grain."

Contemporary feminist Shulamith Firestone has written that "a book on radical feminism that did not deal with love would be a political failure."[10] One of the most profound and comprehensive discussions of this issue occurs in an early feminist classic—Simone de Beauvoir's *The Second Sex*, a treatise I will examine in some detail.

The author begins by making the crucial point that love has a different meaning for men and women—a phenomenon that explains the perennial misunderstandings between them.[11] She then enumerates these distinctions, starting with the discrepant emphasis placed on love by the two sexes:

> Men have found it possible to be passionate lovers at certain times in their lives, but . . . even on their knees before a mistress . . . they remain sovereign subjects; the beloved woman is only one value among others; . . . For woman, on the contrary, to love is to relinquish everything.[12]

Woman is willing to do so because she has very little to lose. Without a career or a respected cultural position, what else is there to structure her life but a *grand amour* that delivers her into the proper roles of wife and mother?

But de Beauvoir makes more subtle points. She notes that women devote themselves to men in order to *partake* of male power—a sphere from which they are otherwise excluded: "The adolescent girl wishes at first to identify herself with males; when she gives that up, she then seeks to share in their masculinity by having one of them in love with her."[13] In adoring a man, woman is allowed to live through him and to experience vicariously what it means to be a subject in the world. Through his admiration, she perceives herself valuable: "Love is the

---

realizing that he is seated in a train car contaminated by typhus. Hoping that Brand will finally recognize her devotion, Lisa goes to his apartment but finds that he does not recall their romantic history—that he treats her like one more casual conquest. Lisa's husband learns that she has seen Stefan and challenges him to a duel. Upon reading the final lines of Lisa's letter (which reveal that she has contracted typhus and is dying), Stefan goes downstairs to fight Stauffer. As he walks out the door where he first met Lisa, he finally has an accurate vision of her.

[10] Shulamith Firestone, in Sheila Ruth, ed., *Issues in Feminism: A First Course in Women's Studies* (Boston: Houghton Mifflin, 1980), 271.

[11] De Beauvoir, 712.   [12] Ibid., 713.   [13] Ibid., 714.

developer that brings out in clear, positive detail the dim negative, otherwise as useless as a blank exposure."[14]

In living through man, however, woman obliterates her own existence, "lets her . . . world collapse in contingence." She becomes "another incarnation of her loved one, his reflection, his double."[15] Thus she is likely to take on his interests: to read the same books, to admire the same artworks, to indulge in the same eccentricities. Given woman's deferential attitude to her lover, it is no wonder that de Beauvoir likens their relationship to master and slave. But de Beauvoir's real insight is to perceive how woman masks her servitude through overvaluation of her mate:

> Since [woman] is anyway doomed to dependence, she will prefer to serve a god, rather than obey tyrants. . . . She chooses to desire her enslavement so ardently that it will seem to her the expression of her liberty.[16]

De Beauvoir's use of the term "god" for the male lover is not gratuitous. She asserts that love is (for the traditional woman) "a religion," an infatuation comparable to a mystical frenzy[17]:

> The same words fall from the lips of the saint on her knees and the loving woman on her bed; the one offers her flesh to the thunderbolt of Christ, she stretches out her hands to receive the stigmata of the Cross, she calls for the burning presence of divine Love; the other, also, offers and awaits: Thunderbolt, dart, arrow, are incarnated in the male sexual organ.[18]

By transforming her master into a deity, woman obscures the nature of her servitude, but she also creates an illusion that is hard to maintain. De Beauvoir suggests that this "ideal" love can endure only at a distance that allows the fantasy to be sustained:

> [Woman's] worship sometimes finds better satisfaction in [her lover's] absence than his presence . . . there are women who devote themselves to dead or otherwise inaccessible heroes, so that they may never have to face them in person, for beings of flesh and blood would be fatally contrary to their dreams.[19]

Woman's overinvestment in romance places her in a precarious mental position. She "is one who waits," and her life hangs in the bal-

---

[14] Ibid., 718.   [15] Ibid., 725.   [16] Ibid., 713–14.   [17] Ibid., 714.
[18] Ibid., 720.   [19] Ibid., 727.

ance of her paramour's comings and goings.[20] She often succumbs to "self-mutilation" and "paranoia."[21]

De Beauvoir stresses the possessiveness that women feel toward the men who occupy such a disproportionate place in their world. Love "comes in the form of a gift," she writes, "when it is really a tyranny."[22] Jealously soon emerges, for she who has all invested in love "feels in danger at every moment."[23] Finally, de Beauvoir speaks of the catastrophe of abandonment for woman—a situation she suffers more profoundly than man: "A break can leave its mark on a man; but . . . he has his man's life to live. The abandoned woman no longer has anything."[24] Interestingly, Freud, in discussing the behavior of an hysterical patient, selects (as exemplary) her fantasy of desertion by a man:

> She told me that on one occasion she had burst into tears in the street, and that, thinking quickly what she had been crying about, she realized the existence of a phantasy in her mind that a pianist well known in the town (but not personally acquainted with her) had entered into an intimate relationship with her, that she had had a child by him (she was childless) and that he had deserted her and her child and left them in misery. It was at this point of her romance that she burst into tears.[25]

If love, for woman, can be an experience of mystical ecstasy, it can also be an occasion for monumental pain.

In characterizing the woman in love, de Beauvoir is not dealing with "the laws of nature." It is not female biology that places woman in this vulnerable position. "It is the difference in their *situations* that is reflected in the difference men and women show in their conceptions of love."[26]

Significantly, de Beauvoir's remarks on women in love—written in the 1940s and based on observation, diaries, letters, and novels—have recently been corroborated. In *Women Who Love Too Much*, Robin Norwood finds that an obsession with romance "is primarily a female phenomenon."[27] And in *Swept Away: Why Women Fear Their Own*

---

[20] Ibid., 736.   [21] Ibid., 722, 732.   [22] Ibid., 728.   [23] Ibid., 735.
[24] Ibid., 739.

[25] Freud in "Hysterical Phantasies and Their Relation to Bisexuality," in *Dora: An Analysis of a Case of Hysteria*, ed. Philip Rieff (New York: Collier, 1963), 146.

[26] De Beauvoir, 713.

[27] Robin Norwood, *Women Who Love Too Much* (New York: Pocket Books, 1986), xv.

Sexuality, psychologist Carol Cassell concludes (from her survey of hundreds of individuals) that women are "love junkies" who consistently place a higher value on amorous relationships than men do.[28] Cassell also advances a rather interesting new theory concerning female romanticism. Women allow themselves to be "swept off their feet" in order to *justify* their repressed sexual attraction to men—an impulse censored by traditional patriarchal society:

> Swept Away is a sexual strategy, a coping mechanism, which allows women to be sexual in a society that is, at best, still ambivalent about, and at worst, condemnatory of female sexuality.[29]

Although Cassell's theory goes beyond that of de Beauvoir, the two formulations converge. Both see the woman in love as propagating illusions—ones that represent her situation as more benign than it is. Cassell states:

> The romantic aura is false and confusing. We become deceived about the meaning of our experience. . . . We use this syndrome to inject the thrill of romance into our lives, lives still subject to the constraints imposed on us because we are women, the female gender.[30]

Letter from an Unknown Woman (based on a story by Stefan Zweig) literalizes and exemplifies the plight of the woman in love, as characterized by de Beauvoir, Norwood, and Cassell. To analyze the film, we will focus on the heroine, Lisa Berndle, and compare her fictional experiences with the theorists more abstract formulations.

V. F. Perkins has stated that "Lisa's offense is the 'excessive' enactment of those qualities which are held out as being woman's nature and woman's glory."[31] This is nowhere so true as in her embodiment of the woman in love. For de Beauvoir, the traditional woman views love as an all-encompassing experience, the structuring principle of life. This is surely our impression of Lisa's passion—an emotion that rules out all other possibilities for her future. As her letter to Stefan informs us (rendered in voice-over narration): "Everyone has two birthdays—the day of his physical birth and the beginning of his con-

[28] Carol Cassell, *Swept Away: Why Women Fear Their Own Sexuality* (New York: Simon & Schuster, 1981), 490, 51.

[29] Ibid., 25.   [30] Ibid., 26–27.

[31] V. F. Perkins, "*Letter from an Unknown Woman*," Movie, nos. 29–30 (Summer 1982): 71.

scious life." For Lisa, reality begins (and ends) on the day Stefan moves into her apartment complex, and she is smitten with love.

In keeping with this view, the narrative focuses every moment on Lisa's relation to Stefan. Even if *she* thought her life began with his appearance, the diegesis might have presented her world independent of that fateful event—but its point of view is consonant with hers. From the moment she meets Stefan, her life (and the filmic story) is consecrated to him, and all subsequent events are subordinated to their encounters. This contrasts with Stefan's world, filled with friends, lovers, and career milestones. Significantly, most of the important events in Lisa's relationship with Stefan occur at railroad stations (their amusement-park ride, his leave-taking, the departure of their son). From the moment she meets him, she leads a decidedly "one-track" existence.

The film does offer some "explanation" for Lisa's monomania by indicating the lack of options in her life. If her energies were not dedicated to a *grand amour*, they would be assigned to a bourgeois marriage. This grim social horizon is invoked in the Linz sequence, in which Lisa dates a young lieutenant. All aspects of the scene (analyzed in detail by V. F. Perkins) attest to the constraints of this cultural world: the couple's dull conversation, the young man's military role, the deafening church bells, the marching-band music, the entrapping camera movements. Although the film's sympathy is obviously with Lisa's romantic, unconventional goal (her desire to have a great passion rather than a pedestrian love), it never questions the assumption that woman's main concern in life should be *love*. Rather, it seems only to inquire what *kind* of love it should be—traditional or otherwise.

If Stefan's creative possibilities include being a renowned concert pianist, Lisa's expressive outlet is limited to that of an "artist of love." As Firestone notes: "Men [have been involved with] thinking, writing and creating, because women were pouring their energy into those men; *women are not creating culture because they are preoccupied with love*."[32]

De Beauvoir also makes the point that women find self-worth in their lovers eyes. For Lisa Berndle, actualization comes through association with Stefan Brand. On the day he moves into her house, she watches his possessions carted in and wonders "about [her] neighbor who owned such beautiful things." The quest of her life is to become another such object that he might possess and cherish. As she remarks

---

[32] Firestone, 271.

in her letter, she "prepared" herself for him by careful grooming. She "kept [her] clothes neater so [he] wouldn't be ashamed of [her]." Throughout the narrative, Lisa's wish to be prized by Stefan eludes her, but at the film's conclusion, her value is finally acknowledged. As though to literalize de Beauvoir's metaphor of love as a "developer," a series of images of Lisa crystallize before Stefan's eyes.

De Beauvoir notes how women live entirely *through* their men. For Lisa Berndle, this is true not only of her relationship with Stefan but also with her father. On the night of Stefan and Lisa's fairground date, they sit in a mock train car, watching false scenery pass outside the window; Lisa tells Stefan of her imaginary childhood travels with her dad. This image of Lisa—stationary (amidst the illusion of movement)—objectifies the way in which her false "travels" in life are predicated on men.

De Beauvoir postulates that woman's intense experience of romance comes from her desire to share in male power—a wish begun in adolescence. Significantly, Lisa is smitten at this precise moment—a period when a girl abruptly learns the constraints of her female role. Her status as Stefan's "double" comes out quite clearly in her statements and actions. She tells him: "Though I was not able to go to your concerts, I found ways of *sharing* in your success," and we see her steal a concert program from a man's pocket on a crowded trolley. Of course, the most profound way that she lives through Stefan occurs in adulthood, when she secretly bears his child and dedicates her life to father and son.

De Beauvoir sees this obsessive quality of female love as a misguided means of appropriating male power. But, as Tania Modleski has noted, in the woman's film "it is . . . not the virile, masculinized male . . . who elicits woman's desire . . . but the feminine man: the attractive, cosmopolitan type . . . or the well-bred, charming foreigner."[33] Stefan Brand stands among this fraternity. Modleski sees woman's attraction to this figure as a means to subvert masculine power, since "the man with 'feminine' attributes frequently functions as a figure upon whom feminine desires for freedom from patriarchal authority may be projected." However, given de Beauvoir's theory, we might read woman's choice of this type of man in an alternate manner. Rather than undermining patriarchy, he may secure it by making a woman's "doubling"

[33] Tania Modleski, "Time and Desire in the Woman's Film," *Cinema Journal* 23, no. 3 (Spring 1984): 26.

of him that much easier, invoking what Mary Ann Doane calls "a thematics of narcissism."[34]

In *Letter*, Lisa fully accepts the fact that her entrée to power comes only through Stefan, and, in his absence, she bears him a child (as surrogate lover). She thereby enacts the Freudian scenario by which woman "adjusts" to her castrated status by converting her desire for a penis into the wish for a baby (a transformation made more "perfect" by the birth of a son). Echoing this sentiment, Lisa writes to Stefan: "My life was measured by the moments with you and our child."

Lisa's love for Stefan also embodies the master/slave dynamic. (At one point she even talks of wanting "to throw [herself] at [his] feet.") Like a vassal, she expects nothing from him. She is content to sit in her bed at night listening to his music, believing that he is "giving [her] some of the happiest hours of [her] life."

If Stefan offers her nothing, she makes of her life a gift to him. The night he first notices her and they enjoy a romantic interlude, she asks, "How could I help you?" And later, when she explains to him why she has never come for assistance, she says, "I wanted to be one woman whom you had known who asked you for nothing." Finally, when they reencounter each other at the opera, she says, "I'd come to offer you my whole life," and regrets that he cannot recognize "what was always [his]." Thus, in love, man is to be the consumer and woman the consumed.

Not only does Lisa make of her life a gift to Stefan but, as in all classical narratives, her love is "present"-ed to him at the conclusion of the story with the arrival of her confessional note. This pattern of "boy getting girl" is traditional in drama: one need only think of Northrop Frye's analysis of comic structure as a case in point.[35] This archetypal narrative pattern also conforms to the male Oedipal scenario, whereby the young boy is "assured" the prize of a woman if he relinquishes his love for mother.[36]

Within traditional literature, woman's position and story is quite different from man's. Her narrative does not recount the achievement

---

[34] Ibid.; Mary Ann Doane, *The Desire to Desire: The Woman's Film of the 1940s* (Bloomington and Indianapolis: Indiana University Press, 1987), 116.

[35] See Northrop Frye, "The Mythos of Spring: Comedy," in *The Anatomy of Criticism* (Princeton, N.J.: Princeton University Press, 1957), 163–86.

[36] Raymond Bellour, quoted in Janet Bergstrom, "Alternation, Segmentation, Hypnosis: Interview with Raymond Bellour," *Camera Obscura*, no. 3–4 (Summer 1979): 90.

of *her* romantic goals but, rather, charts her role in the fulfillment of male desire. She functions as a character in somebody else's plot. As de Lauretis writes:

> The end of the girl's journey, if successful, will bring her to the place where the boy will find her, like Sleeping Beauty, awaiting him, Prince Charming. For the boy has been promised, by the social contract he has entered into at his Oedipal phase, that he will find a woman waiting at the end of *his* journey.[37]

In *Letter*, Stefan realizes the gift of Lisa's love before he faces his fatal duel. Lisa, however, never receives her reward: by the time Prince Charming bestows his kisses, Sleeping Beauty is already dead.

De Beauvoir's perception of woman's deification of the male lover resounds in *Letter*. Critics have noted the film's Catholic sense of fate, and some have even offhandedly characterized Lisa as a "Lady Madonna."[38] But none have surfaced the parallels between her stance and that of a religious novitiate. Her attitude toward Stefan is one of worship for a god, and she seems more like a nun than a schoolgirl. Most evocative is the scene in which she sneaks into Stefan's apartment, and walks through it in a religious thrall. His rooms have more the hallowed ambience of a church than the atmosphere of a bachelor apartment. Her worship of Stefan is apparent in her desire to "throw [herself] at [his] feet" and in her adoration of him playing the piano (see fig. 8). As though aware of her pure transcendent quality, Stefan gives her a white (rather than a red) rose, a tribute to her bloodless holiness. Like the religious devotee, Lisa's god/lover is conveniently absent—someone to adore in the abstract, at a material and physical distance. Significantly, she gives birth to Stefan's child in a Catholic hospital, tended by sisters—and the letter telling Stefan of her death comes on stationery emblazoned with a cross. Both the epistolary format and the transcendent ending of the film are reminiscent not so much of other woman's pictures as of Robert Bresson's *Diary of a Country Priest* (1951). For Lisa, the struggle to maintain a self-negating love seems not so much the achievement of ideal romance as that of spiritual grace.

Stefan's removal from Lisa also insures that his presence will be in

---

[37] De Lauretis, 133.

[38] Robin Wood, "Ewig hin der Liebe Gluck," *Personal Views: Explorations in Film* (London: Gordon Fraser, 1976), 131–32; V. F. Perkins, "*Letter from an Unknown Woman*," *Movie*, nos. 29–30 (Summer 1982): 72.

the form of an illusory mental image. She is with him for only one night, and during the rest of her life she sustains him as a fantasy. Rather than a real flesh-and-blood man, he is like a wax figure—a comparison she suggests on the night of their carriage ride when she predicts that his likeness will one day appear in a museum.

The sense of Stefan as a mere image on Lisa's mind screen suggests certain parallels between him and a male film star. For Stefan, love is an act: on the night of the couple's first encounter, they sit together in a restaurant booth, framed by two side curtains that make the site of their tête-à-tête into a kind of stage. Stefan is also, quite literally, a performer; in the same scene, he autographs a woman's concert program and eight-by-ten glossy photo. If Stefan is a matinee idol, Lisa is a loyal and adoring "fan." Like a classic female viewer, she watches the romantic lead from afar—as an unseen voyeur.

Perhaps, in some sense, all women in love share Lisa's predicament. For traditional heterosexual romance to work, they must assume the role of passive spectators of masculine power and transpose their lovers into distant, overblown images. De Lauretis finds parallels between the act of seduction and woman's film-viewing experience:

8. *Letter from an Unknown Woman* (1948). Lisa (Joan Fontaine)'s worship of Stefan (Louis Jourdan) is apparent as she watches him play the piano.

> If women spectators are to buy their tickets and their popcorn,
> the work of cinema . . . may be said to require woman's con-
> sent; and we may well suspect that narrative cinema in partic-
> ular must be aimed, like desire, toward seducing women into
> femininity.[39]

The situation involves a complex and infinite regression: as Lisa is seduced by Stefan (an ersatz "movie" image), so the female spectator
watching *Letter* is seduced by the image of Stefan seducing her.

Cassell's notion of women as Swept Away is also relevant to *Letter*,
for the film obliquely suggests such repression of female desire. Modleski cites a particular moment in the film when Lisa reencounters Stefan at the opera house and looks at him with the erotic concentration
usually reserved for men: "Here we find . . . the possibility of feminine
desire being actively aimed at the passive, eroticized male." But this
impulse is ultimately denied by Lisa's voice-over narration, which says:
"Somewhere out there were your eyes and I knew I couldn't escape
them." Thus, although the film depicts Lisa enraptured with desire for
Stefan, she conceives of herself as being desired by *him*. Thus, as Doane
notes, the patriarchal "flaw" of the traditional love story is "to posit
the very possibility of female desire." But "for this reason, it often ends
badly."[40]

De Beauvoir tells us that the woman in love is one who waits. On
the evening of Lisa's departure for Linz, she bolts from the train station
and returns to her vacant apartment. She runs to Stefan's door and,
finding him out, decides to stay. Ultimately, he comes back with another woman, and Lisa retreats. But her vigil does not end on Stefan's
doorstep. The rest of her life is lived in suspended animation, marking
time with another man but anticipating Stefan.

In *The Desire to Desire*, Doane discusses Roland Barthes's insight
that woman's conventional pose of waiting generates powers of fantasy. He writes: "It is Woman who gives shape to absence, elaborates
its fiction, for she has the time to do so."[41] But Doane expands the
point by noting that female desire itself can take on an imaginary quality, a fact that is evident in many 1940s love stories:

> The essentially fictive character of female desire is frequently
> demonstrated by the woman's demand for "all or nothing". . . .
> The ultimate consequence of this . . . attitude . . . is illustrated

[39] De Lauretis, 136–37.   [40] Modleski, 25–26; Doane, 118.
[41] Roland Barthes, quoted in Doane, 109. The original citation is from *A Lover's Discourse*, trans. Richard Howard (New York: Hill and Wang 1978), 41.

by those films in which a woman spends almost her entire life loving a man who, when he meets her again, does not recognize her.[42]

Letter stands among these works, and Lisa's desire for Stefan is so fanciful that it sustains an entire life without him.

Doane also makes the point that women's pictures reproduce scenarios of female masochism. In characterizing that syndrome (via Freud), she notes how women's masochistic fantasies are de-eroticized. For men, sexual reveries are utilized in conjunction with masturbation, whereas for women, the "fantasy . . . becomes an end in itself." Masochistic daydreams function not as vehicles for sexuality but *instead* of it.[43] It is this substitution of fantasy for eroticism that we find in the life of Lisa Berndle, who survives on imaginary images of Stefan in lieu of any carnal relation with him. Perhaps there is even a way that the camera work employed in *Letter* accentuates Lisa's fiction. The tracking shot is so omnipresent, so tied to her (in its anthropomorphic fluctuations), that we almost feel it her companion—a dream lover that stands in Stefan's place.

While much of *Letter* conforms to de Beauvoir's portrait of the woman in love, one aspect of her characterization is missing: the experience of malaise. (Robin Norwood will later equate woman's enactment of romance with the sensation of pain.)[44] Whereas de Beauvoir's female lover is possessive and jealous, Lisa Berndle is saintly and selfless. While de Beauvoir's woman veers toward madness, Lisa Berndle seems stoic and sane. On the one hand, this portrayal seems a positive view of woman, avoiding certain stereotypes of neurosis. On the other hand, the film's denial of woman's suffering only encourages martyrdom by imagining that such devotion can be practiced at no psychic cost.

In *Letter*, the difficult periods of Lisa's life have been excised from the text. The narrative cuts directly from Stefan's departure at the train station to Lisa's stay at the maternity hospital, eliminating the undoubtedly stressful period of her pregnancy. Likewise, her letter skips from the nine-year period of her single parenthood to her marriage to the affluent Johann Stauffer. We are allowed to see only the high points of her life when she is seemingly in control. Yet de Beauvoir has indicated how abandonment by a lover precipitates a major crisis for woman. Despite *Letter*'s excision of this trauma, the repressed returns in the form of the heroine's death. As Doane has noted, this conclusion

[42] Doane, 167.　　[43] Ibid., 23, 24.　　[44] Norwood, xiii.

is a staple of the genre and reveals its precarious ideological position: "The inability of a large proportion of love stories in the 40s to produce the classical happy ending . . . is a sign of the love story's vulnerability, the fragility of its project."[45]

In discussing the woman's film, many theorists have linked the configuration of melodrama to conversion hysteria and have likened its heroines to neurotic victims.[46] (Recall, too, the fantasy of Freud's hysterical patient, who imagines an unrequited love affair with a pianist— a virtual "script" for *Letter*.) Modleski, however, questions the applicability of this concept to Lisa Berndle. On the one hand, her struggle could be read as "the classic dilemma of . . . the hysterical woman," and her chronic muteness seen as a sign of this illness.[47] Although Modleski admits that Lisa's life is marked by nostalgia, she does not see her as suffering from reminiscence in the orthodox Freudian sense.[48] Rather, Modleski turns critical clichés on their head and points to *Stefan* as the true hysteric:

> Superficially it appears in the film woman's time is hysterical time. . . . Closer analysis, however, reveals Stefan is the hysteric. . . . For Stefan is the one who truly suffers from reminiscences. . . . Unable to remember the woman who alone gives his life significance, Stefan is doomed to an existence of meaningless repetition, especially in relation to women, who become virtually indistinguishable to him.[49]

In conceiving Stefan as an hysteric, and in positioning the *male* lover as potentially unbalanced, Modleski has pointed to a crucial issue— that heterosexual love, as contained in patriarchal culture, breeds pathology. If women in love hover on the brink of destruction, men will fare no better. Thus the film gives us a sense of the limitations of *both* characters—of the struggles enacted by both individuals in the dynamics of love. Perhaps this is even figured into one of its stylistic tropes, which connects (with a "blur-in"/"blur-out" motif) shots of Stefan reading and flashbacks of Lisa—a technical metaphor for the psychic murkiness of their relationship. Rather than simply reverse polarities, we might also consider whether the classic male pattern is a different one, whose distinctive features explain his perils in romantic engagement.

[45] Doane, 118.

[46] See Geoffrey Nowell-Smith, "Minnelli and Melodrama," *Screen* 18 (Summer 1977): 117.

[47] Modleski, 20.   [48] Ibid., 23.   [49] Ibid., 24.

We might begin by configuring Stefan as a particular type of hysteric, specifically an *amnesiac*. If Lisa is haunted by an inability to *forget* (anyone but herself), Stefan is plagued by an inability to *remember*. In a way, Stefan even suffers a double amnesia by forgetting Lisa twice—as an adolescent and as a young woman. His memory lapse runs even deeper, however. It is the fact that he has forgotten his trip to Milan that leads him to break his date with Lisa after their first night of love. Although he vows to return in two weeks, he forgets that promise as well. Through it all, Stefan even forgets his recurrent amnesia: the night after rediscovering Lisa at the opera, he thoughtlessly tells her that he "couldn't get [her] out of [his] mind."

In its classic configuration, amnesia constitutes a "partial or total loss of memory" and is attributed to "shock, psychological disturbance, brain injury or illness."[50] But, as Freud tells us in *The Psychopathology of Everyday Life*, even quotidian forgetting has its tendentious causes. He refers to such mental lapses officially as "amnesia" and says that "in all cases" they "proved to be founded on a motive of displeasure"[51]: "One . . . finds abundant indications which show that even in healthy, not neurotic, persons resistances are found against the memory of disagreeable impressions and the idea of painful thoughts."[52] Thus Stefan's forgetting of Lisa can be seen as more than accidental. As Freud remarks: "Lack of attention does not in itself suffice to explain . . . the forgetting of intentions."[53] But what does?

To pursue this question, let us analyze the character of Stefan once more—this time looking to the psychic syndrome of *Don Juanism* for clues to his motivation. Stefan is an inveterate womanizer, an "obsessive seducer." [54] He is a selfish man for whom love is a game that he seeks to win at the least possible psychic cost. Hélène Cixous has commented on how the Lothario exemplifies the patriarchal stance to the world:

> Take Don Juan and you have the whole masculine economy getting together to "give women just what it takes to keep them in bed" then swiftly taking back the investment, then reinvesting etc., so that nothing ever gets given, everything gets taken back, while in the process the greatest possible dividend of pleasure is taken. Consumption without payment, of course.[55]

[50] William Morris, ed., *American Heritage Dictionary of the English Language* (Boston: Houghton Mifflin, 1978): 43.
[51] Freud, *Psychopathology*, 68. [52] Ibid., 74. [53] Ibid., 78. [54] Wood, 130.
[55] Hélène Cixous, "Castration or Decapitation?" trans. Annette Kuhn, *Signs* 7, no. 1 (Autumn 1981): 47.

103

But what is the accepted psychological explanation for Don Juan's behavior? In *Beyond the Male Myth*, Anthony Pietropinto and Jacqueline Simenauer advance the theory of the womanizer as a sexually insecure man who is led "to seek new women in order to validate again and again that [he] can satisfy a woman."[56] Although this explanation works up to a point, they note that it does not account for why a man "would repeatedly risk failure and discount the approval of many women in the hope of adding one more to his growing list."[57] Rather, they see this quest for the confirmation of manhood as "only half the story."

The other part involves the idealization of women, the unconscious search for the perfect mother—a quest resulting in inevitable disillusionment and retreat. The Don Juan is a man who has not recovered from the Oedipal shock of maternal separation—and the introduction of the paternal "third term." In his adult romantic relationships, he continues to look for a "doting mother," despite the fact that each successive woman will fail to meet his impossible expectations.[58] This is a theme we have encountered in other incarnations—in our discussions of *The Lady from Shanghai* and *Persona*.

In *Letter*, Stefan enacts an Oedipal scenario. As Modleski has noted, for most of the film he refuses the Law of the Father; only at the end does he learn to "accept the values of duty and sacrifice espoused by his patriarchal society."[59] Furthermore, he flits from woman to woman in a hopeless and repetitious hunt for the mother. The teenaged Lisa observes Stefan kissing a woman on the stairs of his apartment building, and later she occupies the same position herself. In filming her with Stefan, the identical camera stance is adopted, implying that there will yet be others. Stefan's search for the ideal woman is clearly driven and relentless: at one point (when he reencounters Lisa after many years), he questions which of them is the pursuer and which the pursued. This dual sense attaches to Stefan himself, who, in seeking women, is also sought by the maternal imago.

Although Stefan is an adult, sophisticated "older man" who sweeps the pubescent Lisa off her feet, he displays childlike qualities. On the night of their fateful tryst, he says that Lisa "may be able to *help* [him] some day." And during the evening, she acts like a fussing parent, bundling him up on the carriage ride and putting a scarf at his neck. "It's a long time since anyone did that for me," he sighs, and we can guess

[56] Anthony Pietropinto and Jacqueline Simenauer, *Beyond the Male Myth* (New York: New York Times Books, 1977), 295.
[57] Ibid.   [58] Ibid.   [59] Modleski, 19.

what he means. Years later, when he meets Lisa at the opera, though he does not recognize her, he says she's the face he's been waiting for and asks quizzically: "Who *are* you?" Finally, when they rendezvous at his apartment, he tells her of a mystery goddess he has sought but never found—one who (like a mother) could makes his life "begin."

Lisa serves a double function in Stefan's world: she is both lover and maternal surrogate. She is familiar to him not only because he has really met her before but because all women embody for him (and recall) the archetypal mother. Because of this, she must be forgotten—for his attraction represents too great a threat.

Beyond the Don Juan's excessive love for the mother are feelings of a darker nature, perhaps shared by all men. Nancy Friday has commented on this male hostility toward women, ascribing it to the controlling position of the mother. She notes that "power in women produces an enormous rage in men but since their need for us is equally powerful, they bury their anger."[60] Hence, it is easy to see the Don Juan's sadistic treatment of his female lovers as a punitive, misogynistic act—one that misses its mark (the mother) and strikes other women instead. The classic Don Juan has two reasons to repress the mother figure: he loves her too much, and he hates her for claiming that affection. In *Letter*, even the mechanism of Stefan's "amnesia" (his forgetting Lisa instead of his mother) conforms to Freud's model, by which the mind "misses the target and causes something else to be forgotten—something less significant, but which has fallen into associative connection with the disagreeable material."[61]

This sense of Stefan's psychosexual repression of Lisa is particularly intriguing since any representation of the couple's lovemaking is excised from the screen by a fade (as it is from Stefan's mind). Stephen Heath rejects the notion that this absence is merely the result of 1940s censorship:

> As always . . . the centered image mirrors a structure that is in excess of its effect of containment, that bears the traces of the heterogeneity—the trouble—it is produced to contain: sexuality here is also the "more" that the look elides, that is eluded from, the look, and that returns.[62]

Hence the fade, and more crucially Stefan's forgetfulness, represents not only repression but Oedipal blindness—an inability to see the

---

[60] Nancy Friday, quoted in Cassell, 150–51.   [61] Freud, *Psychopathology*, 75.
[62] Stephen Heath, *Questions of Cinema* (Bloomington: Indiana University Press, 1981), 146.

105

psychic roots of his distress; and it seems no accident that his visual nonrecognition of Lisa is at the core of the story. Significantly, there are only two memorable shot/countershot sequences between the protagonists in *Letter* (which is reasonable, considering it is a film about Stefan *not* returning Lisa's look). But even these moments, which, on the surface, emphasize Stefan's apprehension of her, ultimately reveal his failed vision.

The first sequence occurs when he reencounters Lisa as a young woman, as she stalks the square where he resides. After a resonant exchange of glances (when we *hope* that he will recognize her), he says only that he has seen her there before—a few nights ago. The second time this dramatic shot/countershot structure is used occurs during the opera sequence. Stefan tells Lisa, "I have seen you somewhere," but adds that he "can't place [her.]" Only after reading Lisa's letter does he acknowledge his love for a woman, and only then can he "see" her. Significantly, the film ends with a series of Stefan's recollections of Lisa, whereby he finally re-vises their relationship. Ironically, at this moment of insight, Stefan covers his eyes in remorse, as though to underscore his previous blindness. For Lisa, it has always been possible to see the invisible (to imagine Stefan in his absence). But, for Stefan, it has been impossible to see what was there. His forgetfulness is made more poignant by the fact of the cinematic medium. If Stefan forgets, the film constantly "recalls" in its role as re-presentational art. As de Lauretis has noted: "Film re-members (fragments and makes whole again) the object of vision for the spectator."[63]

For final confirmation of Stefan as a Don Juan, we might look to the manner in which he meets his death. After realizing his repression of Lisa (and ostensibly the Oedipal desire at its base), he faces a duel with Lisa's husband—an act that Modleski has noted evokes castration.[64] Johann Stauffer is an older man and the legitimate possessor of the woman Stefan loves; hence, it is not a distortion to see him as a father figure.[65] At the moment of Stefan's comprehension of the *dual* nature of his attraction to women (lover as mother /mother as lover), he faces a *duel* (a challenge of phallic swords) with an elderly opponent worthy of his infantile hostility and fear.

Thus the film configures Lisa's sublime amorous posture not as some hysterical aberration but rather, as a "reproduction of mothering." We should recall that Freud, in his essay on femininity, stated that a heterosexual relationship "is not made secure until the wife has succeeded

---

[63] De Lauretis, 67.   [64] Modleski, 20.   [65] Ibid., 24.

in making her husband her child as well as in acting as mother to him."[66] Like a good parent, Lisa offers Stefan unconditional love—and requires nothing in return. Like a good parent, she accepts the fact that he will abandon her and go off into the world. Lisa even literalizes her maternal/romantic role by bearing Stefan's child—a boy (named Stefan) who stands in his place. Obviously, this role for the woman in love can function only because it satisfies the traditional man, who seeks in his mate a mother substitute.

The sense of male/female relationships as being mired in the infantile past comes out on many levels in the film. Critics have remarked on its temporal complexity which involves (1) the time of Lisa's writing the letter (as represented by her offscreen narration); (2) the time to which the letter refers (as represented by flashbacks to her childhood, adolescence, and youth); (3) the time of Stefan's reading of the letter (the night before the duel); and (4) the time of Lisa's death and the delivery of the letter to Stefan (which we never see). Although this chronological intricacy has been acknowledged, its symbolization of psychic entrapment (like the maze in *The Lady*) has not been underscored. Direct reference to stasis is made by Stefan on several occasions in the film. On the night he first notices Lisa in his neighborhood square, he comments that he "almost never get[s] to the place [he] start[s] out for." And later, on the fairground train ride, he jokes with Lisa about "reliving the scenes of their youth." Finally, on the night following their meeting at the opera, he talks of how "all clocks stopped" the moment he saw her. In truth, for Stefan, all clocks stopped even earlier—at the Oedipal stage. This emphasis on stagnation is made still more poignant in the film by Ophuls's formal reliance on camera *movement*—a technical (and ironic) counterpoint to the narrative impasse.

It would be a mistake to think of the film as naive or sentimental in its depiction of love. Wood, for instance, states that "irony is as essential to the Ophuls tone as his romanticism."[67] What *Letter* shows us, after all, is a case of *amour fou*, one whose consummation comes in death—hardly a very sanguine circumstance. But what remains an open question is how to characterize the film's precise attitude.

Critics have struggled with this issue and arrived at divergent conclusions. Michael Walker, for example, sees the woman's film not

[66] Sigmund Freud, quoted in Luce Irigaray, *This Sex Which Is Not One*, trans. Catherine Porter and Carolyn Burke (Ithaca, N.Y.: Cornell University Press, 1985), 64. From "New Introductory Lectures on Psychoanalysis," in Strachey, 22:117–18.

[67] Wood, 124.

merely as depicting the plight of the woman in love but as confronting the issue head-on:

> In the woman's film . . . what we so often see is how love serves to lead women into positions of oppression: to sacrifice themselves for their families/lovers, to submit "willingly" to suffering and endure wasted lives—in short, to embrace the role of "victim." And so the woman's film raises, very acutely, the *problem* of love.[68]

V. F. Perkins, on the other hand, reads the woman's film in a contrary manner, finding in it only "an indulgence of the stereotyped opposition of emotional woman . . . and rational man."[69]

This is clearly a very slippery issue. How do we know if the hyperbolic strategies of the text (its presentation of an extreme case of the woman in love) amount to an exaggeration of the situation or a critique? To pursue this, we must inquire how the film constructs its two protagonists. Despite *Letter*'s ironic presentation of Lisa's delusional love (its emphasis on her folly and self-destructiveness), melodramatic *heroism* still attaches to her actions. The film tacitly endorses her hopeless passion as a valiant spiritual goal. In this respect, it denies her the tragic position, which would characterize her life as ill spent on unrequited love. Rather, it reserves that stance for Stefan, and the film recounts *his* loss. The tragedy lies *not* in the fact that a woman has made of her life a hollow tribute to a callous male but in the fact that the man has not accepted the gift. Some critics have not only refused Lisa her own tragedy but have seen her responsible for Stefan's. Wood writes:

> The more times one sees the film, the more one has the sense . . . of the possibility of a film *against* Lisa: it would require only a shift of emphasis for this other film to emerge. It is not simply that Ophuls makes it possible for us to blame Lisa for destroying her eminently civilized marriage to a kind (if unpassionate) man, and the familial security he has given her and her son; it is also *almost* possible to blame Lisa and her refusal to compromise for Stefan's ruin.[70]

Lisa's status is also denied through the undermining of her point of view. Although the story seems to be offered from her perspective, her subjectivity is qualified. Wood speaks of how the film frequently vio-

[68] Walker, 43.   [69] Perkins, 71.   [70] Wood, 129–30.

lates the conventions of first-person cinematic narrative, "taking great liberties with such an assumption."[71] If we examine the structure of *Letter*, we find many episodes that validate this observation. During the Linz sequence, the camera leaves Lisa to focus on secret conversations with her parents, who discuss their hopes for her engagement. Later in the film, when she and Stefan go to a café, the camera focuses on Stefan secretly instructing the maître d' to give his excuses to another woman. These are both scenes that delineate actions unknown to Lisa and, hence, obviate her point of view.

Lisa's position is also subverted by the narrative structure of the film. It is true that the screen story issues from her letter, which determines the diegetic events. But her *writing* of the letter (and, hence, her female voice) is subsumed by the act of Stefan's *apprehension* of it. Once more, the presentation of woman's world is mediated by male consciousness; she is "read" by him. But the film is about reading in a broader sense than simply comprehending words on a page; it is about one person "reading" (or "misreading") another. As a teenager and young woman, Lisa "reads" Stefan as a passionate lover and a promising artist—an interpretation that turns out to be grossly distorted. Likewise, Stefan "misreads" Lisa as a shallow, infatuated young woman who will recover from his callow rebuff; furthermore, he mistakes her passion for a "crush." But the film argues for a larger sense of misprision in heterosexual relationships, whereby men and women misread their lovers by seeing them as mythic gods, children, or parents rather than as equal human beings. Ironically, when Stefan eventually "reads" Lisa correctly, on the night he scans her letter, the process kills him. Stefan's tendency to regard Lisa as a text may also explain his inveterate amnesia. As Roland Barthes claims: "It is precisely because [we] forget that [we] read."[72]

Finally, there seems a resonant truth in the film's emphasis on the issue of visibility and invisibility, on presence and absence. Stefan not only has trouble remembering Lisa, he has difficulty envisioning her at all! She is transparent to him as a teenager, and later, as a young woman, she must stalk his street repeatedly before he notices her. For Lisa, the problem is the opposite; Stefan burns such a potent visual impression on her mind that she continues to see him when he is not there—as a haunting "afterimage" on her emotional life. Within the terms of the film, we might say that woman is invisible and man is visible; he is seen and she is unseen.

[71] Ibid., 127.   [72] Barthes, *S/Z*, 11.

Luce Irigaray comments that in Western culture, "the male sex [has become] *the* sex because it is very visible," while "[woman's] sexual organ represents *the horror of nothing to see*. A defect in this systematics of representation and desire. A 'hole' in its scoptophilic lens."[73] She also implies that, within masculine society, what is visible is valued, while what is invisible is worthless; hence, discrepant attitudes arise toward male and female sexuality.

Irigaray also discusses the two sexes' opposing relation to the act of vision: "investment in the look is not privileged in women as in men." With control of the gaze comes male power, for "the eye objectifies and masters" and "sets at a distance."[74] The unseen female sex does not wield or value vision like the specular/spectacular male.

In *Letter*, man is superficially associated with the look—be it Stefan's seductive glance or that of the voyeuristic camera. As Irigaray implies, the look tends to objectify and master woman, establishing her as a figure of desire. In Stefan's case, it clearly "sets" Lisa "at a distance"—one that spans their entire lifetime. But if Stefan *looks* at Lisa, he never *sees* her; thus the master of the eye is blind to more profound in-sights. As Stefan is oblivious to Lisa, so is he to his own motives for spurning her. If she is invisible to him, so is the awesome maternal ghost that haunts him—the *real* "unknown woman" in his life.

In some oblique fashion, these issues circle back to the plight of the woman in love (much as the film circles back to its own beginning). Though conceived as a vision of pleasure, woman remains fundamentally *invisible* to man. If he sees her at all, he looks right through her to the background figure of the maternal imago. Perhaps all female lovers are "unknown women"—unrecognized by the men they love. (Geoffrey Nowell-Smith writes that in melodrama, "Femininity . . . is not only unknown but unknowable."[75]) But it is an even greater loss that these women are "unknown" to themselves. In "doubling" the male lover, in living "through" him, they negate their own existence. Women may be seduced and abandoned not only by their paramours but by their own acceptance of restrictive views on love.

[73] Irigaray, quoted in Heath, 161; and Irigaray, *This Sex*, 25–26.
[74] Irigaray, in Heath, 161.   [75] Nowell-Smith, 116.

Revising Romance

I am more convinced than ever that love is the best, most insidious, most effective instrument of social repression.
—Rainer Werner Fassbinder[76]

Shulamith Firestone asserted that a book of radical feminism that avoided the subject of love would be a political failure. Perhaps we might say the same of feminist film—yet precious few have considered this issue, favoring more "serious" topics like motherhood, rape, political organization, and work. Perhaps female artists, aware of the cost of woman's flirtation with romance, have attempted to ignore it. But the repressed has a way of claiming its return.

Women directors have recently confronted the question, though their attitudes have diverged. Maria Luisa Bemberg accepts the conventions of the love story, believing that one can adapt them to a female perspective. In *Camila* (made in Argentina in 1984), she depicts a forbidden affair between an aristocratic woman and a priest—a relationship that she sees as equal and liberating. The rhapsodic tone of the film, however, is indistinguishable from that of Ophuls.

Rejecting this approach, other women have sought to subvert the assumptions of heterosexual screen romance, bringing to the subject a far more cynical perspective. *Straight through the Heart* and *Recital* fall within this latter group and constitute a challenge to *Letter*. Interestingly, they match the Ophuls work not only in their theme but in their use of an epistolary format. In *Letter*, the narrative is conceived as a posthumous communiqué from a woman to her paramour, while in *Straight Through*, the heroine writes to herself. Finally, in *Recital*, women read love letters aloud as part of a critique of traditional romance.

STRAIGHT THROUGH THE HEART: BLUME IN LOVE

What if we updated the drama of *Letter* and placed it within a contemporary context? What if we portrayed it from a woman's point of view? Then we might have *Straight through the Heart* by West German filmmaker Doris Dörrie. What the director does is to take a romance comparable to Zweig's and shift the balance. In so doing, she

---

[76] The subtitle ("Revising Romance") is a phrase coined by Linda Podheiser for an exhibition of women's video presented by the American Federation of Arts. The quote is from Rainer Werner Fassbinder, in Robert Kolker, *The Altering Eye: Contemporary International Cinema* (New York: Oxford University Press, 1983), 358.

vocalizes elements muted in *Letter*: the pain and suffering of the submissive, amorous woman, the pathology of the man who encourages that dynamic. Dörrie also suggests that love affairs frequently end in violence, not in the spiritual transcendence with which *Letter* concludes. While *Straight Through* reengages the familiar figure of the masochistic woman (and may initially seem retrograde in this regard), it does not do so naively. It restructures the frame in which she is pictured and thereby critiques her perennial constraints and complaints.

Straight Through concerns a young woman, Anna Blume (Beate Jensen), and her relationship with an older man, Dr. Armin Thal (Josef Bierbichler). At the beginning of the film, she lives alone in a shabby flat and works at a local grocery store as a checkout girl. One day she notices a classified advertisement for a house sale and goes there in pursuit of a refrigerator. She meets Armin, who is liquidating the estate of his recently deceased mother. When Anna inquires about the refrigerator, he says it has been promised to someone else. Despite her urging, he refuses to renege on his agreement. She leaves his apartment and seems to have no further thoughts about the man (or the appliance).

We next see Anna in the supermarket, where she undercharges a young mother for food. Anna's boss observes this, and when he confronts her, she quits. In rebellion, she goes to a beauty parlor to have her hair dyed blue. That night a messenger comes to her door with flowers and a note that reads: "I would like to invite you and your new hair color to dine with me this evening." She cannot imagine who has sent the letter, but (in a spirit of adventure) she goes to the specified restaurant. Armin appears and proposes that she move into his house and receive a monthly allowance. He claims to want no sexual or emotional relationship, only the "excitement" of having her around. She first refuses, but then reconsiders and accepts the offer.

After she has moved in, Armin is quite impatient with her, criticizing her for lounging about or for having no table manners. Despite this, she grows fond of him and attempts to pierce the thick emotional wall that surrounds him. When he is at work, she snoops around the house, looking in his drawers and cabinets; she learns that he was once married. His maid discloses that other women have lived there under a similar arrangement.

Anna realizes that she is falling in love with Armin and tries repeatedly to shift their relationship from a platonic to a sexual one. He resists but finally succumbs. In a confrontation following their lovemaking, however, Armin insults Anna; she packs her bags and moves into a hotel. Once there, she finds that she is haunted by him. Obsessively, she tracks down Armin's ex-wife (a ravaged alcoholic) and engineers a meeting with her. Finally, Anna returns to Armin's house and tells him that she is pregnant—a lie.

Armin is overjoyed and wants to have the child, which he is sure will be a daughter. Anna moves in again and for nine months feigns pregnancy, stuffing herself with food, wearing a pillow to simulate a swollen belly. When she is due to "deliver," she leaves town, telling Armin that she is going to a Frankfurt clinic. Instead, she steals a newborn girl from an unsuspecting Arab woman in a grocery and returns to Armin's house with the infant (whom they name Rosa). He is a doting, compulsive father, and Anna feels shut out. Their relationship deteriorates, and Armin orders Anna to leave his house. She blurts out that the child is not his, but he discloses that he already knows about the kidnapping from an article in the newspaper. Anna packs her bags but, before leaving, pleads with Armin, who is taking a bath. When he rebuffs her, she impulsively turns on a hair dryer and knocks it into the water. In a flash, Armin is electrocuted. Anna escapes with the child and runs aimlessly down the street. She follows a crowd of Arabs onto a bus. In the final shot, she sits on the back seat with Rosa as the vehicle departs.

Although the film recounts a very different story than *Letter*, there are obvious parallels that make an intertextual comparison of the two fruitful. Both concern a May/December romance between a young, impressionable woman and an older, experienced man who is jaded about romance. In both films, there is a class difference between the lovers, the man having a more elite status. In *Letter*, Lisa is from an unsophisticated bourgeois family, while Stefan is a bohemian artist who cavorts with the upper echelons. In *Straight Through*, Anna is a rather uncouth working-class girl, while Armin is a cultured, upper-middle-class professional. In both stories, the woman is obsessed by love for a man who does not return her affections. And in both films, the man is a womanizer who has had countless previous affairs. In each work, the narrative concludes with the specter of death. In *Letter*, Lisa has died and Stefan is facing a duel, while in *Straight Through*, Armin has been killed and Anna will likely be punished for the crime. Finally, both films involve an epistolary format: the narrative of *Letter* is fashioned as a note from Lisa to Stefan; and in *Straight Through*, Anna frequently writes letters to herself. Furthermore, Anna's entire relationship with Armin is initiated by an anonymous note from him: a "letter from an unknown man," as it were.

While these parallels exist, the tone and perspective of the films radically diverge. *Letter* valorizes Lisa's martyrdom, whereas *Straight Through* finds Anna's plight absurd and regrettable. Moreover, it offers a critique of the situation of the woman in love and gives us a skeptical (rather than a transcendent) reading of traditional romance. In Riffaterre's terms, we might say that *Straight Through* bears a "complementary" relation to *Letter*, since it offers a "negative" version of the Ophuls intertext.[77]

As we have seen, *Letter* recounts the story of a young woman who views herself as a tabula rasa before encountering her lover. Through him, she becomes a person—learns about art and culture, finds a purpose in life. She literally speaks of her rebirth through romance. *Straight Through* reverses this process. It is the tale of an independent young woman (with a provisional sense of self) who becomes a cipher through her relationship with a man. In the scenes prior to Anna's residence with Armin, she is a feisty person with her own ideas. She lives alone and is coping, although one of her letters mentions loneliness. She allows certain grocery customers to go without paying; she stands up to her boss when he supervises her too closely. She even dyes her hair blue as an act of defiance. When she goes to Armin's house sale, she aggressively bargains for the refrigerator, trying to convince him to break his promise. When Armin propositions her at the restaurant, Anna is flip, calling his proposal "a rotten con." She is also unimpressed with his upper-class status. When they meet at a fancy eatery, she brazenly orders schnitzel and chips, while he chooses French food.

As soon as Anna moves in with Armin, her personality begins to drain from her—like blood from a vampire's victim. She wanders aimlessly around his house, barely leaving the premises. Although he has offered her "a room of her own" (more luxurious than her flat), the site marks the loss of her autonomy, and she behaves more like a prisoner than a boarder. Although her own apartment had been cramped, Armin's roomy house constricts her spirit. Thus Anna's experience of her lover's "space" is different from that of Lisa Berndle, who moved joyously through the sanctified halls of Stefan's chambers.

In a sense, Dörrie plays upon the conventions of the Gothic romance, in which a young woman comes to live in an older man's dwelling. Like a Gothic heroine, Anna is awed by Armin's abode, which seems to shelter some mystery. Like the Gothic heroine, she seems on the verge of being driven mad by her lover. Like a Gothic heroine, she

---

[77] Michael Riffaterre, "Syllepsis," *Critical Inquiry* 6, no. 4 (1980): 627.

thinks to herself: "I should go now . . . and get out of danger." Finally, like the bride in *Rebecca* (1940), she wonders about the "first Mrs. Thal." At one point in the film, Armin comments on how we all "invent our own stories." But Dörrie reveals how women frequently script themselves into romantic clichés. In the Gothic novel, it is traditionally the woman whose life is in peril, whereas here Armin is in danger, a victim of his own victimization of women.

The longer Anna resides in Armin's house, the more her activities center on him, and she spends her time prowling through his possessions or waiting for him to return from work. Like Lisa Berndle, she aspires to learn his ways. During their first breakfast together, he criticizes her technique of eating hard-boiled eggs, demonstrating how to tap and peel them neatly. At that point, she is sarcastic, scorning his advice that to succeed in the world she must know etiquette. "Think I want to get anywhere?" she responds acerbically. After she falls in love, however, we see her meekly trying to imitate Armin's table manners. One day, as she collapses on his carpet, she traces the outline of her body with chalk, as a police detective would a corpse. Clearly, this is a metaphorical image of her status as love's casualty, one who has been shot "straight through the heart." When Armin returns at night, he brings her a "birthday" present, and they celebrate the occasion. Like Lisa Berndle, Anna's "rebirth" is declared upon her submission to a male lover. But while this is romanticized in *Letter*, it is likened to homicide (or sickness) in *Straight Through*. This critique is made even more explicit when, in one of Anna's letters to herself, she refers to her love for Armin as an "insidious illness."

In *Letter*, Stefan Brand's pathology was largely submerged within the text. Though the narrative casts him as an immoral cad, it never investigates the Oedipal nature of his syndrome. In *Straight Through*, Armin's perversity is brought to the surface in countless sequences. At their first breakfast, Anna says "You can't exactly call this [living arrangement] normal, can you?" Throughout the film, she makes reference to his "problems." Even the maid implies that he is crazy. But it is not so much these vague allusions that are important as the scenes that specifically identify Armin's psychic difficulties and suggest an explanation for his behavior.

It is crucial that Anna meets Armin in his *mother's* apartment during a period in which he grieves her death. In one of the few sequences that depart from Anna's point of view, we follow Armin into the bathroom of his mother's flat, where he takes an old box out of a secret com-

115

partment in the wall. Crouching by the bathtub, he opens it, and we see that it is filled with his childhood mementos: a Disney comic, a Hershey Bar wrapper, some fake money. He seems distraught as he looks them over. In the same scene, a woman asks to purchase a deer statuette from the apartment. Armin refuses, saying that it belonged to his mother and is of sentimental value. On the night that he and Anna first make love, he mentions that his father never returned from World War II and that he became his mother's "protector."

These references to Armin's attachment to his mother seem highly pointed in a film that generally refuses psychological depth. We know absolutely nothing about Anna: her parents, her background, her hopes, her fears. Yet this detail (about a maternal fixation) is supplied for Armin, a man who seems to be a classic womanizer. At one point, Anna even inquires whether, if she moves out, he'll simply "get some-one else." Armin refuses to be emotionally involved with women be-cause he knows that his repetitive relationships always have a similar denouement. As he says, "I know exactly how it will end." Seeing his ex-wife, we suspect that his affairs regularly conclude with some wom-an's devastation.

Armin also evinces the love/hate attitude toward women character-istic of the Don Juan, Stefan Brand. On the night that Armin and Anna first make love, he tells her that women "live their feelings to the full, tearfully swear their undying love and then get up and wash their hair." Clearly, though he needs women, he has been hurt by them and feels a compensatory contempt. His enmity comes out in several other sequences of the film, unlike the hostility of Stefan Brand, which is masked by saccharine charm. On the night Armin first propositions Anna, he says that she will accept because she is "a pretty rotten spec-imen." Later, when they play a board game, he criticizes her for losing and mockingly asks if she has any pride. When she says "no," he re-sponds, "Obviously, or you wouldn't be here." It is this dynamic of seducing women, then demeaning them, that is characteristic of the Don Juan, who acts out his dichotomous feelings toward the female sex. As Anna later says, "You pay me to dig you out; then you hit me over the head with a shovel."

For Armin, like Stefan, love is an elaborate contest. But in *Straight Through*, this issue is brought out in bold relief. Armin is fixated on games: we have already mentioned the one that he plays with Anna, and he also plays chess (via radio) with someone in Japan. But it is his relationship with Anna that truly ends in a checkmate situation. For

116

Armin, love is a battle, and what he hopes of woman is simply a viable opponent. As he tells Anna, "It's boring if I always win." On the night he propositions her, he reveals that he sees in her a "dauntless, fearless warrior." When she responds that she is "not fighting anything," he shifts the metaphor and tells her that he sees her as a daring circus artist: "the only one to really put herself at risk." Later, when she has moved in with him, he tells her that it would help if she had "strong nerves." He sees himself as a challenge to women and seeks one who proves her worth by resisting his domination. What he overlooks, however, is that his sadistic behavior attracts a masochist—and the cycle is repeated endlessly. No wonder Armin thinks he knows how his love affairs will end; a womanizer's relationships are always the same.

Other occurrences in the film highlight Armin's particular syndrome. He not only talks about his mother but reveals that he has always had a need to play the father—a symbolic strategy, we surmise, for displacing the patriarch. One night, when Armin and Anna talk, she asks him about his first love. He confesses that, when he was fourteen, he had a crush on an eight-year-old girl with whom he played house. He enacted the husband and she the wife, and they pretended to have an invisible child, named Wacky, whom they kept in a shoebox. Armin realizes that this was not a conventional game for a teen-aged boy, although it was for a little girl. He says the role-playing ended when his friend tired of it, though he did not. Armin later hints that he and his playmate eventually wed. When Armin finishes his story, he tells Anna that it was all a lie, but we suspect that he has spoken the truth.

Armin continues to play the father in other ways. His proposition to Anna seems like a form of perverse "adoption," and when he refuses her sexual advances, she wryly calls him "daddy." One night, when Anna returns to his home drunk, he puts her to bed, as a concerned parent would, refusing her attempts at seduction. And, after Anna has left him, she comes to his dental office, pretending to be a patient, and tells his nurse that Dr. Thal "prowls after little girls in the park at night."

Finally, Armin becomes totally obsessed with the idea of having a child. When he believes that Anna is pregnant, he has a renewed interest in her, imagining that he can play father to her mother. In a sense, their relationship is a rerun of his childhood games—since Anna's baby is as invisible as Wacky. Anna has value to Armin only as a madonna; in one of her letters, she refers to herself as having a "nine-month reprieve" from his rejection. In a sense, this situation surfaces the dynamics of *Letter*, where Stefan's regrets about Lisa come with the revelation that she bore him a son. *Straight Through* underscores the futility of replaying childhood roles in later life. While Lisa really becomes a mother, Anna's maternity is a sham—as specious as her relationship with Armin.

When Anna's baby finally "arrives," Armin becomes a smothering parent. He not only plays the father but subsumes Anna's role as mother, collapsing both functions into one. Armin even relates the infant to his mother: upon seeing the child's black hair, he remarks that it is like his mother's when she was born. Anna has a different reading of his child fixation. She comments that he loves the baby because (unlike a mature woman) she "smiles and shuts up." All of these occurrences locate Armin's problems with women at the Oedipal stage of separation. Significantly, when Armin and Anna first meet, she tells him that she thinks life would be better if it began in old age and worked its way back to infancy. In certain respects, Armin experiences this imagined regression. He even dies in a bathtub, the site contiguous to his hidden box of childhood treasures.

Both *Letter* and *Straight Through* end in death, but this denouement carries a different valence in each work. *Letter* closes with the martyred demise of Lisa, who perishes in the name of motherhood, nobly contaminated by the son she has born to Stefan. In *Straight Through*, the woman escapes alive despite her self-destructive impulses. Her freedom, however, is only provisional, and we expect that she will be caught and punished. Instead of martyring herself, she impulsively takes revenge by killing her lover with a hair dryer—a "weapon" that reminds us of his original "crime" of procuring her for her coiffure. We are not meant to condone Anna's murderous act but rather to understand it as the predictable outcome of a situation of emotional brutality.

In truth, the viewer is as "shocked" by the murder as is Armin. Throughout the film, Dörrie plays with our expectations that Anna will be destroyed. Generally, it is woman who is love's sacrificial victim: think of Joan Fontaine's character in *Letter*, Greta Garbo's heroine in *Camille* (1936), or Bette Davis's protagonist in *Dark Victory* (1939). But how, precisely, does Dörrie subvert our assumptions?

First of all, the eccentric, almost comic tone of the film belies its eventual resolution. In one letter, Anna refers to herself as a clown, and we regard her as such. She is funny in her drunken scene and audaciously amusing throughout, as she slinks around Armin's house in a red satin dress, embarrasses him in his office, ties a pillow to her tummy, or tails young mothers in pursuit of a child. When intimations of death do trickle in, they initially hover around her. In one of Anna's rare moments of intimacy with Armin, she tells him about a recurrent childhood fantasy that ended in her demise. Whenever someone slapped her, she would think "that I'd bleed to death. Then I lie in a coffin, in a white dress, with a lily in my hand and they all stand round about sobbing. All those who had treated me badly and who were sorry, only now it's too late, and they can't do anything about it." Hearing this, we suspect that the drama will end with Anna's death and Armin's remorse for mistreating her—precisely the scenario of *Letter*. Later in the film, this fantasy seems realized when Anna lays herself out amid candles on Armin's pool cover, waiting for his return from the office. When he rushes in, concerned, she tells him that she wanted to "look pretty when [he] came home." She understands that the martyred woman is "attractive" to man. (Hélène Cixous infers that a man sees the woman he loves as "a dead woman."[78]) At another point, Anna traces the outline of her body in chalk as though she were a murder victim—another suggestion that it will be she who expires. Finally, one of her letters states that she does not "dare think how [the affair] will end."

While these incidents encourage us to view Anna as imperiled, there are suggestions that Armin is endangered. One night he tells her of a recurrent dream about a butterfly that perches on his neck and symbolizes death. Another evening, when he returns home to find Anna's chalk drawings on the floor, he asks her if those are her victims and confesses that he "doesn't feel safe anymore." Finally, when Anna critiques Armin's life-style, she tells him that he is "buried alive" in his house. By playing with our hermeneutic urge to solve the plot's enigmas, Dörrie keeps us guessing. Though Armin has bragged that he "knows exactly how [his love affair] will end," both he and we are chilled by the grisly climax, which inverts the paradigm of female sacrifice and asserts a woman's desire for vengeance against an abusive lover. In *Letter*, the conclusion is never in question. The film begins with Lisa's admission that by the time we read her note she may be dead.

Straight Through touches on other issues relevant to heterosexual romance: in particular, the question of male vision. *Letter* revolves

---

[78] Cixous, 41.

around Stefan's refusal to see Lisa—in any profound sense of the term. And this formulation constitutes an ironic transposition of the conventional notion of man as wielder of the gaze. In *Straight Through*, Armin occupies the traditional voyeuristic position. After meeting Anna at his house sale, he spies on her and decides (like Paris) that he likes what he sees. His desire is literally to possess her, and his surveillance constitutes a mode of "window shopping." Dörrie emphasizes woman's own complicity in this matter; in one of Anna's letters, she bemoans the fact that "we need a spectator for everything we do." Armin and Anna's encounter also illustrates Berger's view that life is a beauty contest for women, whose prize is to be acquired by a man—that while men gaze, women appear.[79] When Armin makes his proposal, Anna is incredulous: why should he offer her room and board "just for the way [she] looks?" Unlike *Letter*, which masks Lisa's status as an aesthetic object, *Straight Through* brings this issue to the surface. When Armin tells Anna about his recurrent nightmare, he says:

> I sometimes dream of a man with a black hat. He's walking in front of me, with a beautiful big butterfly sitting on his hat. I want the butterfly. Just as I think that, the man turns around and says I can buy it. It's very expensive, but I pay him. The butterfly then flies off the man's hat and settles on my neck, and the man says: "That's death." That's the end of the dream, every time.

This fantasy has great relevance to the plot of the film, for it presages the fate of Armin and Anna. She is the lovely insect that he purchases— that eventually causes his demise. His dream thereby underscores the pernicious aspect of this behavior for man, as well as for woman. The fantasy also establishes resonant intertextual associations with another work: John Fowles's *The Collector*, adapted for film by William Wyler in 1965. That drama concerns a demented man who captures and imprisons both butterflies and women. He is a clear role model for Armin Thal.

Unlike *Letter*, *Straight Through* also reveals the communication barriers between men and women. As sociologist Nancy Chodorow has noted, the young girl's attachment to the mother allows her to feel close to others throughout her life. Boys, on the other hand, who attempt a radical separation from the mother frequently have difficulties

---

[79] John Berger, *Ways Of Seeing* (London: British Broadcasting Corporation and Penguin, 1978), 47, 52.

establishing emotional ties in their adult lives.[80] In *Letter*, Lisa simply accepts Stefan's coldness and aspires to be the one woman who "asks him for nothing."

In *Straight Through*, however, Anna is devastated by Armin's detachment and rallies against it, trying to pierce through his shell. She sees his aloofness as a form of psychological maladjustment. Their struggle comes out in various sequences of the film. At their first dinner together, Armin specifically mentions that he wants "neither emotions nor obligations of any kind," to which Anna responds that "someone always has to pay into the bargain." When Anna thanks him one morning for putting her to bed inebriated, he rebuffs her by saying, "I'd have done that for any drunken wench." Moreover, in a diary entry, she characterizes Armin as "hard as stone." Finally, when Anna asks him if they might be less formal, he responds, "I don't think we should give up this distance lightly; why should we pretend to be any more intimate than we are?" Anna cynically calls his remarks "rubbish," then says, "You decide; you pay; you're the boss." Her reaction makes clear that Armin's decision to "employ" women (for board and wages) is yet another distancing device. He treats his potential lovers as hired domestics or prostitutes, preferring to place his relationships with them in a "business" context, gaining power through his supervisory position. This sense of a hierarchal relationship between Armin and Anna is extended in the film by her association with Arabs, who (like women) are an underclass within white patriarchal society.

Significantly, Anna's only access to Armin's personality is through his material possessions. When he is gone, she prowls around the house looking for clues to his life and psyche. Armin's isolation not only sickens him, it infects Anna like some contagious disease. While she begins the film an outgoing woman, she ends it a hermit: dissembling pregnancy, she must hide out in her room (as Armin had in his); fleeing from the police, she can expect a life of solitude.

Dörrie not only addresses Armin's emotional detachment within the diegesis but also articulates it on more figurative levels. This sense of his distance comes to us in part through Dörrie's hyperbolic use of shot/countershot in scenes between Armin and Anna. The two are usually separated by film frames, which isolate them like inmates in neighboring cells. Their final exchange in the bathroom is rendered in this

---

[80] Nancy Chodorow, *The Reproduction of Mothering: Psychoanalysis and the Sociology of Gender* (Berkeley, Los Angeles, and London: University Of California Press, 1978), 93.

very mode. In certain sequences (for instance, at the restaurant, or during a chess game at Armin's home), the camera slowly pans between them, measuring the blank space that intervenes. Only in rare moments of intimacy (talking in bed or making love) does Dörrie employ extended two-shots of the lovers together (see fig. 9). As for symbolism on another level, it seems no accident that Anna meets Armin while searching for a refrigerator. The iceman cometh, and she later refers to him as "cold and unassailable." Significantly, the film begins with Anna taking some frozen food from a windowsill and stabbing it with a knife. Retrospectively, this seems a metaphor for the violence she will unleash on the frigid Armin.

It is also telling that Anna writes letters to herself throughout the drama, which are rendered in voice-over narration like the words of Lisa Berndle. The first note is penned before she lives with Armin, and it speaks of her loneliness. But she continues to correspond with herself, even after they have become lovers. In one letter, she confesses that she cannot live without him, and in another that she is feigning pregnancy. Armin jokes with her about the mail she receives, asking if they are "love letters." Obviously, if she is to receive any, she must write them herself, since an affective response from Armin will not be forthcoming. This contrasts with the attitude of Lisa Berndle, who has faith that her words to Stefan will reach their emotional target. And,

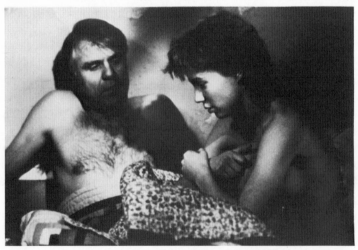

9. *Straight through the Heart* (1983). Only in rare moments of intimacy does Dörrie employ extended two-shots of the lovers (Josef Bierbichler and Beate Jensen).

of course, they do, causing him to rethink and regret his life. For Anna, romance entails a monologue; dialogue is an impossibility.

Letter and *Straight Through* can also be compared on the level of narrative progression and discussed in relation to the paradigm for conventional story structure.[81] Though the drama of *Letter* appears to issue from woman's desire, that dynamic is undercut. Lisa's narrative is bracketed within Stefan's prologue and epilogue, which clamp it like a vise. Furthermore, Lisa's wish is to be desired by a man, hardly a liberating project.

Straight Through is much more honest about traditional heterosexual interaction. Anna and Armin's encounter literalizes de Lauretis's notion of the woman becoming part of the man's story. Anna is largely oblivious to Armin until he scripts her into his drama. This is clearly seen as a "bit part" for her rather than a starring role. Armin is correct to state that people "invent [their] own stories," but he fails to note that the narrative act is reserved for men alone.

Both films also tend to invoke traditional fairy-tale structure. In *Letter*, the adolescent Lisa is a metaphorical Sleeping Beauty, waiting for Prince Charming's kiss. Her wish is magically realized when Stefan finally romances her. By the end of the film, however, Lisa's spiritual sleep has led to her physical death—a fate from which even Stefan cannot save her. We sense, however, that good Prince Charming will join her in the afterlife.

Straight Through is far more ironic about such fabled expectations, making allusions to Sleeping Beauty and to other traditional mythic personae. When Anna is working at the grocery (where her boss refers to her as a "princess"), she threatens to give him a kiss that will turn him into a toad—a clear invocation of the frog-prince legend. According to Madonna Kolbenschlag, in Grimm's version of this tale:

> A beautiful young princess plays with a golden ball which accidentally rolls into a pond. A frog tries to befriend her and retrieves her ball after he extracts a promise from her to allow him to play, eat and sleep with her. The princess soon forgets her pledge, and leaving the frog behind, returns to the castle. He follows her and demands that she honor her pledge. She is repelled, but her father, the king, insists that she keep her promise. The princess is progressively overcome with anger and disgust as the frog intrudes more and more in her life. When he demands to sleep with her, she rebels and in a fit of outrage and

[81] Bellour; De Lauretis, 103–57.

123

revulsion, she smashes the frog against the wall of her bedroom. In that moment, the spell is broken and the frog is transformed into a magnificent prince—a worthy spouse for the princess.[82]

Kolbenschlag points out that "the frog's phallic, assertive qualities identify it as an obvious projection of male sexuality." She notes that feminists might object to conventional interpretations of the tale, which see it as "a cautionary message to females to bear with the atavistic aspects of the male personality, to accommodate themselves to the abrasive, exploitative demands of a male partner."[83]

It is not difficult to see, in Armin, an incarnation of a frog-prince. Anna meets him by accident (as does the beautiful legendary princess), and he extracts from her a promise that he can reside in her presence. Though he appears to exact no sexual price from her, his reticence is a veiled seduction. He knows that the princess will be challenged by his reserve and will make her own erotic demands. Like the princess, Anna becomes more and more angry with the behavior of her newfound companion and more compelled to act as he desires. However, when she erupts in violence, her frog is not turned into a prince but destroyed—an event that cynically rejects the notion of miraculous transformations in romantic life. On another level, the story of Armin and Anna enacts the reversal of the legend, since it can be read as a narrative of a prince turning into a frog. In the beginning of the story, Armin appears regal and desirable, but by the end, his repulsive qualities have surfaced.

There are also inverted references to Sleeping Beauty in the film—a fairy tale that can be seen (in Riffaterre's terms) to "mediate" between *Straight Through* and *Letter*.[84] When Anna relates her fantasy of dying (while her loved ones mourn the loss), we feel that she aspires to the role of Sleeping Beauty. This sense is furthered by her penchant for playing the corpse. From another perspective, it is Armin who assumes the heroine's position and Anna who impersonates the prince. Armin is "buried alive" in his thorny castle, while Anna tries to awaken him with love. What Dörrie manages to demonstrate is that heterosexual romance is no fairy tale, and that even a shifting of its terms fails to bring about true liberation.

Straight Through is a drama with great superficial similarities to *Letter*, since both chronicle the story of a woman consumed by self-de-

---

[82] Madonna Kolbenschlag, *Kiss Sleeping Beauty Good-Bye* (Garden City, N.Y.: Doubleday, 1979), 205.

[83] Ibid., 206.   [84] Riffaterre, 627.

structive love for a man. What is crucial, however, is that the two works place this situation in opposing contexts. In *Letter*, Lisa's devotion is seen as ennobling, while in *Straight Through*, Anna's attachment is seen as entrapping, as what Fassbinder calls an "instrument of social repression." In *Letter*, the Sleeping Beauty tale is preserved, while in *Straight Through*, it is exploded, shown to be a dangerous "time bomb" ticking away at women's lives.[85]

RECITAL: LOVE IS JUST A FOUR-LETTER WORD

Thus far, we have discussed two dramatic feature films that present alternate views of the woman in love. In Stephanie Beroes's *Recital*, we encounter an avant-garde work that distinguishes itself from the dominant cinema on a variety of levels, the most obvious being its form. Instead of delineating a conventional story, it adopts an abstract structure and presents nine autonomous sequences arranged like chapters in a book. In this regard, it bears the same relation to *Letter* as does *Riddles of the Sphinx* to *The Lady from Shanghai*.

Each section of *Recital* depicts a woman situated in some external locale, reading a letter or other text. Several of the documents are love notes or meditations on romance; this sets the tone of the film and provides its thematic focus. In each segment, the orators do not seem to be the authors of their words. Their stilted delivery, their errors in language bespeak their unfamiliarity with the texts. Several women talk with foreign accents, which establishes a further rupture in the verbal presentation. This distances them (and us) from the material at hand, which is traditionally charged with an excess of passion. Furthermore, the camera repeatedly retains the women's images for several moments after their speech is completed, thus defusing the impact of their words. In the intellectual "space" created by these strategies, the viewer has room to contemplate and critique the material presented—a stance unavailable to the spectator of *Letter*.

The structure of *Recital* bears other resonant parallels to the Ophuls film. First, there is the use of the letters in both works, though they are subject to very different modes of analysis. Secondly, there is the emphasis on reading in both films. In *Letter*, woman is "read" by man, but in *Recital*, her words are related by other women, who offer the audience guidelines for apprehending them. Finally, the visual presentation of the female in the two films is different. In *Letter*, Joan Fontaine is photographed in an aestheticized fashion as an object for spec-

[85] Kolbenschlag, 17.

125

tator pleasure. In *Recital*, however, the subjects are placed casually in the frame, with little attention given to their decorative function. Nor are the women chosen for their physical beauty, and the long-shot distance and static camera downplay their bodies.

Taken collectively, the nine sequences of *Recital* make a cumulative statement about heterosexual romance. The first letter is rendered by a woman reclining on a ridge above the sea—a veritable San Francisco postcard setting. She reads a note (to a man named Bob) that expresses the pain of unrequited love, the abyss of frustrated passion. The final credits of the film reveal that it was written by Stephanie Beroes:

> What hurts me so much . . . is that you have no energy for me any more and you are so casual when I tell you I'm hurt. Whenever I have an idea or any thought I always think: what would Bob think of it, how would he like it? I am devoted to you and to the beautiful love you told me we could have. We can be so happy together. But so many doubts and questions trouble my mind. Is it wrong for me to be hurt? Well, if you have to have other lovers, I can accept that. But what about me and us? I want to put all my energy into you. You are my only love, my only lover.

The text (with its devotional tone, its placement of the paramour at the center of the universe, its charge of Don Juanism) might have been written by Lisa Berndle to Stefan Brand. It figures the enamored woman as enraptured and subservient—and, ultimately, in pain. As opposed to the ecstatic tone of Joan Fontaine's delivery, here the letter is read in a monotone, with no apparent feeling. The speaker even stumbles over words, breaking the spell of their lyrical cadence. Although the ocean vista is one we conventionally associate with romance (as in *From Here to Eternity* [1953]), this connotation is undercut by the scene's presentation as neutral backdrop.

The second letter is read by a woman seated in a folding chair near the sea. It is signed "Bobcat," which we assume to be the nickname of the man to whom the first letter was addressed. Once more, it is read in a vacant voice, and the sound of the wind rustling pages nullifies the romantic force of the words. The letter exudes a tone of benign condescension, as the writer relishes his central position in his lover's life:

> I wonder if my presence, my demands on your time are keeping you from experiencing other things which will help you to grow and enrich your life. . . . With me there maybe all your insights and observations would have been altered.

The man clearly sees himself as his woman's mentor—a role not unlike that of Ophuls's hero. Like Stefan Brand, the writer also reveals his deep-seated ties to the maternal imago, as he calls his woman: "My mate, my love, my sister, my *mother*."

In the third segment, a woman stands by the ocean, with the Golden Gate Bridge in the background. She reads a meditation on love, perhaps a letter or a diary entry. The tone is poetic, describing a series of oneiric rhapsodies. This time the reader explodes in outright laughter (like Cixous's Medusa) at the sound of the passage she must recite[86]:

> My eyes became your eyes and I felt my lashes touch your cheek—our cheek. I slept again. And I dreamed and I know that in my dream we were together in another world. [LAUGHTER]

She also curses when she fumbles a word:

> We were walking along a path and our bodies could by—defy— all principles of matter—intermingle and pass through each other . . . and we spoke of it and laughed at the feelings . . . the marvelous physical pleasure it gave us and we—were—understood that this miracle was a magnif . . . a magnif . . . oh shit, I can't say that word.

The phrase she struggles with is a figure of romantic hyperbole that speaks of the lovers' "spiritual oneness." The reader's attitude is highly sardonic—like someone mocking the purple prose of a Harlequin novel.

The fourth segment marks a break with the previous three in that the text recited (by a woman on a rooftop terrace) is more expository in nature. The credits ascribe it to Carolee Schneeman, an avant-garde filmmaker of an earlier generation than Beroes. It speaks of the sexism of the art world, which "is committed to masculine preserves":

> By the year 2000, no young woman artist will meet the determined resistance and constant undermining which I endured as a student. For studio and history courses will usually be taught by women. She'll never feel like a provisional guest at the banquet of life or a monster defying her god-given role, or a belligerent whose devotion to creativity could only exist at the expense of a man. . . . All that is marvelously already falling around our feet.

[86] See Cixous, "The Laugh of the Medusa," trans. Keith Cohen and Paula Cohen, in Elaine Marks and Isabelle de Courtivron, *New French Feminisms* (Amherst: University of Massachusetts Press, 1980), 245–64.

Schneeman's words also speak for Beroes, an artist in a field dominated by men. At the end of the reading, the final words of segment three are repeated: "Oh yes, I love you, I love you"—with its accompanying laughter.

This superimposition of texts is provocative. At the moment Schneeman's words predict the collapse of the patriarchal art world, laughter is heard. But, of course, the laughter's original object was romance—another sphere in which men have dominated. The conjunction of texts also implies that Beroes sees herself as a woman of multiple dimensions—as both artist and lover—two roles that intermingle, like the bodies described in the clichéd romantic prose. In *Recital*, woman is seen to be both artistic and amorous, whereas in *Letter* she is excluded from cultural creation, forced to channel her imaginative energies entirely into romance. There is another reason, not immediately apparent, for Beroes's conjoining art and romance. The credits for *Recital* assign the male-authored letters to Bob Gaylor, a filmmaker and teacher. We infer that Beroes's romance took place within the art-world milieu, making a separation of the two domains impossible.

In the fifth segment, the woman from sequence three reappears, positioned on the rooftop terrace. As she reads, the camera pans right, focusing on a view of the city. She recites a love poem (credited to Kathleen Frazier), in which the writer bemoans the failure of a relationship in which each person "assumed too little" about the other:

> And I assumed too little—kept packaging you with gravity, trying to design space like a shelf I could measure. And I assumed a small sameness in you, a small difference . . . And you assumed too little—planted me, potted me, how it felt good to you.

Rather than the utopian musings on Eros that we heard earlier, here we encounter a paean to the constraints of love. Again we are reminded of the subtext of *Letter*, which contradicts the surface romanticism with a somber vision of love as pathology. When the recitation has been completed, the camera pauses on the image of terrace greenery—a reminder of the previous text equating love with horticulture.

In segment six, a woman sits in a chair by the sea and reads another of Stephanie's letters to Bob, so it is formally matched to section one. But the tone assumed here is quite different. In the first segment, the author was consumed with love (despite her unrequited passion), but here she reveals a growing distance from her affair. As she states: "After two years of all that unbearable pain over you, I have finally come to a void. I am free of my attachment to you, and now I have no feeling for you whatsoever." She analyzes her former amorous posture and realizes the subjection that it represents. She talks of allowing herself "to be totally controlled," of having been "consumed and swallowed and broken down and excreted," of having cared for her lover "more than herself." By the end of the letter, she confesses that "those feelings [have] slipped into the sentimental past."

This is a critical section, for it shows a woman's awareness of the problematic position she has occupied in love. It makes clear that the entire structure of the film has traced the trajectory of a woman's consciousness-raising (from sentimentality to rationality), with each segment representing a progressive point along the way. Rather than the static portrayal of the amorous woman offered in *Letter* (where Lisa Berndle's attitude toward romance is the same as an adolescent and as an adult), here a woman develops and learns, and begins to configure herself within the broader social world. Perhaps we might deem the Beroes film "Letter from a *Known* Woman" to signify that she is understood, at least by herself. But this knowledge has been garnered at a cost. Segment six is extremely bitter; Beroes "thanks" her ex-lover for his deceits and speaks of hating him. The lady doth protest too much and, in so doing, remains trapped in the bonds of masochistic romance.

Section seven is very important in establishing a connection between woman's romantic oppression and her containment in the larger cultural world. A pan shot finds a woman on a rooftop at dusk; she begins to read a passage about the sexism of language.[87] The excerpt stresses that there are far more abusive words for women than for men, and that those epithets are frequently tied to female sexuality:

> Words used to insult men differ from words to insult women. In the first place, there are not as many. . . . Terms for male animals like "bull" and "buck" usually carry the implication of sexual prowess, whereas "cow," "vixen," "bitch" . . . imply passivity or bad temper and promiscuity as well. "Womanizer," "Don Juan," and "stud" can be taken as compliments at the woman's expense.

This treatise on language occupies a central position within the film, for it expands the theme of woman's oppression from the realms of art

---

[87] Beroes credits this passage as "Words Used to Insult Men" by Casey Miller and Kate Swift. I assume it is from their book, *Words and Women* (New York: Anchor/Doubleday, 1976).

and romance to the broader field of semiological production. If woman has no trustworthy language, she has no authentic voice—a fact apparent from the spoken narration in *Letter*, which is merely a ventriloquistic "throw" of male discourse. In *Recital*, women do speak for themselves, but this is acknowledged as a qualified victory. This section also raises (by implication) the question of language and film, and the possibility that traditional cinematic form also subjugates women. Hence, Beroes fashions a more experimental style that refuses voyeuristic camerawork, that employs distancing techniques, that dismisses conventional narrative.

In the next sequence, the woman from segment three sits on a rooftop overlooking the city and reads a text later ascribed to Carolee Schneeman. The material is relevant to the previous section on language, for it discusses woman's fear of talking:

> Can you imagine that whenever I speak, whenever I speak, there is a convulsion of guilt behind my eyes; she should keep quiet. So utterly conditioned not to fight, for fear of our own aggressions; the defeat implied in making defense.

Perhaps these words hark back to segment six and to Beroes's own fears about asserting resentment, about "making defense."

In the final segment of the film, the woman from section one reappears, sitting on rocks overlooking the ocean. She folds a letter in her hand and puts it away, then gets up and approaches the camera, her face in close-up. The camera pans left (the opposite direction from its movement in segment one), framing the sunset on the sea. The sound of music is heard, and the voice of Billie Holiday singing:

> I don't know why but I'm feeling so sad
> I long to try something I've never had
> Never had no kissin', oh what I've been missin'
> Lover man, where can you be?

Holiday continues the verse until applause is heard—a noise that merges with the ocean's roar.

"Lover Man" is a poignant torch song bespeaking need and desperation—the kind of pain apparent in *Recital* and *Straight Through* but excised from *Letter*. It is rendered by Billie Holiday, a woman known for her self-destructive relationships with men. The lyric articulates woman's favored fantasy of Prince Charming arriving to save Sleeping Beauty's life. Fittingly, Holiday is applauded for this stance; she tells the crowd precisely what it wants to hear.

Beroes's attitude toward this song is rather ambiguous. On one level, she clearly empathizes with the words of the singer and shares her attraction to the masochistic pose. Like the singer, having failed in one romance, she truly wonders where (or if) her lover man can be. But although Beroes has experienced the sentiment of the song, we sense that she is now able to discard it with irony, like the love letter folded in segment nine.

In the film's first letter, Beroes spoke of her paramour's wish that she be "liberated"—that she accept his relationships with other women—a posture she ultimately rejects. By the end of the film, however, she has found a more powerful liberation from the illusions of traditional heterosexual romance: its valorization of the submissive woman, its sentimentalization of female masochism, its claim for primacy in woman's life.

Rainer Werner Fassbinder refers to love as an insidious instrument of social control. From the struggle charted in *Recital*, we sense that Beroes has experienced that process for herself. But perhaps in selecting the closing Billie Holiday song, Beroes means not only to debunk an impossible female fantasy but to raise hope for a revised, utopian sense of romance. Possibly, "by the year 2000," women will not only have gained parity in the art world (as Carolee Schneeman so ardently hopes) but will have achieved equality in love—an emotion they should not have to do without.

131

5 Shall We Dance? Woman and the Musical

Introduction

[P]lot, psychology, motivation, suspense—are to such an extent conventional in the musical that they leave little room for variation: we alternate between the male focus and the female focus, working our way through a prepackaged love story whose dynamic principle remains the difference between male and female. —Rick Altman[1]

Since the beginning of the sound era, the musical has been a prevalent genre in the American cinema—from its first essays in the 1920s (*The Jazz Singer* [1927], *Broadway Melody* [1929]) to its more recent incarnations (*Grease* [1978], *Flashdance* [1983], *Footloose* [1984], *The Little Shop of Horrors* [1986]). Like all genres, the musical has revealed a certain formulaic construction. Critics have commented on its predictable segmentation into narrative sequences and production numbers, and have examined the interrelationship of these two registers. Scholars have focused on the genre's reflexivity. Leo Braudy, for instance, finds the musical "self-conscious about its stylization, the heightened reality that is its norm."[2] He also notes the musical's valorization of personal spontaneity, or "the energy from within."[3] Several critics have commented on the genre's presentation of an ideal community. As Richard Dyer has remarked: "Alternatives, hopes, wishes—these are the stuff of utopia, the sense that things could be better, that something other than what is can be . . . realised."[4] Extending this insight, Martin Sutton has seen the genre's central conflict as between imagination and "a restraining, 'realistic' social order."[5]

Although these aspects of the musical are important, there are others that have greater relevance to the question of women and film. Writers have frequently noted the genre's focus on heterosexual romance, which is apparent in the titles of certain works (*Sweethearts* [1938], *For Me and My Gal* [1942], *Royal Wedding* [1951]). Braudy, for ex-

---

[1] Rick Altman, "The American Film Musical: Paradigmatic Structure and Mediatory Function," in Altman, ed., *Genre: The Musical* (London, Boston, and Henley: Routledge & Kegan Paul, 1981), 201.

[2] Leo Braudy, *The World in a Frame: What We See in Films* (Garden City, N.Y.: Anchor/Doubleday, 1976), 141.

[3] Braudy, 139.   [4] Richard Dyer, "Entertainment and Utopia," in Altman, 177.

[5] Martin Sutton, "Patterns of Meaning in the Musical," in Altman, 191.

132

ample, talks of the musical hero's "search for the perfect partner," and Thomas Schatz sees the genre as examining "American courtship rites."[6] Rick Altman finds "a dual focus, built around parallel stars of opposite sex and radically divergent values."[7] And Jim Collins sees the dance numbers as "metaphor[s] for the sexual act."[8] Thus the musical will incorporate the conventions of the love story, treating them either comically (*Swing Time* [1936]) or tragically (*Carousel* [1956], *A Star Is Born* [1954], *West Side Story* [1961]), as the case may be. The previous chapter made clear how such a romantic framework can have problematic implications for the portrayal of woman.

Crucial to a discussion of sexual difference and the musical is the genre's focus on spectacle—often (though not exclusively) an occasion to display women. While some works (like the Astaire/Rogers cycle) allow for a certain equality in the visual depiction of male and female stars, many favor the use of women as decorative/erotic objects. Think of the treatment of actresses like Marilyn Monroe and Jane Russell in *Gentlemen Prefer Blondes* (1953), of Ann Reinking in *All That Jazz* (1979), or of Jennifer Beals (and her stand-in) in *Flashdance*. Within the musical, issues of genre and gender frequently overlap (making its organizing principle "the difference between male and female"). It is precisely this interaction that I will pursue.

In the first part of the chapter, I will examine a classical Hollywood musical—Busby Berkeley's *Dames* (1934), a film that not only represents but *hyperbolizes* various aspects of the musical's form: its split between narrative segments and production numbers, its dichotomy of free and repressive worlds, its focus on looking at women. In this sense, *Dames* is a work that invites a reading "against the grain" as a primer on issues of sexuality and the cinema. In an essay on feminist film criticism and theory, Judith Mayne identifies certain works that reveal the contradictions of Hollywood cinema, that "offer exaggerated representations of woman . . . [that] la[y] bare the very mechanisms which in other films would be concealed."[9] *Dames* is such a text.

In the second part of the chapter, I will discuss several works by women directors that deconstruct the genre. One is a Hollywood

---

[6] Braudy, 140; Thomas Schatz, *Hollywood Genres* (New York: Random House, 1981), 189.

[7] Altman, in Altman, 200.

[8] Jim Collins, "Toward Defining a Matrix of the Musical Comedy: The Place of the Spectator within the Textual Mechanism," in Altman, 143.

[9] Judith Mayne, "Review Essay: Feminist Film Theory and Criticism," *Signs* 11, no. 1 (Fall 1985): 86.

133

film—*Dance, Girl, Dance* made by Dorothy Arzner in 1940. The others are works in the avant-garde—performance pieces by American artist Kathy Rose and a film by Belgian director Chantal Akerman. Although I link the work of these three women filmmakers, their concerns are very different. Dorothy Arzner fashions a rather conventional musical that integrates production numbers and dramatic segments. In the work of the experimental filmmakers, these elements are split. Kathy Rose's *Primitive Movers* and *Strange Ditties* (1983) rewrite abstract film dance (devoid of any narrative context), while Chantal Akerman's *The Eighties* (*Les années 80* [1985]) parodies the romantic drama in which musical numbers are traditionally embedded. The filmmakers' work also varies on the level of ideological approach. Arzner injects an antipatriarchal message within a transparent Hollywood text, while Akerman's film engages such issues more overtly within an anti-illusionist film. Rose, on the other hand, eschews feminist statement entirely. Her work gains meaning in this regard only through a reading "against the grain" of its nonrepresentational discourse on spectacle and specularity.

The Image of Woman as Image: The Optical Politics of *Dames*

> *I never had the intention of making eroticism or pornography. I love beautiful girls and I love to gather and show many beautiful girls with regular features and well-made bodies. It is the idea of spectacle which is expressed in "What do you go for?" What do you come to do, why do you go to a spectacle: It is not the story, it is not the stars, nor the music. What people want to see are beautiful girls. —Busby Berkeley*[10]

In the proliferation of literature on the status of women in film, the most common critical strategy has been that of distilling from the cinematic narrative an abstract "image" of women in film. From the reverential treatment accorded to the Gish persona in the films of D. W. Griffith, Marjorie Rosen extracts the image of woman as posed on a Victorian pedestal. From the relationship of the Doris Day character to her male protagonists, Rosen posits a vision of woman as militant crusader for chastity. To characterize the adolescent film heroines of the 1950s, she conjures the image of Popcorn Venus.[11] Similarly,

[10] Busby Berkeley, "Rencontre avec le grand 'Architecte du Musical,' " *Cinéma* 103 (February 1966): 44.

[11] Marjorie Rosen, *Popcorn Venus* (New York: Avon, 1973), 71, 211, 300ff.

134

Molly Haskell compares the malign erotic presence of Rita Hayworth in *The Lady from Shanghai* to that of a mythological siren and reads from the machismo sexuality of contemporary cinema the image of woman as rape victim.[12]

In approaching the production numbers of Busby Berkeley, however, we encounter cinematic texts of another order. Rather than presenting us with a realistic narrative from which we must decoct a feminine "image," Berkeley's plastic abstractions present us with the essence of image itself—a vision of female stereotypes in their purest, most distillate form.

Berkeley's mise-en-scène, in fact, has a comic propensity to literalize the very metaphors seized upon by critics like Rosen and Haskell in their characterization of the portrayal of women. While Griffith treats Lillian Gish as though she were on a pedestal, Berkeley, in *Broadway Serenade* (1939), situates Jeanette MacDonald physically upon a pedestal. While some directors shroud their virginal heroines in an aura of sexual impenetrability, Berkeley, in "Pettin' in the Park," shrouds Ruby Keeler in a suit of metal armor. While films of the 1950s cast women metaphorically in the role of Popcorn Venus, Berkeley, in *Fashions of 1934*, casts them literally as the goddess and her galley slaves. While certain stars have filled the screen with the sense of mythical sirens, Berkeley, in "By a Waterfall," fills the screen with mermaids themselves. Finally, as Molly Haskell finds the image of rape inscribed in the content of contemporary films, so one finds, in the style of Berkeley's "through-the-leg tracking shots," implications of the sexual act transposed to the rhetoric of camera technique.

Thus Berkeley's production numbers provide a spectrum of images of women that range from Reverence to Rape. On this level, Berkeley's oeuvre constitutes a definitive text on the subject—an illustrated catalogue whose elegant pages display the cinematic image of woman in all its varied embodiments and incarnations.

A privileged work in this respect is *Dames* (1934), a film whose very title seems to propose it as germane to a discussion of women in cinema. What distinguishes *Dames* from other works in the Berkeley repertoire is the manner in which its production numbers (with their symbolic discourse on the feminine stereotype) are implanted within a narrative that deals directly with the same thematic issues. (The dramatic episodes of the film were directed by Ray Enright.) It is nonetheless intriguing to examine this Centaurian construction and disclose

[12] Molly Haskell, *From Reverence to Rape* (New York: Penguin, 1974), 204, 323ff.

135

the ways in which its discrete segments inflect upon one another and create a rather curious cinematic text. In its hybrid totality, *Dames* constitutes an eccentric treatise addressed to three interlocking aspects of the portrayal of women in cinema: (1) the nature of the image of women in film; (2) the character of the relationship between the female screen presence and the male spectator and/or director; (3) the attitude of the Hollywood industry toward the position of women in the commercial film medium.

THE FEMININE MYSTIQUE AND CINEMATIC TECHNIQUE

While conventional film narratives situate their female personae in a realistic universe, the Berkeley production numbers posit their existence in the realm of pure imagery. The space in which his sequences transpire does not conform to that of the concrete external world. It is abstract and, in its fluid chain of spatial metamorphoses, essentially ambiguous. From this perspective, it becomes the perfect decor for fantasy, and often the narrative prologues explicitly locate the numbers in a character's consciousness. "I Only Have Eyes for You," for example, proposes itself as an oneiric meditation occasioned by Dick Powell's having fallen asleep on the subway.

Beyond the motivational ploys of the framing stories, it is Berkeley's cinematic technique that renders screen space as quintessentially fantastic. Often the numbers unfold in a void, black space whose dimensions are unknowable. The mechanics of concealed cuts transport us magically from one locale to another, creating a geography unnavigable by the human body. In "I Only Have Eyes for You," a cutout face of Ruby Keeler falls away to reveal "behind" it a ferris wheel of costumed girls. In actuality, the sites are connected only by a splice, and the implication of spatial relation is merely an illusion. Spatial paradoxes emerge as well. In "I Only Have Eyes for You," we leave Keeler on the exterior rim of the ferris wheel in one shot, only to discover her on its interior surface in another. Movement in the numbers likewise declares itself synthetic, as images rotate, girls fly up to the lens of the camera or advance forward, propelled by Eisensteinian jumpcuts.[13]

If the geography of the numbers is unchartable, their temporality is unmeasurable; it is as far removed from the flow of normal time as is that ebony vacuum from the coordinates of conventional space. The constraints of causality are similarly dissolved. In "I Only Have Eyes

[13] I am referring to the series of triadic "jump cuts" that occur during the coronation sequence in *Ivan the Terrible–Part 1*.

136

for You," the external world responds to Dick Powell's obsessional fantasies, so that a crowd of people can simply be made to "disappear from view."

Given Berkeley's mise-en-scène as the potential environment of fantasy, with what particular visions of the female image is it populated?

One approach to the question entails an examination of Berkeley's formal technique and the manner in which certain myths concerning women are inscribed on the seemingly value-free level of plastic composition. One should keep in mind the obvious fact that, except for their narrative prologues, the production numbers of *Dames* exclude the presence of men. They are, in fact, elaborate corporeo-plastic constructions of women's bodies "composed" in particular decors. Clearly, these compositions are more than just pictorial; from their physical arrangements of the female form can be read covert assumptions about the female "norm."

We might begin with the very concept of *stereotype*, which on one level denotes having no individuality, *as though cast from a mold.* Ironically, this very notion of uniformity constitutes a stereotype in the depiction of women in film. One thinks of female screen personae in terms of types—a reflex that is not so automatic in the case of males. We have, for instance, the "blonde bombshell," the "femme fatale," the "vamp," the "gamine," or the "sex goddess." These are not "career" specifications, as are the masculine labels of "gangster" or "cowboy," but rather categories of sexual proclivity and physical demeanor. Indeed the entire history of cinema can be seen as constituting an ongoing fashion show of popular female "styles."

This sense of the feminine screen persona as conforming to a particular type is nowhere more apparent than in the chorus lines of Berkeley's production numbers. Part of the humor of the numbers, in fact, arises from our perception that the women look remarkably alike. This notion is eventually catapulted into another realm entirely in "I Only Have Eyes for You," where women are not merely similar but disconcertingly identical. Berkeley clearly prides himself on this stylistic penchant. In an interview, he speaks of a particular day of hiring when he auditioned 723 women to select only three: "My sixteen regular girls were sitting on the side waiting; so after I picked the three girls I put them next to my special sixteen and they *matched just like pearls.*"[14]

Ultimately, this conception of female as stereotype is embodied

---

[14] B. Pike and D. Martin, *The Genius of Busby Berkeley* (Reseda, Calif.: Creative Film Society), 64 (my italics).

within the mise-en-scène of Berkeley's work, particularly in the production number also titled "Dames." There, as though to demonstrate
the precise matching of the Berkeley girls, he lines them up one behind
another until their multiplicity is subsumed in an image of apparent
unity. "Dames" also contains a sequence emblematic of woman's alleged conformity to an external image: in depicting a row of showgirls
making up before their dressing-table mirrors, Berkeley deploys yet another row of women to represent their reflections. One thinks of Molly
Haskell's statement on this issue and the way Berkeley's iconography
tends to literalize it. In speaking of the genesis of feminine cinematic
stereotypes, she refers to how the Gish persona was succeeded by a
"long line of replica mirror-image virgins."[15]

Although Berkeley's relish of the chorus line takes on a transcendent
quality, its presence is, after all, a convention of musical comedy. But
his mode of engaging it is not, and it is on this level of stylistic inno-
vation that more significant attitudes toward women emerge. What
happens in most Berkeley numbers (and quintessentially in "Dames")
is that the women lose their individuation in a more profound sense
than through the similarity of their physical appearance. Their identities are completely consumed in the creation of an overall abstract design.

The configurations of those designs can clearly be read for meaning.
The perpetual arrangement of girls in circular format seems closely
associated with symbols of female sexuality. The objects formed by the
chorus line are equally tendentious. In "Dames," the girls delineate the
sentimental boundaries of a heart. And in "The Shadow Waltz" in
Gold Diggers of 1933, they outline a shapely violin being bowed—a
metaphor that any Freudian analyst would be proud to unpack. Thus
in the Berkeley numbers, the notion of women as sexual *objects* takes
on a deviously witty relevance.

The chorus-line patterns also tend to literalize the notion of two-
dimensional feminine screen portrayal. If there is any match for the
"flatness" of the Ruby Keeler character in the Enright narrative, it is
clearly the showgirls in "Dames," whose bodies are pressed into black-
and-white patterns employed interchangeably with animated designs.

This reduction of the female form to biotic tile in an abstract mosaic
is not devoid of overtones of power. It tends to literalize the stereotype
of the male director as potent Svengali who transforms the dull but
malleable female form into an alluring screen presence. The words of

[15] Haskell, 49.

von Sternberg seem particularly applicable to Berkeley's cinematic technique:

> It is the nature of woman to be passive, receptive, dependent on male aggression. . . . In other words she is not normally out-raged at being manipulated; on the contrary, she usually enjoys it. I have plenty of evidence to assume that no woman, as opposed to male, has ever failed to enjoy the possibly mortifying experience of *being reorganized in the course of incarnating my vision of her.*[16]

Even the narrative element of the production number "Dames" alludes to the sexuality of power: it portrays an all-male theatrical board of trustees who choreograph the careers of showgirls from behind the scenes.

Privileged in the canon of female stereotypes is the conception of woman as decoration, which has had its supreme manifestation in the history of film. Once more, in the iconography of the Berkeley sequences, we find this cliché in its rarefied form, unencumbered by the obfuscations of a plot. The function of the women in a number like "I Only Have Eyes for You" is essentially plastic, their status being equal to that of the decor. They are simply elements of the total mise-en-scène—facets of its comprehensive ornamental structure. Even the frills of their white organza dresses seem to tell us that they are, after all, pure "fluff."

Relevant to this impression is the curious fact that Berkeley girls did not (and often *could* not) dance—a phenomenon that accentuates our perception of their role as visual embellishments. As Berkeley himself unabashedly confesses:

> I never cared whether a girl knew her right foot from her left so long as she was beautiful. I'd get her to move or dance, or do something. All my girls were beautiful and some of them could dance a little, some of them couldn't.[17]

In a number like "I Only Have Eyes for You," the women's gestures (swaying back and forth or undulating the folds of their gowns) clearly do not function as choreography. They serve as kinetic designs that interact dialectically with the complex trajectories of the mobile decor and the moving camera. But the awesome proficiency of Berkeley's me-

[16] Josef von Sternberg, *Fun in a Chinese Laundry* (New York: Macmillan, 1965), 120 (my italics).
[17] Pike and Martin, 51–53.

139

chanical decor tends to underscore the technical incompetence of the Berkeley girls and concretize the image of women as essentially passive. The sets of "I Only Have Eyes for You" are elaborate, preprogrammed machines for action that transport the girls through dizzying cycles of aimless, repetitive movement. What heightens this sense of passivity is the zombiism of the Berkeley girls—a quality they exude beneath the surface of their opaque, dissociative grins. The Berkeley girls, in fact, seem to extend passivity virtually to catatonia, proposing the image of female as ambulatory Surrealist mannequin.

Ultimately, what becomes apparent from a reading of Berkeley's mise-en-scène is the way in which he generates an image of woman as "image" itself. This portrayal proceeds on multiple levels. She is represented as image in terms of her embodiment of cultural stereotypes and as image in her posture of conjured male projection. But the presentation of these first two conceptions depends upon the establishment of a third, which is Berkeley's obsession with the status of woman as *film image*—as plastic, synthetic, celluloid screen object. Von Sternberg once said of Marlene Dietrich that "she was a perfect *medium* . . . who absorbed [his] direction and . . . responded to [his] conception of female archetype."[18] While von Sternberg perhaps offered this rhetorically, Berkeley has embraced it literally. Through his articulation of woman as film image, she becomes quite concretely a medium—one that, in its pliancy, can be molded to the configurations of the Berkeley imagination.

All these varied senses of woman as image seem encoded within the iconography of "I Only Have Eyes for You." It is, first of all, a sequence whose feminine imagery is diegetically situated within the realm of Dick Powell's fantasies. Its references to women and advertising (the subway posters for Society Cosmetics and Willard's for the Hair) furthermore invoke the cultural clichés of surface beauty and vanity. But what is most important in the sequences occurs with the magical dissolves on the advertising posters (transforming each model's face into that of Ruby Keeler) and with the fluid bridge from the final poster to the huge Ruby Keeler head adrift in a black amorphous space. Through those shot transitions, we move from the domain of extrafilmic senses of the female image to the possibilities of its embodiment in cinematic imagery itself.

During the course of the number, Berkeley proceeds not only to cat-

[18] Josef von Sternberg, Introduction to *The Blue Angel—Classic Film Script* (New York: Simon & Schuster, 1968), 12.

alogue those possibilities in formal terms but, ironically, to create a fabric of imagery that comments on his very act of creation. One thinks, for example, of a final segment of the number, comprised of an elaborate chain of process shots. First, we see Ruby Keeler step into a mock-up mirror frame, which becomes reduced in scale and supported by a base consisting of small Ruby Keeler figures aligned in apparent unity. The entire "mirror" is eventually grasped by the hand of a large Ruby Keeler figure who enters from offscreen left. What we have here, of course, is a pictorial allegory—one that dramatizes the employment of women through cinematic processes to present and support a stereotypical image of women. But the most evocative trope of the number comes in the form of the giant jigsaw-puzzle vision of Ruby Keeler's face (see fig. 10). What we see is an obedient cluster of three-dimensional women who proceed to cover their bodies with a two-dimensional photographic representation (a process that, significantly, is accomplished by lifting their skirts above their heads). What is most intriguing, though, is the form that photograph takes. It comes to us in the guise of a jigsaw puzzle—a fragmented version of an image that must be sequentially assembled. In his choice of this conceit, Berkeley has again generated an iconography metaphoric of the portrayal of women in film. It is a portrayal involving the constitution of a giant synthetic image through the assemblage of interlocking pieces commonly referred to as "shots."

"SWEET AND HOT"

In addition to translating certain stereotypes concerning women into the figurative discourse of cinematic imagery, Berkeley's mise-en-scène proposes a particular vision of female sexuality. In order to disclose this, however, it is necessary to locate Berkeley's production numbers within the narrative framework of Enright's *Dames* and to situate the film within the historical context of screen censorship.

The Hollywood production code officially came into being in 1930, but since there were no adequate enforcement provisions, it remained for some time merely an advisory document.[19] In the early 1930s, public criticism of film content mounted and, according to Richard Randall in *Censorship in the Movies*, the year 1934 (the release date of *Dames*) marked "the turning point of self-regulation":

[19] Richard Randall, *Censorship in the Movies* (Madison: University of Wisconsin Press, 1970), 199.

141

American Catholic bishops formed the Legion of Decency to review and rate films. At the same time they threatened the industry with a general boycott by Catholic patrons if the moral tone of films did not improve. This pressure resulted in the MPPDA's [Motion Picture Producers and Distributors of America] formation of the Production Code Administration (PCA) as a quasi-independent, self-supporting body charged with enforcing and interpreting the code.[20]

Evidently the power of the MPPDA and the PCA was based on their domination by the five largest companies in the industry, which, in turn, controlled seventy percent of the film theaters.

In this historical perspective the plot of *Dames* seems an ingenious parody of the censorship of movies. In place of the Legion of Decency, we have the Ounce Foundation for the Elevation of American Morals. (The constant reference to the organization as the "O.F. for the E. of A. M." seems to mock the alphabetics of the MPPDA and the PCA as well.) Substituting for the censorship of film is the censorship of theater. In keeping with the economic realities of film censorship, Ezra Ounce (Hugh Herbert) is portrayed as a millionaire, and the opening sequence of the film catalogues the name plaques of the myriad enterprises constituting his monopolistic empire.

Typically, Ezra Ounce's specific objections to the theater focus on

[20] Ibid.

10. *Dames* (1934). The most evocative trope of the production number is the giant jigsaw-puzzle vision of Ruby Keeler's face.

142

the figure of the showgirl. It is the flagrant display of women on the musical stage that he identifies as the source of its moral danger. Clearly, we are to regard Ezra Ounce as a blustering fool, a repressed, adolescent man who mistakes "good clean fun" for sinful prurience. After all, what takes place on the stage of the theater is to be so innocuous as to permit the participation of the antiseptic Ruby Keeler (who plays his niece, Barbara).

But, ironically, what Ezra Ounce supposedly views on the stage as theatrical numbers within the diegesis of *Dames* are, in actuality, the cinematic insertions of Busby Berkeley. This stylistic dislocation is echoed by a shift in sensibility as well. While the Enright narrative proceeds to spoof the need for censorship of female sexuality, the Berkeley numbers intercede to present it in more slyly perverse configurations than Ezra could have anticipated (or even perhaps appreciated). This tonal disjunction seems epitomized in the title of the fictional musical comedy from which the numbers emerge, "Sweet and Hot." The diegesis of the film would have us believe that what transpires on the stage is naively "sweet." But the realities of our viewing experience contradict this and assert that what Berkeley depicts on the screen is unremittingly "hot."

"The Girl at the Ironing Board," for example, presents us with what was called in those days a "specialty number." The epithet seems peculiarly apt since it unfolds as a comic vignette on the sexual "specialty" of fetishism. It begins with Joan Blondell voyeuristically peering through the laundry window at a loving couple in a carriage outside and singing:

> Nobody ever has whispered to me
> The sweet things a girl loves to hear
> Nobody's arms ever twined around mine
> Still I'm not lonely for romance is near——
> A girl who works at the laundry
> Has a dream lover all of her own
> A lover, unseen, whose love she keeps clean
> With water and soap and a washing machine.

As though the subject of erotic symbolism and fetishistic partialism were not sufficiently overt, she continues:

> There is something about your pajamas
> That fills me with sweet ecstasy
> And because it's part of you

143

I'm learning to love you
So bring back your laundry to me.

The rest of the number dramatizes the notion of fetish as symbolic substitute for the "normal" sexual object. We see animated male laundry sing and gesture to her from the clothesline; she even whisks a pair of longjohns from the pile and dances off with them. At the end of the number she is "gang raped" by a mass of laundry that slides down upon her from the lines.

In keeping with the fetishism syndrome, the number represents the fetish in the context of a series from which Blondell chooses a favorite partner with "whom" she departs: "The construction of a series of love objects is exhibited in the [fetishist's] choice of a partner by first imagining a whole row of possibilities and then ... picking one of them as favorite."[21] Significantly, the one aspect of the number that does not conform to the syndrome is the notion of the fetishist as female. Although stereotypes of sexual behavior are currently under re-evaluation for their cultural determinants, it is nonetheless the case that as late as the Kinsey report of 1953, fetishism was considered an overwhelmingly male syndrome.[22] In "The Girl at the Ironing Board," we would seem to have a clear case of the imposition of a classically male fantasy on the behavior of a female screen persona.[23]

Finally, "The Girl at the Ironing Board" abounds in elements that seem to comment parodistically on the idea of censorship. After its eccentric portrayal of sexuality, the sequence ends on the saccharine note of a chirping bird that sings as Blondell and her laundry walk into the sunset. The Griffith-like sentimentality of this touch is comically false, as disingenuous as the stuffed bird itself sitting on an artificial prop tree.

The song lyric that describes keeping love "clean" comes to mind as

[21] Wilhelm Stekel, *Disorders of the Instincts and Emotions* (New York: Liveright, 1952), 33.

[22] A. Kinsey, W. Pomeroy, C. Martin, and P. Gebhard, *Sexual Behaviour in the Human Female* (New York: Pocket Books, 1953), 679.

[23] The overtones of fetishism in the iconography of *Dames* would seem to go beyond this particular number. In the Enright narrative, we have the absurd character of Ezra Ounce, who is depicted on several occasions toying obsessively with a series of ceramic elephants. The image of dozens of masked Ruby Keeler likenesses in "I Only Have Eyes for You" has the distinct sense of fetishistic partialism (the necessity for the love object to display particular attributes). Even the precise "matching" of the chorus girls carries similar implications. Finally, the jigsaw image of Ruby Keeler's "decapitated" head calls to mind Freud's discussion of Medusa as a symbol of castration, the fear of which underlies the syndrome of fetishism.

one views this work, whose implications had bypassed the process of Production Code laundering. The propriety of the numbers is much like the moral status of Horace Hemingway (Guy Kibbee), which Ezra Ounce suspects is "nothing but a snare and illusion."

From the reviews at the time of the film's release, it seems likely that its implications escaped the public eye, as they had that of Ezra Ounce. An innocuous *New York Times* review of August 26, 1934, for example, described it simply as "an original combination of comedy and song . . . which is staged very cleverly."

THE GOLD DIGGERS, OR THE MEN WITH THE MOVIE CAMERAS

Certain things clearly did not escape the public eye, and it is precisely to the subject of spectator vision that one must turn to complete an analysis of *Dames*.

The title number of the film confronts the issue most explicitly. It begins with an all-male theatrical board meeting at which various investors argue about the elements that ensure commercial stage success. One says: "I tell you, gentlemen, if I'm going to put money into this show I want to be sure that we get the best music possible." Others interrupt, advocating the importance of story or publicity, until finally Dick Powell breaks into a song that establishes the economic base of show business on the male desire to look at women:

> Who writes the words and music for all the girlie shows?
> No one cares and no one knows.
> Who is the handsome hero some villain always frames?
> Who cares if there's a plot or not, if it's got a lot of dames?
> What do you go for? Go see the show for?
> Tell the truth—you go to see those beautiful dames.

Then, as a horde of showgirls enters the board room, he expounds on this theme more thoroughly and reveals that the true gold diggers are to be found in the corporate male bureaucracy, not in the chorus line, as generally supposed.

> Leave your addresses, my big successes
> All depend a lot upon you beautiful dames.
> Oh dames are necessary to show business.
> Dames—without you there would be no business.
> Your knees in action, that's the attraction
> What good's a show without you beautiful dames.

145

After this framing episode, the sequence erupts into the actual production number. Significantly, it emphasizes women's "knees in action," the black-stockinged legs being employed to create geometric designs against a pure white floor.

Aside from "Dames," however, the theme of vision is referred to in almost every lyric of the score. One song is entitled "Try to See It My Way"; another (a fantasy of prenatal love) has Powell confessing that he adored Keeler when she "was a smile on her mother's lips and a twinkle in her father's eye." There is, of course, "I Only Have Eyes for You," which alternately represents the love of a woman as optical illusion and optical obsession.

The act of looking is not only alluded to in the song lyrics of *Dames* but also invoked in the mode of presenting the imagery of the production numbers themselves. Inscribed in Berkeley's optical stylistics is a virtual discourse on voyeurism and its relation to the female screen presence: the "Kino-Eye" has become that of a Peeping Tom. This notion is even brought to the literal surface of the narrative, with one shot revealing an insert of a gossip column, "On the Rialto," whose byline is none other than Peeping Tom.

The implicit thesis of cinema as voyeuristic enterprise (as spectacle) is advanced on many levels in Berkeley's production numbers. One thinks immediately of the anecdote concerning his introduction of the close-up to the vocabulary of the film musical. Sam Goldwyn evidently came on the set of *Whoopee* and questioned Berkeley about his motivation for the technique. Berkeley responded: "Well, we've got all the beautiful girls in the picture. Why not let the public see them?"[24]

Just as Berkeley comprehended the difference between the choreographic potential of theater and cinema, so, too, he seems to have grasped the difference in their voyeuristic appeal. For the close-up has the power to annihilate the spatial gap that distances the theatrical spectator from the female stage presence.

The number that most clearly transposes the issue of voyeurism into stylistic terms is "Dames." Berkeley fills the screen with chorines clothed in provocative negligees à la Fredericks of Hollywood and has them engaged in the visually taboo pursuits of sleeping, bathing, and dressing. As though to shame the camera for its intrusion, however, the lens is continually punished by withdrawing the girls from sight. A whole chain of such instances occurs in the beginning of the number.

[24] Tony Thomas and Jim Terry, *The Busby Berkeley Book* (New York: New York Graphic Society, 1973), 25.

In the first such shot, women run up to the camera and obscure the lens with the fabric of their nightgowns. Then, in a masked cut (with attendant change of decor), the fabric is removed to reveal a girl in a bathtub. She proceeds to cover the lens with a powder puff, which (through another masked cut) is removed by another girl at a dressing table. Eventually, that girl takes a bottle of perfume and sprays the surface of the lens. We next see the lens wiped clean, but this time our vision is identified with a particular male stagehand, and the lens has become a window through which he watches the showgirls approach.

The dialectic of seeing and being prevented from seeing is epitomized in the number's final voyeuristic character, a "blind" man who sheepishly removes his dark glasses to stare at the showgirls passing on the street. (We should remember that, as English legend has it, Peeping Tom was a Coventry tailor who went blind after peering at Lady Godiva.)

Although Berkeley plays on the notion of camera as voyeuristic tool, he nonetheless conceals its presence. While mirrors figure dominantly in the imagery of the numbers (the "mirror" of women in "I Only Have Eyes for You" and the dressing-table "mirrors" in "Dames"), they are most often false surfaces that refuse to reflect an image of the camera or of the man who stands behind it.

But the iconography of the Berkeley numbers seems to go beyond engaging the female screen persona as the source of mere voyeuristic pleasure. In addition to the numbers whose effect depends on the presence of *actual* women, one is struck by the existence of sequences content with their photographic image.

We might recall, for example, that on the subway in "I Only Have Eyes for You," Dick Powell conspicuously ignores the corporeal reality of Ruby Keeler to embark on a fantasy digression based on her photographic likeness. The issue seems crystallized in the final sequence of "Dames." What we see on the screen is a shot of the Berkeley harem arranged in pyramidal fashion against a complex decor. Imperceptibly, the image of the actual women transmutes to that of a photographic representation. And, in a parody of sexual entry, the number ends with Powell's head breaking through the image surface.

What emerges in *Dames* is yet another sense of "the image of woman as image," for it is not so much the physical feminine presence that is celebrated as it is her synthetic cinematic *image*. Ultimately the privileged status of that image and its mode of presentation propose it as a virtual *substitute* for woman herself. Von Sternberg had spoken of

147

manipulating the female screen image into a "visual aphrodisiac."[25] But in *Dames* it seems, like Blondell's laundry, to have acquired the dimension of a fetish.

Once more we find ironic reverberations of the issue within the Enright narrative. In an early scene of the film, Horace Hemingway goes to visit his millionaire cousin, Ezra Ounce, and with polite duplicity remarks that his daughter, Barbara, sends her love. The following comic dialogue casually ensues, but in retrospect seems to encapsulate the dynamics of the portrayal of women in *Dames*:

> EZRA: Barbara sends her love to me? Why should Barbara send her love to me? She's never even seen me!
> HORACE: She's seen your picture.
> EZRA: Well, then. . . . *Maybe she's sending her love to my picture.*

Anything Goes: Rescoring the Musical

DANCE, GIRL, DANCE: WHEN A WOMAN LOOKS

Like *Dames*, *Dance, Girl, Dance* is a backstage musical. It concerns a troupe of female dancers under the tutelage of Madame Basilova (Maria Ouspenskaya), a former ballerina with the Russian Ballet. Within the group, the narrative focuses on two performers: Bubbles (Lucille Ball), a burlesque queen who has mastered and embraced the role of showgirl, and Judy O'Brien (Maureen O'Hara), who rejects that posture and aspires to artistry in the field of modern ballet. As the film opens, the women are appearing in an Akron, Ohio, nightclub, which is closed down by the police. In the audience is Jimmy Harris, who defends the dancers and helps them get their pay. Though he seems initially attracted to Judy, he is inexplicably turned off when he notices her blue eyes. He leaves with Bubbles, and the two spend an evening together on the town. When Bubbles returns to the girls' apartment, she complains that Jimmy abandoned her at the Club Ferdinand when he found a toy bull on the floor. Disgusted, she throws the stuffed animal at Judy, who keeps it as a memento of Jimmy, whom she obviously desires. Subsequent scenes reveal that Jimmy is divorcing his wife, Elena (who has blue eyes), and that he is highly ambivalent about their separation.

When the dancers are reunited in New York, Madame Basilova

[25] Von Sternberg, *The Blue Angel*, 12.

complains that the only performances she can book are burlesque rou-
tines. When Judy mentions that she is creating a ballet, Madame Basilova asks, "Where could I sell a *Morning Star*?" and reveals that all the
male impresarios "want Bubbles." In the following scene, a theater
owner from Hoboken, New Jersey, comes to audition girls for a hula.
Since Bubbles has not yet returned from Akron, Madame Basilova convinces Judy to attempt the dance. The man is unimpressed, and claims
that she has "too much class." When Bubbles appears, she performs
the erotic number and is hired on the spot.

Judy continues choreographing *Morning Star*, and Madame Basilova sets up an appointment for them with Steve Adams (Ralph Bel-
lamy), the head of the American Ballet. On their way to the meeting,
Madame Basilova is hit by a bus and dies; the interview does not take
place. A few weeks later, Judy returns to Mr. Adams's office and, while
waiting for him, observes the ballet dancers rehearsing. Losing her
confidence, she runs away. On leaving, she unknowingly shares the
elevator with Adams, who notices her and is attracted to her.

Meanwhile, Bubbles has become a successful burlesque artist, using
the name of Tiger Lily White. She tells Judy that she needs a "tony
number" for her act and asks her to perform *Morning Star*. Judy accepts. At her first performance, she realizes that, within Bubbles's routine, her dance is a joke; it elicits laughs and jeers from the male audience, who demand the showgirl's return. Though humiliated, Judy
decides to continue because no other options are available to her, and
she desperately needs the money. Bubbles's act achieves tremendous
popularity, working its way up through the burlesque circuit. Judy is
billed as her little "stooge."

Jimmy Harris attends the theater one night and protests the treatment of Judy. When they meet after the show, he recalls their first encounter in Akron. A romance develops. She reminds him of the bull he
had given to Bubbles and confesses that she has kept it. He takes her
to the Club Ferdinand, where he had frequently gone with his ex-wife.
When the latter appears with her new husband, a fight breaks out between the men, and Judy leaves, having realized that Jimmy is still enamored of Elena. When pictures of the debacle appear in the newspaper, Bubbles is jealous of the publicity given to Judy; she is also upset
upon learning that Jimmy is wealthy and that he prefers Judy to her.
When Jimmy shows up drunk at Judy's apartment house, Bubbles
picks him up and rides off with him.

When Judy appears at the theater that night, Bubbles brags that she has married Jimmy (obviously while he was in an alcoholic stupor). Judy is tremendously distressed but goes onstage. This evening, however, she finds her role of stooge intolerable. She stops her performance and talks back to the male audience, chastising them for their voyeurism, indicating that she finds them laughable and pathetic. Steve Adams and his secretary are both in the audience and applaud Judy's diatribe. When Bubbles perceives what Judy has done, she charges onstage and slugs her; a fight between them erupts, which amuses the audience. The women are arrested and, in defending themselves, come to a rapprochement (see fig. 11). The Harrises are reconciled in the courtroom. The film ends with Judy in Adams's office. He tells her: "Silly child, you've had your way long enough; now listen to me." We sense that he will be her impresario, and suspect that he will also be her lover.

While *Dames* offers us only one model of the female performer—that of visual spectacle—*Dance* proposes two women who represent clear alternatives. Claire Johnston conceives of the film as based on a central character opposition:

> Bubbles' desire to please, to exploit her sexuality for success and money, to "get her man," is contrasted with Judy's desire

11. *Dance, Girl, Dance* (1940). Judy (Maureen O'Hara) and Bubbles (Lucille Ball) are arrested and, in the courtroom, come to some rapprochement.

150

for self-expression, for work and the achievement of physical grace, and for acknowledgement within the terms of bourgeois culture.[26]

Thus Arzner does not simply adopt the stereotypes of vamp versus naif; she employs them self-consciously to "generate within the text of the film an internal criticism of it and of the function woman has within the narrative."[27] By contrast, while *Dames* offers us a treatise on the showgirl, it presents no real challenge to that system. Furthermore, though Barbara (like Judy O'Brien) is portrayed as a "good girl," she does not reject woman's role as erotic vision; the only female who does is Barbara's mother (played by Zasu Pitts), and she is seen as an asexual prude. In *Dance*, although Arzner positions Bubbles and Judy dialectically, she makes them both rather sympathetic. Though we are urged to reject Bubbles's values, we nonetheless like her spunk, and, in the final courtroom scene, Judy realizes that her enemy's behavior is symptomatic of a broader patriarchal system. Thus Arzner uses the musical's notion of a "restraining social order" to focus particularly on the situation of women.

While *Dames* may constitute a primer on the strategies of voyeurism (as practiced in the musical), it in no way surfaces the problematic aspects of this phenomenon. However, this is precisely what *Dance* achieves, lending a feminist thrust to the genre's penchant for self-reflexivity. When Madame Basilova contemplates booking her girls for a hula, she complains that she is a "flesh peddler, a jelly-fish salesman," and decries the fact that men always request "the hot one." It is during the sequence when the Hoboken impresario auditions the women that Arzner's formal style interrogates the process of specular consumption. As the man observes Judy's dance, shots alternate between her performing and him watching. His eyes remain immobile, his cigar stuffed in his mouth. When Bubbles takes over, however, there is a parallel, but different, shot/countershot sequence. As Bubbles hulas, she smiles and winks offscreen, articulating an eyeline match with the gaze of the man. This time his eyes are alive as he looks her body up and down and chews aggressively on his cigar. The close-ups get larger and larger until his face looks almost distorted. Here we have a documentation of voyeurism at work: the man's engagement, as well as the woman's complicity—the surveyor and the surveyed. The grotesque,

[26] Claire Johnston, "Dorothy Arzner: Critical Strategies," in Johnston, ed., *Dorothy Arzner: Towards a Feminist Cinema* (London: British Film Institute, 1975), 5.
[27] Ibid.

lustful quality of the man's response establishes a pejorative context in which to view his behavior. In *Dames*, it was treated as a harmless joke.

This sequence is not frequently discussed in studies of *Dance*, but another one is: the moment when Judy renounces her role as musical stooge and aggressively scolds the audience (like Liz in *The Girls*). She admonishes them for paying admission to stare lasciviously at women. She reveals (like Wakoski's belly dancer) that the female performers ridicule them. Clearly, in this scene, a woman looks back and thereby destroys male voyeuristic pleasure. Some have argued, however, that when Judy receives applause for her speech and becomes embroiled in a catfight with Bubbles, her status as spectacle is restored, thereby qualifying her subversive act.[28] Nonetheless, this sequence stands in stark contrast to an earlier one of Bubbles shining a spotlight on her audience—not in order to "illuminate" the specular process but to single out certain men for flirtation and conquest.

Arzner maps a typology of alternate looks into the film, which allow the female dancer to be viewed more humanely than in a musical like *Dames*. Immediately following the Hoboken audition, Judy goes to the attic of Madame Basilova's studio to practice her ballet. Her teacher mounts the stairs and watches her. This scene of Madame Basilova looking at Judy stands in radical opposition to the one preceding it.

Some of the men in the film also resist the voyeuristic position as they observe dancers perform onstage. When Jimmy Harris and Steve Adams are in the audience, they are unimpressed by Bubbles's coyly seductive numbers and horrified by the mockery made of Judy's ballet. When Steve watches his dancers (one of whom looks like Bubbles), the male gaze is devoid of any sexual component. Within *Dance*, the world of high art is represented as one in which the female performer can achieve respect, while low art is a realm in which she remains an erotic object. This class formulation is problematic; John Berger's analysis of European nude painting, a decidedly "respectable" art, makes that abundantly clear. But devoid of the bias, this antithesis of "ways of seeing" woman remains viable.

There is another important manner in which the concerns of *Dance* circle back to those of *Dames*. The Berkeley film is extraordinary for the way in which it surfaces the fetishistic use of woman that obtains surreptitiously in the cinema: through its iconography of the photo-

---

[28] Ibid., 6.

graphic image and its specialty number of girls who adore men's laundry. Though this issue is underscored in *Dames*, the text does not critique it.

The narrative of *Dance*, however, can be read as a resistance to fetishism—an issue that has not been addressed in the previous critical literature. Within the world of the film, Bubbles is a woman who has adopted a fetishistic demeanor in order to please men. Her street clothes and costumes bear all the telltale signs: fur trim, sequins, phallic hats. In the film's first musical number, Bubbles and her chorus are even clothed in Dietrich-like costumes: top hats, garters, and stockings. When Bubbles has achieved notoriety, her most popular musical number is "My Mama Told Me," which configures her as a childlike maiden—a pose that simultaneously defuses her sexual threat and offers her up as spectacle. When her skirt blows up repeatedly in this routine, it calls attention to the bodily site of male discomfort: the female genital "lack." Judy, on the other hand, rejects the role of fetishistic object, both in her dress and in her style of dance. She also opposes this assignment in her relationship with Harris.

Throughout the film, Jimmy is presented as a sympathetic figure (who prefers Judy to Bubbles, who defends the former's art), but he is also characterized as disturbed in his liaisons with women. He is in the midst of a divorce but remains highly ambivalent about his wife. Though attracted to Judy in Akron, he leaves with Bubbles—as though drawn to the fetishistic woman against his will. Significantly, he abandons Judy when he notices her blue eyes, which remind him of those of his wife. Jimmy's obsession with eye color comes up frequently in the film, as though it were a symptom of his obsessive partiality to certain modes of female appearance. On the night he reencounters Judy, he calls her "the girl with the blue eyes." And when he takes her to the Club Ferdinand, he says that "sometimes he wishes that [her] eyes were brown." At one point, his wife even mocks his preference for things blue. His neurosis about women works itself into the dialogue of the film. On the night he meets Judy, he tells her he is "rotten" and urges her to "keep away from guys like me." When he takes her to the Club Ferdinand, he refers to himself as "being cured."

The nightclub is important in other ways, for its symbol is the bull—a masculine icon. It is here that Jimmy likes to take women (his wife, Bubbles, Judy), as though the male aura of the place can liquidate their female danger—or compensate for their lack. While Judy has a crush on Jimmy, she carries around the toy bull (with its prominent phallic horns) as a sign of her attachment to him. Significantly, she realizes how mixed up he is *at* the Club Ferdinand, and it is there that she rejects him and his view of women. In many ways, the romantic structure of the film is asymmetrical and unconventional. When Jimmy is introduced as a romantic lead early on, we expect that he and Judy will form a couple. This logical resolution, however, is subverted, along with the positioning of Judy as fetishistic object. It is regrettable, however, that in the final scene, Judy winds up with Steve Adams—a man who treats her as a child, not as a woman.

Claire Johnston characterizes Arzner's heroines as violating the societal norms established for woman:

> The central female protagonists react against and thus transgress the male discourse which entraps them. The form of transgression will depend on the nature of the particular discourse within which they have been caught. These women do not sweep aside the existing order and found a new, female, order of language. Rather, they assert their own discourse in the face of the male one, by breaking it up, subverting it and, in a sense, rewriting it. It is this form of rewriting which then becomes the structuring principles of the text.[29]

As the heroine of *Dance*, Judy "transgresses the male discourse" in her oppositional speech to the audience. And, through her formulation of a new kind of dance, she "re-writes" the discourse of spectacle as well. It is not only Judy who engages in these processes but also Arzner, who revises the classical musical film, as embodied in *Dames*.

DANCING IN THE DARK: THE FILM/CHOREOGRAPHY OF KATHY ROSE

If we could imagine that Judy O'Brien achieves her goal in the Arzner film and becomes a modern dancer, we might have a figure like the contemporary choreographer/performer/filmmaker Kathy Rose. Shunning conventional "musical" structure, Rose creates avant-garde pieces that integrate cinema and dance. Surprisingly, her work even has relevance to *Dames*, where the musical sequences functioned both as pure abstraction and as potent ideological discourse. The same might be said of the experimental "production numbers" of Kathy Rose. Despite their lack of narrative reference (like the lovers on a subway in "I Only Have Eyes for You" or the laundresses at work in "The

[29] Ibid., 4.

154

Girl at the Ironing Board"), Rose's creations can be seen as reworking the conventions of musical spectacle and posing a challenge to the aesthetics of voyeurism. Though Rose's work does *not* propose itself as feminist in its orientation, I will read it "against the grain," surfacing its unintentional and unconscious discourse on the issue of imaging woman.

Kathy Rose began her cinematic career as an independent animator, and *Pencil Booklings* (1978) serves as a particularly useful introduction to her later dance/film work. It starts with a sketched (possibly rotoscoped) image of Rose at her drawing table; some of her cartoon personae float around in midair. Soon they begin to rebel, complaining about their voice effects and expressing displeasure at being in her movie. She tries to gain control of the situation by putting them through an animation "cycle," then requiring them to do bizarre calisthenics. She shouts, "One and two and three and four; hand into legs and up through neck," and they respond with bodily contortions possible only for drawn figures. Ultimately, Rose gets disgusted with them and leaves the room, at which point they pick up the pencil and make their "own" film. When she returns, she is told, "If you really want to make good cartoons, you have to be in one first." Her face is then transformed from a realistic line drawing to a comic caricature. The camera moves into her eye, and a chain of diverse characters emerge from it. At the end of the film, her creations applaud her and the ostensible lessons she has learned.

What is most striking about *Pencil Booklings* is not its self-reflexivity (although that is clearly at issue), but the *democracy* that reigns between Rose and her cartoon figures. Rather than the animator as dictator or benevolent despot, Rose presents herself as an equal, a creator devoid of the need for separation or mastery. This ethic and aesthetic surface again in her cinema/dance work, for what Rose does in these pieces is both to animate figures on film and to dance with them as a live, three-dimensional presence before the screen. In this respect, Rose differs radically from Busby Berkeley, whom, Leo Braudy described as a "nonparticipating choreographer-director."[30]

Clearly, her consciousness has been raised in *Pencil Booklings*; she has learned that "to make good cartoons, you have to be in one first." In so doing, her method also revolutionizes film terpsichore, which Amy Greenfield defines as "the *opposite* of the documentation of live

[30] Braudy, 142–43.

dance."[31] In Rose's work, however, the two modes productively inter-mix and create a third option championed by Roger Copeland:

> Rather than envisioning the ideal dance film as an artwork sit-uated as far as possible from the "constraints" of live perfor-mance, why not conceive of it as a . . . hybrid that *intentionally* preserves certain aspects of live performance, embellishing them cinematically, rather than simply eliminating all "theatri-cal" qualities on the misguided assumption that they will render the resulting film "impure"?[32]

Aside from forging a new form of film dance, Rose's experimental compositions (*Primitive Movers* and *Strange Ditties*) can also be read in relation to Berkeley's production numbers—texts to which they have no obvious ties. One of the primary issues that surfaced in *Dames* was the objectification of the female body in spectacle—the chorus girls used as decorative design, woman transformed into image. Rose also employs "chorines" in *Primitive Movers*, but they are animated figures, truly two-dimensional personae (rather than females rendered as such). Their flatness is emphasized by the nature of her iconography, which suggests an Egyptian graphic style. When woman's body is in-voked, Rose eschews photographic representation, preferring to ap-pear as a live dancer herself. Rose's image appears on film only at the end of the work: she exits from the stage, and a shot of her (in the same costume) appears momentarily on the screen, then disappears.[33]

Rose not only performs with her animated chorus line but also en-gages in their choreography—in a democratic gesture we recognize from *Pencil Booklings*. ("I think of them as dancers," she told an in-terviewer for the *Philadelphia Daily News*.)[34] Avoiding distanced con-trol of her creations, she operates at their level, inventing with them an original form of film dance. At the opening of *Primitive Movers*, a line of female figures stretches out across the screen, almost to the right-hand border. In the remaining space, Rose interjects herself, standing close to the screen, striking an angular pose like that of her animated dancers. The figures have been drawn and projected so that their size

[31] Amy Greenfield, ed., *Filmdance: 1890–1983* (catalogue for a program of films at the Public Theater, New York, November 29–December 11, 1983, published by the Elaine Summers Experimental Intermedia Foundation), 1 [my italics].

[32] Robert Copeland, "The Limitations of 'Cinedance,' " in Greenfield, 10.

[33] A subsequent piece (*Syncopations*) utilizes both dancers and film footage of dancers. This represents a change from Rose's animated work.

[34] Dan Geringer, "An Animated Time with Kathy Rose," *Philadelphia Daily News*, 19 October 1984, 59.

is equivalent to hers; distinctions between them are tenuous. Rose's movements onstage are synchronized with theirs, and all arms, feet, and heads shift in unison; at one point they even seem to hold hands. The effect is partly comic, as we laugh at the unlikely spectacle of an artist dancing with her cartoons—Kathy Rose and the "Rosettes," as one reviewer called them (see fig. 12).[35] Many scholars have discussed the musical's elimination of distinctions between high and low art; the humor in Rose's performance is, in part, linked to her merger of modern dance and movie cartooning.[36]

As *Primitive Movers* progresses, Rose's own movements begin to vary from those of her drawings; at one point, as they lean left, she veers toward the right. Her spatial relationship to the chorus line also changes: in one shot, an area is reserved for her at screen left; in another, the figures part in the center, and she fills the void. Although *Primitive Movers* starts out as a flat composition, it expands into depth. Breaking with their horizontal blocking, the drawn figures regroup "behind" one another, with Rose taking a position at the apparent "front" of the line. She also experiments with her own relation to the screen, creating certain depth effects. At the beginning of the piece, she stands close to it, so that her equivalence to her figures is emphasized. As the piece unfolds, however, she moves forward, ahead of the screen, and begins to play with the throw of her shadow. Thus both Rose and her silhouette dance with the animated figures—a move that has resonant theoretical implications. Beyond literalizing the notion of cinema as a play of light and shadow, Rose "projects" such specters from her own dance/body, circumventing the more illusory photographic form so problematic for women in *Dames*.

In *Strange Ditties*, Rose uses her shadow more emphatically. Much of the piece proceeds against the background of a black screen (a variation on Berkeley's "void"), which opens up into a central abstract white shape. If the performance space allows, Rose leaves the stage and dances through the audience toward the apparatus. There she moves her arms in the projector beam and casts playful shapes upon the screen, sometimes obliterating the image entirely. When she stands before the light source, her huge blurry shadow appears upon the screen. One can think of few artists who invoke so graphically the tension between woman's presence and her screen re-presentation.

Many writers have noted the musical's strong appeal to the spectator, its simulation of "live entertainment." As Jane Feuer has hypoth-

[35] Ibid., 59.   [36] Braudy, 143–44.

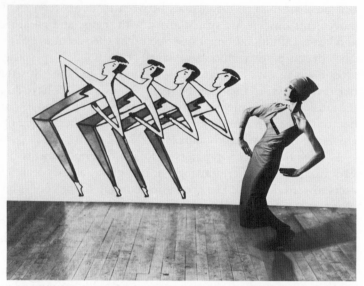

12. *Primitive Movers* (1983). We laugh at the unlikely spectacle of an artist (Kathy Rose) dancing with her cartoons.

esized: "Maybe that's why so many musicals are about putting on a show rather than about making films."[37] Collins has also stressed the musical's invocation of "direct address," a process by which the film audience feels that it is in the same time/space sector as the screen performers.[38] In *Dames*, we can see this process at work when we are made to feel as though we were in the theater, watching live performers sing and dance, despite the "impossibility" of Berkeley's extravaganzas. In Rose's work, this sense of direct address is literalized, for while we view a film, a live performer dances before us. Although she makes forays into the audience, this process works against the notion of spectacle. The more she approaches us, the more she projects shadows, and the more our attention is drawn to the screen. If we do turn around to find her, she eludes us, hidden by the glare of the projector.

It is also significant how aggressively Rose takes on the projector light and uses it to suit her purposes. In *Primitive Movers*, when Rose reserves a space for herself in the filmic mise-en-scène, she is really employing the beam as pure *spotlight*, for no image is registered on the segment of the filmstrip that "hits" her. Here again she literalizes an

[37] Jane Feuer, *The Hollywood Musical* (London: Macmillan, 1982), 23.
[38] Collins, 139.

158

impulse of the cinema: its framing of woman as spectacle. Although the light searches her out, she resists its voyeurism, refusing to be the "showgirl" it seeks. Altman has noted how woman, in the musical, is associated with conventional beauty, a fact apparent in the demeanor of the Berkeley chorines.[39] Rose's appearance, however, is extremely harsh and stylized (like a Noh actor): with white makeup, wine-colored lips, and a coif that strikes a geometric pose. A male reviewer once described her appearance, simultaneously revealing his own discomfort with it:

> Even her hair is impatient—dark, short, cut severely, possessed of the need to fall *femme fatale* style over her left eye whenever the spirit moves it. Mystery hair. *Dangerous* hair. Hair you wouldn't trust at midnight in the fog on the deck of a tramp steamer bound for a port where they sell diamonds below wholesale.[40]

Rose also resists the voyeurism of the light by escaping into shadow. In *Strange Ditties*, she dances frequently in a dark space, allowing only portions of her body (hands, legs, arms) to fall within the sphere of illumination. When they do so, they are not fetishized but used as a means for creating chiaroscuro effects.

Finally, Rose escapes the frame of spectacle by drawing on modern dance tradition—an area in which women artists have achieved great stature and have used their bodies more for aesthetic than for erotic purposes. As critic Jennifer Dunning writes: "Modern dance in America is an art that has been forged by women."[41] Clearly, this is the world that Judy O'Brien seeks to enter in *Dance*. Rose's work is laced with references to various female precursors of her art. The title, *Primitive Movers*, is an homage to "Primitive Mysteries" (1931) by Martha Graham; *Strange Ditties* is influenced by Katherine Dunham's technique; other work draws on the choreography of Mary Wigman. Rose is also familiar with the dance films of Maya Deren and Doris Chase, although she seeks to forge a very different style from theirs. Rose's use of the female body draws on the conventions of dance art. In *Strange Ditties* she wears a highly transparent top that reveals her bosom—a costume that could be seen as inviting voyeurisim. When asked about this, she discussed her interest in the human form as "sculpture" and cited traditions of nude modern dance. For Rose, to

---

[39] Altman, in Altman, 203.   [40] Geringer, 59.
[41] Jennifer Dunning, "Do Women Prevail in Modern Dance?" *New York Times*, 17 April 1987, C 15.

ignore the body is to leave out "a whole part of what your art is about."[42] Although one might argue with the filmmaker about the possibility of using the female form without invoking the pitfalls of spectacle, she is clearly in control of the strategy, using it for her own (not patriarchal) purposes.

Rose's work is also intriguing for its use of the female body as a screen. In *Primitive Movers*, after she and her "doppelgängers" have danced together for a period of time, the animation leaves the figural realm and moves into pure, colorful abstraction.[43] At this point, Rose sheds a layer of her costume and emerges in a white leotard decorated with lines. As the film light washes over her, this outfit seems alternately yellow, turquoise, and red. Again, her method seems to literalize a certain tendency in film (exemplified in *Persona*): to use the female body as a "dream screen" for fantasies. In Rose's case, however, the projections have no tendentious implications, comprising, as they do, pure form and color. If fantasies circulate in her pieces, they are largely hers rather than those of the film spectator. Rose has described the mental state in which she performs:

> I am enclosed in a world of light. . . . I'm locked into a world of fantasy. I am meshed into an abstraction. I cannot see the audience. I can only keep track of where I am on the stage by watching my shadow. It is hard to keep my balance. I cannot see the floor.[44]

Rose's use of the female body as a reflective surface brings to mind an article by Judith Mayne. In "The Limits of Spectacle," she discusses how the film screen functions both as a plane for spectacle and as an opaque barrier, a "threshold separating two spaces."[45] Mayne identifies several films in which the screen metaphor is literalized within the mise-en-scène: *The Big Sleep* (1946), *The Cheat* (1915), and *Uncle Josh at the Moving Picture Show* (1902). It is the latter film that seems most relevant to the work of Kathy Rose.

In *Uncle Josh*, a man seated in a theater box watches several movies. The first (*A Parisian Dancer*) depicts a showgirl, and Uncle Josh leaps onstage to join her number. With the third selection, however—a romance entitled *A Country Couple*—Josh goes one step further and tears down the movie screen. Instead of entering the storied world, as he had hoped (and as Buster Keaton later would do in *Sherlock Jr.*

---

[42] Rose discussed this in an interview I conducted with her in the spring of 1986.
[43] Geringer, 59. He calls her animated figures "doppelgängers."   [44] Ibid., 59.
[45] Judith Mayne, "The Limits of Spectacle," *Wide Angle* 6, no. 3 (1984): 6.

[1924]), Josh finds only an apparatus for rear projection. Mayne draws several provocative conclusions from this little film, which she sees encapsulating certain tendencies in the cinema. First, although the dancer had excited Josh, it is only with the romance (and a heterosexual couple) that he attempts to enter the film: "An image of a dancing woman may be seductive, but it . . . simply oil[s] the machinery that *A Country Couple* sets in motion." Secondly, she sees the film as enacting certain "primal scenes of the cinema":

> *Uncle Josh* does not conclude, as well it might have, with Uncle Josh overcome and overwhelmed by the screen. Instead, Uncle Josh confronts the rear-projectionist and his machine. . . . If there is something of lifting a woman's skirts suggested by Uncle Josh's reaction to the screen—as the flouncing dress of the dancer surely suggests—then the projectionist appears, precisely, in order to block any sight of what might be underneath those skirts.[46]

Thus the screen simultaneously facilitates spectacle and blocks access to that which is displayed.

In Rose's work, we have a rather bizarre and inverted reincarnation of Uncle Josh and his project. In the primitive film, it is the male spectator who wishes to dance with the image and "get into the movies"— in order to possess a female screen persona (the dancing girl, the woman in *A Country Couple*). But his decision is based on a mistaken belief that if he jumps onstage he will find the film image real. He is, of course, thwarted in this pursuit by the screen—a site that offers spectacle and then blocks entry to it.

In Rose's work, however, this model is rewritten and reversed: when "Aunt Kathy" jumps onstage, it is not through any misunderstanding. Furthermore, her desire is not to possess an image but to *be* one, for she is both spectator and spectacle, Uncle Josh and the Parisian dancer, performer and screen. Finally, in Rose's work, the screen does not act as a barrier, hiding a mechanical apparatus that projects a locus of desire. Rather, a real woman dances onstage, confronting the light of a projector that illuminates her body through a filmstrip that she controls. It is only when Rose finally exits the stage (at the end of *Primitive Movers*) that her film image appears—a shot that momentarily invokes the limits of movie spectacle identified by Mayne. If, at that point, Uncle Josh arose from the dead and attacked the screen, he might find the real Kathy Rose standing there.

[46] Ibid., 7.

In *Dames*, the theme song addresses the question of dance/spectacle by asking: "What do you go for? Go see the show for? Tell the truth—you go to see those beautiful dames." And surely this ethic applies to Uncle Josh's philosophy of film viewing as well. In Rose's work, however, the director is simultaneously filmmaker and "dame," animator and dancer, spectator and text. This radically restructures the dynamics of the cinematic musical number, releasing it from the realm of voyeurism and mastery in which it has, for so long, been contained.

TORCH SONG: *THE EIGHTIES*

The performance pieces of Kathy Rose address dance spectacle devoid of the narrative and thematic content generally associated with the musical. In contrast, *The Eighties* by Chantal Akerman focuses on the integration of production numbers within the genre's larger dramatic structure. Part I of the film (which lasts some sixty minutes) consists of fragmented rehearsal scenes for a work that chronicles a love triangle, a staple of the musical genre. In Part II (approximately twenty-five minutes), these vignettes are contextualized within a musical romance.

When we first watch Part I, however, we have no way of knowing that the scenes belong to a musical because they are rendered as spoken text and chronicle a melodramatic story of unrequited love. But given that the root of the word "melodrama" implies a play with *music*, the linkage between Parts I and II becomes clear. In Part I, Akerman not only alludes to the sentimental love story on which the musical is based (for example, Jimmy and Barbara's romance in *Dames*) but also dismantles it, revealing its gestures, postures, poses, and choreographic moves. Even her division of the film into rehearsal and performance segments lays bare the structure of the musical, which so often concerns putting on a show.

THE LIBRETTO: *The Eighties* begins with a black screen, as a woman's voice intones: "At your age, grief wears off." While the image remains blank, we hear another female voice coaching the first, telling her: "Don't move," "Simpler," or "That's too emphatic." Over and over, the same dramatic line is recited, as the director offers advice ("A little more high-pitched," or "That's too subdued"). By the end of this sequence, we comprehend that we are witnessing a rehearsal—an event we will follow for the next hour. The very nature of the initial shot (its total refusal of visual sensation) also suggests that, in *The Eighties*, the notion of theatrical spectacle will be revised.

162

Specifically, what Akerman addresses is the paradigm of melodrama—whether functioning as a genre itself (as in *All that Heaven Allows* [1955]) or as a support for other forms like the musical. The phrase "at your age, grief wears off" is emblematic of melodrama, with its references to emotional excess and suffering. This focus is made even clearer when a woman rehearses a romantic scene. She shouts: "Robert, you're the one I love," and, from offscreen, another woman's voice answers: "But *she's* the one *he* loves." With this revelation of betrayal, the first actress responds: "I've lost him," "I love him so dearly," "No one will ever love me." Obviously, the play in progress is a romantic melodrama, perhaps not unlike *Letter from an Unknown Woman*. Akerman's approach to the material, however, is more in the spirit of Stephanie Beroes and Doris Dörrie than of Max Ophuls.

Akerman deconstructs the sentimental story in several ways, using a series of variations to structure the film. One of her principal methods is sheer repetition. In the first shot, the line about grief is reiterated numerous times, and recognizable clusters of lines reappear periodically for the duration of the film. The treatise on Robert first arises in the beginning of *The Eighties* but is revived some ten minutes later. The opening line about grief resurfaces in a closing segment, lending a circular shape to the film. This radical use of repetition (which Akerman forged in such films as *Jeanne Dielman* [1975]) underscores the redundancy of certain tropes in the romantic melodrama, as well as their endless replay in the lives of real women.

Akerman also distances us from the drama by using multiple actors to fill one role. Because we are watching a rehearsal in Part 1 and not a completed musical, we have great difficulty identifying characters or reconstructing plot, but each fragmentary scene allows us to make certain conjectures. The dialogue concerning Robert hints that the play is about a triangle between a man and two women who fight for his affection. Other scenes (which refer to clothing stores and hair salons) allow us to surmise that the play takes place in a shopping mall. But any sense we begin to glean of dramatis personae is subverted by the scrambling of actors spouting the same dialogue. The lines about Robert, for example, are delivered by one woman at the beginning of the film and by another some ten minutes later. Similarly, other lines (about a girlfriend's marriage) are uttered by two different actresses during the course of the film. This strategy reveals the existence of a certain dramatic stereotype of woman as masochistic victim and emphasizes its duplication in real life. The use of multiple actors (many of whom resemble one another and wear similar clothes) also prevents the spectator from an easy identification with the sentiment of the story, forcing the viewer to recognize his/her anxiety with this unanchored stance.

Akerman also accomplishes a great deal with her use of the female voice-off. It is most frequently identified with the play's director, who advises the actors on their delivery. The opening shot illustrates how that voice comments on the players' presentation of dialogue, but it frequently confronts the performers' gestures. In one shot, the camera focuses on a woman, while offscreen the director's voice is heard coaching her: "They're behind you. You struggle not to look; you can't resist." In another scene, the director's voice talks about how "emotion has to show." These coaching sessions not only reveal the artificiality of the melodramatic form (where lines must be "slightly above a whisper" but not "too subdued") but also reduce melodrama to a series of gestural poses—a body language. In particular, that discourse attaches to the actress who is both the protagonist and the victim of the melodramatic text.

The female voice-over also feeds actors cues that are the "prompts" for their lines. This technique reduces any emotional power the scenes might have (since the director recites the lines unconvincingly). It also serves to scramble gender roles, since the female director often reads male lines.

Interestingly, when the first actor speaks, he does so assertively (in contrast to the more passive delivery of the actresses), and no directorial voice is used to comment on his performance. This seems to underscore the traditional power of the male (both onscreen and off). Rather than pine away about romance, he discusses commerce, declaiming how the strong shop owners will survive and how his store will prosper because women will always wear dresses. "Who has ever seen a naked woman running around the streets?" he inquires.

This vignette has great relevance to Altman's observations that, in the musical, man is "seen as an endless source of gold, while woman is identified by her beauty."[47] It also makes clear the link between the genre's romantic story line and its fascination with the American Dream. As Collins has stated: "The economic success that is so highly considered in the 'real' world is replaced in the fictional world of the musical by success in love and the dance."[48] In Akerman's film, there is no such substitution; one register is merely superimposed upon the other.

47 Altman, in Altman, 205.   48 Collins, in Altman, 141.

It is also telling that Akerman's libretto situates the drama in a shopping center. During the rehearsal, we see no sets; actors repeat their lines against blank walls (perhaps an homage to Jean-Luc Godard). But the dialogue (which mentions business, clothing, and hair salons) makes a commercial location clear. Several rehearsal scenes revolve around this world—one in which the store owners are generally male and the sales help and customers female. One of the boutiques is a dress shop and a scene depicts a male store owner advising a female customer. She complains that the slit in a skirt is too pronounced, to which he replies that she will "make heads spin." He continues: "As a man, I know what a woman should wear to please a man." She finally storms out of the shop, shouting: "What if I don't want to please anyone?" In another rehearsal scene, a woman is reluctant to buy a red garment, although she states that her "husband insists on [her] wearing it." In yet another episode, a shopgirl complains about working in a store, being cooped up waiting for customers, listening to a noisy air conditioner. "This is not life," she concludes.

The choice of this milieu raises the question of consumerism as attached to the female subject. Just as women are the principal customers for musical and melodramatic films (which contain them within a patriarchal structure), so are they consumers (and saleswomen) of other products that leave women in a similar bind. Madonna Kolbenschlag has commented on the addictive quality of consumerism and the manner in which it helps sublimate other desires in women's lives:

> When the sense of self-worth is diminished, when sexuality is muted and functionalized, when access to power and decision-making experiences are minimal, women often compensate by a compulsive indulgence in acquisitive behavior. The "shopping syndrome," with all its quasi-entrepreneurial activity-choices, opportunities (bargain days), mobility, plus the visual and social excitement of the marketplace—can be a substitute for creative work and the experience of power.[49]

The sites of clothing stores and hair salons also allude to the figuration of woman as spectacle, be it within the film musical or more quotidian circumstances. The choice of a shopping-center locale is also significant on another level, particularly because it is portrayed so negatively. Recall that the classic musical conceives of a utopian world that is counterposed to banal reality. As Sutton has written, in the musical,

[49] Madonna Kolbenschlag, *Kiss Sleeping Beauty Good-Bye* (Garden City, N.Y.: Doubleday, 1979), 19.

"the romantic/rogue imagination" does "daily battle with a restraining 'realistic,' social order."[50] In the scenes rehearsed in *The Eighties*, however, no such struggle is being waged; all the characters are conformists before the fact.

Although Part I seems to proceed as a conventional melodrama, there are momentary gaps during which the musical form intervenes. The film's second shot presents a series of women's feet, in high-heeled shoes, walking across a tiled floor. Some of them execute a dance-type shuffle. Both the close-ups of the feet (a staple of production numbers) and the choreographed gestures invoke the musical film.

Other episodes in Part I allude to this more directly. Early on, we hear a chorus of female voices singing a jaunty tune. Onscreen, a woman (who looks like one of the actresses pining for Robert) is shown in long-shot, doing a little dance. It is clearly improvised and spontaneous rather than a professional routine. Another woman later moves around to the same music. Further along, we are introduced to a large ambiguous space (like a huge hall or underground parking lot) in which various actors walk, strut, and/or dance to music. The score for this sequence is disjunctive—rendered alternately by a full orchestra, a single clarinet, and a tinkling piano. The actors' gestures again seem largely unrehearsed. Some of their poses satirize melodramatic tableaux—as when a woman leans theatrically against a pole (see fig. 13, a still from *The Golden Eighties* [1983], an earlier version of the piece). Other gestures seem like parodies (or inadequate imitations) of professional stage dancing. (They remind one of those attempted by Angela [Anna Karina] in Godard's *A Woman Is a Woman* [1961]—a character who wants to be in a Bob Fosse show.)

Besides accompanying moments of dance, music wends its way into other areas of the text. In certain rehearsal segments, a background score is heard (as though to remind us of the musical roots of *melodrama*). In one shot, a piano plays as an actress stands against a wall; in another, a woman paces as music is heard on the soundtrack.

Throughout Part I, the rehearsal segments are interrupted by shots of performers singing a cappella for the camera. A man presents a song in Arabic; a woman offers a tune about lovers parting in a café; another renders a lyric immortalized by Marlene Dietrich in *The Blue Angel* (1930)—"Falling in Love Again." One of the most powerful episodes centers on a close-up of a woman singing a torch song in the style of Edith Piaf: "It's crazy how I love you," "If you leave me I'd

---

[50] Sutton, in Altman, 191.

13. *The Golden Eighties* (1983). Some of the actors' poses satirize melodramatic tableaux.

die." Here we have the merging of the melodramatic and musical imaginations.

The final section of Part I asserts its connection to the musical more emphatically by taking place in a recording studio. It begins with a medium shot of a woman (wearing headphones) who sings a song into a microphone; in the foreground, a female conductor directs her. The woman sings a love song about a failed romance and her hope for another. The lyrics tell of how her lover adores Lily, of how "should love come along," she will "drop everything, burn her bridges, say goodbye to the Magasin Toison d'Or." The references to a love triangle, and to the mall setting, make us associate this song with the vignettes rehearsed earlier. We realize that we have already heard this tune as background music during rehearsal scenes.

What is important about this sequence, however, is its focus on bodily and gestural language—the same kind of physical display that has been coached in the melodramatic scenes, here executed by both the singer and her conductor. It also reveals how centrally the score functions in the love story (be it musical or classic melodrama), both to represent emotional excess and to kindle a response in the film viewer. At the end of the recording session, the singer is so energized that she dances around to the score.

In the next sequence, this gestural discourse is extended when we see the conductor sing a song. We recognize its lyrics as the words of a letter that we have heard recited by one of the actresses in a previous scene. It is a love song (reminiscent of one from Claude Lelouch's *A Man and a Woman* [1966]), sung in a throaty, breathy style. The camera again emphasizes the singer's bodily language, as she grimaces in response to the emotion of the song. She interrupts the recording session several times, commenting that she has "gone wrong" or veered "off the track." She listens to an instant replay of her taping session, then begins to record again. This scene and the previous one are musical rehearsals for the film-within-a-film, as the earlier sections have been run-throughs of the drama. They both share in the classic musical's tendency toward self-reflexivity. But while that genre only demystifies to remystify, as Feuer has pointed out, *The Eighties* accomplishes a more consistent modernist deconstruction.[51]

THE FILM-WITHIN-A-FILM: At the end of the recording session, a title appears that reads "Part II: project." With the next cut, we move from rehearsals to the "movie" itself, presented to us directly onscreen. The musical begins with a shot of a woman working at a soda fountain; she is one of the actresses we have seen in Part I. From behind, another woman runs into the restaurant; she utters lines about a friend's marriage that she has delivered in rehearsal. She asks the countergirl if she has gotten a letter, at which point the latter takes out a sheet of paper and begins to read. We recognize the text from the rehearsal sequence. After a brief recitation, she starts to sing the song recorded by the orchestra conductor at the end of Part I. As the woman performs, she continues to scoop out ice cream mechanically, and people proceed to call out food orders from offscreen. As she moves away from the counter, a group follows her, listening to her song. She hands out sandwiches and drinks as she intones the steamy lyrics. At the end of the number, as she sings "there's only you," she approaches the camera and smiles. Another woman enters the restaurant and inquires: "What's going on here?"

With this sequence, the viewer can retrospectively position certain fragmentary rehearsal scenes witnessed before: the recitation of the letter, the recording of the song, the dialogue sequence about a friend's marriage. They are finally placed within the framework of a musical romance. With this contextualization, however, their tone is entirely transformed: what at first seemed melodramatic now seems comic, as the artificiality of the situation is revealed. The scene becomes a *parody*

[51] Feuer, *Hollywood Musical*, 43.

168

of the musical-romance. It mocks the *bricolage* of using the ice-cream scoop as a prop; it burlesques the chorus of passersby commonly used as a stand-in "audience"; it even travesties the quotidian locales chosen for such segments by juxtaposing a romantic love song with orders for ice cream or coffee.[52] (Significantly, one of the love duets between Barbara and Jimmy in *Dames* occurred in a soda fountain.) In its status as parody, it also becomes a "negative" or "complementary" text for *Dames*—in Riffaterre's sense of the terms.[53]

The satire becomes stronger in the next segment, which takes place in a beauty salon. We rediscover the actress who had pined for Robert. She is talking to another worker about how he is infatuated with Lily. She then begins to sing a song that inquires what Lily has that she does not, how Lily took him away from her. After her solo, a chorus of shop girls poke their heads into the frame, responding to her lament. It is a melody and lyric we recognize as a background tune in the earlier rehearsal scenes. The advice they give her is tough, not the usual poetic fluff. They taunt her for making a fuss, for always complaining. The young woman's lyrics also become quite explicitly sexual. She mentions how she loves it when Robert "breathes down [her] neck" or "rocks with all [his] might" as they make love. This takes Collins's notion of the musical as metaphorically inscribing eroticism and makes it ridiculously explicit.

In the next shot, some female customers (sitting in barber chairs) turn magazine pages in time with the music, as a chorus of women continues the song from offscreen. Female operators stand behind them, washing their hair and spraying hoses in a synchronized manner. The chorus tells the bereft shop girl to "throw [her lover] in the gutter," to "break the spell and wish him hell." They chastise her for "losing her head and her curlers" and tell her to "turn punk rock or new wave," "to put on mascara but not to cry." We then cut to a group of men having their hair washed in a unisex salon. They chime in on the chorus and give her equally harsh advice: one verse tells her to "make fun of that fathead." Another suggests that "he's handsome but he's dumb." As she runs out of the shop, a woman embraces her and says: "At your age, grief wears off." We recognize the line from the first rehearsal scene and realize that we have come full circle to the opening segment.

Once more, this musical sequence is rather ridiculous, with its cho-

---

[52] Ibid., 26–34; Feuer, in Altman, 163.
[53] Michael Riffaterre, "Syllepsis," *Critical Inquiry* 6, no. 4 (1980): 627.

reography of magazine pages and water hoses and its utilization of antiromantic lyrics. According to Schatz, although the classic musical shows us a courtship in conflict, the resolution of the film pretends that the tensions "will magically dissolve once the performance is over."[54] The musical number we have witnessed (with its gritty lyrics and tough-love advice) can leave us with no such illusions.

The final musical vignette takes place in a clothing store, another locale implied in the rehearsals of Part I. We see a close-up of red high heels under a dressing-room curtain. A salesman begins to talk to the woman with words we have heard before; the scene ends with the couple embracing in the fitting room. Two other women witness this tryst; both are shocked and disturbed. We suspect a love triangle with not only one victim but two.

As one woman leaves the shop, she walks into a café and begins to sing the lyric we have heard her record in Part I: about how Robert loves Lily, how she'll leave the Magasin Toison d'Or, how if love comes her way again, she'll respond. Once more the words seem rather inappropriate for a conventional musical. She sings about how her lover is always drunk, how he is a "handsome bastard," how she must look for him "at every joint." As she sings, the people in the café begin to waltz around her (in both heterosexual and homosexual couples); the crowd becomes so large that it literally blocks her out and comically upstages her. At the end of the number, the young woman who pines for Robert runs toward the camera with tears in her eyes—a final sentimental tableau. The film ends with a circular pan of Brussels at dusk—a movement repeated several times. From offscreen, Akerman's voice is heard thanking people for their work on the film, listing its various citations and credits.

Clearly, Part II has shown us a performance of the project rehearsed in Part I—a film that is both an homage to, and a parody of, the standard romantic musical, a form whose conventions look ridiculous when revised from a feminist perspective. In Part I, Akerman has emphasized the artifice of the musical libretto (its melodramatic bias, its romantic victimization of woman), while in Part II, she has revealed the pretense involved in its status as spectacle, as theatrical work.

Throughout the film (in both the rehearsal sequences and in the final credits), Akerman actively asserts her creative presence, through her voice-off and her stand-ins (the orchestra conductor and theater director)—an orientation she shares with Dorothy Arzner and Kathy Rose.

[54] Schatz, 200.

170

While Busby Berkeley choreographs his musicals indirectly, from on high, the women who challenge the genre script themselves into the production, choosing to transform it from within. If *Dames* asks "what [we] go to see the show for," and answers that it's "woman as spectacle," the work of Arzner, Rose, and Akerman rewrites that equation. The "dames" we celebrate in their work are not showgirls, but film directors who rescore and restore the cinematic musical form.[55]

[55] A special thanks to Marcia Landy for her comments at a screening of *The Eighties*.

171

6 Sisters: The Divided Self

Two-Faced Women: The "Double" in Women's Melodrama of the 1940s

THE DOUBLE

It is the phantom of our own Self, whose intimate relationship with and deep effect upon our spirit casts us into hell or transports us to Heaven. —E.T.A. Hoffmann[1]

One of the most compelling branches of the genre of the fantastic is the literature of the double, of the split or multiple self. As many historians have noted, the theme is quite ancient and can be found in various primitive rituals and superstitions. In certain societies, for example, when twins are born, either one or both are slain, for fear of their embodying evil spirits.[2] The double theme also appears in archetypal myths and legends, such as the fable of Narcissus, with his haunting duplicate mirror image, or the legend of Romulus and Remus, the twin founders of Rome. Even fairy tales reveal a similar fascination with the doppelgänger. A Swedish folk story centers on a maiden who mysteriously loses her shadow upon making a pact to retain her beauty.

The figure of the double has been manifest in diverse forms. At times the doppelgänger has shown itself as an ethereal being—a shadow, a reflection, or an animated portrait. At other points, it has taken the shape of an identical being—a person of kindred appearance, a relative, a twin.

While the theme of the double has existed in ancient rites and rituals, it has also appeared in various arts. In literature, its apogee came in the German Romantic period of the nineteenth century—the writings of E.T.A. Hoffmann, Jean-Paul Richter, Heinrich von Kleist, Ludwig Tieck, De La Motte Fouqué, and Heinrich Heine.[3] The cinema, which followed on the heels of this literary tradition, soon spawned its own brand of doppelgänger vehicle. *The Student of Prague*, first filmed in

---

[1] E.T.A. Hoffmann, quoted in Otto Rank, *The Double: A Psychoanalytic Study*, trans. Harry Tucker, Jr. (Chapel Hill: University of North Carolina Press, 1971), 69.

[2] C. F. Keppler, *The Literature of the Second Self* (Tucson: University of Arizona Press, 1972), 16.

[3] These writers are all mentioned in Robert Rogers, *The Double in Literature* (Detroit, Mich.: Wayne State University Press, 1970), 53.

Germany by Stellen Rye in 1913, recounts the tale of a young man plagued by his mirror-image alter ego. It was, in fact, this expressionist work that inspired psychoanalyst Otto Rank in his renowned study of the double.[4]

Whether the theme of the double is expressed in literary or in cinematic form, it has, in modern times, been consistently subjected to a particular kind of critical analysis. In general, it has been read as a symbolic discourse expressing psychic conflicts, wherein dual characters represent facets of the unified self. C. F. Keppler, for example, in *The Literature of the Second Self*, speaks of the typical polarity that exists between the two personae: "oppositeness is the main link that unites them, for it is the complementary oppositeness of the two halves of the being whom they comprise, a being sometimes suggesting the total human personality."[5] By and large, critics have seen the source of such psychic tension as issuing from the author's consciousness: Otto Rank, for instance, examined the quasi-pathological personalities of E.T.A. Hoffmann and Edgar Allan Poe.[6] Theorists like Keppler, however, have admitted a broader social view, noting that the double can also function to resolve "the wider problems of [the artist's] culture."[7]

In this regard, the cinema is, as always, a special and interesting case. As a collective product, less tied to creation by an individual auteur, it resists scanning for the traces of a unique psyche. Rather, as a mass-produced medium, marketed for wide appeal, it is more readable for its revelation of larger social attitudes.

WOMAN AS DOUBLE

Woman is, in essence, a dual being. Can such an assertion be contested? . . . moreover, . . . because of this essential duality she belongs, of her very nature, to that world of ghosts and vampires and demons and monsters and automatons and lunatics and evil geniuses that we call the realm of the fantastic. —Gérard Lenne[8]

As catalogued by such scholars as Rank, Keppler, and Robert Rogers, the double theme has predominantly centered on a male protagonist, but it is important to realize that there have occasionally been instances involving a female subject. Heinrich Heine's story *Nights in*

---

[4] Rank, 3–7. Although it is not clear from the edition of Rank's study that I have, it seems that he is referring to the 1913 and not the 1926 version of *The Student of Prague*.

[5] Keppler, 11–12. [6] Rank. [7] Ibid., 189.

[8] Gérard Lenne, "Monster and Victim: Women in the Horror Film," in Patricia Erens, ed., *Sexual Stratagems* (New York: Horizon Press, 1979), 31.

Florence, for example, concerns a woman with a dual existence.[9] However, the most interesting group of texts on the female doppelgänger is found in the cinema, not in literature. During the World War II years, as part of the broad category of women's melodrama, a particular genre emerged, focusing on female identical twins played by the same actress. The trend actually began in 1939 with *A Stolen Life*, starring Elizabeth Bergner. But it reached fruition in the mid-1940s with the triptych: *Cobra Woman* (1944) and *The Dark Mirror* (1946), both by Robert Siodmak, and the remake of *A Stolen Life* (1946) by Curtis Bernhardt.[10]

It is this triad of "double films" that will form the subject of this section. In examining them, we will find that there are significant differences between the dramatic configurations of female versus male doppelgänger narratives, and that these divergences reflect established patriarchal assumptions about women. Finally, we will show that in order to analyze the female doppelgänger tale, we must go beyond the methodologies of traditional literary and psychological criticism into the field of recent feminist thought.

In order to discuss these films, however, it is first necessary to grasp the broad sweep of their plot lines. *A Stolen Life*, which stars Bette Davis in dual roles, is the story of twins, Katy and Pat. In the beginning of the film, the good sister, Katy, meets up with a lighthouse keeper, Bill Emerson (Glenn Ford), while visiting her cousin, Freddie (Charles Ruggles), in New Bedford, Massachusetts. The two start to date and seem mutually enamored. When Katy returns to her cousin's home, we learn that she has a twin sister, Pat, who seems very curious and jealous of her relationship with Bill, whom she has yet to meet. The next day, as Bill awaits Katy for a luncheon appointment, he spots Pat and mistakes her for his date. Mischievously, Pat goes along with the game, leading him on to believe that she is Katy. Bill is shocked to find himself more attracted to "Katy" and confesses that up till now there had been something "lacking" in her. As he is about to kiss Pat, the real Katy comes on the scene and reveals her sister's trick. From that point on, Pat openly pursues Bill, and they soon wed; Katy tries to drown her sorrow in artwork.

She periodically hears from the Emersons and learns that Pat has greedily convinced Bill to abandon his beloved lighthouse-keeping job

9 Mentioned in Rank, 19.

10 For a discussion of women's melodrama, see Molly Haskell, "The Woman's Film," in Gerald Mast and Marshall Cohen, eds., *Film Theory and Criticism*, 2nd ed. (New York: Oxford University Press, 1979), 505–34.

and go into business in South America. While Bill is away, Katy and Pat visit Freddie's cottage and spend a tense weekend together. Pat insists that she and Katy go for a sail, even though a storm is brewing (see fig. 14). Once afloat, Katy suggests several times that they turn back, but Pat seems excited by the danger. Their boat capsizes near the lighthouse, and Pat is swept into the water. Katy grabs her hand to save her, and as her sister sinks into the ocean, she is left holding only Pat's wedding band.

In the next scene, Katy awakens in the lighthouse-keeper's bed and finds, to her surprise, that she is wearing Pat's ring. When people in the room refer to her as Pat, she fails to correct them, and we realize that she has decided to capitalize on this fortuitous exchange of identities. She pretends that it is Pat who has survived and Katy who has drowned. She looks forward, nervously, to her reunion with Bill, since he will now be *her* husband, but finds, to her chagrin, that he is estranged from his wife. He chides her for her adulterous affairs and indicates that he wants a divorce. She tries to convince him that they can start anew, but, ultimately, cannot endure the sham. Pat has been so cruel to Bill that even though Katy wants him, she cannot bear to inhabit her dead sister's shoes. She flees to Freddie's cottage, where her cousin admits that he knows her true identity. Suspecting the same, Bill soon follows. He confesses his feelings and tells Katy that he has loved her all along.

14. *A Stolen Life* (1946). Pat (Bette Davis) insists that she and Katy go for a sail, even though a storm is brewing.

The Dark Mirror—more of a *film noir* than is *A Stolen Life*—concerns the twins Terry and Ruth Collins, both played by Olivia de Havilland. As the film opens, we learn that a psychiatrist (Dr. Peralta) has been murdered and that the police suspect a woman named Teresa Collins. When detectives investigate the crime, they learn that she is a twin who secretly trades identities with her sister. Though a man has testified that, on the evening of the murder, he saw one twin in the park, he cannot be sure which one. In a protective gesture, the women refuse to cooperate with the police and fail to reveal which of them has the alibi. As a result, the police cannot prosecute, and officially drop the case.

But this situation troubles the chief detective, who wishes to foil the murderess in her commission of a perfect crime. He enlists the help of a psychiatrist, Dr. Scott Elliot (Lew Ayres), who works in an office building where the sisters have sold candy. He is an expert on twins and convinces them to undergo certain tests in order, ostensibly, to further his research. Ruth seems reluctant to cooperate, while Terry (who is obviously smitten with Elliot) is eager, and we suspect that the former is the killer. However, conversations between the sisters later reveal that Terry was at Dr. Peralta's apartment on the night of the crime, and that Ruth is the one with the valid alibi. Dr. Elliot proceeds with the tests. He soon falls in love with Ruth and becomes convinced that Terry is a psychotic murderer. Suspecting the doctor's affection for her sister, Terry becomes extremely jealous and, through various sadistic tricks, tries to make Ruth believe that she is going mad. From Dr. Elliot's discussions with Ruth, we learn that Terry's jealousy is long-standing, dating back to a foster father's preference for Ruth. Ultimately, Dr. Elliot decides that he must warn Ruth about her sister and make her face up to the suspicions that she has previously suppressed. He calls Ruth on the phone, but Terry answers, not revealing her true identity. As she makes an appointment to meet Dr. Elliot, we suspect that she will kill him, as she did Dr. Peralta.

In the nick of time, the real Ruth arrives, so Dr. Elliot is warned of Terry's scheme. When she appears, he confronts her with his psychiatric opinion and urges her to get help. Meanwhile, Terry has left Ruth at home, half convinced that she is hallucinatory and insane. There are hints that she will commit suicide. But the police detective, who has also feared for her safety, rescues her in time and convinces her to feign death in order to bring Terry's psychosis to a head. Terry and Dr. Elliot arrive on cue at the girls' apartment, and when Terry is told of her sister's death, she pretends to be Ruth and accuses the deceased

176

"Terry" of murder. She is foiled when the real Ruth emerges from the bedroom and, in a gesture of rage, smashes her sister's image in the mirror. We learn that ever since the twins were children men have preferred the more saccharine Ruth. Dr. Peralta (who did not realize he was dating identical twins) was killed by Terry because he grew to love the sweeter "side" of what he thought was a single schizophrenic woman. The film ends as Dr. Elliot gazes into Ruth's eyes and asks: "Why are you so much more beautiful than your sister?"

Cobra Woman, is more bizarre and fantastic than *A Stolen Life* or *The Dark Mirror*. The film revolves around the sisters Tollea and Nadja, played by Maria Montez. Set in an exotic island decor, *Cobra Woman* is the least melodramatic of the three and clearly crosses over into the jungle-action-film genre. *Cobra Woman* opens with a love scene between Tollea, an island girl, and Ramu, a Western adventurer, which establishes that they are shortly to be wed. Soon, however, Tollea is mysteriously kidnapped, and a native man is found dead with two fang marks on his body. In discussing the crisis with another island resident, Ramu learns of Tollea's mysterious background. She was apparently born on the nearby Cobra Island and brought to her present home as an infant by a Scotchman who found her as a stowaway on his boat. Ramu and his sidekick, Kado (Sabu), leave for Cobra Island to rescue her.

On the island, Tollea has met her grandmother, the queen of the region, who is responsible for her abduction. The older woman tells Tollea that she is the firstborn of royal identical twins and is the rightful leader of her people. At birth, however, both girls were submitted to a cobra-venom test, and since she was vulnerable to its poison and her sister immune, it was decided that Tollea should die. In order to spare her, however, her grandmother hid her aboard a Scotchman's boat, thus saving her life. Her grandmother has sent for her now to wrest power from her evil twin sister, Nadja, who rules the island with a cruel hand. As evidence of their heritage, both sisters bear cobra-fang scars on their wrists.

Meanwhile, Ramu has arrived on the island and has encountered Nadja, whom he mistakes for Tollea. As he sees her swimming in the ocean, he rushes into the water and kisses her, a gesture she does not rebuff. As he grabs her for a second embrace, Nadja says seductively: "You don't have to hold me; I won't run away." Though somewhat confused by her behavior, Ramu assumes that Nadja is his fiancée. Having been observed kissing the sacred priestess, however, he is rounded up by islanders and put in prison.

After her swim, Nadja goes to the temple, where she enacts the King Cobra ritual for a throng of devotees. As the snake is brought in, she performs an erotic dance, mesmerizing the creature into submission. When it finally lunges at her, she goes into a quasi-erotic frenzy and points at those individuals to be sacrificed to the island's smoking volcano. Through this sadistic rite, Nadja terrorizes the masses into giving her more and more gold.

Meanwhile, Ramu's friend Kado has helped him escape from prison, and he goes to the priestess's palace in search of Tollea. Once there, Nadja tries to convince him that she is his love, but Ramu soon realizes that she must be Tollea's twin sister. At the mention of her sibling, Nadja becomes violent and threatens to hunt Tollea down and sacrifice her to the virulent mountain. Cunningly, she offers Ramu an alternative plan: her sister will be given safe conduct off the island if only he will remain. Clearly, Nadja wants Ramu for herself.

Tollea eventually confronts Nadja, claiming the island's rule for herself. In the ensuing struggle, Nadja trips and falls out a palace window, plunging to her death. Tollea then dresses in Nadja's priestess garb and goes to the temple to claim her rule. When she arrives, people assume she is Nadja and call on her to perform the King Cobra rite. Unlike Nadja, however, she is terrorized by the sight of the giant snake and faints dead away. Fortunately, Kado saves the day and kills the cobra before he can lunge at her. A fight then takes place in the temple, but when people realize that the volcano is finally still, they declare themselves "under the rightful queen."

Ramu and Kado leave Cobra Island dejectedly, assuming that Tollea has remained to rule her nation. But once at sea, they find her on board as a stowaway, and she pledges to Ramu: "Thy people shall be my people."

There are certain broad narrative structures apparent in these twin films that posit them as cinematic "triplets." One sister is good and the other is evil, and the audience's sympathies are directed toward the former. Similarly, the sisters are cast as rivals for the affections of an eligible man, and their competition forms the crux of the drama. Furthermore, we have the sense that the sisters' problems derive from some spoken or unspoken childhood trauma. Finally, the twins undergo a symbolic exchange of identity that leads to one sibling's symbolic death and to the other's real demise.

Clearly, we recognize certain attributes of the broad theme of the double, whether the protagonist is a man or a woman. This similarity is evident if we compare the plots of *A Stolen Life*, *The Dark Mirror*, and *Cobra Woman* with Rank's summary of the basic doppelgänger scenario, in which he assumes a male hero:

> We always find a likeness which resembles the main character down to the smallest particulars. . . . Always, too, this double works at cross-purposes with its prototype; and as a rule, the catastrophe occurs in the relationship with a woman, predominantly ending in suicide by way of the death intended for the irksome persecutor.[11]

Although Rank cites amorous relationships as the fulcrum of the male doppelgänger struggle (and speaks of the hero as exhibiting a "defective capacity for love"), the dual personae are not always open rivals for a paramour, as they are in the female-twin films.[12]

When one considers the case of the male-twin film, other sexual differences emerge. Historically, most of these works have been comedies rather than melodramas, lending the masculine equivalent a far lighter tone. One thinks, for example, of *Our Relations* (1936), with its duplicate set of Laurel and Hardy; of *Wonder Man* (1945), with Danny Kaye playing comically incompatible twins; or of *Start the Revolution without Me* (1970), in which both Donald Sutherland and Gene Wilder are given identical brothers. As Martha Wolfenstein and Nathan Leites note in their book, *Movies: A Psychological Study*, often in these comic films: "any love conflict is avoided by providing another beautiful girl for the hero so that he has no need to covet his brother's wife. The solidarity of the men who might be rivals . . . is achieved by eliminating any cause for rivalry."[13]

Even the male-twin films of a more melodramatic bent exhibit distinctions from their female counterparts. *The Corsican Brothers* (1942), for example, stresses the spiritual ties between Siamese twins separated from birth rather than their competition. And *House of Numbers* (1957) tells the story of a good brother who selflessly takes the place of his jailed twin.[14] It is true that in this film the good brother falls reluctantly in love with the convict's wife, establishing a romantic tension, but even here, the paradigm of the evil twin temptress who cunningly steals her sibling's lover is eschewed.

---

[11] Rank, 33.   [12] Ibid., 72.

[13] Martha Wolfenstein and Nathan Leites, *Movies: A Psychological Study* (Glencoe, Ill.: Free Press, 1950), 142.

[14] Since I have not been able to view all of the male-twin films discussed, my understanding of their plots is based largely on *New York Times* reviews as well as other sources.

Female siblings in the cinema, however, are represented in a far more malevolent fashion. Wolfenstein and Leites note:

> Sister relations are apt to be more overtly hostile than brother relations. Sisters tend to be love rivals, and the defeated one may have little scruple about killing the other. When a twin is thrown by chance into her sister's place, she is not apt to feel, like a brother, that this is an embarrassing situation, from which she would be happy to escape. She is likely to have desired this position for a long time.[15]

The question arises as to why films with female identical twins are apparently so different from those with males, and, beyond that, how the particular cast of the sister films reveals broader social attitudes toward women. If Keppler is correct that the double figure can function symbolically to resolve the "problems of culture," what precisely might those problems be that are expressed in this highly specialized doppelgänger genre?

A promising approach to this issue is through an examination of the polarity between good and bad twins and the qualities associated with each. If we analyze the traits of the nice sisters versus the evil ones, it becomes clear that the sympathetic women are identified with attributes assumed desirable in female behavior, while the hateful twins are not. In *A Stolen Life*, for example, Katy is portrayed as extremely passive. When her sister cruelly steals her boyfriend, she does nothing to fight back. She is entirely self-sacrificing and masochistic, thinking of Bill's happiness and feelings above her own. Similarly, she is loyal and honest, incapable of deceiving a man. In the beginning of the film, when she fabricates a ruse to encounter Bill, she ends by confessing it to him. At the end of the movie, after secretly exchanging identities with her dead sister, she guiltily abandons the scheme. As Freddie tells her: "You were never a liar. . . . How did you think you could live a lie?" Moreover, Katy is represented as being safely asexual, without the erotic luster that can ensnare a man. Bill describes her as a "cake without frosting," and later an artist friend questions whether she is a "real woman."

In a similar fashion, Ruth, in *The Dark Mirror*, has qualities associated with the classic good girl. Her psychiatrist-boyfriend, Dr. Scott Elliot, notes that she exudes a "warmth" that is lacking in her twin sister and refers to her as "sweet." Like Katy, she is shy and demure in

---

[15] Wolfenstein and Leites, 143.

her dealings with men, assumes a childlike role, and allows Terry to protect her "like a mother."

The characterization of Tollea in *Cobra Woman* reveals the same basic structure. She is portrayed as passive—constantly subjected to abduction—ultimately relinquishing political power to follow her man. Her sexuality is also depicted as rather tame, and she is finally unable to perform the boldly exotic cobra dance.

At the opposite end of the spectrum are the three "bad" sisters. In *A Stolen Life*, Pat is cast as a kind of modern-day femme fatale, the type whose love is treacherous and even perverse. At one point, Bill tells Katy that her sister is "dangerous," the kind that "could worm the secrets out of a Sphinx." She is a perilous woman for a variety of reasons, in part because she is frequently deceptive and lies. But she is particularly threatening because she is sexually aggressive and takes a domineering role with men. When Bill escorts Katy to a party, Pat whisks him away in a reel dance and boldly kisses him on the lips. In Bill's own words, she is a "well-frosted" woman and, unlike Katy, "all dolled up." Her erotic aura is manifest in her dramatic clothing—hats, veils, rhinestones, and sequins—and seductive gestures, which are lacking in Katy. Finally, Pat is represented as highly competitive, never an attractive manner in a woman. Unlike Katy, who backs off from a confrontation, she is excited by a challenge and treats her conquest of Bill as a stimulating game.

Similarly portrayed is the figure of Terry in *The Dark Mirror*, although her negative features are more gothically delineated. As a murderess, she is quite literally a fatal woman whose friendship brings men to their death. Furthermore, she is characterized by attributes that are not conventionally thought appealing in a female. She is described by Dr. Elliot as lacking in warmth, and, worse than that, she is clearly intelligent: at one point Ruth even tells the doctor that Terry is the "smart one." Like Pat in *A Stolen Life*, she is sexually forward, directly propositioning the doctor on several occasions. She is also represented as beguiling, giving Dr. Elliot false accounts of her past. She seems strong and commanding, calming her hysterical sister who is distraught over their run-in with the law.

Cast in the same mold is Nadja, in *Cobra Woman*, who is portrayed as a dangerous female—a viper woman who sentences people to death. She is a political leader and, as such, socially powerful—never a favored quality of the Eternal Feminine. Like her counterparts, she is aggressively sexual: without hesitation she seduces the stranger, Ramu, and regularly performs the erotic cobra dance (see fig. 15).

181

While the character of Pat, in *A Stolen Life*, is portrayed in rather restrained terms, Terry and Nadja are depicted in a more baroque manner. In *The Dark Mirror*, Terry not only tries to steal her sister's boyfriend but also attempts to drive her to suicide, creating gothic nighttime "special effects" that stimulate hallucinations (see fig. 16). In these bedroom scenes, Terry is cast as a kind of vampire, preying on her sibling victim. Moreover, the extent of her perversity is narratively manifest in her ultimate diagnosis as insane—a paranoid creature who is "poisoned" and "twisted" inside. In a similar vein, Nadja's status as an exotic priestess in *Cobra Woman* lends her evil female nature a rather supernatural dimension. While the depiction of Pat in *A Stolen Life* is tame, by comparison, there is one scene in which her portrayal approaches that of Terry or Nadja. Before the audience is aware of Pat's existence, Katy returns to the bedroom one night after a date with Bill. As she crosses the darkened chamber, we notice something lurch in the shadow and see her sister ominously appear.

In all three films, the audience is meant to sympathize with the good sisters, those with laudable traits. This strategy is entirely in keeping with the literature of the double, in which both author and reader tend to identify with the more naive of the split selves.[16] In *The Dark Mir-*

[16] Keppler, 3.

15. *Cobra Woman* (1944). Nadja (Maria Montez) is aggressively sexual and regularly performs the erotic cobra dance.

182

ror, for example, the primacy of the figure of Ruth is expressed clearly in the use of the mirror iconography. In many scenes, Ruth is shown sitting at her vanity table, while Terry is positioned so that *her* reflection dominates the mirror frame. Only at the end of the film, when Ruth has finally triumphed, is her own image caught in the glass.

The audience is encouraged in other ways to side with the good girls. In *The Dark Mirror*, for example, the viewer (like the characters in the narrative) is initially tricked and confused about the girls' identities, about who is innocent or guilty. By the middle of the story, however, this anxiety is relieved when it becomes clear that Ruth is virtuous and Terry is evil. For the rest of the film, the girls wear nameplate necklaces or monogrammed robes identifying them, so the viewer feels on safe "moral" ground.

Another reason why the audience identifies with the good girls is that they are preferred by men. In *The Dark Mirror*, Dr. Elliot's affection for Ruth is never in doubt, but in the other films the situation is more complex. Though initially attracted to Katy, in *A Stolen Life*, Bill falls passionately in love with Pat, only to return to Katy in the end. In *Cobra Woman*, though Ramu is temporarily seduced by Nadja, he eventually penetrates her deception and realizes that his love is Tollea.

But what is the precise significance of the split between good and

16. *The Dark Mirror* (1946). Terry (Olivia de Havilland) attempts to drive her sister to suicide, creating nighttime "special effects."

bad girls in these films? The figure of opposing twins seems not to represent dual lobes of the female psyche, but rather two aspects of the broader cultural conception of woman. There are many reasons why woman might be seen in this bifurcated manner, given conventional views of femininity. Simone de Beauvoir, for instance, in *The Second Sex*, speaks of woman as having a "double and deceptive visage"—not because of her essential nature but because of the contradictory expectations with which she is viewed by men.[17]

> There is no figurative image of woman which does not call up at once its opposite: she is Life and Death, Nature and Artifice, Daylight and Night. Under whatever aspect we consider her, we always find the same shifting back and forth.[18]

Other critics have noted that, among the myriad female stereotypes, the polarity of good girl/bad girl, of virgin/whore has held particular sway. Robert Rogers, in his book on the double, devotes a chapter to this opposition, which he sees as derived from the male's ambivalent attitude toward the mother. Consequently, he notes the ease with which woman is subsequently "dichotomized."[19] Likewise, in their book on psychology and the cinema, Wolfenstein and Leites discuss the American fascination with the saintly versus the evil female and explain how they try to combine the two into a single persona.

> American films thus provide an eat-your-cake-and-have-it solution to the old conflict between sacred and profane love. The exciting qualities of the bad woman and the comradely loyalty of the good one are all wrapped up in one prize package, which we have called the good-bad girl.[20]

Wolfenstein and Leites's conception has particular relevance to *The Dark Mirror*, *Cobra Woman*, and *A Stolen Life*. In each film, sacred and profane lovers are represented by identical twins, who, when spliced together, constitute the ideal "good-bad girl."

But the split between good and bad twins has deeper implications than can be explained by the stereotypes of saintly and evil females, or virgins and whores. Rather, the fissure that they represent seems not so much demarcated along the lines of morality (of vice versus virtue) as it does along the lines of gender identification—of "masculine" versus "feminine" poles. Thus the positive qualities associated with Ruth,

[17] Simone de Beauvoir, *The Second Sex*, trans. H. M. Parshley (New York: Vintage, 1974), 223.
[18] Ibid., 210.   [19] Rogers, Chapter VII, 126–37.   [20] Wolfenstein and Leites, 20.

Tollea, and Katy (passivity, warmth, sweetness, masochism, modesty) are culturally defined as "feminine," while the negative traits identified with Pat, Nadja, and Terry (aloofness, intelligence, competitiveness, strength, sexual boldness) are decidedly not. It, therefore, seems no accident that the bad sisters' nicknames are frequently androgynous and could be associated with men. We are not surprised when Bill tells Katy in *A Stolen Life* that Pat could "worm the secrets out of a Sphinx," thereby positioning her in the male/Oedipal stance. Similarly, it seems fitting that Katy is said to have something "lacking," while Pat does not; the latter is clearly a "phallic" female.

But it is in *Cobra Woman* that the masculine nature of the evil sister is most obvious, and is expressed on a highly symbolic level. Only Nadja can perform the erotic dance that mesmerizes the patriarch, King Cobra, rendering him dazed and erect, immobilized in a trance. She alone can evade his aggressively sexual "lunge" and save herself from his deadly bite. Thus she is "immune" to his masculine "poison," while her feminine sister, Tollea, is vulnerable and subject to fainting at the sight of his terrible phallic presence. She seems, rather, identified with the vaginal volcano that erupts during Nadja's rule and is calmed by Tollea's succession. The narratives of *The Dark Mirror*, *Cobra Woman*, *and A Stolen Life* seem not so much to depict battles between good and evil as they do psychic struggles between alleged "masculine" and "feminine" lobes of the female consciousness.

This sense of the narratives can easily be read from the scenario of *A Stolen Life*, which is cast in the mold of a traditional allegorical journey of the self. Katy first meets Bill by the ocean, and they travel together across the waters to the magical-sounding Dragonhead Island. Their next encounter is at the awesome lighthouse, where they begin to fall in love. Katy then loses Bill to her more "masculine" sister, whom Bill seems facilely to "exchange" for his former love object. Ultimately, Pat is killed on the rocks of the phallic lighthouse, where upon Katy temporarily "murders" her feminine self and assumes her sister's identity. Learning, however, that being such a virile woman is shameful, she resumes her original persona and eventually wins her man. As the narrative comes full circle, she and Bill are back on Dragonhead, with him urging her to forget all that has intervened. "Pretend," he says "that we have never left the island." It is as though the story had moved us nowhere in real time and space, but only in the psyche of the female protagonist. Thus, in losing her twin sister, she has rejected a facet of her identity, finding her "feminine" half more satisfying than her "masculine."

185

This conception of the doppelgänger narrative as enacting a drama of self-growth is conventional, as is the use of double figures to symbolize diverse aspects of a single identity. According to theorists, however, the particular qualities that the dual personae represent will vary with each author's personality. What is striking about these female-twin films is how stable the characterizations remain. The split is between "feminine" and "masculine" attributes, cast in the guise of good and evil sisters. This consistency suggests that the films deal not with the split of a particular psyche but rather with a rupture in the social conception of woman. As Freud once noted metaphorically, in speaking of the dissociated mind: "If we throw a crystal to the floor, it breaks; but not into haphazard pieces. It comes apart along its lines of cleavage into fragments whose boundaries, though they were invisible, were predetermined by the crystal's structure."[21] Following Freud's line of thought, we might inquire of these female-twin films: what are the predetermined crystalline social structures that have caused the women to break in this particular manner?

THE FEMALE DOUBLE INTERPRETED

The woman as sign . . . becomes the pseudocenter of the filmic discourse. The real opposition posed by the sign is male/ nonmale. . . . The image of the woman becomes merely the trace of the exclusion and repression of Woman.
—Claire Johnston[22]

In order to examine this issue concerning the cultural representation of woman, we have to scrutinize more closely the opposition posed by the twins and to question their characterizations as "masculine" and "feminine." For an analysis of this paradigm of the double, however, such traditional critics as Rank, Keppler, and Rogers are not especially helpful. More fruitful are the writings of diverse postwar feminist theorists: Simone de Beauvoir in the 1940s and, more recently, Claire Johnston, Luce Irigaray, Julia Kristeva, and Nancy Chodorow. Such feminist thinkers have made clear that there are no objective, value-free standards for masculinity and femininity; rather, such conceptions have been historically defined and authored by men. What patriarchy has deemed acceptable in a female has been labeled "feminine," and what has been unacceptable, "masculine." We can imagine, however, that from a woman's point of view, no such dichotomization

---

[21] Sigmund Freud, quoted in Rogers, 16.

[22] Claire Johnston, "Myths of Women in the Cinema," in Karyn Kay and Gerald Peary, eds., *Women in the Cinema* (New York: Dutton 1977), 411.

would need to exist. Rather, varied qualities of her persona (the so-called "masculine" and "feminine") might be integrated into a conception of a complex, unified, female self. Thus the split between the twins in *The Dark Mirror*, *Cobra Woman*, and *A Stolen Life* need not be viewed as a real break in the psyche of woman. Instead, it is more aptly seen as a cleft in the male view of her.

Simone de Beauvoir's existentialist-derived concept of woman as "Other" is most useful here. If man can see in woman only his opposite, then it is not surprising that a female who dares to share some of "his" qualities (intelligence, strength, eroticism) might be viewed as suspect or unnatural. Patriarchy rejects the allegedly "masculine" woman—the woman who claims her total human range and refuses to be entirely "non-male."

A similar point has been made more recently in regard to film by Claire Johnston, whose work has been influenced by developments in Marxism, semiology, and Lacanian psychoanalysis. She sees the figure of woman in the cinema as a male-constructed sham, a patriarchal "front" that actually signifies the "trace of the exclusion and repression of Woman."[23]

It is this sense of a male perspective that informs the characterization of the twins in *The Dark Mirror*, *Cobra Woman*, and *A Stolen Life*. The two sisters do not represent real poles of the female psyche, but rather two opposing male views of woman. Though the narratives would seem to revolve around female characters, they are only its "pseudocenter." Instead, women are largely evacuated from the scene, and the twins signify male consciousness in "drag." The true mirror images reflected in these films are not the light and dark sides of the female mind, but rather the dialectical fantasies of man. This fact should not really surprise us, for, as Johnston has indicated, "within a sexist ideology and a male-dominated cinema, woman is presented as what she *represents* for man."[24]

The pivotal role of male consciousness (as the lens through which to view and evaluate the twin women) is made most explicit in *The Dark Mirror* by the central function of Dr. Scott Elliot. It is he who is the "expert" on twins, who wants to add Ruth and Terry to his "collection." It is on his authority that we learn that Ruth is desirable and normal, that Terry is unattractive and demented. As Mary Ann Doane has made clear in her work on the 1940s "woman's film," the figure of the male doctor is prominent in that period:

[23] Ibid. [24] Ibid., 410.

187

> *In the "woman's film," the erotic gaze becomes the medical gaze.* The female body is located not so much as spectacle but as an element in the discourse of medicine, a manuscript to be read for the symptoms which betray her story, her identity. Hence the need in these films for the figure of the doctor as reader or interpreter, as the site of knowledge which dominates and controls female subjectivity.[25]

Beyond simply positioning a doctor within the narrative to mediate and direct the viewer's estimation of the sisters, *The Dark Mirror* evinces certain techniques by which audience identification with the male medical gaze is assured. The central scenes in this regard are those in Dr. Elliot's office, where Ruth and Terry are given psychological exams: a Rorschach, a word-association quiz, and a polygraph test. We, the audience, are secretly present at the scene, monitoring the women's responses along with Dr. Elliot's reactions, but certain filming strategies give us an especially privileged view. During the Rorschach tests, we look directly at the inkblots, in shots positioned over the female subject's shoulder, so that we (like Dr. Elliot) can judge the results. We grow suspicious when Terry sees a lamb of death, with men caught in its paws, and feel relieved when Ruth sees only innocuous ice skaters, a drum majorette, and a maypole. Similarly, during Terry's polygraph test, we are privy (like the doctor) to close-up views of the graph paper and can watch the lines swerve madly as she lies about men's preference for her over Ruth.

These strategies of identification seem to have been mirrored in the studio's public-relations gimmicks designed for marketing the film. In a paper on the woman's picture, Janice Schuler notes how Universal International suggested that sample inkblots be run in newspapers, so that the readership could analyze them for themselves. It was also proposed that lie-detector machines be placed in theater lobbies to allow patrons to experience the procedure on a firsthand basis.[26] Because of these techniques (both intrinsic and extrinsic to the filmic discourse), the viewer's personal conclusions about the twins were bound to mesh with those of Dr. Elliot: the spectator would see Ruth as a good, feminine woman and Terry as a disturbed, masculine girl.

Dr. Elliot's views can be seen to coincide as well, with someone

[25] Mary Ann Doane, "The Woman's Film: Possession and Address," in Doane, Patricia Mellencamp, and Linda Williams, eds., *Re-Vision: Essays in Feminist Film Criticism* (Frederick, Md: American Film Institute and University Publications of America, 1984), 74.
[26] Janice Schuler, "The Woman's Picture: Promotional Address and Femme Fans," Unpublished paper, 5–8.

else's, and in this regard we might conceive of him as a fictional stand-in for Dr. Freud. Does not the Freudian conception of woman paint the same picture, casting her in a lifelong struggle between opposing masculine and feminine drives? According to Freud, this drama begins in early childhood when the young girl must make a unique and traumatic switch of allegiance not required of the male. While the young boy (who desires his mother) can later extend that impulse in his love of a wife, the young girl must radically shift from a female to a male love object. In addition, according to the Freudian school, this transfer of love from mother to father imbues the young girl with hostility toward her own sex—an emotion that may later flare up in rampant jealousy. Thus we are not surprised that, in *The Dark Mirror*, the sisters are cast as vicious opponents, or shocked when Dr. Elliot declaims that "all women are rivals, fundamentally."

The Freudian view, however, articulates an even more dramatic war between masculine and feminine forces, which is fought on the battleground of the female body itself. Freud sees the maturation process of the female psyche as involving a topographical move from clitoral (or masculine) eroticism to vaginal (or feminine) sexuality. In the ultimate denouement, a woman's clitoral desire for a penis is eventually satisfied by her vaginal delivery of a child. Thus her "masculine" half is repressed—like a bad erogenous twin sister. This Freudian notion of woman's lifelong psychic struggle is well summarized by critic Evlyn Gould:

> In order for a young girl to become a woman, the ambivalence of the female child towards her mother must be transformed into hatred and the clitoral erogenous zone given up for the vagina. Freud further explains that this transfer of erogenous zones predisposes women to hysteria since it requires the repression of the virile, phallic pleasure of clitoral masturbation. In fact, hysteria . . . is almost inevitable in female sexuality because of the double erogenous zones: one masculine, one feminine.[27]

Given this psychic and physiological view of woman, the twin films take on added significance. Perhaps the fact that the twins are consistently split along lines of masculinity and femininity (rather than some other more neutral trait) is due to the ubiquity of the Freudian conception, which sees woman as fundamentally bisected by two opposing sexual modes. Surely, one can imagine *other* ways to read woman's

[27] Evlyn Gould, "On Sara Kofman's *L'Enigme de la Femme*," *DisCourse* 4: 34.

situation than the manner chosen by Freud, and contemporary feminists have offered such new interpretations. Luce Irigaray, for example, sees female erogeny as diverse but coherent—multiply contained within the bounds of the feminine:

> ... woman does not have a sex. She has at least two of them, but they cannot be identified as *ones*. Indeed she has many more of them than that. Her sexuality always at least double, is in fact, plural. . . . Indeed woman's pleasure does not have to choose between clitoral activity and vaginal passivity. . . . Both contribute irreplaceably to woman's pleasure but they are only two caresses among many to do so.[28]

By contrast, the Freudian view positions woman at the hub of a psychic vortex that spins her sexuality out centrifugally into two antipodes.

In a similar manner, the traditional notion of women as inevitable antagonists has been subjected to recent revision by Nancy Chodorow. Rather than seeing the mother/daughter relationship as necessarily mired in hatred—the Freudian scenario—she stresses the importance of positive maternal identification as a central feature of a young girl's development:

> For a girl . . . there is no single oedipal mode or quick oedipal resolution, and there is no absolute "change of Object." Psychoanalytic accounts make clear that a girl's libidinal turning to her father is not at the expense of, or a substitute for, her attachment to her mother. . . . Instead, a girl develops important oedipal attachments to her mother as well as to her father.[29]

Thus it would seem that the conventional psychological view of women's rivalry bespeaks an unstated fear of female bonding—be it parent to child, sibling to sibling, or political "sister" to "sister." In this regard, it is interesting to note that the publicity material for *The Dark Mirror* reveals this masculine anxiety. A press release, for example, nervously queries whether it is "true that twin girls regard each other with more affection than they can ever give their husbands."[30]

Hence, the Freudian narrative for female sexual maturation can be seen not as a real developmental blueprint but rather as a fictional sce-

---

[28] Luce Irigaray, in Elaine Marks and Isabelle de Courtivron, eds., *New French Feminisms: An Anthology* (Amherst: University of Massachusetts Press, 1980), 102.

[29] Nancy Chodorow, *The Reproduction of Mothering* (Berkeley: University of California Press, 1978), 127 (my italics).

[30] Schuler, 7.

190

nario—a projection of male consciousness onto woman's body and mind. It is for this reason that the twin films hold a special fascination. In their use of one actress in dual, simultaneous roles, they depend on special effects that tend to literalize this ideological process. When Bette Davis or Olivia de Havilland play both good and bad sisters, it becomes clear that the same woman can be regarded in contradictory ways, depending on the perspective from which she is viewed. (In this respect, one is reminded of the current feminist reevaluation of a figure like Freud's "Dora," whom contemporary critics see, in a far different light than did the Victorian doctor.[31])

Furthermore, the optical processes necessitated by the twin film almost concretize the imposition of an external masculine view on women. In order to cast the same performer in two different (but simultaneous) roles, the films rely on a wide use of matting and rear-screen projection—techniques that confuse reality and illusion. For example, in one scene in *The Dark Mirror*, Ruth and Terry stand diagonally in a courtroom as the police question them about a murder. One image is projected on a back screen, while the "real" actress stands in the foreground. In a similar manner, certain sequences employ a deceptive use of optical printing. While the "real" de Havilland (playing Ruth) sits at a vanity mirror, a photographed image of her as Terry (standing behind) is matted into the mirror frame.

It is the metaphorical, psychological resonances of these optical practices that are most intriguing—the sense in which they parallel the kind of psychic processes by which people "project" aspects of themselves onto other individuals. Seen in this regard, the good and bad twins in the films seem like nothing so much as dichotomized male projections of opposing views of the Eternal Feminine.

The concept of projection screens is particularly suggestive within this context. The female characters in all three films function not so much to reflect the image of women as they do to "screen out" the true female form—and to constitute a surface on which to duplicate the masculine visage.[32] As Jung once remarked, in discussing the "anima" and "animus": "Projections [can] change the world into the replica of one's unknown face."[33]

One wonders, on a broader social/historical level, why these partic-

---

[31] I am thinking particularly of the film *Sigmund Freud's Dora* (1979) by Anthony McCall, Claire Pajaczkowska, Andrew Tyndall, and Jane Weinstock.

[32] The issue of woman as "screen" is discussed in another context by Shoshana Felman in "Rereading Femininity," *Yale French Studies*, no. 62 (1981): 19–44.

[33] C. G. Jung, in Violet S. de Laszlo, ed., *Psyche and Symbol* (Garden City, N. Y.: Doubleday/Anchor, 1958), 8.

ular male anxieties regarding women may have been exacerbated during that period. Was there something in American culture of the late 1930s to middle 1940s that heightened a fear of female bonding or of woman's "masculine" side? Though such a question cannot be adequately tackled in a critical essay, certain speculative suggestions do come to mind.

These films appeared during, or immediately following, the war years—a time when women were alone on the home front, left to function collectively without their men. They were required to enter the work force in unprecedented numbers and even to perform such "unfeminine" jobs as that of Rosie the Riveter. In an essay on the subject, Michael Renov speaks of woman as driven to "schizophrenia" in this era—torn between social pressures to take the place of men and yet remain "attractive" for their return.[34] Thus the uneasy fascination with the female double in this period would seem to have cultural determinants, since woman's persona was seen as divided, and its aspects as mutually exclusive.

DOUBLING AND MOTHERHOOD

The "uncanny" is that class of the terrifying which leads back to something long known to us, once familiar. —Sigmund Freud[35]

Gérard Lenne, as previously quoted, characterizes woman as fundamentally "a dual being" and asks whether "such an assertion [could] be contested." He then goes on to question whether the doppelgänger is not somehow more applicable to woman than to man:

> Now I must ask if this essential duality is true only for woman or if it applies as well to all humanity. But is not the female sex in some way more human than the male? Can we not see the concept of the double . . . etched to perfection in woman's appearance and behavior?

Interestingly enough, Lenne also cites the figures of identical female characters, played by the same actress, though his concern is not with twins but with the animate and inanimate women in Fritz Lang's *Metropolis* (1926).

[34] Michael Renov, *"Leave Her to Heaven:* The Double Bind of the Post-War Woman," Unpublished paper presented at conference of the Society for Cinema Studies, Los Angeles, 1982.

[35] Sigmund Freud, "The 'Uncanny,' " in Benjamin Nelson, ed., *On Creativity and the Unconscious* (New York: Harper & Row, 1958), 123.

Clearly, Lenne's view of woman, as expressed in this passage, taps into sexist ideology and, in that respect, is problematic.[36] As de Beauvoir has made clear, the conventional view of woman as a dual creature (as mother and whore, as life and death) is not an essential quality of her being but rather a mark of man's own ambivalence toward her. Similarly, the Freudian notion of female sexuality is hopelessly polarized between the incompatible domains of masculinity and femininity.

Despite the lapses in Lenne's formulation, we might inquire if there is any way in which we can "redeem" his statement and see the female human being as having a privileged relation to the double. One speculative thought comes to mind, but it has nothing to do with the realm of the gothic. Rather (as Freud suggests in speaking of the " uncanny"), it concerns something natural and even familiar—woman's special role in childbirth. While male authors have conceived of baroque fictions to conjure an aura of the double—animated portraits, living shadows—woman's body, in its quotidian biological potential, constitutes a ready-made theater for such spectral scenes. In the possibility of pregnancy (whether realized or not), of growth of a second self within the primary being, every woman comes closer to a lived sense of the double than do most men.[37]

Once more, it is a contemporary feminist critic, Julia Kristeva, whose work is most suggestive of this theory. In discussing motherhood, for example, she writes:

> Pregnancy seems to be experienced as the radical ordeal of the splitting of the subject: redoubling up of the body, separation and coexistence of the self and of an other. . . . This fundamental challenge to identity is then accompanied by a fantasy of totality—narcissistic completeness—a sort of instituted, socialized, natural psychosis.[38]

Thus, while the real and benevolent possibility of the female body for doubling is ignored in the male-oriented literature of the doppelgänger, a false bifurcation is imposed on it as the battleground of hostile masculine and feminine forces.

In many ways, this neglect of the maternal dimension participates in a larger cultural repression of the mother's role. (Witness, for example,

[36] Lenne's quote is decidedly slippery on this point. At times he is clearly aware that he could be accused of sexism, but he seems to slip into conventional attitudes nonetheless.

[37] The exception, of course, is male twins.

[38] Julia Kristeva, "Women's Time," trans. Alice Jardine and Harry Blake, *Signs* 3, no. 1 (Autumn 1981): 31.

that in *Cobra Woman*, the bad sister is identified with a matriarchy, which the good sister rejects to follow her man. Similarly, the evil twin in *The Dark Mirror* is seen as "maternal" in her perverse control of her sister.) Interestingly, Rank's discussion of the double takes particular note of how many twin legends involve a pointed denial of motherhood: "twins [are] considered self-created . . . generated through their own magic power, independent of the mother."[39]

The double figure in literature may ultimately be based on a primal suppression of woman's birth function—perhaps the only natural sphere of the doppelgänger drama. Hence, it is not surprising that when female alter egos do appear, they are denied association with the specifically feminine possibilities of doubling and, instead, are split falsely into warring "masculine" and "feminine" poles.

Woman is thereby driven in these narratives to the hysteria that Freud predicted—to the paranoia of Terry in *The Dark Mirror*, the religious dementia of Nadja in *Cobra Woman*, or the suicidal frenzy of Pat in *A Stolen Life*. Meanwhile, as Kristeva's thoughts make clear, woman's real relationship to the phenomenon of doubling is erased—an experience that would be felt not as a malevolent terror but as a natural, benign, and even creative "psychosis."

The Return of the Repressed

PANDORA'S BOX

Fair is foul and foul is fair
Hover through the fog and filthy air.

Double, double, toil and trouble;
Fire burn, and cauldron bubble.

—*William Shakespeare*, Macbeth[40]

The Bad Sister (based on a novel by Emma Tennant) was made by Laura Mulvey and Peter Wollen in 1983 as a feature video for England's Channel Four television. Like *Riddles of the Sphinx*, it is an experimental narrative, though its style is not as radically innovative as the earlier work. Wollen characterizes its stance as the "half-way house approach," including "some of the mainstream . . . and some of the

[39] Rank, "The Double as Immortal Self," in *Beyond Psychology* (Camden, N. J., 1941), 91.
[40] William Shakespeare, *Macbeth*, ed. G. K. Hunter (New York and London: Penguin, 1985), 53, 105.

avant-garde grammar."[41] The decision to shoot in video was an economic (as opposed to an aesthetic) one, and, overall, the piece retains
its cinematic feel. Mulvey and Wollen, in fact, call it a "video feature
film."[42]

The title suggests that there will be thematic parallels to *The Dark
Mirror*, *Cobra Woman*, and *A Stolen Life*. A brief plot summary
makes those correspondences abundantly clear. The film opens in a
television studio, where a man and a woman discuss a program they
are producing. At certain points, the viewer sees the videomakers talking; at other times, the spectator watches the images they discuss, as
pictured on a monitor. The show concerns a case of domestic violence
in Scotland, in which a man, Dalzell, and his daughter, Ishbel, have
been murdered. One of the prime suspects is Dalzell's other child,
Jane—his illegitimate offspring by a servant/mistress. As the male videomaker recounts the story, he reveals that the drama hinges on Jane—
and on her problematic relationship with her late half-sister. Though
there are no twin figures in this work (as in the Hollywood cycle), the
film clearly counterposes good and bad sisters (who are the very same
age). Moreover, in invoking the trope of the double, the narrative suggests a divided image of the female self. But, in *The Bad Sister*, the
ideology of the dominant film is entirely opposed and its values completely reversed. Thus, in Riffaterre's terms, the Mulvey/Wollen piece
represents a "complement," or photographic "negative" of the earlier
canonical works.[43]

As *The Bad Sister* progresses, the scene shifts between segments of
the production team talking and sequences that represent footage they
are examining on the screen (filmed interviews, home movies, photographs, etc.). A portion of the narrative is offered as a dramatization
of Jane's tape-recorded diary. As the videomakers create their program, they attempt to solve the crime under investigation and to make
sense of the puzzling Dalzell family dynamics. As one of them states in
the beginning of the work:

> Mystery adds spice to crime. Mystery adds charm; it attracts
> our curiosity. We ward off the shock of death by setting out in
> search of a second surprise, the perpetrator of death.

[41] Peter Wollen, interview in *Opsis* (Spring 1984): 35–40. Reprinted in a program
note for *The Bad Sister*, Carnegie Museum of Art, Pittsburgh, December 5, 1984.
[42] Wollen and Laura Mulvey, quoted in a press release for a showing of the film at The
Kitchen, New York City, November 1983. The quote is reprinted in the Carnegie program note.
[43] Michael Riffaterre, "Syllepsis," *Critical Inquiry* 6, no. 4 (1980): 627.

In addition to penetrating the conundrums of the Dalzell deaths, the videomakers (both within the film and without) offer the viewer a solution to the "mysteries" of the female psyche: one different from that advanced by the mainstream cinema.

To surface those distinctions, we must begin by investigating certain similarities. In discussing *The Dark Mirror*, *A Stolen Life*, and *Cobra Woman*, we stressed that the difference between sisters lay in their "adequacy" as women—the good ones seen as feminine and the pernicious ones as masculine. In *The Bad Sister*, the contrast between Jane and Ishbel is registered, in part, on this basis. As the videomakers study Jane's tape diary, the images present us with a dramatization of a party she attended one evening. When we first see her, she has a soft, "womanly" appearance: her strawberry blonde curly hair is long, and she is wearing a fancy purple dress. She looks for her boyfriend (and roommate), Tony, and when she finds him talking with his ex-lover, Miranda, she leaves the gathering in a rage and returns to her apartment. In a scene reminiscent of "The Execution of Rita Hayworth," she stands before her bedroom mirror and cuts her golden locks. The camera renders a close-up of the fallen tresses; the soundtrack augments the noise of the scissors snipping. She then puts on a denim pants suit and continues shearing her hair; an image of her former self appears (via dissolve) in the mirror. Finally, she picks up a gun and leaves the apartment.

We have witnessed not a gender-neutral transformation but one that represents a move from "feminine" to "masculine" demeanor. Her acquisition of a gun (an image that is superimposed on her face in the opening-credit sequence) also associates her new self with phallic power, as well as with violence. At first glance, Jane seems to be the "bad" sister, since she is identified as a possible murderess. Clearly, this bears comparison with a film like *The Dark Mirror*, in which the dangerous sibling is seen as masculine and homicidal. Opposed to Jane stands Ishbel—a figure we encounter only as a fleeting vision. What we do see, however, is stereotypically feminine: she has a prim, Victorian presence and long, flowing dark hair. Her legitimacy, her beauty, her status as a murder victim mark her (conventionally) as "good."

While the narratives of *The Bad Sister* and the twin films converge in establishing this dichotomy between women, their orientation is completely antithetical, the former constituting a critique of the latter. It is important that the "bad" sister of the Mulvey/Wollen piece works as a *film critic*, thereby objectifying the adversarial stance of the movie in which she appears. Even the style of the video piece "revises" the more traditional film, constituting a "bad sister" to its "good." As Wollen states:

> I was quite intrigued with doing [the video piece] "properly," i.e. doing the eye-line matches and getting the continuity right, and yet producing something which clearly in some ways was wrong from the point of view of the well-made television product. On one level it does look just like how it ought to look, but on another level it's somewhat unsettling.[44]

The first difference that we note between *The Bad Sister* and the twin-film genre is that the Mulvey/Wollen piece takes the point of view of the "evil" sibling, whereas the Hollywood films do not. Although it is through the videomakers' review of Jane's diary that we come to know her, it is, nevertheless, *her* story that we hear. We have access to her consciousness, and Ishbel is seen only through Jane's eyes. Thus our sympathy will be with the "bad" sister, despite her alleged crimes. Through her voice, we come to hear her justifications for the murders and, hence, to comprehend her motivation. In framing the narrative from the perspective of the "bad" woman, Mulvey and Wollen repeat a strategy used in *Riddles*, whereby the Oedipal tale was told from the vantage point of the Sphinx.

In *The Bad Sister*, the traits of "masculinity" displayed by the "pernicious" woman are not regarded in a negative light. Rather, they are seen as marks of justified rebellion against the constraints of femininity, as defined by patriarchal culture. In one segment of Jane's diary, she calls herself the "other" sister. If woman has conventionally been seen by men as the male "other," Jane sees herself as *other* than that.

In fact, her "masculine" behavior is regarded as an act of valid opposition to traditional society. It seems crucial that most of the men involved in Jane's life are represented as oppressive figures (with the exception of her clergyman friend, Stephen Pauling). Her father is an upper-class Scottish aristocrat, the lord of a landed manor, who runs his household like a feudal estate. A brutal and alcoholic man (whom one of the videomakers describes as "drunk, lazy, and wealthy"), he treats his servant/mistress and daughter like the hired help they are. Thus he has both legitimate and illegitimate families, separated by propriety and class.

Several sequences in Jane's diary focus on moments of domination

[44] Wollen, *Opsis*, 35–40.

by her father—a patriarch in both a domestic and an economic sense. In one flashback, we see her, as an adolescent, garbed in a maid's black dress—mocked by some rich young men playing tennis on the estate. As she walks through the formal garden, her father appears and becomes annoyed with her. He clips her ear with a hedge pruner and calls her a "disobedient slattern." This violent act (with its overtones of symbolic castration) recalls the earlier scene of Jane cutting her hair. These matching segments encourage us to see her murderous act as retaliation against the subjection of women.

In a later recollection, Jane is a young girl at Christmastime, as her father distributes gifts to the children on the estate. His wife and daughter, Ishbel, sit beside him, while Jane sits among the others on the floor. He calls her up last for a present and omits a surname. After the ceremony, Ishbel leads Jane upstairs, and they play together in a closet. Their game is interrupted by Dalzell and his wife, who abruptly pull the two girls out. In response, Jane stabs Ishbel with a hat pin and runs away. Again, associations are made between this memory and later events—specifically, Jane's murder of her sister. Once more, her hostility to Ishbel seems justified by her father's insensitive rupture of their sibling bond.

Jane's boyfriend, Tony, is also presented as an unsympathetic character. Significantly, he is a screenwriter of commercial films, underscoring the fact that men create the movies that women (like Jane) can only suffer and critique. Though Jane and Tony are not husband and wife, the domestic scenes between them bespeak the ennui and tensions of a bad marriage. In most of these encounters, Tony tends to nag Jane about her unconventional behavior. He is annoyed when she cuts her long hair and upset when she has to go to a press screening on a Sunday. He also complains about her lack of interest in culinary chores: she does not check on the roast or prepare the onion sauce. Their sexual life is clearly unsatisfying to Jane, whom we see distracted, repulsed, or alienated during intercourse. Finally, it is suggested that Tony may be having an affair with his old girlfriend, Miranda (whose photo Jane finds in a drawer).

Unlike Jane, Tony comes from a proper, middle-class family. His mother visits the apartment en route to an embassy reception. She, too, is an unattractive figure—superficial and intrusive—which further distances us from Tony. As spectators, we empathize with Jane's rejection of her mate, as we do with her opposition to her father. Thus her "masculine" qualities are not viewed as pernicious but as logical responses to social abuse.

198

Her "masculinity," however, is seen not merely as an opposition to men but also as a rejection of the feminine ideal. This theme is advanced by her hostility to the two women who represent that stereotype: Ishbel and Miranda, inverted "doubles" of herself. As Jane lies in bed one evening, we hear her thoughts on this issue through voice-over narration:

> As I sat hating the girl in the photo [Miranda], I wanted to expel her—to throw her from my body—she, my shadow, as a definition of that vague thing—womanhood. Men like her because she is so finite; she never dreams; there's no static around her head; this is reserved only for me—only for the other sister—and then the terrible competitiveness; it's a battle she always wins.

Jane attempts to exorcise this feminine archetype from her consciousness. Because we identify with her and sanction her struggle to oppose the Eternal Feminine, the poles of the twin films are reversed. "Good" sister becomes bad, and "bad" sister becomes good—and our sympathies are decidedly with the latter.

In addition to distinguishing itself from the Hollywood cycle on the basis of what it rejects (patriarchy, the feminine mystique), *The Bad Sister* also separates itself on the strength of what it *embraces*. While the earlier films instruct the viewer that the "good" sister's salvation lies in repudiating her sibling and aligning herself with a man, *The Bad Sister* urges Jane to associate herself with other women. If she abandons Ishbel and Miranda as ideal female models, she accepts others—women normally excluded from society.

One of the women with whom she is linked is her mother. Like the Sphinx in *Riddles*, she stands outside of male culture—as a servant, a mistress, the parent of an illegitimate child, a battered woman. Through one of Jane's flashbacks, we witness the denouement of her mother's relationship with Dalzell. One afternoon, she and Jane return to the servants' quarters and learn that a sum has been deducted from their wages to pay for an iron they have broken. Jane picks up a hammer, and the two walk to the main house and knock on the door. Dalzell answers and announces that he will evict them from the estate. As Ishbel looks on from an upstairs window, Jane and her mother kill Dalzell, maiming his eye (like that of Oedipus) in the process. As her mother is taken away, Jane sobs in her attic bedroom.

In commenting on the events, the videomaker says that "the eviction may be one of the clues of the murder." But it is not merely the

199

events of that particular day that lead to her violent eruption. Rather, it is the fact that as a servant woman, she has *always* been excluded from the male social world. The narrative of *The Bad Sister* not only recounts Jane's excision of her "good" woman doubles (Ishbel and Miranda) but also her growing engagement with the image of her mother.

Jane also adopts an older woman, Meg, as a mentor—a figure whom the male videomaker denotes as a "crucial character" in the drama. He learns about her largely from an interview with Stephen Pauling—the clergyman who has befriended Jane. Pauling explains that Meg once led a commune of women on the Dalzell estate—a group Jane and her mother had joined upon their eviction. Meg later moved to England, where she established a similar society of "wild women." Stephen notes that it was "a most peculiar setup—a big house in Notting Hill, lived in exclusively by women."

Pauling clearly regards Meg as a witch, and her commune as a coven. He tells the videomaker that "it bears the marks of something supernatural, something evil." He also implies that Jane is under Meg's unnatural sway:

> [Jane] was in a trance. I wonder whether she was under some sort of spell ... possession—or hypnosis. She could have stabbed her sister without knowing anything about it. God knows what sort of powers Meg had transmitted to her.

Stephen says that Jane was looking for a "spiritual center," and that she found it in Meg.

The Scottish setting, the wild women all spark associations with *Macbeth* and the weird sisters. In Shakespeare's play, they invoke a world in which good and bad are dangerously reversed—in which "fair is foul and foul is fair." In *The Bad Sister*, such conventional polarities are also inverted, but the "witch" is seen in a more positive light. In recouping the figure of the sorceress, Mulvey/Wollen participate in a trend of feminist art that seeks to rescue certain marginal legendary female figures (like the Sphinx). As Nina Auerbach notes: "Woman's freedom is no longer simple initiation into historical integrity, but the rebirth of mythic potential."[45]

Although Jane admits Meg's awesome powers ("[she] can control my life and my thoughts"), she mocks Stephen's religious theory that

45 Nina Auerbach, *Woman and the Demon: The Life of a Victorian Myth* (Cambridge, Mass., and London: Harvard University Press, 1982), 12.

Meg is allied with the devil, who wants Jane's soul. Rather, she praises the "travels" that Meg sends her on. These psychic excursions are all associated with the sea: swirling water imagery appears in the film's opening credits, and, at the end of the piece, a ship arrives to take Jane away. (Its gangplank appeared in an earlier fantasy, which followed Jane's transformation through wearing masculine garb.) Furthermore, in one of her meetings with Stephen, the two discuss the ocean and what it "means." Jane links it to death, but Stephen ties it to madness. Clearly, the sea—with its dark, vast, mysterious waters below the surface—is a suitable metaphor for the unconscious. A similar association circulated in *A Stolen Life*, where the trope of an ocean journey was used as a metaphor for a voyage of self-identity.

If, in *The Bad Sister*, Meg and her sea travels are linked to the psyche, it is especially interesting to note how Jane describes those supernatural trips:

> [Meg] can take me to another world and I think it's because she knows what happened to my mother; she has that knowledge she knows I need; it's like an invisible movement beneath the surface that draws me irresistibly. It's the adventure I've always wanted.

Meg has access to Jane's mind because she can lead her to her mother—an important figure who has been "evicted" from her psychic and social world. One is reminded again of Chodorow's theory that a daughter's bond with her mother is far more important than Freud may have supposed—with his emphasis on female rivalry and the daughter's rejection of her mother's "castration."

But Meg does more than encourage Jane's rapprochement with her female parent; she is also the one who urges Jane to purge herself of her bad sister, Ishbel, and to consider violence. At one point, the following exchange takes place between the two women:

> MEG: You've got to get rid of your bad sister. That's what your mother wanted; it was her last wish.
> JANE: Where is she, Meg? Did she sail on the ship?
> MEG: You can only find out if you get rid of your bad sister, it will set you free. You can travel further than anywhere I've shown you. Vengeance. Without it, the pain can never be assuaged.

Because of Meg's powers over Jane's unconscious, and her seeming ability to relieve her of her psychic demons, she resembles a *psychia-*

trist more than a witch. Perhaps this is why Jane and Tony's apartment has a poster for Hitchcock's *Spellbound* (1945), a film that centers on a female analyst and whose title conflates supernatural and psychological powers.

Other aspects of *The Bad Sister* emphasize the theme of the unconscious. The narrative structure continually focuses on Jane's mind through her tape diary—which the male videomaker calls "a message written in code." Furthermore, within the dramatizations of her life, there is a continual shift between conscious and unconscious thought, between dream and waking states, between imagination and reality. Claire Johnston has stated that "a desire for change" in woman's art "can only come about by drawing on fantasy," and clearly, in *The Bad Sister*, this is what Mulvey/Wollen attempt to do.[46] Jane's flashback to Christmas on the Dalzell estate, for instance, occurs in a daydream as she peers out a window. Her recollection of her father's murder comes while she sleeps. A reverie concerning childhood occurs as she sits, distracted, in a press screening. Finally, one particular sequence of the film (when Jane wanders into a surrealistic dock-side bar) is reminiscent of the work of Kenneth Anger (*Fireworks* [1947]) and Jean Cocteau (*Blood of a Poet* [1930])—both artists known for their focus on the psyche.

Aside from reading Jane's sea escape as a trope for her descent into the unconscious, another interpretation offers itself—and it has more to do with Meg's invocation of vengeance. The image of Jane departing on a ship that magically arrives is reminiscent of Bertolt Brecht's Pirate Jenny and the vessel she describes in her song of fantasy revenge:

> And a hundred men will come ashore before it's noon
> And we will go where it's dark and chill
> And every man they find, they will drag along the street
> And they'll clap him in chains and lay him at my feet
> And they'll ask: now which of these are we to kill?
> And when the clock strikes noon it will be still down by the
>   harbor.
> When folk ask: Now just who has got to die?
> You will hear me say at that point: All of them!
> And when their heads fall, I'll say: Whoopee!
>   And the ship with eight sails and

[46] Claire Johnston, ed. *Notes on Women's Cinema* (London: British Film Institute, 1973, 1975/ *Screen* Pamphlet 2), 29.

> With fifty great cannon
> Will sail off with me.[47]

Jane's sea travels involve her rejection of the "good" woman models offered by patriarchal culture and her alignment with females who stand outside the city walls: Pirate Jenny, the wild women, her mother. In this respect, *The Bad Sister* does not entirely cast off the symbolism of doubling; rather than choose a man (as does the good sister in *The Dark Mirror*), Jane selects new female alter egos. On this level, the film reflects certain feminist theories that accept, but reinterpret, the notion of duality in woman. For Luce Irigaray, *"[Woman] is neither one nor two. Rigorously speaking, she cannot be identified either as one person, or as two."*[48]

When Meg speaks of Jane's ties to other oppressed women, she mentions the emblems of "the bound foot, the burning pyre, the Pharaoh's knife, and the stake through the womb." Her last image touches upon another variation on the doubling theme—vampirism—a motif that previously surfaced in *The Dark Mirror*. Thus, in Riffaterre's sense, the horror film (and its expressionist mode) "mediates" between the twin films and the Mulvey/Wollen piece, acting as third terms in the intertextual network.[49] In *The Bad Sister*, Jane is bitten by Meg and becomes pale and wan, and she later ravages her sister's neck as a seeming prelude to her murder. Furthermore, Jane's mother is exhumed from her grave by a caretaker on the Dalzell estate and declared "avenged." Perhaps, too, when Jane goes off on her eerie ship, she is not only like Pirate Jenny but like Murnau's Nosferatu, who transports his plague to distant lands. Thus *The Bad Sister* also inverts the values of the traditional vampire narrative, seeing the "monster" as a more promising figure.

The Bad Sister is also more self-reflexive than its mainstream counterparts. In *The Dark Mirror*, we witness a crime and follow its solution, while in the Mulvey/Wollen piece, we watch a video being made *about* a crime. Hence, there exists a distancing commentary (by the producers) on the stereotypical aspects of the drama—the "murder room," the "mystery," the "good" and "bad" siblings. By implication,

[47] "Pirate Jenny Song," from Bertolt Brecht, *The Threepenny Opera*, trans. Desmond Vesey and Eric Bentley (New York: Grove Press, 1984), 25.

[48] Luce Irigaray, *This Sex which Is Not One*, trans. Catherine Porter with Carolyn Burke (Ithaca, N.Y.: Cornell University Press, 1985), 26.

[49] Riffaterre, 627.

203

their dialogue comments not only on the program they are making but on all such media projects, including the twin films themselves.

In addition, many of the self-conscious references in *The Bad Sister* have particular relevance to the question of "good" versus "bad" women. When Jane cuts her hair, on her dresser is a picture of Louise Brooks, an actress known in the 1920s for her flapper coiffure and her portrayal of sexually rebellious females. Her most notable role was Lulu, the prostitute in Pabst's *Pandora's Box* (1929)—a title that might equally apply to the dangerous opening of Jane's unconscious. At other points in the video, Tony (who is a screenwriter) makes reference to the performers who may be cast in one of his films: Meryl Streep, Isabelle Adjani, and the like—all paragons of femininity. Since we deplore Tony's superficiality, we also reject those women and find his mention of them ludicrous. In one of the flashbacks (just before Jane and her mother kill Dalzell), there is a high-angle shot of a staircase that mimicks an image in Hitchcock's *Vertigo* (1958). Again, the quote is significant, since that film is about a man who fetishizes women and tries to remake one lover into a replica of another. In Jane's exorcism of her sister/double, she is also rejecting women's tendency to duplicate the male ideal. Finally, there is at least one reference in *The Bad Sister* to *Riddles of the Sphinx*. When Jane leaves her apartment to go to a party (at which she will kill Ishbel), she wears an acrobat's costume. In *Riddles*, the image of female acrobats was used as a symbol of liberation. In all these respects, *The Bad Sister* utilizes Riffaterre's final sense of intertextuality—the "intratextual" inclusion of direct quotes.[50]

Given the film's multivalent symbolic discourse, the real enigma it confronts is not the details of a murder but the riddles of female consciousness—a theme familiar to Mulvey/Wollen. As the videomaker states in the opening of the piece, through mystery, "We ward off the shock of death by setting out in search of a second surprise, the perpetrator of death." In *The Bad Sister*, the crime narrative, the "whodunit" format, deflects a more substantial shock: the truth of female desire, the nature of her "plague"—the contents of Pandora's Box. In so doing, *The Bad Sister* opposes the ideology of the Hollywood twin film, identifying the female psyche with such subversive qualities as masculinity, violence, witchcraft, and female bonding.

The root of the term "mystery" is in the Greek word for "secret ritual." By dramatizing and recapitulating the Dalzell crime, the video

[50] Ibid.

piece performs a palliative "rite" and restores the bad sister to her "rightful" place.

MASCULINE/FEMININE

What do I want from you? closeness without sameness support without competition loyalty without betrayal an ending to those ancient dualities an ending to living in comparison. —"Sister/Sister"[51]

Another work that confronts the female double is Margarethe von Trotta's *Sisters, or The Balance of Happiness* (*Schwestern, oder die Balance des Glücks*), made in West Germany in 1979. Unlike the Mulvey/Wollen piece, it is a rather conventional film, viewed by some critics as an updated "woman's picture"—the genre to which *The Dark Mirror* and *A Stolen Life* belong.[52] However, *Sisters* takes a different attitude toward its subject than either the Hollywood films or the British experimental video. While the former bifurcates the female, banishing her "masculine" side, and the latter reverses this polarity by celebrating the "bad" woman, *Sisters* rejects such dichotomies and argues for a synthesis of gender identification in human life.

On a narrative level, the film concerns the relationship between two sisters who live together. The elder, Maria (Jutta Lampe), is an executive secretary who supports the younger sister, Anna (Gudrun Gabriel), while she studies biology at the university. The two women display symbiotic ties: Maria is assertive and needs to dominate her sibling, while Anna seems to relish her own passivity and dependence. A crisis occurs in their lives when Maria begins to date the boss's son, and Anna sinks into a depression, finally taking her life. After Anna's death, Maria reads her sister's diary, which accuses her of having precipitated the suicide. To compensate for her loss, Maria befriends Miriam (Jessica Fruth), a young secretary in her office, and attempts to replicate her perverse and controlling relationship with Anna. When Miriam rebels, Maria is shattered but learns that she must strive for a certain balance in her life.

In many ways, von Trotta's film is similar to *The Dark Mirror*, *A Stolen Life*, and *The Bad Sister*. All tell the story of female siblings

[51] Clare Closs, Sondra Segal, and Roberta Sklar, "Why Do I Weep" from "Sister/Sister," in Hester Eisenstein and Alice Jardine, eds., *The Future of Difference* (Rutgers, N.J.: Rutgers University Press, 1985), 197.

[52] See E. Ann Kaplan, "Gender and Genre: Margarethe von Trotta and the Woman's Film" (unpublished paper).

whose relationship is torn asunder through jealousy over a man. Most deal with the death of one sister and her "haunting" of the other. All are imbued with an aura of fantasy and are "mediated" by the horror film.

Many factors contribute to the expressionist ambience in *Sisters*. Primary is the film's periodic use of a fairy-tale motif, reminiscent of those of the Brothers Grimm—specifically, Hansel and Gretel. As the drama opens, a story is being read aloud about two sisters walking in a dark forest; the younger one repeatedly asks if she can stop to rest, while the older one spurs her on. (Here we have a presaging of Anna's eventual decline and of Maria's attempts to prevent it.) As the camera tracks into a dense, barren woods, the light eerily shifts from bright to dark. As the narrative unfolds, these fairy-tale sequences are positioned as flashbacks to the sisters' childhood—one imbued with awe and fear. The film continually "regresses" to the imaginary state, in which no distinctions exist between self and other, between fiction and reality.

Other elements contribute to the film's gothic tone. Anna is continually presented as a figure of mystery and is frequently posed in some symbolic decor. Once, for example, she is photographed through the glass of an aquarium in which lizards reside. She also keeps a diary in which she collects grotesque icons: faces frozen in postures of pain and suffering, like the drawings of Edvard Munch. The lighting in the women's apartment also has an expressionistic feel, with its darkness and shadow, simultaneously evocative of the psyche and the womb.

Certain images in the film seem invested with a supernatural taint. One thinks, for instance, of a two-shot of the sisters on a ferryboat, sailing through a cloud of fog and mist, or of the images of Maria looking up (from the street) at her apartment window to find Anna (like Dracula) peering down. Expressionist tropes are openly quoted in the diegesis as well. After Anna dies, Maria finds certain passages in her diary that allude to vampirism—a theme found in *The Dark Mirror* and *The Bad Sister*. In one entry, Anna writes: "When I am dead, drive a stake through my breast to keep me from haunting you." In another, she states: "Chop off my head when I am dead so I won't rise up and torment you." Certain scenes that follow Anna's death resemble a ghost story. On one occasion, Maria is startled when a door inexplicably slides open. On another, she hallucinates a vision of Anna's specter.

Like the Hollywood twin films and the Mulvey/Wollen video, *Sisters*

17. *Sisters, or The Balance of Happiness* (1979). *Sisters* highlights the figure of the double through myriad visual and narrative strategies.

also highlights the figure of the double, using myriad visual and narrative strategies (see fig. 17). Recurring iconic two-shots are invested with a sense of the doppelgänger. In the first scene, when Maria returns home from work, Anna affectionately places her head on the nape of her sister's neck. Later, the two lean their heads on one another in an image reminiscent of *Persona*. In yet another sequence, Maria cradles Anna to her breast in a shot evocative of Bergman's *Cries and Whispers* (1972), which is also about siblings.

Like the other works, *Sisters* is dominated by a mirror iconography as metaphoric of the double. In one flashback, we see the women as children, sitting at a vanity putting on lipstick. As they move the mirrored panels, their images multiply in an infinite regression suggestive of a retreat to the imaginary. At another point, Anna looks into a mirror as she takes Polaroid photographs of herself—"mirrors" of yet another kind. Significantly, *three* snapshots develop, symbolizing the interconnections between Anna, Maria, and Miriam. Following Anna's death, Maria looks at her own face in a mirror and, in a Magritte-like vision, sees the back of her head. When it turns around, it bears the face of Anna peering back at her. One evening Maria dreams of Anna's death but casts herself in the role of the bloody corpse.

The doubling theme is also invoked in the diegesis. When Anna returns home from a lecture on cell transplantation, she asks Maria if she believes there could be "copies" of herself. And clearly, Maria's eventual use of Miriam as her sister's "replica" invokes this theme on a dramatic level. Significantly, Miriam and Maria first meet in an office bathroom as they primp in front of a mirror.

There is yet another sense of narrative doubling in the film. While the relationship of Maria and Anna is that of siblings, Maria frequently assumes a maternal position, "superimposing" a model of parent/child on that of sisters. It is as though both women were "stuck" or "lost" in the imaginary (that dark forest), each endlessly replaying roles in the nuclear family.

Another significant dramatic doubling occurs in the film. Anna takes a job transcribing letters for an old blind woman. The lady lives with her older sister, and their relationship is as problematic as Anna and Maria's. If the flashbacks provide us with an infinite regression into the sisters' past, this sequence accords us an infinite progression into their future—a stage that promises to be equally dim.

The sisters in von Trotta's work also stand in opposition to one another and are configured along the accustomed lines of "masculinity" versus "femininity." Maria is clearly the "manly" one—a fact apparent in her appearance, personality, and world view. As an executive secretary, she wears "dress-for-success" suits that mold the female body to masculine dimensions; her hair is pulled back in a harsh chignon. She seems most at ease in her skyscraper office, with its high-tech decor devoid of all organic materials. On an emotional level, she eschews "feminine" warmth: two of her male colleagues joke that the fur most appropriate for her is that of a "polar bear."

Maria's interactions with Anna also place her in the traditionally "masculine" position. She is the one who has money and supports them. Like a wage-earning man, she feels the right both to protect and dominate her sister. In the opening scene, Maria returns from a day at work to find Anna studying at her desk. Maria's first gesture is to fuss over her sister, to worry whether she has had enough to eat. When Maria goes into the kitchen and finds a mess, however, she becomes annoyed that Anna has not cleaned up. Von Trotta has commented on how the sisters replay the relationship of a conventional heterosexual couple: " Maria is the efficient one who works, makes money, is tired in the evening; Anna is like a housewife waiting for her husband."[53]

[53] Margarethe von Trotta, in Annette Insdorf, "Von Trotta: By Sisters Obsessed," *New York Times*, 31 January 1982, 19.

She notes: "In a certain way [Maria] reacts like a man who is oppressed in his job—she comes home and turns the oppression on her
sister, as a man does his wife."[54] There are moments of the film in
which a strong sensual tension exists between the sisters, reinforcing
this view of them as a heterosexual couple: once, when Maria comes
home, Anna loosens her sibling's hair and runs her fingers through it.

Maria also assumes the "masculine" position by trying to make de-
cisions regarding Anna's life, such as discouraging her from quitting
school. She will eventually attempt to dominate Miriam as well, urging
her to take English lessons to advance her career, offering to support
her while she does so. Maria's assertiveness alienates others. After
Anna's death, Miriam reads one of Anna's diary entries that states:
"Maria doesn't know how offensive her proficient manner is with
others. She slaps me in the face with it." And later Maria's friend Fritz
accuses her of having wanted to make Anna into a version of herself.

Maria's identification with rationality—her suspicion of intuition or
imagination—also aligns her with the traditionally "masculine." She
serves male language in her role of secretary; several scenes focus on
her taking dictation in her boss's office, formulating the "Italian Trade
Board Address" or "Procedural Rules for Multi-National Undertak-
ings." This discourse, however, has little to do with her: in one episode,
following Anna's suicide, Maria's boss insensitively dictates a letter of
condolence for a business associate without ever according that cour-
tesy to Maria. She also agrees to type her boss's son's thesis, entitled
"The Hero and His Weather." In her action, we find both the exploitation of the female worker and her role of transcribing male-authored
texts—ones that valorize heroes versus heroines. Later in the film,
Maria advises Miriam to learn English—the internationally dominant
language of commerce and culture.

Although Maria does not question this discourse, von Trotta does
through various subtle aspects of the film. In the scenes in Maria's office, the sound of mechanical typewriters is deafening, lending them a
harsh, inhuman quality. In one sequence, a close-up reveals Maria elec-
trically sharpening pencils, which seem more like pointed weapons
than innocuous tools of writing. Finally, certain long-shots of Maria's
office depict the secretarial "pool"—with numerous women working
like automatons—faithfully typing men's words.

As one who accepts the dominant male culture, Maria is entirely
goal-oriented and supportive of the system. When Anna confesses that

---

54 Margarethe von Trotta, in Amy Taubin, "Theories of Relativity," *Soho Weekly
News*, 2 February 1982, 48.

she has lost faith in education and wants to drop out of school, Maria counsels her not to quit when she is so "close to finishing." Later on, Maria cannot understand why Miriam has little interest in succeeding in her secretarial career. After Anna's death, Maria has a conversation with her friend Fritz that reveals her general attitude. While he bemoans the fact that Anna did not have the necessary "packaging" to be successful, Maria blames her sister for refusing to prove herself and states: "What a man can do and what he is worth is shown in his profession and work." When Fritz asks her if she really believes that "nonsense," she replies. "Yes; I couldn't get up each morning if I didn't." Typically, she has worded her paraphrase of the Protestant Work Ethic in terms of the masculine, talking about what "a man" can or cannot do. She is truly an "executive" secretary, in that she is identified with the male boss she serves. She is also, in some sense, a highly "fetishized" woman—one in whom all traces of the threat of femininity have been eradicated through a transvestite mimicry of the masculine attitude.

Von Trotta makes clear how the roots of Maria's male orientation lie in the history of her immediate family. After befriending Maria, Miriam visits the latter's mother and learns that Maria was her father's favorite. She is also told that, after his death, Maria's mother put her in professional school so that she might gain the earning power to become head of the household.

If Maria is configured in classically "masculine" terms, Anna is portrayed as highly "feminine." Her looks are soft and pretty, and her face has a girlish quality. Like a figure of female mystery, her expression is opaque; she wears an enigmatic, Mona Lisa smile. Like a conventional woman, she is highly dependent and plays the role of "wife" to Maria's "husband." She is clearly an hysteric, and von Trotta gives us several scenes that delineate her emotional disintegration. In one episode, Maria returns home to find Anna crouching in a corner sobbing. She takes her to bed and cradles her to her bare breast, like a nurturing mother. Anna is also a masochist, as evidenced by her suicidal act. Toward the end of the film, Maria explains to Miriam how her sister died: she slit her wrists and *watched* the blood flow from her body. This death scene conforms to female masochistic fantasies, as configured by Freud, who claimed that women position themselves as spectators more than as participants of some imaginary painful event.[55]

[55] See a discussion of Freud's essay, "A Child Is Beaten," in Mary Anne Doane, "The

Significantly, throughout the film, there are close-up shots of Anna looking vacantly into space.

Like a classic female, Anna is identified with nature, in that she is a student of biology. Just before taking her own life, she writes in her diary that she will break a natural "law." As a woman, she questions the transformation of nature through male science—a practice she finds more concerned with death than with life. In one of her diary entries, she regrets that people are concerned with gene manipulation when they have not mastered the ability to love. Throughout the film, incidents point to the perversion of life through science and technology. When Maria comes home from work one day, she turns on the radio and hears a story about scientists experimenting to determine which animals could survive a nuclear explosion. The theory is advanced that rats will inherit the earth. Later in the film, when Anna attends a biology lecture, we hear the male instructor discuss nuclear transplantation for the purposes of reproduction. In Anna's rejection of the discourse of science and technology, we are reminded of Mary Daly, who writes:

> The products of necrophilic Apollonian male mating are of course the technological "off-spring" which pollute the heavens and the earth. Since the passion of necrophiliacs is for the destruction of life and since their attraction is to all that is dead, dying and purely mechanical, the father's fetishized "fetuses" (re-productions, replicas of themselves), with which they passionately identify are fatal for the future of this planet. Nuclear reactors and the poisons they produce, stockpiles of atomic bombs, ozone-destroying aerosol spray propellants . . . these are the multiple fetuses/feces of stale male-mates in love with a dead world that is ultimately co-equal and consubstantial with themselves.[56]

It seems significant that a musical theme recurring periodically in *Sisters* is reminiscent of a melody from Alain Resnais's *Hiroshima, Mon Amour* (1959)—a film about the atomic explosion that ended World War II. And in the discussions of genetic engineering that occur in Anna's class, we are also reminded of certain Nazi "experiments" that

---

'Woman's Film': Possession and Address," in Mary Ann Doane, Patricia Mellencamp, and Linda Williams, *Re-Vision*, 67–82.

[56] Mary Daly, *Gyn/Ecology* (Boston: Beacon Press, 1978), 63.

occurred during the same period. In support of this reading, von Trotta has claimed that *Sisters* is about "the suppression of our Nazi past."[57]

Speculating even further on this theme of the misuses of science, one is struck by certain parallels between *Sisters* and Fritz Lang's *Metropolis*. Both works invoke the theme of doubling: in the Lang film, a real woman (named Maria), who is identified with humanism, is replicated by a robot who stands for science and evil. (In *Sisters*, Anna even queries Maria as to whether copies of herself might exist.) In a sense, the older sibling of *Sisters* seems like the "bad" Maria and the younger like the "good." In the plot of *Metropolis*, the chief industrialist's son loves Maria, as does the boss's son in *Sisters*. Both films also critique the mechanization of society. In the Lang film, this phenomenon is not viewed primarily in terms of sexual difference, whereas it is in *Sisters*—with science and technology linked to the male.

Throughout *Sisters*, Anna is associated with other "feminine" qualities. Unlike Maria, she is not success-oriented and refuses to conform to the requirements of the cultural world, to "package" herself correctly, as Fritz would have it. Von Trotta empathizes with her position:

> Germans and Americans have very little sympathy for losers. But if you lose in such inhuman societies, it is a sign that you have preserved your best qualities. Anna's suicide is in that sense a positive and conscious act of resistance.[58]

Unlike Maria, Anna tends to avoid social discourse and barely speaks at all; her muteness is also symptomatic of hysteria. What language she does employ is personal—notes written to herself in diary entries. The only other language associated with her is poetic—the lyrics to an opera (sung by a woman), which is heard in the background during scenes in her apartment. Instead of being tied to the rational world, Anna has a mystical bent: she gives Maria a Buddha and later lectures her on the magical properties of trees. Anna is also associated with the unconscious. She writes in her diary in a stream-of-consciousness mode and, on one occasion, speaks of how "the dream of life robs her of life."

Within the family structure, she is identified with her mother. When the sisters visit their parent, Anna finds that her mother is reading sad poetry, a fact that links her to the depressed Anna. After her daughter's death, the mother reveals that she shared with Anna a tendency toward

[57] Von Trotta, in Insdorf, 19.   [58] Von Trotta, in Taubin, 48.

212

melancholy—the only difference being that, as a conventional house-wife, she had little time to dwell on it.

Within the plot space, Miriam eventually "stands in" for Anna, and, in so doing, is also identified with the feminine. Like Anna, she is not career-oriented and opposes the male system of which Maria is a part. She resists studying her English lessons and, when she has passed the course, rejects Maria's offer of a "better" secretarial position. (Miriam realizes that in such a new job she will continue to do the same work, merely typing in English instead of German.) Significantly, while Miriam has her language lessons (sitting in a prisonlike cubicle, wearing headphones that feed her business phrases), she uses a kitschy Statue of Liberty pencil sharpener—a symbol of the phony freedom offered by Maria's life plan.

In other respects, Miriam's "femininity" is posed in terms that differ from Anna's. While Anna embodies certain stereotypically female traits, she is not male-identified. In one scene, she sits in her school cafeteria, smiling blankly into space. Misinterpreting her glance as a come-on, a young man approaches her table, and Anna abruptly leaves. Miriam, on the other hand, is obsessed by men. When she first learns that Maria is the boss's secretary, she asks to be introduced to his son. Her plan is thwarted, however, when she falls in love with a nonconformist computer programmer who quits his job to follow a singing career. In many ways, Miriam is attracted to the female roman-tic posture of masochism. She wants to sing "like Billie Holiday," and, in one sequence, even lip synchs "The Man I Love," a torch song that envisions woman as the passive Sleeping Beauty.

But although von Trotta configures her women along the familiar opposition of masculine/feminine, her attitude toward this dichotomy swerves from the Hollywood twin film and the Mulvey/Wollen work. First of all, she contextualizes this opposition within the broader social world. We see Maria not only as the "masculine" one but also as spe-cifically adopting the values of the dominant business culture, and we understand how she is encouraged to do so. Rather than view Anna as some purely archetypal figure of nature, we regard her as a woman resisting contemporary formulations of male science. Even Anna's stereotypically feminine masochism is positioned differently than in the twin films. As E. Ann Kaplan has noted:

> If [von Trotta's] heroines fall into masochism, it is a result of a choice arising out of a particular political and personal context. Von Trotta reveals how this position has been externally con-

structed as against appearing . . . inevitable as in Hollywood films. The female spectator thus sees the masochism as a result of how patriarchy limits and defines the feminine rather than as something to identify with unproblematically.[59]

Furthermore, while the twin films invoke dualities in order to validate the "feminine," and the Mulvey/Wollen video raises them in order to reclaim the "masculine," von Trotta argues for some balance. In *Sisters*, although we can identify some women with the "masculine" and others with the "feminine," we cannot easily decide who is "good" and who is "evil." Rather, each woman has positive and negative features—to the extent that those moralistic terms apply at all.

While we may recoil from Maria's domineering and critical attitude, we must admire her willingness to care for her sister. While we may reject her pliant attitude toward the status quo, we must admit that she has made the most of her limited situation. While we may empathize with Anna's warmth and vulnerability, we are critical of her tendentious jealousy over her sister's romance. While we may feel sympathetic toward Anna for her psychological problems, we are repulsed by the vindictiveness of her death act. While we may admire Miriam for her gutsy refusal to climb the secretarial ladder, we reject her passive attitude toward men.

Just as we fail to categorize the women as good or evil, we are unable to embrace either pole of "masculinity" or "femininity." While we sympathize with Anna's "womanly" suspicion of the male scientific enterprise, we can hardly applaud her classically feminine hysteria or masochism. While we may disparage Maria's fetishized appearance and fascistic dominance, we must admire her "masculine" qualities of strength, independence, and responsibility. While we may sympathize with Miriam's spontaneity, we are critical of her willingness to assume the victim's position in her relationship with Maria and men. Thus, throughout the film, von Trotta keeps the spectator in a fluid position, denying him or her the rigid modes of identification typical of more traditional films. In this regard, her film evinces the "critical subjectivity" that Mary Gentile detects in the best feminist films:

> This is not simply a text that deconstructs itself, for in the process of deconstruction, the defusing of one system of form and content may yet imply the validity of some other system. Rather this is a text that attempts to hold contradictions in tension, to

[59] Kaplan.

214

deconstruct and construct equally, to deflate no "truth" in favor of another but rather to affirm and deny them all.[60]

Unlike the Hollywood twin film, which exorcises the evil sibling, and unlike *The Bad Sister*, which restores her to a dominant position, the von Trotta film questions those very dichotomies. Moreover, by dramatizing the poles of "masculinity" and "femininity" in a story of two women, *Sisters* demonstrates how those roles are socially constructed, not biologically determined.

In the final moments of the film, von Trotta imagines the possibility of some synthesis of the extremes. As Maria sits alone in her apartment, she lifts a pen and writes in her sister's diary: "I will attempt to dream in the course of my life; I will endeavor to be Anna and Maria." As she does so, the camera tracks through the fairy-tale forest, invoking a world of childhood that predates the splitting of the personality into opposing poles. Von Trotta argues for this sense of wholeness in both men and women, for only through such psychic integration will the dominance/submission dynamic be avoided—whether enacted by two sisters, two friends, or two lovers. In this regard, *Sisters* goes beyond the limited parameter of the "woman's film" to imagine a more healthy stance for the whole of humankind.

[60] Mary Gentile, *Film Feminisms* (Westport, Conn., and London: Greenwood Press, 1985), 22.

215

7 Girl Groups: Female Friendship

Introduction

*When we look at friendship in society we can see many
variations. But there is no social factor more important than
that of sex in leading to friendship variations. —Robert Bell*[1]

In the final chapter of *From Reverence to Rape* (1974), Molly
Haskell discusses the previous decade of international cinema, examining the representation of women. Despite the political
gains of the feminist movement, she finds those years the most dis-
heartening in film history.[2] "[T]he closer women came to claiming
their rights and achieving independence in real life, the more loudly
and stridently films [told them] it's a man's world."[3] As evidence, she
cites the absence of screen portrayals of female friendship—at the very
time male "buddy" movies proliferated:

> Not only in film but in plays . . . the sixties and particularly the
> seventies may go down as the time when men, released from
> their stoical pose of laconic self-possession by the "confes-
> sional" impulse and style of the times, discovered each other.
> They were able to give voice, or lyrical vision, to feelings for
> each other they had been keeping under their Stetson hats.[4]

Haskell is, of course, referring to such works as *M*A*S*H* (1970),
Easy Rider (1969), *The Odd Couple* (1968), *Butch Cassidy and the
Sundance Kid* (1969), *Husbands* (1970), and *Midnight Cowboy*
(1969). While this genre burgeons, films depicting female friendship
decline, even as compared with earlier epochs of film history. Haskell
inquires:

> Where, oh where, is the camaraderie, the much vaunted mutual
> support among women? It was there, without advertising itself,
> in the twenties: among Griffith's women, with Clara Bow and
> her college pals; in the thirties, among the gold diggers, with
> Kay Francis and Aline MacMahon and Eve Arden, and in the

---

[1] Robert R. Bell, *Worlds of Friendship* (Beverly Hills, Calif., and London: Sage Publications, 1981), 55.
[2] Molly Haskell, *From Reverence to Rape: The Treatment of Women in the Movies*
(Baltimore: Penguin, 1974), 323.
[3] Ibid., 363.   [4] Ibid., 362–63.

216

advice and support of older women like Binnie Barnes and Billie Burke: in the forties with Bette Davis and her female costars; even in the fifties, with Marilyn Monroe and her millionaire-hunting friends. *But where, in the movies and out, are their modern equivalents?*[5]

Some seven years later, critics writing for *Jump Cut* validate Haskell's conclusions about the portrayal of female friendship in the cinema:

In the multitude of buddy films, pairs of men get to act out their adventure fantasies. . . . [W]omen friends are shown as either: trying to get "the man's something" and fighting over who gets it (*All About Eve*), turning against each other (*Little Women*), or accepting the Judgment of Paris that splits women into narrowly defined "I'm This/You're That" sets of roles (*The Turning Point*). In cinema, even women's friendships revolve around men.[6]

In this chapter, I will examine the filmic representation of female friendship through a study of two contemporary works: George Cukor's *Rich and Famous* (1981) and Claudia Weill's *Girlfriends* (1978). In some respects, my approach will differ from that of earlier sections. First of all, the male-authored text under consideration was made *later* than the woman's film, thus reversing the chronology of other essays. I will still maintain, however, that Claudia Weill's film is a "response" to the Cukor work—in that it addresses stereotypes of female friendship that have circulated for centuries in our culture. Hence, *Girlfriends* critiques a larger "social text," of which *Rich and Famous* is only a single "quotation." As it happens, *Rich and Famous* is a remake of *Old Acquaintance* (1943); hence, its reiteration of clichés is more literal.

In previous chapters, I have largely focused on experimental feminist works, ranging from the avant-garde films of Rose, Akerman, and Beroes to the essay-narratives of Mulvey/Wollen and the modernist dramas of Zetterling. While *Straight through the Heart* is more traditional, its cynical comedy is unorthodox and its presentation quite stylized. *Girlfriends*, however, is a conventional fictional work—though its subject matter precluded Hollywood financing. Instead, the

5 Ibid., 371 (my italics).
6 Edith Becker, Michelle Citron, Julia Lesage, and B. Ruby Rich, "Lesbians and Film/Introduction," *Jump Cut*, nos. 24–25 (March 1981): 18.

film was independently produced through grants from the American Film Institute, the New York State Council on the Arts, the Creative Arts Public Service Program, and the National Endowment for the Arts. Despite *Girlfriends'* mainstream narrative and formal mode, it is a crucial work to consider. Few experimental feminist films were ever viewed by the general public, but *Girlfriends* was—and it made a forceful impression on the average viewer.

I must also admit that my reaction to *Rich and Famous* differs from my response to other films in this book. Regardless of my ideological reservations about *The Lady from Shanghai, Persona, Dames,* or *Letter from an Unknown Woman,* I find them tremendously impressive and compelling works of the cinema, which part of me truly likes (the part that never behaves as it "should"). However, *Rich and Famous* is, for me, an altogether unappealing film—both in its execution and in its portrayal of woman. I have nonetheless considered it because it so aptly demonstrates Haskell's insight concerning the contemporary cinema.

Because *Girlfriends* and *Rich and Famous* adopt an essentially realist aesthetic and aspire to a "seamless" style, I will pay less attention to formal analysis than in previous sections. There are no tour-de-force sequences in these films to match Berkeley's terpsichore, Welles's Magic Mirror Maze, Ophuls's crane shots, or Bergman's poetic editing. Therefore, I will place more emphasis on reading the ideological implications of narrative structure, characterization, and point of view. In this regard, the chapter will take advantage of certain strengths of the sociological approach to film analysis—a methodology that has waned over the past two decades.

Because the films under consideration seek to portray an apparent "slice of life," I will also engage the debate over realism that has reigned in feminist film criticism of the 1970s and 1980s. In my discussion of *Girlfriends,* I will attempt to demonstrate how sociological and semiological modes of investigation are not mutually exclusive, and to show how subtle self-reflexive techniques can qualify the classic realist text.

Not a Pretty Picture

Theorists agree that friendships between women have traditionally been ignored. Writing in 1868, William Rounseville Alger notes the "small number of recorded examples of the sentiment," as well as the common belief that "strong natural obstacles make friendship a comparatively feeble and rare experience with [women]."[7] More recently, Lillian Rubin has confirmed this characterization: "just as women have been invisible in public life throughout the ages, so their private relations with each other have been unseen as well."[8]

In contrast, male relations have been valorized. Rubin notes:

> For as long as the word has been written, men's friendships have been taken to be the model of what friendship is and how it ought to be. From the Greek philosophers to modern writers . . . major treatises have been devoted to friendship among men—to the depth of their bonding, the intensity of their love, their enduring commitment.[9]

In a similar vein, Robert Bell finds an absence of any ancient myths of female friendship comparable to those of Achilles and Patroclus or Roland and Oliver.[10] When female friendships *have* been considered, they have been devalued. Bell notes:

> The "traditional wisdom" about female friendships has been to see them as inferior to those of men. This undoubtedly has been a reflection of a more general notion of female inferiority.

Beyond such dismissal, female friendships have been portrayed with certain unkind stereotypes. Bell notes that they are typically seen as "trivial" or "amusing."[11]

> Women in small groups were not seen as teammates or colleagues, but as the "girls" trooping off to have lunch in a tearoom. The image was often of women dressed up to impress one another having a terrible time splitting the check.[12]

Similarly, Virginia Curlee Koenig catalogs popular misconceptions about female friendship: "that women tend to mistrust each other . . . compete with one another for men" and resist a "tendency to bond."[13]

Stereotypes of female friendship have also manifested a fear of lesbianism—part of a broader cultural anxiety about homosexuality. In writing about male friendship, C. S. Lewis regrets that he must first engage in "a tiresome bit of demolition":

---

[7] William Rounseville Alger, *The Friendship of Women* (Boston: Roberts Brothers, 1868), vii.

[8] Lillian B. Rubin, *Just Friends* (New York: Harper & Row, 1985), 59.   [9] Ibid.

[10] Bell, 58.   [11] Ibid.   [12] Ibid., 67.

[13] Virginia Curlee Koenig, *Intimacy in the Marital and Female Friendship Relationships of Women*, Ph.D thesis, School of Education, University of Pittsburgh, 1983, 36.

219

It has actually become necessary in our time to rebut the theory that every firm and serious friendship is really homosexual. . . . Those who cannot conceive Friendship as a substantive love but only as a disguise or elaboration of Eros betray the fact that they have never had a Friend.[14]

There may be even greater fears about lesbianism than about male homosexuality, since women typically display more physical and emotional affection toward one another. Ann Seiden and Pauline Bart quote actress Jane Fonda concerning her experience of filming Joseph Losey's *A Doll's House* (1973):

Nora's relationship with her one woman friend in the film is deliberately intended to show two women who cared for each other, who were more open to each other than they could ever be to men. . . . Nora's warmth toward [her friend] . . . was immediately interpreted by every man on the set as homosexual.[15]

Aside from the existence of stereotypes, there have been other reasons why female friendships have been denigrated. As Bell points out, women have been seen to operate exclusively within kinship structures—as opposed to men, who venture out into the world. It is assumed that all nonfamilial relations will be secondary to them: "In many societies men have friends and women have relatives."[16] Moreover, women themselves have had reason to devalue female friendship because they need to cultivate male power:

Many women, even today, find that their adult status or prestige depends on their attachment to a male. And many women are willing to give up female friends, if necessary in order to win a man.[17]

If these are the old misconceptions about female friendship, how have they been revised today? Once more, there is agreement on the subject. Bell states:

I would argue that the historical beliefs in the inferiority of female friendship are wrong. The evidence clearly indicates that

[14] C. S. Lewis, "Friendship," in Martha Rainbolt and Janet Fleetwood, eds. *On the Contrary: Essays by Women and Men* (Albany: State University of New York Press, 1984), 44.

[15] Jane Fonda, in Ann M. Seiden and Pauline B. Bart, "Woman to Woman: Sisterhood Powerful?" in Nona Glazer-Malbin, ed., *Old Family/New Family* (New York: D. Van Nostrand, 1975), 194. Quoted in Koenig, 35.

[16] Bell, 59–60.   [17] Ibid.

220

the friendships of women are more frequent, more significant and more interpersonally involved than those commonly found among men.[18]

Rubin concurs:

The results of my own research are unequivocal: At every life stage between twenty-five and fifty-five, women have more friendships, as distinct from collegial relationships or work-mates, than men, and the differences in the content and quality of their friendships are marked and unmistakable.[19]

The stereotypes are untrue: relations between women are more numerous and substantial than those between men. Hence, we must suspect that the derogatory images that circulate are, in fact, male projections of their own discomfort with friendship.

Rubin notes how relations between men are marked primarily by shared activities: "that they tend to *do* rather than *be* together is undeniable."[20] Even when a man has a "best friend," he confides little of his interior life.[21] Furthermore, Rubin finds men more overtly competitive in their friendships than women—a factor that works at cross-purposes with trust.[22] When men want real closeness, they usually turn to women, not to other men.[23] Hence, while female friendships involve "intimacy," male relations entail a more superficial "bonding."[24]

Women have been more successful than men at establishing interpersonal ties because the social structures in which they conventionally operate (home, family, community) are more conducive to forming friendships than are those of men. According to Bell, male friendships are often compromised because the two men "are in the same work world and are in competition with [each other] or are in positions of greater or lesser power."[25] Woman's domain, on the other hand, is usually less cutthroat or hierarchal. Even when women enter the work force, they befriend their female co-workers—either because their career drive is less obsessive than men's or because they find female solidarity functional in countering sexism.[26]

Bell also notes that women are traditionally "more socialized to the skills of . . . interaction" than men and thus can establish links with people more easily.[27] But it is Rubin who probes the question in greatest detail, drawing on the research of Nancy Chodorow. She finds that the difference in men and women's potential for friendship originates in their early childhood experience of the traditional nuclear family, in

[18] Ibid., 60.   [19] Rubin, 60–61.   [20] Ibid., 61.   [21] Ibid., 66.   [22] Ibid., 82.
[23] Ibid.   [24] Ibid., 68.   [25] Bell, 61.   [26] Ibid., 71.   [27] Ibid., 61.

FEMALE FRIENDSHIP

which the mother is the primary care giver. It is within this context
that "children develop a sense of self and gender identity."[28] For the
young girl, it is difficult to establish borders between self and other
because of her likeness to the primary role model, her mother. Hence,
in adult life, she tends not to create barriers against other people. For
the boy, separation from the mother is required in order to configure
his male sexuality. As Rubin notes:

> This is the beginning of the development of the kind of ego
> boundaries so characteristic of men—boundaries that are fixed
> and firm, that rigidly separate self from other, that circumscribe
> not only his relationships with others, but his connection to his
> inner emotional life as well.[29]

Rubin views the grown man's tendency to turn to women for intimacy as a replay of his original relation to the mother. She also sees
the competitive aspect of men's friendship (and woman's discomfort
with rivalry) as tied to early childhood experience:

> The boy child, whose developing sense of himself is so separate
> from others, easily learns to become the competitor. If relation-
> ships cannot be trusted to provide safety and security, then
> strength is the answer and winning the goal.[30]

For the girl child, competition with the same-sex parent is far more
threatening and complex: while vying with the mother, she must also
identify with her for gender integration. Rubin describes the "fear and
foreboding" that attends the girl's wish to compete with her.[31] The
anxiety that arises in this primal setting later causes a repression of
competition in adult female friendships:

> In adulthood, a close connection with another woman is likely
> to reawaken the old fantasies and the feelings that accompanied
> it—the same envy, the same wish to compete, and the same
> combination of triumph and fear at the prospect of winning.
> Better to leave the field than to take a risk.[32]

Thus, while female friendships are often more superficially amicable
than those between men, woman's discomfort with rivalry is a potential problem:

> It's a paradox, isn't it? Because we're women, we have learned
> to abjure competition, have been taught to believe it to be a

[28] Rubin, 90.   [29] Ibid., 95–96.   [30] Ibid., 98.   [31] Ibid., 87.   [32] Ibid., 88.

222

destructive force in human relationships, especially when it arises between us. So rather than acknowledge our competitive feelings . . . we distance ourselves from the object of competition, thereby damaging the very closeness we wish so much to protect.[33]

Given this psychosocial configuration, it is not surprising that female friendships have been more successful than male. What is astounding is that they have been culturally ignored. In recent years, however, the women's movement has focused attention on this issue. Historians like Carroll Smith-Rosenberg have studied relations between women in earlier eras, and feminists in all fields have stressed the need for mutual support, for "sisterhood."[34] This has legitimized friendship as a crucial relationship in female life.

Distorted images of female friendship still obtain, however, within the broader culture—as an analysis of *Rich and Famous* will demonstrate. In this Hollywood film, the subject of female friendship is legitimized only as a box-office ploy, while the illegitimate stereotypes remain.

Rich and Famous: Not So Tender Comrades

To speak the truth, I never yet knew a tolerable woman to be fond of her own sex. —Jonathan Swift[35]

Rich and Famous, released in 1981, is based on the play *Old Acquaintance* by John Van Druten, a work first adapted for the screen in 1943.[36] It was made by the veteran Hollywood filmmaker George Cukor—by then an octogenarian. From the 1930s through the 1950s, Cukor was especially well known as a "woman's director," working with such actresses as Jean Harlow, Joan Crawford, Judy Garland, Sophia Loren, and especially Katharine Hepburn. Gary Carey writes:

If [Cukor] has a continuing subject, it is Woman, her emotions, her intelligence, her attempts to find herself and express herself in an often inimical society. . . . His heroines and the actresses

[33] Ibid., 86.
[34] Carroll Smith-Rosenberg, "The Female World of Love and Ritual: Relations between Women in Nineteenth-Century America," *Signs* 1 (1975): 1–29.
[35] Quoted in Koenig, 36.
[36] John Van Druten, *Old Acquaintance* (New York: Random House, 1941). It was first produced at the Morosco Theatre in New York City on December 23, 1940. The film version in 1943 starred Bette Davis and Miriam Hopkins.

he has chosen to portray them chronicle, even if only inadvertently, *the changing styles of and attitudes towards women* during the more than four decades in which he has been making films.[37]

For Carey, Cukor not only depicts women, he "sees them less from a man's point of view than from the view of the women themselves."[38] Of all Cukor's films, Carey finds only *Our Betters* (1933) and *The Women* (1939) misogynistic.[39] His essay was, written, however, before *Rich and Famous*—and surely he would have wanted to add it to his list. Though Carey finds that Cukor's films delineate "changing . . . attitudes toward women," *Rich and Famous*, ironically, demonstrates how conceptions persist—and remain intractably the same.

The film traces the friendship of two women over a period of years: from their college days in the 1950s through their adult life in the 1980s. The casting is done in the standard mode, with two gorgeous women playing the leads. Candice Bergen (Merry Noel Blake) is known for her classic WASP beauty and Jacqueline Bisset (Liz Hamilton) for her natural sensuality. Appropriately, one of the characters ends up living in Beverly Hills, writing for the movies, and hobnobbing with the star set. Thus the discourse of Hollywood operates both within and without the film's diegesis.

The very first sequence of *Rich and Famous* signals its ideological project. It takes place in a Smith College dormitory room, as Liz helps Merry elope with her fiancé, Doug (David Selby). As they prepare to leave, Merry grabs her childhood teddy bear, but Liz suggests that she leave it there. Merry offers it to her as "company," but Liz declines the gift. At the railroad station, Merry asks Liz if she is "jealous," and notes that Doug is more "Liz's type." She also reminds Liz that Doug was Liz's blind date first. The train arrives, and Merry prepares to depart. She runs back to kiss Liz good-bye and impulsively hands her the teddy bear. The final shot shows Liz standing alone, hugging the stuffed animal.

On the level of narrative structure (and its implications), it seems significant that this film on female friendship begins at the precise moment when the relationship ruptures—when one girl is leaving the other. What is excised from the story is any representation of the bond

[37] Gary Carey, "George Cukor," in Richard Roud, ed., *Cinema: A Critical Dictionary, Volume One* (Norwich, Great Britain: Martin Secker & Warburg, 1980), 238–39 (my italics).
[38] Ibid., 239   [39] Ibid.

between them during the years they lived together as roommates. It is this intense period that ostensibly anchored their friendship and sustained it through separation. Yet we are given no idea what brought them together, what interests or aspirations they shared.

Another crucial aspect of the opening scene is its immediate invocation of the themes of jealousy and competition for a man. This taps the familiar notion of females as opponents, particularly as configured in a heterosexual triangle. As the videotape "jacket" tells us: "This [is the story] of two friends who knew exactly what kind of lives they wanted—each other's." Yet, as Rubin has shown, although women have envious feelings toward one another, they attempt to suppress them because of their original love for the mother. When competition arises, women tend to be less direct about it than Merry and Liz, who behave more like men.

The next sequence takes place some twelve years later. Liz has become an established author and is giving a talk at UCLA. Merry, who is a Malibu housewife and mother, comes to hear her address. From what transpires, one assumes that the screenwriters of *Rich and Famous* felt the need to situate Liz's character within the women's movement—because the film's subject is female friendship and because she is an unmarried intellectual. Thus the precise words of her talk and of her host's greeting are important. The professor who introduces Liz states that "although [Liz] doesn't identify herself specifically with feminist politics, her works are themselves an evocation of the feminine life—a plea for the feminine ethic—a demand for a space to be just that—female." When Liz begins her speech, she confesses that she is not active in feminist projects, and some women in the audience aggressively shout: "Why not?" She responds that she is too obsessed with her craft and with the "paralysis" that accompanies it. She then quotes an "old writer friend" on the subject and launches into an unrelated diatribe regarding her love of elderly men. Significantly, the writer she mentions (James Cain) is an American author of the "hard-boiled" school, who is responsible for the literary properties on which the following films were based: *Double Indemnity* (1944), *Mildred Pierce* (1945), and *The Postman Always Rings Twice* (1946)—all works involving problematic representations of women.

Several things are clear from this scene. To be "modern," the film casts one of the friends as a somewhat "liberated" woman—a single artist living in New York. But the UCLA sequence demonstrates that the narrative must declare its distance from feminism. Liz's novels speak

225

instead for the "feminine"—for what is "female"; and we will learn, in short order, just what *that* represents.

The scene also works to undermine the credibility of the "liberated" woman,—be she feminist or not. We immediately learn that Liz suffers from "paralysis," and that her second novel is long overdue. Furthermore, her remarks concerning her love of old men seem not only irrelevant but peculiar—and they shake our confidence in her psychological health. Her comments are so tangential that they seem a shameless, gratuitous valentine to the elderly George Cukor himself.

The next scene advances several more misogynist themes. Liz leaves a party at Merry's house to walk with Doug, and confesses that she has recently broken up with a man. She also discusses her psychoanalysis and her therapist's prediction that she will start writing again when she resumes loving. Thus Liz is not only intellectually blocked, she is "frigid"—a familiar conflation of woman's artistic and sexual drives. The scene further advances our sense of the friends' potential rivalry over men; when Doug and Liz return, Merry is furious at them, since her guests have been "talking." Despite the fight that occurs (and Merry's unwarranted suspicion), Liz later thanks her for "being there" in times of crisis. This tribute rings hollow because we have never witnessed any supportive moments between the women.

This sense of the pretense of a friendship is further confirmed by an encounter between Liz and Merry that occurs later the same evening. Merry discloses that she has written a novel in her spare time and asks Liz to listen to her read it aloud. Liz grudgingly agrees and stays up all night to hear it. When Merry finishes, Liz erupts in an envious rage because the novel is good, because it is pure pulp, because Merry has penned it quickly, because she has experienced no pain, and because she wants Liz to show it to her literary agent. "Do you know what it is to be blocked?" Liz screams at Merry, who calls her a "bitch." Such is the reunion of old college pals who are "there" for each other at critical times. As Carrie Rickey has noted, the women's friendship seems as likely as that between Susan Sontag and Judith Krantz.[40] When Doug takes Liz to the airport the next day, they embrace in a casual manner—and he departs. But in a shot/countershot sequence, Liz steals a glance at him, fueling the themes of jealousy and betrayal.

At this point, the film begins to concentrate on Liz and her sexual and psychological hang-ups. This focus clearly attempts to exploit the persona of Jacqueline Bisset, known for her erotic screen presence.

[40] Carrie Rickey, [Review], *Village Voice*, 14 October 1981, 50.

(The videotape "jacket," for example, promises that the film will be "elegantly raunchy.")[41] As soon as Liz is on the plane for New York, she drinks and converses with a man who sits nearby. We hear snatches of conversation regarding the death of his wife and his resulting loneliness. As the flight ends, Liz excuses herself to go to the bathroom, and the man follows her to the rear of the cabin. As she emerges from the lavatory, he presses his way in. They begin to make passionate (though cramped) love—and the scene is intercut (in a satirical manner) with images of the plane's ailerons moving and engines reversing. As they groan with pleasure, the stewardess says: "The sound you now hear is that of the wheels being lowered." When the plane lands, and the two say good-bye, the man's wife and kids surprise him at the airport: apparently, his seduction has been an elaborate ruse. Liz smiles wryly and departs, despite the fact that the joke has been on her. In the final scene of this segment, Liz is back in New York, meeting with her literary agent—hyping Merry's manuscript.

The next narrative section occurs in 1975, when Merry has become a successful novelist/screenwriter residing in Beverly Hills. The first scene is a "match" with the previous one of Liz, for it establishes Merry's sexual problems as correlated with her new productivity. Rather than being cast as the promiscuous woman, she is configured as the castrating bitch—the flip side of the coin. Doug is now unemployed and resentful of her success. As the pair make love one night, Merry leaves the room to diagram the plot of her next novel. When she returns, Doug says he has finished "by himself." He will later tell Liz that "a few parts of [his] anatomy are missing."

The drama then uses the occasion of Merry's marital problems to advance the theme of rivalry between the two women. When Doug and Merry are in New York (for her appearance on a talk show), Doug leaves the television studio and shows up early for a dinner date the two have with Liz. Before Merry arrives, he tells Liz that he wants a divorce and reminds her of the flirtation they once shared. He later confesses that he has fantasized about marrying her. Though Liz remains loyal to Merry, we sense that her rebuff of Doug involves a sacrifice, and the seeds of doubt are planted.

The final segment of the story takes place in New York in 1981. Merry is in town because she is a candidate for a prestigious book award, and Liz is there because she is one of the judges. This section

41 That phrase is taken from Sheila Benson, [Review], *Los Angeles Times Calendar*, 9 October 1981, 1.

further develops the notion of Liz's instability: her alcoholism, her sexual and psychological maladjustment—all seemingly the fate of an unmarried, intellectual woman. In one scene, she is interviewed in her hotel room by a young writer from *Rolling Stone* magazine, Christopher Adams (Hart Bochner). A shot/countershot sequence (in which he eyes her legs) makes clear that he is attracted, and we suspect that she returns the feeling. As they talk, however, she upbraids him for his obsession with youth. He leaves her room, and she storms out to walk on Fifth Avenue. At a stoplight, a handsome teenaged boy (Matt Lattanzi) eyes her and asks for directions to Cartier. She points out the store and continues on her way, and he tags along beside her. In the next shot, they are both in the store, with no explanation of why she has allowed this unabashed pickup. The young man walks her to the hotel lobby and forces his way into the elevator. In her room, she drinks and watches him slowly undress, clearly lusting for his flesh. A rear-angle shot (from behind) shows him pulling down his pants, as she sits (at his pelvis level) on the bed. They make love. In the next scene, she is again with Christopher Adams, but this time their sexual attraction is consummated. Hence, this woman who loves "older men" is also attracted to young boys. Liz falls in love with Christopher Adams, though plagued by the difference in their ages, and the relationship fails.

This narrative segment also chronicles the travails of Merry's life. She has now been divorced for several years and is raising a teenaged daughter. Their relationship is troubled, and the child is rebelling. Debbie (Meg Ryan) is currently involved with a Puerto Rican poet—not exactly a match her Rodeo Drive mother sanctions. As teenagers frequently do, Debbie has chosen an alternate role model in the bohemian Liz. She frequently appears at her "aunt's" hotel room, trying to avoid her mother's scrutiny and control. In one of these visits, she meets Christopher Adams, and when his relationship with Liz flounders, he turns to his younger friend.

Through this plot configuration, the theme of female rivalry (traced in Liz and Merry's "friendship") is doubled in their relationship with her daughter. Merry and Debbie are at odds with each other in a manner reflecting stereotypes of mother-daughter interaction (e.g., *Mildred Pierce* [1945], *Imitation Of Life* [1934/1959]). Beyond that, Debbie and her maternal surrogate even vie for the same man. Yet, as Rubin and Chodorow have shown, it is precisely the young girl's connection to her mother that makes later friendships with women relatively easy.

Though the film's symbol for friendship (Merry's teddy bear) harks back to earlier days, the narrative itself denies woman's childhood lessons. Despite the ostensible theme of female bonding, there seems no possibility of female support—either within or without the nuclear family. Characteristically, Liz and Merry are shown to have absolutely no other relationships with women in the film. And the ones depicted are fraught with tension and violence.

The scene that epitomizes this brutality occurs in the final narrative segment. Liz is in her hotel room, having just learned that Chris has gone off with Debbie. Merry arrives distraught and, with typical selfishness, does not notice Liz's depression. Merry has just seen Doug and learned that he will remarry. He has also confessed that he once loved Liz. Merry is furious and says that the women must "examine the terms of their friendship." This process amounts to a catty girl fight: Merry accuses Liz of "cradle snatching" and asks how many men she has "had." She says that she hates Liz, who calls her a "cunt." As the fight becomes physical, the women grab Merry's old teddy bear (which Liz keeps as a memento), and they pull it apart, stuffing and all. (Ostensibly, scenes like this led one critic to call the film "bitchily entertaining.")[42]

Here we have one more instance of how the film depicts female betrayal in the guise of portraying friendship (see fig. 18). Beyond that, we sense that this is *not* how women fight with one another: attacking each other's sexuality, envisioning each other as "cunts." Rather, this seems entirely a male fantasy of female confrontation and reflects masculine modes of hostility. (Significantly, the stuffed animal they destroy sports the male label of "teddy" bear.) In "Myths of Women in the Cinema," Claire Johnston has labeled woman the "pseudocenter of the [classical] filmic discourse."[43] As she writes: "Within a sexist ideology and a male-dominated cinema, woman is presented as what she represents for man."[44] This seems nowhere so true as in *Rich and Famous*; the combative figures in this culminating scene are not so much women as male images of women—positioned for the pleasure of the masculine viewer, like female mud wrestlers.

It is interesting that filmmaker Yvonne Rainer (whose work will be considered in Chapter 10) recalls a scene of women fighting in a movie

[42] David Denby, [Review], *New York*, 8 October 1981, 87.

[43] Claire Johnston, "Myths of Women in the Cinema," in Karyn Kay and Gerald Peary, *Women and the Cinema: A Critical Anthology* (New York: Dutton, 1977), 411.

[44] Ibid., 410.

18. *Rich and Famous* (1981). The film depicts female betrayal in the guise of portraying friendship.

she saw as a child. She recounts this experience in *Film about a Woman Who . . .* (1974), couched in the third person:

> She remembers a . . . scene—was it Dorothy Lamour or Betty Grable?—in a movie she saw when she was no more than 9 or 10. One woman had ripped another woman's dress off. She had stayed in the movie theater long after her friends had left until the scene came around again.

Analyzing her naive thrall, Rainer first hypothesizes that her pleasure arose from "vicarious satisfaction in the eruption of female anger on the screen, an anger that I was not permitted to express in my own family." But she states that she is now more interested in reading her reaction as "an example of male sadistic identification":

> The spectacle of two women fighting over a man provoked in me the pleasure that was clearly intended for the male spectator who would "naturally" identify with the absent . . . male character they were fighting over. I don't remember rooting for either woman, neither the one who would eventually "get her man" nor her rival. The perversity of the situation was that I took pleasure in the humiliation of *both* women.[45]

[45] Yvonne Rainer, "Some Ruminations around Cinematic Antidotes to the Oedipal

230

It is this quandary that faces the female spectator of *Rich and Famous*.

It is perplexing that so many reviewers glossed over the film's tendentious tone. Sheila Benson of the *Los Angeles Times* said it had "the best women's roles ... in recent memory."[46] David Ansen of *Newsweek* said Cukor "demonstrates why he has long been regarded as Hollywood's foremost 'women's director.' "[47] Carrie Rickey, in the *Village Voice*, said Cukor's camera "lovingly captures Bisset's deglamorized ecstasy," and praised him for lovemaking sequences shot "from Bisset's point of view."[48]

Several writers specifically lauded the film's conclusion. Dean Billanti, in *Films in Review*, said *Rich and Famous* is "a touching and elaborate summation of [female friendship] especially at the end, when the two women realize that their relationship has been the most important thing in their lives."[49] And Joseph Gelmis of *Newsday* found the final scene "strangely touching, sentimental and bold."[50]

But, in truth, the film's denouement is utterly unconvincing, for, after the strife we have witnessed, we are to imagine that some poignant rapprochement occurs. Merry has won the book award and is grimly hosting a New Year's Eve celebration. Liz, who has refused to attend, is back at her Connecticut home. Merry leaves her party and takes a taxicab to the country, appearing at Liz's door. As the two sit by the fire, Merry says: "Our oldest friend, what else do we have in life?" And Liz replies: "Our oldest enemies." Here, perhaps, we find the only honest moment of the film, when the true nature of their relationship is unveiled.

But the film is more mean-spirited than that. As the women ponder their future, Liz suggests that they take a long trip together around the world and "sleep only with guys who can't pronounce [their] names." She says that while she used to want men to find "mystery" in her writing, she now wants them to find it in her body. As the clock chimes midnight, Liz asks Merry to kiss her. Merry queries whether there's something "strange" about Liz, but they toast each other and embrace.

What this scene attempts is to bring to some happy resolution this most unsettling relationship between two women. But it does so in a highly devious manner. It is so uncomfortable with physical displays

Net(les) while Playing with De Lauraedipus Mulvey, or, He May Be Off Screen, but . . ." *The Independent* 9, no. 3 (April 1986): 23.

[46] Benson, 1.   [47] David Ansen, [Review], *Newsweek*, 21 October 1981, 98.
[48] Rickey, 50.   [49] Dean Billanti, [Review], *Films in Review* (December 1981): 622.
[50] Joseph Gelmis, [Review], *Newsday*, 9 October 1981.

of female friendship that it must make a cheap joke about lesbianism—about being "strange." It also suggests that the women's hope lies in abandoning work for sex—in having men find poetry in their bodies rather than their minds. Is this, perhaps, what Liz's UCLA host meant about her speaking for the "feminine," for the "female"? Finally, given the misogyny of the film—its transvestite projection of male fantasies onto women—it seems fitting that Merry and Liz's imagined future together (screwing around on a worldwide tour) is a perfect scenario for a macho "buddy movie"—the kind whose ubiquitous screen presence Molly Haskell so ruefully deplored.

Girlfriends: Odd Couples

> *Pausanias in his "Description of Greece" . . . gives an account of an elaborate painting by Polygotus of the under-world—the scenery and fate of the dead in the future state. Among the images of the departed . . . were two women, Chloris and Thyia, locked in a fond embrace. Of these two women . . . Pausanias says that they were a pair of friends extraordinarily attached to each other in life. Their story is lost.* The imagination of womankind ought to compensate for the missing narrative, and make the names of Chloris and Thyia live with the names of Damon and Pythias. —*William Rounseville Alger*[51]

Girlfriends was made three years prior to *Rich and Famous*, in a period that saw the release of several Hollywood films about female friendship: among them, *The Turning Point* (1977) and *Julia* (1977). Weill saw the film as an antidote to the buddy movies that Haskell vilifies:

> I thought they were really boring. They were a little simplistic in their notion of what friendship was. . . . They had two men with beautiful faces, and the adventures they have together.[52]

Girlfriends began in 1975 as a short film, made for $10,000 through a grant from the American Film Institute. When Weill received positive feedback on her work, she decided to expand it and began reshooting. The final cost of the feature production was a mere $500,000. Many women worked on the project: Suzanne Pettit as editor, Vicki Polon as

---

[51] Alger, 16 (my emphasis).

[52] Claudia Weill, in Judy Klemesrud, "*Girlfriends* Director on Female Friendship," *New York Times*, 4 August 1978.

screenwriter, Jan Saunders as producer, and many others on the crew. Weill says: "I trained a great many women on this film—a lot of women gaffers, a lot of women assistant editors, a lot of women sound people."[53] Though made as an independent piece, *Girlfriends* gained distribution by a major company (Warner Brothers Pictures) when it received critical acclaim.

If we compare the stories of *Girlfriends* and *Rich and Famous*, certain parallels become clear. Both are dramas about friendship between women and its disruption through marriage. While *Rich and Famous* traces this process over several decades, *Girlfriends* examines a period of about a year and a half. In both films, one of the women remains single, and the narrative concentrates on the struggles of her independent life. In both works, the friends are artists. In *Rich and Famous*, Liz and Merry are writers; in *Girlfriends*, Anne is a poet and Susan a photographer. In both narratives, the friendship crests in an emotionally charged altercation between the women, which is ultimately resolved. Even these confrontations bear comparison. In *Rich and Famous*, the fight occurs at the moment when Merry has won the book award, and equilibrium is reestablished when she visits Liz in the country. In *Girlfriends*, the conflict occurs at the moment when Susan gets a gallery show, and a rapprochement ensues when she leaves her opening to visit Anne in her pastoral retreat. Even the final shots of the films (of the friends by a fireplace) are precisely the same, and both hark back to the conclusion of *Old Acquaintance*—a work that seems (in Riffaterre's sense) to "mediate" them.

But there are vast differences between the films that mark *Girlfriends* as more generous in its portrayal of friendship between women. Instead of two beautiful movie queens, it utilizes actresses of more average appearance. It is true that Weill, as an independent artist, might not have had access to superstars, but she could easily have cast gorgeous unknown performers. Typically, some male reviewers felt the need to disparage the looks of Melanie Mayron, who plays the lead character, Susan Weinblatt. Gordon Gow, for example, writes that she "is not a prepossessing wench" and describes her "full moon face and recalcitrant hair that improves only marginally when she has something done about it."[54] Stanley Kauffmann, on the other hand, seems to appreciate Mayron's eccentricity and charm:

[53] Claudia Weill, in Diane Jacobs, "What Are Friends For?" *Soho Weekly News*, 17 August 1978, 30.
[54] Gordon Gow, "*Girlfriends*," *Films and Filming* (September 1978): 34.

At first sight she looks redundant: she seems a stereotype of Plain Girl chosen to show that this independent low-budget film is deliberately renouncing movie slickness. But Mayron is much more than a negative symbol. With her vernacular truths, she opens a plump bespectacled type into a unique and appealing individual.[55]

Beyond being physically ordinary, Susan is also Jewish—and her ethnic appearance contrasts with the Aryan beauty of the dominant culture.

The narrative structures of the films diverge as well. The Cukor film begins at the moment when an intense friendship disintegrates—when Merry is leaving Liz to elope with Doug. In *Girlfriends*, although the fulcrum of the drama turns on Anne's marriage, we do at least get some scenes of the women living together before the issue of separation is raised. In the opening sequence, we see Susan early one morning photographing Anne as she sleeps. In the next scene, we watch Anne read her poem to Susan, soliciting an opinion. Clearly, the women share a spirit of creativity. Some of the small details of these scenes are also particularly telling. As Anne reads her work, Susan sits on the toilet, demonstrating the mundane intimacy of the roommates' lives. We also see the women together in a laundromat and in a new apartment they have rented.

While this portrayal of the women's friendship is superior to that in *Rich and Famous*, it is not as deep as we might like, and a competing romance is introduced precipitously. Instead of dedicating a significant portion of the narrative to the women's relationship, only a few scenes must serve to sum it up. Some writers have justifiably criticized the film for this. Rebecca A. Bailin notes that because of Anne's impending marriage, the friends have few moments together, and "[w]hen they do, the focus . . . is not on what binds them but what pulls them apart."[56]

While both narratives quickly introduce an outside heterosexual romance into the dyad of female friendship, they do so in opposing ways. In *Rich and Famous*, the sense of a triangle is emphasized, with Merry's husband, Doug, at its apex. Hence, the women are positioned in competition for a man. In *Girlfriends*, the theme is far more submerged and is configured in another manner. At no point in the narrative are the women seen as rivals for Anne's beau (and later husband), Martin.

[55] Stanley Kauffmann, "Small Film, Large Hurrah," *New Republic* 5/12 (August 1978): 21.

[56] Rebecca A. Bailin, *"Girlfriends*: No Celebration of Female Bonding," *Jump Cut*, no. 20 (May 1979): 3.

Rather, if any triangle exists, it is Susan and Martin's competition for Anne. Thus, a woman vies with a man for her female friend, not with her friend for a male lover. In this model, it is men, not women, who threaten female friendship—a very different thing.

In *Rich and Famous*, Liz and Merry's rivalry was doubled in the presentation of mother and daughter. In *Girlfriends*, this latter interaction does not figure centrally in the narrative, but where it does arise, it seems unproblematic. When Anne reads Susan one of her poems, "I Have a War with My Mother," it is about generational struggle. Susan, who seems dubious about the verse, suspiciously asks Anne if she ever really fought with her mother, and Anne replies, "No." This brief sequence contains an implicit critique of the stereotype that sees women perpetually engaged in battle. Another reference to the maternal relationship occurs later in the film (at Susan's show)—and it is equally benign. At her opening, she proudly introduces her mother to people; the character is played by Melanie Mayron's real parent.

Girlfriends is quite subtle in its presentation of the awkward moments that arise in a female friendship with the introduction of the masculine third term. When Susan visits the newlyweds, they project their honeymoon slides, and she is embarrassed when nude photos of Martin and Anne flash on the screen. Though Anne apologizes for showing them, we empathize with Susan and her sense of exclusion. Later, when the girl friends fight, Susan complains that the only time she sees Anne alone is when her husband is busy. At another moment, we hear Martin confess that he does not think Susan likes him very much. Even at the end of the film, when the women have survived the transition in their friendship, Martin is perceived as a continuing threat. When Susan arrives at Anne's country home, the two women spend time talking and laughing by the fire, finally at ease with each other again. In the last shot, however, as we stare at Susan's face, we hear a car arrive offscreen, and Martin calls Anne. It is on this ambiguous unstable image that the film closes.

Beyond this variation on the theme of rivalry, *Girlfriends* articulates a more important message—that friends are *couples* in the same way as lovers, and that the disruption of their bond is as traumatic as divorce. As Weill herself has stated: "What I tried to do was show that female friendship is as fragile, delicate, supportive, complex, nourishing, painful, and difficult as a love affair. . . . It is not unlike a marriage."[57]

57 Weill, in Klemesrud.

Given this view, it is understandable that the film focuses on Susan's struggle to live alone. While we may regret the paucity of scenes with Anne (the tendency to portray the friendship as an absence rather than a presence), the centrality of their relationship is inscribed in the profound gap left in Susan's life by Anne's departure. Early on, Susan meets an artist, Eric (Christopher Guest), at a party and spends the night at his apartment. The next morning, she sneaks off to be alone. When she next encounters him, some months later, he asks why she left. She replies that she was "coming out of a heavy relationship." When he inquires whether "they" were living together, she nods, and it is clear he assumes she is talking about a man. The film means, on some level, to establish the equivalence of female friendship and heterosexual romance as the two most important relationships in straight women's lives. This opposes the stereotype of female friendships as entirely peripheral to women's romantic ties. Beyond equating friendship with a love affair, Weill also uses another metaphor to explain its centrality. As she states, it is "like a kinship, like family."[58] Whereas traditional views allow woman only blood relations, Weill sees woman as creating new kinship structures in the broader female social world.

As the narrative unfolds, it is clear that Susan experiences a genuine crisis over Anne's leave-taking. Like someone recently separated or newly moved from home, she must first become acclimated to living alone. Poignant scenes communicate her pain. In one episode, she glumly paints the apartment that she and Anne were to rent, while recollecting fragments of conversation from the wedding. In another sequence, Susan attempts to install a security gate. She gives up in frustration, flips the channels of her television, and cries. In another segment, she telephones several friends, only to get their answering machines; she reaches for a Hershey Bar in compulsive desperation.

We also witness her struggle to fill the vacuum left by Anne's departure. After visiting the couple in the country, she picks up a hitchhiker, Ceil (Amy Wright), whom she eventually invites to stay with her, despite the woman's rather annoying habits (like wearing Susan's clothes and using her developing trays to wash stockings). Susan also explores the possibility of a relationship with an older married man, Rabbi Gold (Eli Wallach), for whom she photographs weddings and bar mitzvahs (see fig. 19).

At a certain point, she comes to terms with her independence and finally relishes it: she tells Ceil that she wants to live alone again and

[58] Ibid.

asks her to leave. It is then that she is also ready for a liaison with a man. When Eric reappears in her life, she seems more willing to get involved, though Anne's leaving has made her wary of all emotional ties. In the final scene, she confesses to Anne: "I'm the biggest turtle I know." Thus, by delineating Susan's struggle and the impact on her life of Anne's departure, the film validates the importance of friendship in female existence.

Girlfriends also establishes its distance from *Rich and Famous* in its handling of the single woman. In the latter film, when the narrative follows Liz, we get a catalogue of her sexual exploits and psychological quirks. In *Girlfriends*, we find a far more positive depiction of the independent woman. Though Susan has several relationships with men (a "one-night stand" with Eric, a flirtation with Rabbi Gold), these are all treated with respect. Though Susan is in pain, we feel no sense of her maladjustment—only of her struggles with the complexities of life. This did not stop some critics, however, from reading Susan according to the single-girl stereotype, exemplified by Cukor's Liz. Harold C. Schonberg, for example, writes in the *New York Times* that "[any] big city is full of sad, unfulfilled girls [like Susan] who lead desperately lonely and frightened lives."[59] This is decidedly *not* Polon and Weill's

[59] Harold C. Schonberg, [Review], *New York Times*, 19 August 1978.

19. *Girlfriends* (1978). Susan (Melanie Mayron) explores a relationship with an older married man, Rabbi Gold (Eli Wallach).

conception of Susan. There are other single women in the film who seem reasonably satisfied. Ceil, for example, hitchhikes happily across country, finding acquaintances where she can, and Susan's colleague, Julie (Gina Rozak), breaks up with her lover and adores life on her own. The film goes so far as to mock the image of the liberated single woman that circulates in *Rich and Famous*. Following the night Susan first meets Eric, she leaves his apartment in the early morning hours and takes a taxicab. We overhear her discussion with the driver. He asks her if she is one of those "women's libbers" and inquires whether she knows karate. When she coughs uncomfortably, he begins telling her of the dangers of mumps and how it can make adult men impotent. "I bet that would make you mad, eh?" he chortles. In the final shot of the sequence, she runs from the cab as though fleeing a psychopath. Clearly, the mention of the women's movement is not a ploy to discount it but rather to identify the malicious prejudices it engenders in men.

If any woman is desperate in *Girlfriends*, it is Susan's married friend, Anne. In *Rich and Famous*, though Merry is as pathetic as Liz, it is not marriage per se that causes her problems. When we find her in 1969, she has already been wed for twelve years and has a young child. Despite this, she has managed to write a novel (in her "spare time")—one that gets published and brings her immediate financial success. Thus we envision no conflict between domestic and artistic life. In *Girlfriends*, however, although the narrative somewhat ignores Anne, we do get a sense of her difficulties. We see her typing Martin's dissertation—a scene signifying the submergence of her creative interests in his. Furthermore, after having a child, she gives up thoughts of school and career. When she tries to write again, we see her attempting to work against the inhospitable background of her baby's cries.

Throughout the film, Susan is critical of Anne's dependence and of her denial of her own needs. At certain moments, she reminds Anne kindly that she can "take care of herself." At other moments, she jokes, insensitively, about Anne's being a "helpless blonde" (as Martin parodies a King Kong attack on his wife). By the end of the film, Anne seems to have learned a lesson from Susan. For the sake of her career, she secretly aborts her second pregnancy and sneaks away from her family to spend time alone at their country home.

Aside from the more positive delineation of friendship in *Girlfriends*, the film opposes *Rich and Famous* in its acknowledgment of a broader female network. In the Cukor film, Liz and Merry relate to no other women (except Merry's daughter), either in a private or professional context. In *Girlfriends*, however, we are made aware of many women in Susan's life. Through her work as a photographer, she meets Julie, who is a bit older and somewhat more successful in the field. She asks Julie if she needs an assistant, and the latter offers her part-time work. Later, when Susan gets a gallery show, she suggests that Julie contact the curator, and the two have a joint exhibition. The women soon become rather friendly. When Julie needs a place to stay for the opening, Susan lets her use her apartment. And when Susan fights with both Eric and Anne, she comes to Julie for comfort. Beatrice, the gallery owner (Viveca Lindfors), is also portrayed as a supportive woman. When Susan declines to give instructions on the hanging of her show, Beatrice encourages her to be more assertive and professional. Thus, between Julie and Beatrice, we get the sense of a "good old girl network" and how it might function in women's lives.

The film also examines the way Susan attempts to find other friends to fill the gap that Anne has left in her life. We see her form a relationship with Ceil, one that ultimately does not flourish. Through the figure of Ceil, the film also raises the issue of lesbianism (a theme to be considered in Chapter 8), though its position is decidedly problematic. When Ceil reveals a romantic interest in Susan, her move is rebuffed in a manner that seeks to avoid any judgmental overlay; and the two live happily together for several more weeks. This attitude is more progressive than that of *Rich and Famous*, which makes a joke about Liz being "strange." But, as Claudette Charbonneau and Lucy Winer have pointed out, this episode is, finally, unsatisfactory. They find it one of many "obligatory anti-lesbian" segments in contemporary women's films (*The Bell Jar*, *The Turning Point*, and *Julia*). Furthermore, they view the "kookie" characterization of Ceil as tantamount to a dismissal of lesbianism:

> *Girlfriends* offers a more sophisticated treatment of the lesbian menace. Claudia Weill does not entertain us with grim, outdated stereotypes. Her lesbian is not tormented and twisted, just somewhat confused. . . . The specter has been reduced to an anomalous flower child, incapable of causing serious discomfort to any "with it" woman.[60]

Another scene in the film, described by Rebecca A. Bailin, seems even more condemnatory:

[60] Claudette Charbonneau and Lucy Winer, "Lesbians in 'Nice Films,' " *Jump Cut*, nos. 24–25 (March 1981): 26.

Susan is seen at a party, talking with her lover-to-be, Eric. He has just asked her to go home with him and she has refused. Over Susan's shoulder, in the background, we can see a couple kissing. It is not totally clear that they are two women—they are in shadow. But they are of equal height and certainly *not* clearly a man and a woman. Susan turns, looks over her shoulder and sees the couple. A look of disgust (?), jealousy (?), passes across her face and she now asks Eric to go home with her. The subtlety of the scene itself is insidious. The couple is not clear. The filmmakers would probably respond to being accused of homophobia by saying that the couple is a man and a woman. Yet they could easily be two women. The scene allows a person to project his/her homophobia onto it and yet remain unaware of it. The scene undercuts the liberal "tolerance" of homosexuality stated in the film.[61]

Weill defends her allusion to lesbianism on the basis of wanting to make clear the platonic nature of Anne and Susan's affection:

When Susan is so upset with Anne's marriage one can wonder whether she's in love with her. The scene with Ceil gives Susan the opportunity to see if it is so. The film is about the whole range of experiences a young woman can go through. A love relationship with another woman is one of those real possibilities, but one that Susan doesn't choose.[62]

Weill feels that she must introduce and dismiss lesbianism to clarify the fact that Susan experiences profound love for her friend in an asexual way. Unfortunately, by taking this defensive position, she only validates cultural anxieties about homosexuality—constructs the lesbian as a troublesome "Other."

Beyond its rejection of lesbianism, there is a more submerged way in which *Girlfriends* is decidedly a film about the "straight" woman. Psychologists claim that, for the young girl, heterosexual identification begins in childhood with a shift of love from the mother (the traditional, primary care giver) to the father as preparation for future relations with men. While Freud configures this move as involving hostility toward the mother, contemporary thinkers (like Nancy Chodorow) hypothesize that the girl simply adds this new paternal affection to that

---

[61] Bailin, 3.

[62] Claudia Weill, in Marsha Kinder, *"Girl Friends," Film Quarterly* 32, no. 1 (Fall 1978): 48–49.

already felt for the mother.[63] *Girlfriends* can be said to restage this drama in the configuration of Susan's emotional life. Susan's break with Anne and her eventual move toward Eric seem to replay the young girl's split from the mother and turn toward the father. *Girlfriends* even literalizes this paradigm by making Susan's first love interest (following her break with Anne) the paternal Rabbi Gold. Significantly, at Susan's photo exhibition, the rabbi exits as Eric arrives.

Girlfriends is more convincing than *Rich and Famous* in its portrayal of female jealousy. In *Rich and Famous*, the confrontations between women, the open competition, had a false ring. In *Girlfriends*, these moments are handled with more sensitivity. Early on, as the girls talk in a laundromat, they exchange important information. Susan reveals that she has just published her first photographs, and Anne discloses that she will be married. Though the women feel anxiety about each other's success, they swallow their words and congratulate each other. After Anne is married, the jealousy finally erupts. Although the women argue, and confess a certain envy of each other, we have no shrewish fights to match those of *Rich and Famous*, and there is a far greater sense of how women subdue competitive feelings. Later in the film (when Susan gets a show), Julie humorously confesses her jealousy, calling Susan "a squirt." But this conflict is nullified by Susan's thoughtful suggestion that Julie approach the gallery owner herself. Weill based her film on Katherine Mansfield's short story *Bliss*, but specifically toned down the theme of rivalry.[64]

In addition to more honestly depicting the world of women, the film delineates the world of men—the sphere in which most females must operate. In *Rich and Famous*, although the women are writers, there is absolutely no critique of the male publishing world. In *Girlfriends*, through Susan's trials and tribulations as an artist, we get some sense of the constraints of working in a patriarchal domain. In one conversation, Julie urges Susan to hound an editor who has published her pictures, since men "love to be pursued by women." When Susan sees him, he criticizes her for not aggressively sticking the camera lens into people's faces. In another scene, Susan attempts to get past a female receptionist who works for a powerful male gallery owner and finds that she can do so only by concocting a specious reference from another man. Finally, one night as Susan watches television, we hear a

[63] Nancy Chodorow, *The Reproduction of Mothering: Psychoanalysis and the Sociology of Gender* (Berkeley, Los Angeles, and London: University of California Press, 1978), 92–93.
[64] Weill in Klemesrud.

241

snatch of dialogue from a game show. A man is asked what kind of movie he would take a girl to see on their first date, and he responds, "A John Ford film—because I identify with John Wayne."

Girlfriends seeks to offer women a variation on that male model by conceiving heroines to whom they can relate—female "ego-ideals," as Laura Mulvey would have it.[65] Marsha Kinder writes that the film "presents the most likable heroine [she's] seen in American feature film."[66] This stance is unavailable to the female spectator of *Rich and Famous*, who must identify, at her own expense, with the protagonists, embodying, as they do, images of the castrating bitch, harlot, or sexual object.

But is the positive identification encouraged by *Girlfriends* ultimately enough? Does it pose a substantial challenge to the cinema or to mainstream culture? To assess this, we must focus on the style with which the film's representation of women is articulated. Earlier on, we characterized *Girlfriends* as a rather conventional fictional drama. On one level, its typicality resides in its adoption of a "realist aesthetic," a paradigm described by Annette Kuhn:

> What is seen on the cinema screen appears to the spectator to be constructed in much the same way as its referent, the "real world". . . . This is what makes realist films easy to watch and follow: they seem to duplicate spectators' everyday ways of experiencing the world.[67]

This mode contrasts with the avant-garde experimentations of Nelson, Beroes, Rose, and Akerman, and even the modernist techniques of Zetterling. Weill speaks of the film in terms of its verisimilitude: "The only criterion I had by which to judge performances, sets, was whether they felt real."[68]

The reviews of *Girlfriends* demonstrate that critics found the film almost newsreel-like in its representation. Stanley Kauffmann talks of its "documentary 'feel,' "[69] and Susan Dworkin notes that Claudia Weill has the "fix of a news cinematographer."[70] Significantly, Weill

[65] Laura Mulvey, "Visual Pleasure and Narrative Cinema," in Gerald Mast and Marshall Cohen, *Film Theory and Criticism*, 3rd ed. (New York and Oxford: Oxford University Press, 1985), 810.

[66] Kinder, 46.

[67] Annette Kuhn, *Women's Pictures: Feminism and the Cinema* (London: Routledge & Kegan Paul, 1982), 131.

[68] Weill, in Jacobs, 30.   [69] Kauffmann, 20.

[70] Susan Dworkin, "*Girlfriends*: A Reality Fix," *Ms.* (August 1978).

began her artistic career as a photographer and then made such film documentaries as *Joyce at 34* (1973) and *The Other Half of the Sky: A China Memoir* (1975).

Another important feature of realist texts is their seeming "transparency," their denial of the process of making. As Kuhn notes, this "is in fact brought about not by a duplication of 'real world' referents but by certain conventions of cinematic signification."[71]

But what exactly are the codes of the classic realist work? In terms of narrative structure, the traditional film generally follows several individualized characters who are rendered in psychological depth. As E. Ann Kaplan notes, they tend to be "seen in the autobiographical mode, as having essences that have persisted through time and that reveal growth through individual change outside of influence from social structures, economic relations, or psychoanalytic laws."[72] Such personae typically function as a source of identification for the audience, who is "stitched" into the text. As Kuhn explains: "Suture is the process whereby . . . the spectator . . . becomes the 'stand-in,' the subject-in-the-text . . . being 'sewn in' to, or caught up in, the film's enunciation."[73] The dramatic fulcrum of the conventional film centers on heterosexual courtship, with woman defined as the locus of male desire; and closure is generally established around this issue. The classical storytelling stance is that of *histoire*—"that mode of address characteristic of narrations of past events, in which the narrator is not foregrounded as a 'person.' "[74]

Within classical fiction, woman has a special role. She serves as object of the male gaze—a figure of both pleasure and threat. As "structure, character or both . . . [she] constitutes the motivator of the narrative, the 'trouble' that sets the plot in motion."[75] Frequently, she is "recuperated" at the story's end to her "proper place" within patriarchal culture.[76]

Beyond these broad plot configurations, specific stylistic devices are typical of the realist text: continuity editing, classical framing and composition, and narrative linearity. These tropes make the drama co-

[71] Kuhn, 132.

[72] E. Ann Kaplan, *Women and Film: Both Sides of the Camera* (New York and London: Methuen, 1983), 128. Kaplan is actually speaking of characters in two documentary films, but she states elsewhere that frequently the codes of Hollywood realism and documentary realism overlap.

[73] Kuhn, 53.   [74] Ibid., 49.   [75] Ibid., 34.   [76] Ibid., 35.

herent for the spectator, and the viewing process relatively "facile."[77] Finally, they cause the screen world to appear "natural" and gloss over contradictions concerning class, race, and/or sexual difference.[78]

In *Girlfriends*, we appear to have a linear, rational story that presents a virtual window onto the real world. Through a utilization of standard cinematic tropes, the narrative seems relatively "seamless" and does not boldly call attention to its own construction. The viewing process is fairly simple, presenting minimal intellectual challenges to us. Rather, meaning seems to issue from the film itself.

Although *Girlfriends* circumscribes a white, bourgeois world (and does not address working-class females or women of color), it does not "suture over" *all* social contradictions—as does *Rich and Famous*, whose very title is a giveaway. (Never is it mentioned in the film that the very notion of long-distance friendship is tied to an elite class with money for jet-set travel.)[79] In *Girlfriends*, Susan is ethnic and decidedly lower-middle class, supporting herself through bar mitzvah and wedding photography. She does, however, feel the "luxury" to pursue an artistic career—an issue that the film never surfaces. Susan's experience as a single Jewish woman is contrasted with that of her WASP married friend, who honeymoons in exotic places, is a lady of leisure, and has both city and country residences.

Girlfriends presents us with several individualized characters with whom we are urged to empathize, and who are rendered in some psychological depth. Though these women figure prominently in the narrative, they are not formulated as objects of the male gaze. Instead, voyeuristic strategies are avoided.

A woman's actions do set the plot in motion (or cause the "problem")—specifically, Anne's decision to move out. But the narrative revolves not so much around heterosexual romance as around same-sex friendship, although the former plays a strong peripheral role. By the end of the film, woman is not entirely "recuperated" to her proper patriarchal place: Anne has secretly aborted her pregnancy and temporarily left her husband; Susan is struggling with independence and has achieved no marriage comparable to Anne's (though we suspect she will). Furthermore, the friendship between the two women has not reached any final equilibrium: as they sit together by the fire, Martin's offscreen voice disrupts their female tête-à-tête.

---

77 These issues are discussed in Kuhn and in E. Ann Kaplan, 125–41.

78 Kaplan, 128.

79 See a discussion of class and friendship in Graham A. Allan, *A Sociology of Friendship and Kin* (London: George Allen and Unwin, 1979), 119.

Annette Kuhn comments on the narrative structure of *Girlfriends*, explaining why it cannot attain stasis:

> Within the trajectory of lack to liquidation of lack ... resolution in *Girlfriends* might be brought about by the establishment of love relationships for Ann and Susan: either with each other, or with new partners. Although the first option would fit in well with the structural demands of classic narrative, as well as with the powerful Hollywood "romance" model, its content is excluded by rules, conscious and unconscious, currently governing representations of homosexuality in dominant cinema.[80]

Here, perhaps, Kuhn stumbles upon (but does not pursue) another reason why Weill felt impelled to disclaim the theme of lesbianism, for the submerged narrative structure of her film points in that very direction. Kuhn mentions other reasons why the film resists closure:

> The second option—re-establishment of equilibrium through the setting up of new [heterosexual] relationships—is also ruled out, in this case by the demands on the narrative set up through the characterisations of the two women: it would simply not be plausible. However ... there is a constant movement towards the latter resolution—in Susan's relationship with a rabbi, for instance, and in Ann's with her husband—it is never quite brought off, partly perhaps because it would undermine the "buddy" structure that governs the organisation of the narrative.[81]

The diegesis remains caught in its own contradictions, unable to bring itself to any final stance.

In refusing narrative closure, the film avoids woman's containment within patriarchy. As Kuhn writes:

> The pleasure for the female spectator of films of this kind lies in several possible identifications: with a central character who is not only also a woman, but who may be similar in some respects to the spectator herself; ... or with fictional events which evoke a degree of recognition; or with a resolution that constitutes a 'victory' for the central character. The address of the new woman's film may thus position the spectator not only as herself a potential 'winner,' but also as a winner whose gender

---

[80] Kuhn, 139.   [81] Ibid.

is instrumental in the victory: it may consequently offer the female spectator a degree of affirmation.[82]

Reading the reviews of *Girlfriends*, one perceives this "affirmation," and the film was celebrated for its progressive features. Susan Dworkin called it a "major event,"[83] and (despite her other criticisms) Rebecca A. Bailin acknowledged it as a significant "departure from the traditional movie images of women."[84] Its alignment with mainstream models made it easily accessible to many female viewers who might be intimidated by works of the feminist postmodern fringe. The question remains, however, whether these positive aspects of the film outweigh its possible "entrapment" of the audience in a realistic mode.

Closer examination of the text reveals elements that qualify its seamless realism and lend the film a self-reflexive dimension. Claire Johnston has asserted that "it is not enough to discuss the oppression of women within the text of the film: the language of the cinema/depiction of reality must also be interrogated, so that a break between ideology and text is affected."[85] Although her rhetoric envisions a feminist avant-garde, in her writing, she has examined the work of Hollywood director Dorothy Arzner, who (as we have seen) inserted strategies of resistance into conventional texts. It is this approach that we must bring to *Girlfriends*. It is not an experimental film that aggressively asserts its construction; nonetheless, there are dimensions of the work that draw attention to the process of its making, and they center around the figuration of woman.

It should not be ignored that the heroine of *Girlfriends* is a photographer. This has autobiographical ramifications for Weill, and even for Mayron, who also pursued the art. Beyond that, it is crucial that the lead female character is a creator of images—a vocation that has particular resonance in a film.

Weill avoids a voyeuristic stance in her own cinematography, and even in her casting of actresses. But the issue of female versus male vision proposes itself continually—though frequently in a manner so submerged that it escapes us at first viewing. One thinks of the credit sequence that unrolls against a backdrop of dime-store-machine snapshots of Susan and Anne—the kind of self-portraits that girls have fashioned when they chum around together. These are not the glamorous icons of *Rich and Famous* (*Vogue* magazine illustrations), but neutral, candid poses.

---

[82] Ibid., 136.   [83] Dworkin.   [84] Bailin, 3.
[85] Claire Johnston, "Women's Cinema as Counter-Cinema," quoted in Kaplan, 131.

This discourse on female imagery arises elsewhere in *Girlfriends*. In the first shot, Susan is filming Anne as she sleeps. Later, when the photos are accepted for publication, Anne is concerned about her partial nudity (which we, as viewers, had not noticed). Susan assures her that her body is not prominent in the image, that it is obscured by the diffuse light. Here we sense that a very different kind of photograph would have been fashioned by a male artist.

Susan's other photographic subjects are also interesting. While she eschews a conventional family structure in her own life (preferring independence or the kinship of friends), her work documents those very relations; she photographs bar mitzvahs and weddings—rites of male and female passage, as constructed by the broader culture. Significantly, when she serves as photographer at Anne's wedding, someone asks her to be in the picture—a stance she seems to avoid. By documenting such rituals, she prevents her own participation in them, using her art as a defense. The fact that Susan desperately wishes to move beyond these jobs signifies that the images she creates professionally have little to do with her own vision. Despite this, she transcends their limitations and creates photographs of artistic worth.

The film establishes a subtle dissonance between her own images and those circulating in the mainstream society. When she visits a male editor who will publish her photos, his office walls are plastered with close-up portraits of women, and he tells her to "take that lens and get right in [people's] faces." When Susan examines the proofs of her work, she finds that her photographs have been cropped—a metaphor for how men truncate female vision. Later, when she maneuvers her way in to see a prestigious gallery director, he sits at his desk, below a huge painting of a female torso: we see the crotch and thighs of a woman wearing only panties. The woman is lying on her side, her torso positioned frontally. Here, as John Berger would have it, is a painting aimed at the male spectator, who is accorded a satisfyingly voyeuristic view.[86] As Susan shows the dealer a portfolio of her work, we notice one image depicting the torso of a nude woman. The shot must have been taken by the photographer herself, for the woman's knees are up directly in front of the camera. Though picturing a female nude, this view is conceived from a woman's perspective: rather than being arranged laterally (for the voyeuristic gaze), the spectator's eyes are identified with the subject herself. Finally, the woman's pubic hair

[86] John Berger, *Ways of Seeing* (London: British Broadcasting Corporation and Penguin, 1978), 54.

is visible—a "forbidden" feature excised from more idealized representations of the female body.

This question of female versus male vision resurfaces in one comic moment of the film. Depressed by Anne's leave-taking, Susan decides to get a haircut. She hands the male stylist a photograph of a hairdo she has clipped from a magazine, and he tells her that it will not work on her face. "Will anything?" she asks glumly. He orders her to take off her glasses so that he can look at her, and she complains: "But I can't see!" "*I* can," the young man responds, "trust me."

Various issues are raised in this sequence. It is significant that when Susan is feeling low, she thinks of "making over" her appearance—a reflex action encouraged by the media and cosmetics industry. She picks out a magazine image that she wishes to copy but is told that she cannot measure up to its standard of beauty. The Judgment of Paris rears its ugly head once more. In order to become glamorous, she must take off her glasses—a symbolic act described by Mary Ann Doane as recurrent in film.[87] Finally, when Susan protests that she cannot see, the hairdresser reassures her that *he* can and asks her to have faith in him. Here, in this brief sequence, apparently a mere slice of life, we have a rather sophisticated series of references to the question of the female image—its formulation by men, and women's complicity in that dynamic.

Through these various scenes and allusions (planted subtly within the cinematic narrative), *Girlfriends* offers a submerged discourse on the subject of woman as image, and as image maker—a substratum that qualifies the film's seamless realism. *Girlfriends* does not simply depict women on screen but interrogates (in an understated manner) the issue of that naturalized depiction. This level of the film was ignored by feminist critics, even ones as sympathetic to the work as Kuhn. She writes that the new women's cinema "cannot . . . deal in any direct way with the questions which feminism poses for cinematic representation."[88]

Girlfriends does not offer the radical challenge to the mainstream film proposed by *Take Off, Riddles of the Sphinx, Recital, The Eighties,* or *The Bad Sister.* But if, in the process of deconstructing traditional film form, the general audience is lost, for whom can it be said that the critique is raised? Should a mode of cinema be endorsed

[87] Mary Ann Doane, "Film and the Masquerade: Theorising the Female Spectator," *Screen* 23, no. 3–4 (September–October 1982): 82–84.
[88] Kuhn, 140.

exclusively that is comprehensible only to a feminist, intellectual elite? Is it advisable to deny female spectators the viewing pleasure that results from identification with positive (albeit realistic) heroines?[89] Filmmaker Bette Gordon thinks not. In discussing her independent feature *Variety* (1984), she writes: "My work is in the mainstream, but I insert questions and discomfort into images, narrative and stories." While other feminist artists are interested in creating an alternate cinema, she fears that this consigns them to "marginality — the 'other place' outside of culture that women have already been assigned."[90]

Unfortunately, there are no simple answers to these questions, for the solutions are ripe with contradictions. If feminist filmmakers remain stylistic "purists," they may lose some viewers they wish to address (conversing instead with the "already convinced"); if they adopt traditional strategies, they may dilute their antipatriarchal stance. At the present moment, "closure" to this debate seems to elude us, just as it did the resolution of *Girlfriends*. As we must look for new models of friendship that negotiate woman's role in both male and female worlds, so we must search for new styles of cinema that traverse the gap between experimental and classical modes.

As an independent women's feature, *Girlfriends* was a step in that direction—and a comparison with *Rich and Famous* has highlighted its distance from the traditional paradigm. The names of Susan and Anne do not rank with those of Chloris and Thyia (or Damon and Pythias), but they help dispel those of Liz and Merry. Despite *Girlfriends'* limitations, it stands as a watershed work for its time. Regrettably, when Claudia Weill entered the Hollywood world of the Cukor film (to make *It's My Turn* in 1980), her movie was a major disappointment. In her own quest to become "rich and famous," the promise of *Girlfriends* was not fulfilled.

[89] For an article that argues for the justification of Hollywood realism in certain cases, see Florence Jacobowitz and Lori Spring, "Unspoken and Unsolved: *Tell Me A Riddle*," *CineAction*, no. 1 (Spring 1985): 15–20.

[90] Bette Gordon, "*Variety*: The Pleasure in Looking," in Carole S. Vance, ed., *Pleasure and Danger: Exploring Female Sexuality* (Boston: Routledge & Kegan Paul, 1984), 194.

8 Women in Love: The Theme of Lesbianism

"My wife left me for another woman."
—Woody Allen (as Issac Davis) in Manhattan *(1979)*

In her 1973 essay on "Lesbianism in the Movies,"[1] Joan Mellen reiterated what we all suspected: that few Hollywood or European feature films had treated the subject, and those that did were largely pejorative. Mellen found that the films she examined (Radley Metzger's *The Lickerish Quartet* [1970], Robert Aldrich's *The Killing of Sister George* [1969], Ingmar Bergman's *The Silence* [1964], and Claude Chabrol's *Les Biches* [1968]) were circulating familiar stereotypes of the lesbian: "They appear either compulsively sadistic or masochistic, always possessive, jealous, hateful and indeed 'sick.' "[2] Few of the films imagine the lesbian as possibly bisexual, limiting her sexuality to one mode; few of them "recognize that her homosexuality may not be the organizing principle of her life."[3] None of the works configure the lesbian as a woman rebelling against the traditional feminine role. Many of them portray her sexuality voyeuristically, exploiting a sense of her "perversion." Mellen finds only a few films that evince a degree of sensitivity or empathy: William Wyler's *The Children's Hour* (1961), Paul Newman's *Rachel, Rachel* (1968), Paul Morrisey's *Flesh* (1968) and *Trash* (1970), Radley Metzger's *Therese and Isabelle* (1968). These works were all directed by men, although two of them were based on women's literary properties: Lillian Hellman wrote *The Children's Hour* and Violette Leduc the novel on which *Therese and Isabelle* was based.

In March 1981, *Jump Cut* devoted a section to lesbianism and film. The editors' introduction comes to much the same conclusion as Mellen concerning the commercial cinema:

> Lesbians are nearly invisible in mainstream cinematic history, except as evil or negative-example characters. There is the lesbian as villainess. . . . There is the lesbian as vampire. . . . There is the brutal bull dyke.[4]

---

[1] Joan Mellen, *Women and Their Sexuality in the New Film* (New York: Dell, 1973), 71–96.

[2] Ibid., 71.   [3] Ibid., 72.

[4] Edith Becker, Michelle Citron, Julia Lesage, and B. Ruby Rich, "Lesbians and Film/ Introduction," *Jump Cut*, nos. 24–25 (March 1981): 18.

250

The writers caution feminist critics to pay attention to these negative images "because they are not only about lesbianism but, in fact, are about the containment of women's sexuality and independence." They also fault theorists for accepting "heterosexuality as [the] norm" and for refusing "to deal with a lesbian perspective."⁵

While the *Jump Cut* writers can envision a mainstream cinema in which the lesbian is portrayed with a positive valence, they are pessimistic about the likelihood of its happening:

> There are instances in which we could imagine the progressive nature of substitution. For example, the substitution of a lesbian couple for a heterosexual one could in fact substantially alter the narrative structures of film romance. Yet the economic pressures of marketing and film production guarantee that in a homophobic society, any authentic "positive image" of lesbian romantic love will remain too great a risk ever to find direct expression on the screen.⁶

While they find the commercial cinema a void, the *Jump Cut* critics note that, in the pornographic sector, lesbianism makes an assertive appearance:

> the most explicit vision of lesbianism has been left to pornography, where the lesbian loses her menace and becomes a turn-on. . . . As long as lesbianism remains a component of pornography made by and for men . . . lesbian sexuality will be received by most sectors of the dominant society *as* pornography.⁷

In the same issue, Claudette Charbonneau and Lucy Winer (whose writing we examined in the previous chapter) discuss the emergence of lesbian subthemes in a group of "women's films" of the 1970s: works like *Girlfriends*, which contain "an obligatory anti-lesbian scene" superfluous to their plot and major theme.⁸ In several other articles, the *Jump Cut* critics applaud avant-garde films by women, which confront the question of lesbianism. Jacqueline Zita writes on the erotic works of Barbara Hammer, and Michelle Citron examines the gender comedies of Jan Oxenberg.⁹

⁵ Ibid., 18, 17.   ⁶ Ibid., 18.   ⁷ Ibid.

⁸ Lucy Winer and Claudette Charbonneau, "Lesbians in 'Nice' Films," Ibid., 25.

⁹ Jacqueline Zita, "Films of Barbara Hammer—Counter-Currencies of Lesbian Iconography," Ibid., 26–30; Michelle Citron, "Films of Jan Oxenberg: Comic Critique," Ibid., 31–32.

Since the publication of that *Jump Cut* issue, more feature films about lesbianism have circulated in the commercial sector. In these works, the "substitution" (of lesbian for heterosexual romantic couple) has taken place, defying earlier predictions. One of the first contemporary movies to address the subject, *Lianna* (1983), was made by John Sayles. Subsequently, several women artists have confronted the question, some successfully and others not. In the former category is French filmmaker, Diane Kurys, who made *Entre Nous* in 1983, and American cinéaste Donna Deitch, who released *Desert Hearts* in 1985. In the latter category is Italian director Lina Wertmuller, whose *Sotto, Sotto* (1984) is as problematic as the retrograde works cited by Mellen et al. Although *Sotto, Sotto* avoids the obvious lesbian stereotypes (perverse seducers, social outcasts), it offers a variety of more original and elusive strategies for discounting this sexual preference.

Sotto, Sotto: The Impossible Dream

This negative characterization of Wertmuller's work should not surprise us. Athough one of the first women filmmakers acclaimed in the 1970s, she was also one of the first attacked by feminist critics, despite their desire to support female artists. Tania Modleski, for example, was shocked by the progressive readings of *Swept Away* (1975) and feared "that some of the film's 'feminist' defenses only indicate[d] that we have developed more sophisticated means for justifying our titillation at seeing women put down."[10] Similarly, Molly Haskell lambasted the film for sailing "on a wave of sexism" and criticized it for using Marxist politics as a ploy for misogyny.[11] She describes the work's romantic plot as follows:

> Thesis and Antithesis are stranded on a deserted island. Thesis ("rich capitalist bitch") is overthrown—abused, beaten, degraded, penetrated—by Antithesis (sexy Sicilian communist male), and in the reversal of the master-slave relationship a temporary synthesis is struck.[12]

Haskell is aware that some have attributed irony to the film, but she discounts this interpretation, since Wertmuller orchestrates "lush mu-

[10] Tania Modleski, "Swept Away by the Usual Destiny," *Jump Cut*, nos. 10–11 (Summer 1976): 18.

[11] Molly Haskell, "Lina Wertmuller: Swept Away on a Wave of Sexism," in Patricia Erens, ed., *Sexual Stratagems: The World of Women in Film* (New York: Horizon, 1979), 244–47.

[12] Ibid., 245.

sic, lighting, and seminude love scenes to convince us of the bliss of sexual surrender, and the genuine passion of two lovers released at last to enjoy their 'natural' roles."[13] Haskell also finds validation for her reading of *Swept Away* in the ideology of other Wertmuller films:

> [Her] male chauvinism, her identification with the male sex, is insidious. All of her women are treated as nonpersons, as types—the whore, the bitch, the devouring wife—while the man . . . is always treated as a person, a character who extends by virtue of his emotional complexity beyond the class or sexual function that defines the others.[14]

Haskell also notes that Wertmuller has publicly distanced herself from the women's movement and has argued for an "androgyny" in artistic creation.[15] (As an interesting footnote, in certain laboratory studies of the effect of pornography on men, researchers use *Swept Away* as an appropriate text to represent male rape fantasies.)[16]

In *Sotto, Sotto*, we again find the textual subterfuge indicative of *Swept Away*. On the surface, the film might appear to be a sympathetic (though comic) treatment of lesbianism and an attack on masculine prejudices about it. But closer analysis reveals opposing forces that work to annihilate this initial exegesis, proposing a far more traditional and pernicious view.

Sotto, Sotto concerns the marriage of Ester (Veronica Lario) and Oscar (Enrico Montesano) and certain sexual tensions that develop within it. During a weekend the couple spends with some friends at Bomarzo, Ester is attracted to Adele (Luisa de Santis), an acquaintance who has recently returned to Italy from Switzerland. When Ester and her husband return to Rome, she acts distant, and Oscar realizes that something is wrong. One night, as they make love, Ester confesses that she has been thinking of someone else. (In truth, she has been watching a window across the courtyard, where Adele and her estranged husband have made love.) Oscar, a traditional Italian husband, assumes that Ester is infatuated with another man and begins a mad, inebriated search for his rival. As part of this quest, he enlists the aid of Adele, who secretly suspects that she is the object of Ester's desire. After Oscar accuses (and almost kills) his friend Amilcare, Ester is forced to confess that her love is for a woman. This precipitates yet another farcical crisis in Oscar's life, as he tries pathetically to grapple with a love

---

[13] Ibid., 246.   [14] Ibid.   [15] Ibid., 246–47.
[16] Henrik Hertzberg, "Big Boobs: Ed Meese and His Pornography Commission," *New Republic* 195, no. 2–3 (July 14/21, 1986): 23.

he cannot understand. At one point, Ester and Adele arrange to meet at Bomarzo, where Ester confesses her attraction—a feeling that Adele tentatively reciprocates (see fig. 20). The women kiss each other shyly but decide that the consummation of their relationship would be folly, that it is an "impossible love." Ester returns to her house, and when Oscar comes home, he begins to brutalize her, mocking her "inversion" and infidelity. Ester flees to Adele's apartment, and when Oscar sees the women embrace, he comprehends their liaison. He attacks them and, in the raucous chaos that ensues, is stabbed. The police arrive, and Oscar tries to nullify the scandal by claiming that he has injured himself. The film ends with Oscar and Ester going off in an ambulance, as Adele looks on from the street.

At first glance, the film's narrative seems to support a feminist interpretation: the story surfaces woman's lesbian or bisexual impulses and mocks the male denial of them. (One newspaper review of the film, in fact, calls it "A Satirical Look at Italian Men.")[17] But an examination of the film's textual systems and modes of spectator address reveal that this reading is ultimately suppressed. To chart that repression, we might begin by investigating the portrayal of Ester, for the manner in which she is presented will affect our attitude toward her sexual crisis. From the opening moments of the film, she is characterized as an avid film viewer. The credit sequence depicts a television set positioned on a bedroom bureau. On the screen are images from *Casablanca* (1942)—those of Humphrey Bogart and Ingrid Bergman in the final scene, as the airplane is about to leave. The camera pulls back to reveal Ester and Oscar in bed. It is immediately clear that he has contempt for her obsession with the cinema. He calls her an "idiot" for being moved by the melodrama and tries to destroy her pleasure by arguing that Bogart was probably "gay." Ester responds: "Cinema—either you like it or not."

Clearly she does. Elsewhere in the film, references to movies abound, frequently invested with the same kind of sexual innuendo present in the credit sequence. During her first visit to Bomarzo, Ester walks with Adele and describes a dream she had the previous night. She reminds Adele of a scene in *Notorious* (1946) in which Cary Grant and Ingrid Bergman engage in an extended kiss—an embrace that shocked the censors of the era. She confesses that, in her reverie, she enacted the

---

[17] Malcolm L. Johnson, "*Sotto*: A Satirical Look at Italian Men," *Hartford [Connecticut] Courant*, 21 February 1986.

20. *Sotto, Sotto* (1984). Ester (Veronica Lario) and Adele (Luisa de Santis) arrange to meet at Bomarzo, where Ester confesses her attraction.

part of Bergman and that Adele stood in for Cary Grant. This is Ester's first revelation of her attraction to her friend.

Later in the film, she makes reference to other movies. On the night she reveals her "infidelity" to Oscar, she is watching *Picnic* (1955) on television and is annoyed when Oscar interrupts her concentration by repeatedly blocking the screen. After she has confessed her love to Adele, she compares their situation to an ill-fated romance suffered by Gérard Philipe in *Le Diable au Corps* (1947). At another point in her emotional crisis, Ester claims that her hair hurts like that of Monica Vitti in *The Red Desert* (1964). Finally, when she makes known to Oscar her attraction for a woman, she likens their marital strife to *Divorce Italian Style* (1962).

While we have found that other women directors use intertextual cinematic allusions to mark their distance from the mainstream cinema, Wertmuller's references anchor woman in her traditional place— that of gullible, naive, sentimental film viewer—a posture disdained by the director. Ester is not only mocked for her intoxication with these movies, but it is also implied that her obsession with cinema has "caused" her lesbian fantasies. She realizes her feelings for Adele through a dream of *Notorious* and later compares their love to that of characters in a film. Hence, her entire attraction to Adele is likened to a ridiculous screen romance—one in which the actors (like Bogart in

Casablanca) are probably "gay." Ester is a film-era Madame Bovary, who has only "the desire to desire."[18] But Wertmuller's portrayal of her heroine lacks the sympathy of Flaubert's, as well as his sense of the social constraints that she aspires to overcome.

Other aspects of the film trivialize Ester's lesbian impulses, relegating them to the make-believe. Significantly, Ester's first encounter with Adele takes place in Bomarzo, a landscape populated by huge fantastic statues. Furthermore, the style in which the setting is rendered lends it an eerie and magical quality. As the women walk through the woods on the first day of their holiday, an asynchronous sound track provides choral voices. The women promenade among the statuary, while female couples pass by. Finally, they notice two women kissing at a window in a castlelike structure—a sight that awes but disturbs them (especially since the women seem to be their "doubles"). When the women later return to the woods and admit their attraction, Adele tells Esther that the place has "bewitched" them. This sense of lesbianism as sorcery undercuts any serious portrayal of its possibility for women. The Bomarzo sequence also has intimations of *A Midsummer Night's Dream*—an allusion that reduces Adele and Ester's coupling to a comic mix-up.

Though no other locale in the film compares with Bomarzo, many settings seem equally artificial. The section of Rome that Oscar and Ester inhabit is a composite of ruins rather than a credible neighborhood. As one critic put it, the film employs "a dream landscape that now seems to be Imperial Rome, now a provincial village."[19] When Oscar pursues Amilcare (for allegedly having an affair with his wife), he barges into the film studio at which the latter works, playing out his drama of infidelity amid an eighteenth-century background. When he exits the studio and meets Ester on the street, the two wander into a warehouse and discuss their problems amid a bevy of plaster busts. This mise-en-scène lends the drama a synthetic quality—one that underscores the notion of Ester's overactive fantasy life. Thus, in *Sotto, Sotto*, the antirealist aesthetic functions not to liberate woman from her conventional portrayal but to repress her unconventional impulses.

Ester's lesbian attraction is also undercut by the manner in which the narrative resolves her relationship with Adele. The two return to Bomarzo, which is enveloped in a mystical fog. They wander into the

---

[18] Mary Ann Doane, *The Desire to Desire: The Woman's Film of the 1940s* (Bloomington and Indianapolis: Indiana University Press, 1987).

[19] Johnson.

edifice in which they had seen the two women embrace. After an awkward and chaste kiss, they conclude that they have been ridiculous (what fools these mortals be) and joke about eloping to Lesbos. As fast as the attraction has appeared, it disappears, and the possibility of their love is never even entertained. Thus *Sotto, Sotto* is more about the *fantasy* of lesbianism than about lesbianism itself—a subject about which Wertmuller seems uneasy.

The director also shows her hand in the lesser weight she assigns to the female characters. Although the narrative disequilibrium is initiated by Ester's actions (her sudden interest in Adele), the plot focuses almost exclusively on Oscar and his reaction to his wife's behavior. Once again, it is the man's story, with woman functioning only as the cause of his "problem" or as an obstacle to his quest.[20] Although, on one level, Oscar's fixation can be read as a means of attacking machismo—an opportunity to lambast the male for his inability to accept female bisexuality—on another, this emphasis bespeaks Wertmuller's attraction to Oscar, a sense that he is far more engaging than Ester or Adele could ever be. It is Oscar who is always cute, despite his jealous rantings and ravings; it is he who always gets the best mug shots, soliciting the viewer's sympathy and identification. He is, in every respect, a Magnificent Cuckold. Wertmuller's direction of Enrico Montesano parallels her earlier use of Giancarlo Giannini: they are the men she loves to hate. But it is her adoration of them (with all their foibles) that stays with the viewer rather than her critique of their sexual politics.

Various sequences in the film emphasize this narrative imbalance. When Ester confesses to Oscar her interest in another lover, the diegesis abandons her entirely and follows Oscar through a night of debauchery. What ensues is an extended drunk scene—a staple of burlesque comedy. Over and over, we hear Oscar shout that "all women are whores," and we watch his friends try to sober him up. Although it is clear that we are to mock Oscar and reject his view of women, his status as narrative focus makes him rather sympathetic, and despite our reservations, his message is drilled into our brains. At the end of the sequence, Wertmuller craftily "covers" herself by having a passing woman say that men are whores, too. But Oscar's vitriolic charges echo in one's mind.

Oscar is given further opportunity to vent his hostility toward women. When a female tourist wants to look through a telescope (that

[20] Teresa de Lauretis, *Alice Doesn't: Feminism, Semiotics, Cinema* (Bloomington and Indianapolis: Indiana University Press, 1984), 103–57.

he is using to spy on Adele and Ester), he calls her a "tart"; at another point, he rants that all women should be killed at birth; in the final scene (when he understands that Adele is the object of his wife's affections), he asks whether she will grow a mustache, or whether the couple will become "engaged." Oscar is made ridiculous in his prejudices; it is not that they are advanced as reasonable positions. But given the likelihood that the audience harbors identical misconceptions, it is improbable that they will discount Oscar's point of view. We may laugh when Charlie Chaplin bumps into a fat man, and wince at the insensitivity of his act, but that does not mean that the Little Tramp's behavior minimizes our prejudice toward corpulence.

Oscar's violence toward Ester is also viewed as a joke—a comic symptom of his knee-jerk masculinity. When Ester returns to their apartment, he beats her up and says that he will treat her as a whore. When the two run over to Adele's flat, his fight with the women borders on attempted rape, and yet it is seen within a humorous context. Oscar is to be excused because he has been emasculated: it is *his* drama and not theirs. Wertmuller's attempt at levity does not succeed here any better than it did in *Swept Away*. As Modleski has noted, sexual violence may be an inappropriate subject for travesty, "for the would-be satirist must wind up defusing the subject and unwittingly defeating his/her purpose."[21]

In addition to being barraged by Oscar's mockery of lesbianism, the audience is introduced to other gay characters who seem entirely unattractive. Following his attack on Amilcare, Oscar encounters several actors who are having a discussion of homosexuality. They predict that within twenty years, eighty percent of all people will be gay, with a higher proportion being female. One woman brags about how many women she has "had," and in response, Oscar jokes about one's mother "getting it off with one's aunt." When Oscar asks the actress if she found it "disgusting" to embrace another woman, she launches into a lecture about deep kissing. Another reference to homosexuality surfaces in a story about a crazy neighbor who is a transvestite/transsexual—a fate seen as revolting and ridiculous.

Other aspects of the film reveal its masculine bias—particularly the visual presentation of the gorgeous Ester. Veronica Larios bears a striking resemblance to Brigitte Bardot. Modleski has noted that Wertmuller "despises women who are not beautiful."[22] The very first sequence of the film stresses Ester's sexual appearance in a manner con-

[21] Modleski, 1.   [22] Ibid., 16.

258

ventionally associated with the male spectator's position. The camera pulls back from the television screen and in panning to Oscar, passes over her prominent breasts, which overflow the bodice of her night-gown. From that moment on, the camera delights in her sensuous face and full lips, in a manner consonant with the traditional cinematic pre-sentation of woman. Nowhere are these shots associated with female desire (Adele's point of view). Rather, they are linked to the omniscient perspective of the camera, which seems to function as a surrogate for Oscar.

This sense of male mediation is apparent in another sequence. The precise moment Ester realizes her passion for her friend is when she spies on her (through a courtyard window) having intercourse with her estranged husband, Mario. This voyeuristic excitement leads Ester to desire Oscar and to make love to him more passionately than ever be-fore. Thus female desire (albeit homosexual) is inspired by, and ex-pressed through, a man. Symbolically, this economy is summed up in Ester's dream, which casts Adele as a surrogate for Cary Grant.

Woman's sexuality is derided in other ways. When Adele and Ester wander into a church (so that Ester can confess her "perversion"), they mingle with a group of tourists listening to a lecture on the statue of St. Teresa. Although the priest stresses the martyr's "mystical love" for God, we are, clearly, to find her stance ridiculous and are reminded of Jacques Lacan's famous theory that (in Bernini's sculpture) St. Teresa is "coming."[23] Thus woman's *jouissance* is a joke, and her spiritual longings merely displaced, lustful desires.

Sotto, Sotto is a most unstable film. On one level, its comedy de-clares Oscar a buffoon and discredits his prejudices toward lesbianism, but on another register, the work is aligned with him and tacitly vali-dates his perspective. This instability erupts in the final sequence in Oscar's attack on Ester and Adele. The scene is not really funny: he cruelly mocks the women's feelings and assaults them physically and sexually. This is an inappropriate denouement for a comic film, more suitable to a television drama on battered wives. This textual disequi-librium is extended further when Oscar is stabbed and temporarily thought dead. Having let the violence progress this far, Wertmuller does not know how to resolve it. When the police arrive, Oscar tries to minimize the scandal (as does Wertmuller), claiming that he has hurt himself. Although Ester accompanies Oscar to the hospital, Adele

[23] Lacan's thoughts on the statue of St. Teresa are discussed in Stephen Heath, "Dif-ference," *Screen* 19, no. 3 (Autumn 1987): 51–112.

watches the ambulance pull off and exchanges tortured glances with her friend. Wertmuller tries to put a narrative "tourniquet" on the bloodbath by having the sequence end with a feeble joke: Oscar asks Ester whether he will have to bleed to death to recoup her affections. He might as well ask the same question of the female viewer. As one critic put it, if this "doesn't sound like a comedy, that's because there's a violent message to *Sotto, Sotto*. . . . Men throw women around and hit them . . . and in the end, the man gets the woman back."[24]

Curiously, Wertmuller's title for the film is fitting *beyond* the ways she might have intended. It is not only Ester's psychic impulses that are "sotto, sotto" (beneath the surface) but also those of Wertmuller, who has fashioned a work that reveals certain tendencies she might not have wished to disclose. Wertmuller has called *Sotto, Sotto* "an abnormal comedy about sex and sexism"—a statement that reveals the same ideological "slippage" to be found in the film.[25] Clearly, what Wertmuller finds "abnormal" in *Sotto, Sotto* is not its mode of humor but the sexual practice that is the butt of her joke.

Lianna: Ordinary People

John Sayles's *Lianna* offers a strong contrast to the Wertmuller film. While *Sotto, Sotto* denies the existence of lesbianism and slyly circulates pernicious stereotypes about it, *Lianna* attempts realistically (in the manner of *Girlfriends*) to portray sexual love between women, and to see it as a natural rather than an unnatural act.

The film follows the life of Lianna Massey (Linda Griffiths), the thirty-three-year-old wife of a film professor in some unspecified college town. She is the mother of two young children and a rather conventional homemaker. We learn that she married Dick (Jon DeVries) when she was his student, and that she gave up her studies after the wedding. Now she spends her days taking care of the kids, doing volunteer work for a local dance group, and enrolling in miscellaneous college classes. The Masseys are apparently experiencing marital stress because of Dick's infidelities with young coeds. While taking a course on child psychology, taught by Professor Ruth Brennan (Jane Hallaren), Lianna grows attracted to her teacher. One night, after having dinner together at Brennan's house, the women make love and begin a sustained romantic relationship. When Dick returns from a trip,

[24] Eric Stange, "Silly Story Line Ruins *Sotto, Sotto*," *Boston Herald*, 7 February 1986.
[25] Lina Wertmuller, quoted in Eleanor Ringal, "*Sotto, Sotto* Is Much Less Than So-So," *Atlanta Journal*, 14 March 1986.

Lianna confesses her affair and reveals that her paramour is a woman. Dick orders her out of the house and threatens to use her lesbianism as a tool to gain custody of the children. Lianna gets her own apartment and struggles to live alone, to accept her homosexuality, and to deal with her eventual breakup with Ruth. The concluding scene finds her reunited with, and comforted by, her best friend, Sandy (Jo Henderson), a straight woman who had rebuffed Lianna because of her lesbianism. It is clear that their friendship has been renewed.

Superficially, there are certain parallels between *Lianna* and *Sotto, Sotto*. Both focus on the situation of a traditional married woman experiencing her first lesbian affair. Both depict the shocked and hostile reaction of the woman's husband to this unexpected development. Both are laced with self-reflexive references to the cinema. But, ultimately, the films handle the material in opposing ways, and it is in their diverse textual positions that the difference between them resides.

While *Sotto, Sotto* concerns the issue of lesbianism, it focuses on a man's problem in dealing with it, not on a woman's experience. In the Sayles film, the situation is reversed. The narrative tracks Lianna's perception of marital distress and her growing attraction to Ruth. There are even "matching" scenes within the two films that make clear how their perspectives diverge. In the beginning of *Sotto, Sotto*, Wertmuller seems equally intrigued by Ester and Oscar. But from the pivotal moment that Esther reveals her love for a woman, the narrative belongs to Oscar and to his plight as a "wronged man." A parallel vignette occurs in the Sayles film on the night Lianna confesses her affair to Dick. He reacts as sarcastically as Oscar, asking if she has met "the man of [her] dreams." When he learns that her lover is a woman, he states that she has "come a long way from Alberta," then vilifies her for "engaging in an unnatural act." But rather than chart *his* reaction, the narrative remains with Lianna and sketches her response to the changes in her life. From then on, the film adheres rather strictly to a first-person point of view, veering from it only a few times, when we are privy to information that Lianna does not know (when her husband tells her children she is gay; when Sandy and one of Dick's colleagues discuss her homosexuality).

The two films also configure the married woman in different ways. While *Sotto, Sotto* mocks Italian machismo and a husband's sexual egotism and possessiveness, it fails to place marriage within a broader social framework. *Lianna* achieves this more successfully—at least for the small segment of American society it examines: the white, middle-class, academic community. Sayles takes pains to depict the life-style of the male college teacher's spouse—a subject treated earlier in Irwin Kershner's *Up the Sandbox* (1972). In the first scene, Lianna and Sandy meet in the local playground and talk. Sandy (who is also taking the psychology class) mentions her respect for Ruth Brennan and confesses that she would be impressed with any woman "who [wasn't] typing her husband's doctoral thesis." Lianna responds with a sarcastic "Thanks!" recognizing herself in her friend's characterization. Sandy (who is married to the college athletic director) also discusses how she has tutored "the entire [football] defensive line" and jokes about being called "Mrs. Coach."

Later scenes reveal Dick Massey's resentment of Lianna's studies. When she mentions her class, he seizes the opportunity to defame the subject (associated with women) and her instructor as well: "Child psychology's an easy ride. [Professor Brennan] must have gotten into it when it was getting respectable." At another point, he complains that Lianna is now too busy to do research for his writing projects. When she admits that she is not interested in "looking up . . . the clapper boy on the silent version of *A Star Is Born*," he cattily humiliates her, noting that clapboards were used only for sound films. When she claims that taking classes will give her energy, he converts her remark into a sexual come-on, asking: "Do you want to work some of it off with your old man?" In a later episode, Dick is enraged when Lianna chooses to go to class rather than attend a cocktail party that will further his career. When Lianna must look for a job, she meets another female applicant, and they talk about the glut of faculty and graduate student wives on the market. Finally, part of the Masseys' marital difficulties stem from Dick's infidelities with his students—a typical syndrome for an aging male college teacher. Clearly, Lianna's marriage suffers not only from the couple's personal problems but from the stresses of the subordinate social status assigned to traditional academic wives.

The attitude toward men is also divergent in the two films. Although *Sotto, Sotto* critiques Oscar and makes fun of his insensitivity and machismo, it fundamentally adores him, with all his comic quirks. There is no affection, however, in Sayles's treatment of Dick Massey, and little levity either. One might even criticize the film for making him too cruel, too unattractive, too much a cardboard "male chauvinist pig." One might also have reservations about the implication that it is a bad marriage, rather than more neutral circumstances, that hurtles Lianna into homosexuality.

Sayles attempts to balance this ideological position in other portrayals in the film. Although Sandy's jock husband, Bob, is mocked, when we finally meet him, he is a rather likable fellow, far more sympathetic than the intellectual Dick. Bob tells Lianna that her homosexuality does not offend him, and he reveals his empathy for one of his own gay athletic students. Rather than discourage Lianna's contact with his wife, Bob urges the two toward a rapprochement. The portrayal of Dick's colleague Jerry (played by Sayles) is also rather offbeat. He is the closest figure to Oscar, since his masculine failings are treated rather humorously. When we first meet him, he asks Lianna if she is going to a party, and when she replies that she is not, he asks: "Then whom will I corner in the kitchen?" Such lewd innuendos surface again when he visits Lianna in her new dwelling, following her separation from Dick. When he walks in, he asks, salaciously, "if he's interrupting anything." Later, when she describes the morning light in her apartment, he responds: "Good, I'll like that." He then propositions her— a move that Lianna summarily rejects. While Jerry is unsympathetic (though ludicrous in his sexual ego), he is later shown to have rather progressive views. In a conversation with Sandy, he mocks her prejudices about lesbianism and her assumption that it is "catching." And in a subsequent scene, he apologizes to Lianna, saying that his botched seduction was not really a "pick-off attempt."

Most significant, however, is how the films diverge in their portrayal of lesbianism itself. In *Sotto, Sotto*, attitudes toward female homosexuality are expressed either in men's caustic responses to it or in women's fears of it. On only two occasions in *Lianna*, however, do characters refer to lesbianism in a pejorative fashion: when Dick calls it an "unnatural act" (on the night of Lianna's confession), and when her young son (who is striving to be cool) deems his mother a "bull dyke." In the first case, the epithet is a predictable, angry response to a perceived betrayal, and in the second case, it is rather unexpected and amusing. Nowhere in the film do we have the relentless string of aspersions launched in *Sotto, Sotto*. Significantly, it is Lianna herself who utters the most tendentious line—but it is delivered with a sense of pride rather than shame. On the morning after a tryst with a woman she meets in a bar, Lianna awakens and says: "Lianna Massey eats pussy!"

The film is also devoid of the many pernicious clichés that have in-
fected the screen portrayal of lesbians. Ruth Brennan is no devious
seductress, no *femme manquée*: she is a physically attractive professional woman who seems conventionally "feminine" and nice. Lianna
is also beautiful and could have her share of men; there is no sense of
these women turning to each other as a "default" position. Above all,
Ruth and Lianna are ordinary women rather than freaks. Neither expresses regret about her sexual choice or considers herself a social out-
cast. Though Lianna suffers greatly over the failure of her marriage
and the breakup of her affair with Ruth, she has no second thoughts
about her erotic preference.

While Sayles does not denigrate lesbianism, he tempers its idealization. Lianna's love affair with Ruth ends, and she admits harboring the
fantasy that "when [she] found somebody everything would be all
right." Clearly, this is as naive in homosexual as in heterosexual relationships. She also is forced to learn of the constraints of lesbian life:
its deceits and paradoxes. When she embraces Ruth on the street, the
latter cautions against their holding hands. "This is the real world,"
she reminds Lianna. In another scene, the women meet at an indoor
swimming pool (see fig. 21), and Ruth jokes that on the beach they
could "play with tanning lotion." The *Jump Cut* editors had warned
against romanticization, against the "positive image" approach: "Les-

21. *Lianna* (1983). Ruth (Jane Hallaren) jokes with Lianna (Linda
Griffiths) that, on the beach, they could "play with tanning lotion."

bian films cannot be considered outside the context of the lesbian community. Within this community, we face daily contradictions (passing
at work but being out with friends, public oppression versus private
pleasure)."[26]

It is significant that Lianna's first lesbian experience is with a professor, making clear that people frequently repeat old neurotic patterns
in new contexts. As Dick says: "So you're still fucking your teachers."
Later on, Ruth points out Lianna's repetition compulsion, noting that
she has again fallen for someone older and more professionally established than herself. Ruth suggests that Lianna stop functioning as her
research assistant in order to escape a subservient position. In Ruth's
attempt to subvert the dominance/submission model, we perhaps see a
reidealization of lesbianism—the implication that relations between
women will be freer of exploitation than heterosexual ones. One reviewer, for example, criticizes the film for making the women "virtual
saints."[27] This schematic black-and-white contrast (between gay and
straight love) surfaces most fully in a montage sequence toward the
end of the film, when Lianna does lighting for the dance company.
Intercut are scenes of a man and woman dancing and flashbacks of
Lianna and Ruth making love. While the heterosexual ballet seems
strife-ridden and violent (reminiscent of Lianna's marriage), the homosexual encounter seems gentle and supportive.

A refreshing aspect of the film is the manner in which Sayles handles
the scene of Ruth and Lianna's first lovemaking. Rather than stage a
crisis or moment of angst, he portrays their sexual encounter as arising
gradually and easily. Lianna talks with Ruth about occasions when she
was attracted to women—incidents she had dismissed. She mentions
having had an adolescent crush on a female counselor, whom she followed out of the bunk at night (with a friend) to watch her liaisons
with a young man. Lianna recollects how she and her girl friend would
then get into bed together and "reenact" the erotic event. She also recalls her closeness with her mother. What these remembrances accomplish is to imply that most women have had bisexual impulses, whether
or not they are ever actualized.

Sayles choreographs scenes of Ruth and Lianna's lovemaking in a
manner that both breaks and confirms certain cinematic stereotypes.
When Dick learns of Lianna's affair, he cruelly asks her if it was like a

[26] Becker et al., 19–20.
[27] David Baron, "*Lianna*: An Honest Refreshing Look at a Lesbian Affair," [*New
Orleans*] *Times-Picayune*, 28 September 1983.

"drugstore paperback." This is precisely the tone that Sayles avoids. As one reviewer notes, there is "no 'sexploitation' here because lesbianism merely serves as a catalyst for one woman's courageous demand for sensuality and meaningful romantic contact."[28] The erotic scene is realized in a highly aestheticized manner: rendered in a bluish haze, with a set of dreamy dissolves that lead from one sensual tableau to another.

There are, however, certain criticisms that might be made. Although the scene is not sensational, the camera does maintain an external stance that is, by definition, somewhat voyeuristic. (Some lesbian filmmakers, like Barbara Hammer, have tried to solve this problem by taking part in the lovemaking scenes themselves and by giving the camera a more participatory role.)[29] On the other hand, Sayles might be praised for not avoiding an explicit scene, for not deeming it too *risqué*. As the *Jump Cut* editors note: "While lesbian filmmaking is not solely 'a matter of a woman plus a woman in bed,' . . . sexuality cannot, and should not, be avoided."[30]

Sayles's erotic sequence could also be denigrated for being a cinema cliché (with its whispered, voice-over track and idealized images)— "New Wave love"—the legacy of Alain Resnais and Jean-Luc Godard. But in employing the kind of visual strategy generally reserved for heterosexual love, the scene at least conveys a sense of stylistic "equality." Elsewhere in the work, Sayles draws upon other established film conventions (such as the poignant exchange of glances) to mark the women's sexual attraction. While there is no originality in his mode of handling female desire, neither is there a sense of titillation.

In certain sequences, however, "the look" can be said to take on new meaning—and it is here that Sayles achieves a dissonant effect by applying established romantic codes to love between women. In the cinema, the gaze generally belongs to the man; we have seen this in our discussions of *Fatima*, *The Lady from Shanghai*, *Rich and Famous*, *Dames*, and *Sotto, Sotto*.[31] There are certain scenes in *Lianna*, however, that focus on women looking in a radical way. After Ruth and Lianna have been dating awhile, they go to a gay bar. Lianna is at first very self-conscious, worried when she spots a woman from the PTA (oblivious to the implications of *that* woman's being there). Ultimately, Lianna relaxes and enjoys dancing with another woman. Throughout

[28] Dennis Fiely, "Film: A Sensitive Look at Lesbianism," *Columbus [Ohio] Dispatch*, 14 September 1983.

[29] Zita, 28.   [30] Becker et al., 20.

[31] E. Ann Kaplan, "Is the Gaze Male?" in *Women and Film: Both Sides of the Camera* (New York: Methuen, 1983), 23–35.

the scene, Sayles intercuts (in a shot/countershot mode) extreme close-ups of eyes looking—although it is not clear whether they are Lianna's or someone else's. These sequences invert the normal paradigm of men looking at women, but they do not seem to convey the same sense of voyeurism and control. Rather, they connote woman empowered to gaze in a new way. Significantly, the lyrics of the background music say: "Women of the world, you know that you are free."

The next scene extends this issue. A montage of shots depicts Lianna walking down the street to the accompaniment of the film's theme song ("Nevertheless"). As she passes various women, she glances back at them: a lady crossing the street, a mother walking with two kids. As Lianna makes eye contact, we surmise that she wonders about each woman's sexual preference (does she or doesn't she?)—and realizes that certain women she has known have always been gay. Her confusion is rather comical because Ruth had reassured her (after their first lovemaking) that "there's nothing written indelibly on your face." Now Lianna wishes there were.

In *Sotto, Sotto*, intratextual and self-reflexive elements functioned in an ideologically conservative manner around the question of woman. *Lianna* makes an interesting match for the Wertmuller work because it, too, has many filmic references. Dick Massey (the most unsympathetic character in the narrative) is a film professor. And Sayles casts himself (the director/screenwriter) as the most blatant male chauvinist of the lot. Throughout the drama, various aspects of cinema are mocked: at a faculty party, the students who are filming it collide with their cameras; before Dick leaves for a film festival, he says he will need aspirin to get through the Eastern European contingent. These references seem to be ironic in jokes, without major implications for the theme of the work. Certain self-conscious episodes, however, do impinge on the subject of the text.

At one dinner-table conversation, Dick tells Lianna about his class and how his students champion the purity of documentary form and critique Robert Flaherty for his control. Dick retorts that he "wanted to shake the bastards up a little." At a cocktail party, one of Dick's students corners Lianna and lectures her about how cinema is "more than reality." Given that Sayles's style in the film is classic realism (rather than Wertmuller's hyperbolic anti-illusionism), these remarks make us consider the problematic aspects of his form: our tendency to view the narrative as "real life," its characters as "ordinary people" rather than fictive constructs. On reflection, we realize that *Lianna* seems a little *too* pat to be true: Lianna's painless "coming out" into lesbianism, her piggish husband who deserves to be abandoned, her supportive feminist lover, her straight girl friend who accepts Lianna's homosexuality. Such a scenario does not necessarily occur in everyday life, and *Lianna* has the verisimilitude of *Nanook of the North* (1920–21).

At other points in the film, Sayles's reflexivity takes the form of references to other movies or film personae. At the supper table, the Masseys' son, Spencer (Jesse Solomon), asks to be excused to watch a film on television, William Wellman's *Battleground* (1949). As Lianna and her daughter, Theda (Jessica Wight MacDonald), finish their meal, the sound of military fighting wafts into the dining room. Spencer watches the film a second time, along with a Japanese horror flick. At another point, Dick sarcastically relates that his best graduate student is doing a thesis on Audie Murphy. When Lianna runs into this woman at a cocktail party, the student waxes poetic about Murphy as the "perfect tragic hero."

From these various allusions, we have a sense of the cinema as a decidedly *male* preserve (war and horror films, a soldier as quintessential protagonist). Significantly, Theda does not want to watch *Battleground* with her brother but remains in the dining room as Lianna brushes her hair. The Massey children are obviously named for screen personalities (Tracy and Bara). Whereas the male actor honored has a wholesome aura, the actress celebrated is a dangerous vamp.

The film also engages references to spectatorship. When Lianna is seen viewing television (either a soap opera or TV movie), there are negative connotations. She sits in bed watching, with the set in the foreground (a direct parallel to the opening scene of Wertmuller's film). On the sound track, we hear voices spouting lines from a typical melodrama: "I have to stand by her; she's my wife." While Ester, in *Sotto, Sotto*, was enthralled by such theatrics, Lianna seems apathetic; and this scene occurs in a sequence chronicling her momentary retreat and depression; she even compulsively eats potato chips as she watches. While Ester is the "typical" vulnerable female viewer, hooked on impossible movie dreams, Lianna finds the cinema a simple irrelevance, be it macho films or women's weepies. When neighbors ask her to accompany them to a screening of *The Magnificent Ambersons* (1942), she declines, knowing that it is her husband's turf.

Clearly, Sayles is trying to make a new kind of film in *Lianna* that speaks to, and about, women. It is this (and not the practice of lesbianism) that has been, for Wertmuller, the truly "impossible dream."

9 Murder, She Wrote: Women Who Kill

Introduction

*The female of the species is more deadly
than the male.* —*Rudyard Kipling*[1]

One of the classic stereotypes in the cinema is the femme fatale, the "deadly woman." In general, this epithet is meant metaphorically. The female in question is not necessarily one who kills but one who "ruins" men, hence establishing an equation between the loss of male ego and death. Among the members of this sorority are Lola Lola in *The Blue Angel* (1930) and The City Woman in *Sunrise* (1927). The two characterizations occasionally overlap, as they do with Elsa Bannister.

But what of the figure of the outright murderess? How has she been viewed within contemporary culture? In reading the literature, it becomes clear that the female killer has been deemed *more* perverse than the male, for she violates obtaining views of woman as life giver and nurturer—figurations that do not apply to men. Jane Totman writes: "[O]n the behavior scale from evil-doing to humanitarianism, women are seen to weigh heavily on both ends. . . . Women, when they take to crime are seen to be 'worse' than men."[2] Similarly, Eileen Leonard notes that murderesses are thought to be "more vicious and dangerous than their male counterparts."[3] Though considered more pernicious than men, female killers are also seen to display "masculine" tendencies, both in their behavior and their physical attributes. Cesare Lombroso found, in 1893, that all "female criminals approximate more to males . . . than to normal women, especially in the superciliary arches in the seam of the sutures, in the lower jaw-bones, and in peculiarities of the occipital region."[4]

Other clichés have circulated about the female offender—conceptions that reveal malign assumptions about women. Otto Pollak, a

[1] Rudyard Kipling, quoted in Richard Deming, *Women: The New Criminals* (Nashville, Tenn., and New York: Thomas Nelson), 27.

[2] Jane Totman, *The Murderess: A Psychological Study of Criminal Homicide* (San Francisco: R and E Research Associates, 1978), 8–9.

[3] Eileen Leonard, *Women, Crime and Society* (New York and London: Longman, 1982), 2.

[4] Cesare Lombroso, quoted in Ann Jones, *Women Who Kill* (New York: Holt, Rinehart and Winston, 1980), 6.

269

criminologist writing in the 1950s, believed that women committed crimes more frequently than supposed, but that their felonies went undetected. He called this phenomenon the "masked character of female crime."[5] Pollak trotted out a host of misconceptions about women to explain these hidden transgressions. He claimed, for example, that females were secretive in their sexual affairs, which primed them for deceit in legal matters:

> [W]oman's physiological make-up permits successful concealment of her true feeling in the important sphere of sex relations, while the male in this respect is biologically forced to show the true state of his feelings. It cannot be categorically denied that this differential experience may well result in a greater degree of confidence in successful misrepresentation on the part of woman.[6]

Women's capacity to "fake" orgasm has been blamed for many things but never before seen as paving the road to crime!

Elsewhere, Pollak mentions woman's tendency to hide her menstrual period as another example of how femininity is correlated with deceit.[7] But Pollak indicts woman's complete biological makeup as predisposing her to criminality:

> Actually . . . menstruation, pregnancy and the menopause have to be considered of central research interest. . . . The student of female criminality cannot afford to overlook the generally known and recognized fact that these generative phases are frequently accompanied by psychological disturbances which may . . . become causative factors in female crime.[8]

Modern medicine has indeed found a correlation between female violence and the premenstrual period, but Pollak would incriminate woman's entire life cycle!

Pollak offers another explanation for the "masked character of female crime"—chivalry on the part of victims and law enforcers: "Men hate to accuse women and thus indirectly to send them to their punishment, police officers dislike to arrest them, district attorneys to prosecute them, judges and juries to find them guilty, and so on."[9] Hence, according to Pollak, women frequently get away scot free.

[5] Otto Pollak, in Freda Adler and Rita James Simon, *The Criminology of Deviant Women* (Boston: Houghton Mifflin, 1979), 37–44.

[6] Ibid., 38.   [7] Pollak, in Leonard, 4.   [8] Pollak, in Adler and Simon, 41–42.

[9] Otto Pollak, *The Criminality of Women* (Philadelphia: University of Pennsylvania Press, 1950), 151.

270

Pollak's claims have been questioned by other criminologists. Dorie Klein notes that the females most likely to commit crimes are poor, third-world, or marginal white middle-class women, and for these individuals, favors are not extended[10]:

> Chivalry is a racist and classist concept and founded on the notion of women as "ladies" which applies only to wealthy white women and ignores the sexual double standard. These "ladies," however, are the least likely women to ever come in contact with the criminal justice system in the first place.[11]

Finally, Pollak finds that woman's role as a homemaker has provided her with numerous opportunities for murder and has assured that her family homicides will go unpunished:

> Woman's task of preparing food for the members of the family has made her the poisoner par excellence, and her function in nursing the sick has had a similar effect. The helplessness of children as victims of crime has brought within her realm a group of victims least equipped to put up any resistance against criminal attacks and practically unable to enlist the help of the law for purposes of prosecution.[12]

Thus woman is damned if she does and if she doesn't. On the one hand, Lombroso sees her deviant "manliness" as the root of her criminality. On the other, Pollak finds that, in her "feminine" domestic position, she faces endless temptations to transgress. Furthermore, woman's criminal nature has been associated with her biology, as though there were a natural correlation between two "X" chromosomes and a tendency toward crime.

Theorists have also suppressed any social reading of female crime, preferring to focus on woman's "essential" being or on isolated cases of "deviance." As Leonard notes:

> Female patterns of crime are generally viewed as emerging from individual female characteristics that are, unfortunately, all too familiar. Women are jealous, revengeful and sneaky; they love to gossip, they cannot be trusted, they instigate crime. These traits might be influenced by social conditions, but the impression is unmistakable: more than social conditions are at work. Men would not act this way.[13]

---

[10] Dorie Klein, "The Etiology of Female Crime," in Adler and Simon, 75.
[11] Ibid.   [12] Pollak, in Adler and Simon, 39.   [13] Leonard, 15

Clearly, misconceptions have been formulated about the murderess—errors that reflect more fundamental attitudes toward the female sex. In this respect, we must concur with Ann Jones when she states: "The story of women who kill is the story of [all] women."[14]

In this chapter, we will probe the issue through an examination of two films: Claude Chabrol's *Violette* (made in France in 1978) and Marleen Gorris's *A Question of Silence* (*Stilte Ronde Christine M.*) made in Holland in 1981. While the former film conforms to traditional views of the femme fatale, the latter does not, offering a feminist perspective on the subject.

Violette: Mourning Becomes Electra

> *I fell in love with Violette Nozière long before I understood her. Many before me have been taken by her: Eluard, Aragon, Magritte, Simone de Beauvoir, Pierre Brasseur. In trying to revive her, I felt the fascination of her ambiguities: murderer and saint, liar and faithful woman, childish yet ingenious. I had to tear at her ghost, peel away at her dreams, go through her everyday life. . . . I didn't wish to judge her but to understand her. —Claude Chabrol[15]*

Claude Chabrol's *Violette* is based on an event in the annals of crime that occurred in France in 1933. An eighteen-year-old girl, Violette Nozière, poisoned her parents. Her stepfather died, but her mother survived to press charges against her. At the trial, Violette was condemned to death by guillotine, despite a clemency appeal by her mother, who had finally forgiven her. In many respects, the Nozière case delineates a classic female crime: murder by poisoning and family violence. As theorists have noted, women more frequently kill their intimates.[16]

The Nozière incident struck a responsive chord in French society and became both a scandal and a cause célèbre (much like the case of Lizzie Borden in turn-of-the-century America). For surrealists (like Paul Eluard), the young woman stood as a symbol of rebellion against bourgeois existence—a view immortalized in his poem "Violette Nozière's Complaint":

> She will poison her parents
> The cruel Violette Nozière

[14] Jones, xvi.   [15] Chabrol, quoted in Gaumont Press book for *Violette*.
[16] Jones, xv–xvi.

Laughing at their miseries
Taking their money
Without pity for the white hair
Of those who gave her life
This wandering sow
Will commit a monstrous crime.[17]

For feminists (who seized upon Violette's claims of paternal rape), she was an emblem of resistance to patriarchy. For others, she was merely a sordid (but compelling) tabloid star.

The question, however, is not so much what Violette represented to her contemporaries as what she means to Claude Chabrol, who "revives" her in his cinematic work. How does he read her as a social "text"? What is it that fascinates him about this "skirted terror"? Does he achieve his goal of "understanding" rather than "judging" her? It will not be simple to answer these queries because *Violette* presents itself as a militantly ambiguous work, one that, ostensibly, reflects the contradictions of its subject. However, the film's semiotic uncertainty is something of a sham—as illusory as the fantasies projected by Nozière herself.

A sense of ambivalence informs the initial image of the film, which functions as a backdrop for the credits. A long shot depicts a gate leading to the Nozière apartment courtyard. Imperceptibly, the camera tracks in and, by the end of the shot, moves through the bars. Two readings of the image are possible. On one level, it seems to presage Violette's eventual incarceration and indicate her possible guilt. On another level, however, it portrays her bourgeois home as prison—a fact that would explain or justify her crime. This textual duality is registered within the shifting focus of the shot. At first, the gate is clearly imaged and the building blurry; by the end of the shot, the figure/ground clarity has been reversed. This continual change of perspective operates on a hermeneutic level within the film, keeping the viewer perennially off-balance in the act of reading Violette.

In certain ways, Chabrol visualizes Violette as the traditional femme fatale, reflecting the press's view of her. As criminologist Florence Monahan has noted: "To newspaper readers and avid consumers of the stuff served up in detective and confession stories about female criminals, they are exciting creatures known as 'The Sphinx Woman,' 'The Tiger Murderess,' 'The Hammer Slayer,' 'The Coma Woman,'

[17] Paul Eluard, "Violette Nozière's Complaint," trans. Tiffany Fliss, in Gaumont Press Book.

273

'The Twentieth Century Borgia.' "[18] In the credit sequence, Violette leaves her house at night (like Nosferatu emerging from his coffin). She is clothed in a black fur coat, with a dark hat angled over her eyes—an outfit she will wear repeatedly. In other sequences, we witness Violette dressing herself in this garb in the communal bathroom in which she hides the costume from her trusting parents. Likewise, we later see, in Violette's hotel room, a photograph of Bette Davis in *Jezebel* (1938), which she has tacked to her mirror as iconic role model. Hence, her cultivation of a vampish *image* is at issue here, which calls into question the film's appropriation of that stereotype. Does the femme fatale represent a schema that the film uncritically projects upon Violette Nozière, or merely the latter's clichéd sense of herself?

This ambiguity is registered in the visual discourse of the film. We frequently think we see certain characters "directly," only to find that we are looking at mirror images of them. In one scene, as Violette climbs the stairs of the Hôtel de la Sorbonne (a place where she trysts with lovers), we find retroactively that we have been viewing a reflection of her. Elsewhere, characters are visibly framed in mirrors: Violette primping in the apartment bathroom or making love in her hotel bed. On the one hand, Chabrol's visual style calls attention to the problematic aspects of imaging Violette—of obtaining direct access to the "truth" of her existence. On the other hand, his strategy makes us wary of his own mediation in configuring a portrait of his heroine.

The very form of the film bespeaks contradictions. In describing his protagonist, Chabrol has said:

> The attempt to delve into Violette's soul is bound to fail. If psychology consists of explaining human beings, then *Violette* is not a psychological film. Her character remains opaque, inexplicable. . . . It doesn't displease me that in the final count, *Violette* is a film about the impossibility of penetrating the human psyche.[19]

We see evidence of Chabrol's view translated into the performance style of Isabelle Huppert, who plays Violette with a dense, catatonic veneer that advances a sense of her opacity. She is posited as an Archetypal Enigma, like the elusive Elsa Bannister.

But the film's narrative structure works at cross purposes to that conception. Much of the work is realized from Violette's point of view,

[18] Florence Monahan, *Women in Crime* (New York: Ives Washburn, 1941), 260.
[19] Claude Chabrol, in Dan Yakir, "Innocents with Dirty Hands: Claude Chabrol on Violence and *Violette*," *Village Voice*, 23 October 1978, 67.

organized around memories, fantasies, and dreams. In the very first sequence, Violette sneaks out of her apartment and boards a bus. In a flashback during the ride, she remembers an encounter with her girl friend in a bar. When we see Violette again mount the stairs of her building, we assume that the narrative has taken us forward in time to the next day. Only much later do we realize that most of the tale has been told in reverse order, and that the opening scene of the film occurs after she has already poisoned her parents. Thus a large part of the narrative is told as her mental recollection. The story "catches up" with itself only when we see her return to her apartment and drag her parents' bodies into another room. From this point on, the narrative moves ahead to the time of her trial and conviction.

Beyond the flashback structure, there are various scenes that represent her visions or remembrances—that "peel away at her dreams," as Chabrol had promised. When she lies in bed at the Hôtel de la Sorbonne, the screen blurs and we see two consecutive images: the ocean and a young man approaching the camera. We then cut back to the dozing Violette. She has had an oneiric episode and has envisioned Jean Dabin (Jean-François Garreaud), a lover she has yet to meet. At other times, the film screen becomes hazy and we see images from her childhood: scenes with her grandmother in the country, vignettes of her waving good-bye to her engineer stepfather at the train station. At one point, we even enter her mind at the moment of fainting. Violette and her mother (Stéphane Audran) have argued when her parents learn that she has syphilis. Violette goes downstairs to the communal bathroom, and suddenly the image becomes distorted. What follows is a shot of Violette and her mother quarreling, and then the image blacks out. In the darkness, we hear a thump; when the picture resumes, we see Violette's stepfather (Jean Carmet) pick her up from the lavatory floor. All of these sequences promise entry to Violette's consciousness at the same time that Chabrol declares the impossibility of that pursuit. What a curious narrative structure to choose for a study that posits the elusiveness of the human mind. Few critics have realized that although Chabrol renders the story from Violette's perspective, it does not speak her point of view. An exception is Stanley Kauffmann, who remarks: "We are not made to feel *with* Violette so that we participate in her acts."[20]

In truth, Violette's psyche is not as illegible as Chabrol asserts, and despite his disclaimers, the film presents a rather coherent picture of

[20] Stanley Kauffmann, [Review], *New Republic*, 14 October 1978, 24.

her tendencies and motivations. His portrayal conforms to certain stereotypes of the female criminal that link her deviance to sexuality or insanity. This view of Violette precludes any social reading of her crime, any sense of her as a feminist "heroine." Essentially, the text positions her (through the device of her own memories) as a maladjusted young woman who has not accepted the fact of sexuality—in her parents or in herself. In particular, it configures her as suffering an *Electral* malaise, fixated on her stepfather and hostile to her mother-rival. Several registers of the film urge us to accept this interpretation.

In our first introduction to Violette's apartment, one item is so prominent in the mise-en-scène that it elicits laughs from the audience: her mother's bridal picture, which sits on a table near the entrance. At first we regard this simply as an emblem of bourgeois social arrangements, but it comes to have deeper implications. During the first sequence of Violette at home, we find her engaged in an adolescent re-creation of the primal scene. The film intercuts shots of Violette in bed (awake and listening) and images of her parents in their room, looking at erotic drawings and having intercourse. The presentation of their lovemaking is hardly idealized: the mother seems reluctant, the stepfather insistent; their cramped living quarters make the mother nervous that Violette will overhear. She asks, "Suppose she wakes up?" and the stepfather replies, "She knows a husband and a wife. . . ." (his voice trailing off). In the next shot, we see Violette stuffing her bed with clothes (to give the illusion of her presence) and sneaking off into the night. She sits outside on a bench and is picked up by a man in a car. When he tries to embrace her, she pulls away; he throws her out of the car, shouting "hussy" and "bitch." We are already led to believe that she rejects the sexual nature of her parents' relationship and compensates for this with a grim, conflicted promiscuity.

Other aspects of the film support the likelihood that she suffers from an Electral syndrome. We learn quite early that she claims her stepfather rapes her: two young men discuss the matter in a bar while eyeing Violette and her friend, Maddy (Lisa Langlois). Yet we never see any evidence of this. On a few occasions, her stepfather kisses her rather emphatically or lingers a bit too long in an embrace, but this is all we can say of his advances. We do see Violette recoil from his physical affection, but this gesture is typical of a teenaged girl. In general, he is an indulgent, loving stepparent whose worst crime is an occasional desirous glance toward his pubescent child. In one of the investigation scenes, following his death, we have strong evidence that she is lying about his sexual overtures. In the "primal scene" sequence, we saw her stepfather use a cloth as a contraceptive device while making love with his wife. During the inquiry, this towel is exhibited by a police detective who reveals Violette's charge that her stepfather used it with her. It is not impossible that he did so (in an episode to which the audience is not privy), but this seems highly unlikely. Our impulse is simply to discount her claims. In classic Freudian psychology, the female Oedipal complex specifically involves the fantasy of having a child by the father, a means ostensibly of compensating for the girl's sense of phallic lack. It is not hard to see Violette's rape fantasy as a convolution of this—a fact that seems implied in Chabrol's view of her assertions.[21]

Perhaps the most damning evidence of Violette's Electral problems comes through her own memories. On several occasions, she recalls scenes from her childhood: in a recurrent reverie, she happily waves good-bye to her engineer stepfather, who departs on a train. On another occasion, she recollects being bounced on his knee—a scene marred by her mother's displeasure. She also remembers spying on her parents while they made love and being slapped on the face by her mother for her voyeurism. Finally, she envisions a scene at her grandmother's house in the country, in which she asks her to reveal some secret involving Violette's parents. What these memory traces indicate is a young girl attached to her stepfather, perceiving her mother as a punishing rival—a child who wishes to learn (but cannot accept) the mystery of adult sexuality. We are urged to conclude that Violette has unconsciously inverted her true feelings, believing that she loathes her stepfather and loves her mother, while the opposite is closer to the truth. As though to seal the connection between past and present, we are often aware of train sounds in the background at her crowded apartment—noises that take us back to the idyllic image of her waving good-bye to her stepfather. It is clear from their mythologically derived names that the Oedipal and Electral complexes involve thoughts of murder. In describing this childhood stage, Jung specifically makes the point:

> Children are small primitive creatures and are therefore quickly ready to kill—a thought which is all the easier in the unconscious, because the unconscious is wont to express itself very dramatically. But as a child is, in general, harmless, this seem-

[21] See Robert L. Watson, *The Great Psychologists* (Philadelphia and New York: J. B. Lippincott, 1963), 452.

ingly dangerous wish is as a rule harmless too. I say "as a rule" for we know that children can occasionally give way to their murderous impulses, not only indirectly, but in quite direct fashion.[22]

Chabrol's Violette is one exception to the rule: an adolescent who literalizes an infantile wish.

Several other moments in the film support this interpretation. While in prison, she awakens from a nightmare and tells her cell mate that she dreamed she had ruined her mother's life. Given Violette's knowledge that she is an illegitimate child (whose birth father deserted the family), her response toward her mother would be riddled with guilt as well as hostility for having to accommodate those feelings. Furthermore, if her stepfather seems unavailable to her (because he is the mate of her mother), this sense of exclusion would be exacerbated by the fact that her real father rejected her. As an adolescent, she makes contact with the man, a prominent socialist leader, and blackmails him for the money she requires to support her underground life-style.

Her Electral complex would also seem to explain her love/hate relations with men. On the one hand, Violette is tremendously cynical and promiscuous, treating men cruelly at the moment of seduction. In one of the first scenes, she approaches a young student in a bar and boldly props her leg up on his table. This gesture is not so much a come-on as an assault. On the other hand, she is romantically fixated on Jean Dabin, whom she loves heedlessly and naively. In fact, she attempts to murder her parents in order to steal funds to support his dissipated life. She also showers him with the cash she obtains from her birth father—clearly an effort to regain the elusive male affection.

Thus Chabrol's reading of the text of Violette Nozière posits her as an insane young woman who is acting out her Electral fantasies—her psychosexual maladjustment. Toward the end of the film, she seems to slip into madness altogether, as we see her enter a bathhouse and take a shower fully clothed. There is no validation of the claims of parental rape, no evidence that her act might have been one of protest over patriarchal power. As Stanley Kauffmann puts it, "She is not 'placed' so that we can see her as a product of contemporary disorders."[23] This Violette is simply a bad seed who grows into a predatory and mutant organism. During the film, when Violette overhears students at a bar

[22] Carl Jung, in *The Collected Work of C. G. Jung*, trans. R.F.C. Hull, Vol. 4/Bollingen Series xx (New York: Pantheon, 1961), 152.
[23] Kauffmann, 24.

talk of politics, she says "it's a bore." One has the sense that this statement speaks for Chabrol, too—through a psychological model, he frames out all social implications of her act.

There are other ways in which Chabrol contains and negates her rebellion while simultaneously delineating the causes that might have justified it. He presents a bleak picture of bourgeois existence. All the scenes of Violette's home characterize it as claustrophobic and imprisoning. When she mounts her apartment-house stairs, we often see her through the bars of the balustrade—a trope that places her within a restrictive context. Shots of Violette in the hallway, approaching her front door, emphasize the narrow corridor that engulfs her from either side. The environment is cramped not only on a spatial but on a psychological level. In one scene, we see Violette bathing her breasts at a washstand, while her stepfather, who is talking with her, tries to avert his eyes (see fig. 22). Chabrol emphasizes this incestuous tension by placing them within the same frame. It is also clear that her parents' marriage is based on a lie. Although we view Madame Nozière's bridal portrait, we know that Violette is illegitimate—a fact her mother seems to have hidden from her husband. Violette's existence—which is based on dissembling—seems to mirror her mother's, as her promiscuity mocks her parents' narrow morality. Even the Nozières' neighbors seem unattractive: at a dinner party, a man talks proudly of having gassed people during the war. Finally, during her trial, a shot/countershot sequence ensues of Violette looking at her all-male jury. She calls them "bastards"—an epithet that condemns herself. Given this view of her middle-class milieu, we can understand why the surrealists perceived her as a spokeswoman for human liberation.

Despite this portrayal of Violette's social suffocation, Chabrol does not make us empathize with her plight. He constructs the film so that the viewer's sympathies are with the parents, despite the fact that they are ridiculous and pathetic fools. (Jung claims, for example, that in their denial of Oedipal conflicts, "parents, like lovers, are mostly blind.")[24] Though we are to believe that Violette's stepfather rapes her, we see no evidence of this. Instead we find indications of his sexual interest in his wife. Despite the fact that Violette continually steals from her parents, we see no hints that they are stingy with her. Chabrol even emphasizes the vampire-like nature of her thievery by framing a shot of her parents sleeping, with Violette pillaging a nightstand in the background. The same composition is used in a shot of Nozière drink-

[24] Jung, 153.

279

22. *Violette* (1978). Violette (Isabelle Huppert) bathes her breasts while her stepfather (Jean Carmet) tries to avert his eyes.

ing the fatal poison: he is depicted in a foreground profile, while Violette regards him from behind; we marvel at her distanced composure.

Chabrol's denouement also closes down any social reading of Violette's act—a perspective he has taken pains to assemble. As she sits in her prison cell (humming the popular song about her), a male voice-over is heard cataloging the events of her later life. The death penalty will be commuted to a life sentence of hard labor. After several years of exemplary behavior, her term will be reduced to twelve years. She will then be fully pardoned by De Gaulle and will marry the prison clerk. Her civil rights will eventually be restored. Given that her birth father is a prominent socialist minister, these developments do not surprise us and may have nothing to do with her innocence or guilt.

Chabrol's own testimony makes it clear that he sees her fate as nullifying any liberating aspects of her vengeful act:

> It's an ironical situation really: Violette poisons her father because he has them all crowded together in a little apartment that is too small for her spirit. So what happens? She ends up in a prison cell, which is smaller still, but she doesn't feel imprisoned there. I did a lot of research and I know for a fact that Violette was happy in prison. She liked it. And later she married and had five children, lived in a small provincial town where she ran a

restaurant . . . and led exactly the *petit bourgeois* life she had killed.[25]

Hence, the life of Violette Nozière is essentially a sardonic joke, an exercise in futility—a view implied by the male narrator's voice that ends this woman's story—like the blade of a guillotine. For Chabrol, her aspirations are also banal. In one interview, he states that she is "tragic and ridiculous,"[26] and elsewhere that she "is no Shakespeare"[27]:

> [She] is not a very intelligent person even though she is a genius at lying. Her immediate aspirations are silly: to go to the sea-shore in a Bugatti and find money for her sad lover. . . . In my opinion, if she chooses her crime, it's because she is not suffi-ciently imaginative, nor does she have enough potential equilib-rium to create a world of her own. She's no artist: she can't paint, write or make music.

Finally, he imagines that if she had been alive in 1968, she would not have been part of the social revolution but would have been "home watching television."[28] The only skill Chabrol will grant Violette is that she is a "genius at lying"—a fact that reflects Pollak's characteri-zation of woman as a mistress of deceit. There is also clear condescen-sion in Chabrol's voice for this pathetic female consumer of popular culture who must kill because she is a creator *manquée*. Chabrol, how-ever, is not; and he subsumes her lack of imagination within his own more potent vision.

Yet, despite Chabrol's negative view of Violette, he "fell in love" with his heroine—was "taken by" her like countless male intellectuals before him. Why does such a figure attract men at their own apparent risk? Why (as Claudette Charbonneau and Lucy Winer inquire) "is Chabrol drawn to a tale which is bound to be so profoundly reaction-ary?"[29]

On one level, Violette's appeal is that she fulfills the male desire to flirt with danger, to confront their worst fears about the female sex.

---

[25] Claude Chabrol, in Diane Jacobs, "A Little Bit Puritanical," *Soho Weekly News*, 19 October 1978, 37. The issue of Chabrol's negation of Violette's rebellion is discussed in Claudette Charbonneau and Lucy Winer, "*Violette*: Skilled, Delicate, Pernicious," *Jump Cut*, no. 21 (November 1979): 6–7.

[26] Chabrol, in Yakir, 67. [27] Chabrol, in Jacobs, 38.

[28] The first quote from Chabrol is in Yakir, 67; the second Chabrol quote is in Jacobs, 38.

[29] Charbonneau and Winer, 7.

On the other hand, she is amply punished for her crime: through incarceration and the sheer futility of her act. Furthermore, she is entirely male centered, tied to her two fathers and to the men who replay their traumatic role in her life. Though she challenges the middle class, she does not challenge *patriarchy* but merely offers a bizarre response to it.

The love/hate emotion that Violette allegedly feels toward men is doubled in their experience of her. They see her as both "murderer and saint, liar and faithful woman." This mystical duality is encapsulated in the two photographs displayed on Violette's hotel mirror: of Lillian Gish and Bette Davis, the virgin and the whore. But in her status as Mystery, Violette is also (like Elsa Bannister) woman as archetypal ambivalent text.

Despite Chabrol's apparent cultivation of a contradictory discourse, his film lacks the ambiguity that he seeks, or ascribes to his heroine's behavior. The text dissembles as does Violette, concealing its tendentiousness with an air of duplicitous detachment. Thus it is not so much Violette's crime that has a "masked character" but Chabrol's rendition of it. Despite his goal of "understanding" Violette, he unwittingly judges her—and from his verdict, she receives no pardon.

A Question of Silence: Ritual in Transfigured Time

> [W]hen women concretize their modes of seeing, the result is
> very vehement, very violent . . . this violence manifests itself
> differently than it does with men. Women's violence is not
> commercial; it is beyond description. —Chantal Akerman[30]

In her essay on misogyny and the female offender, Meda Chesney Lind charts the long lineage of myths concerning female rebellion and points to the character of Lilith as an early embodiment of such tendencies. According to Hebraic tradition, Lilith was created as Adam's first wife:

> More independent than Eve, she objected when Adam said she
> must obey him. Saying: "We are equal. We are made of the
> same earth," she, according to legend, flew up in the air and

---

[30] Chantal Akerman, quoted in Silvia Bovenschen, "Is There a Feminine Aesthetic?" *New German Critique*, no. 10 (Winter 1977): 123. From Claudia Aleman, *Frauen Und Film* 7 (March 1976).

became a night demon who ate children and seduced men in their sleep.[31]

For Lind, a similar folklore has attached to the female criminal, another rebel who is seen as monstrous. She writes: "The fear of defiant women is as old as the history of male domination and has necessitated the creation of . . . figures . . . to serve as warnings to all women that those who defy male authority suffer ignominious consequences."[32] Not only does the defiant woman inspire fear in the male public, she encourages obedience in the female citizenry—perhaps a more important goal of her formulation. In *A Question of Silence*, filmmaker Marleen Gorris confronts head-on this mythification of the woman criminal, bending the process to her own feminist purposes. While legends (like that of Lilith) caution women against insurrection, Gorris's contemporary tale radically reorients the target of that admonition: it no longer warns women against their own defiance, but men against the rebellion of women.

Like *Violette*, *A Question of Silence* concerns a shocking murder—one based on fact. Three women who have never before met show up one day in the same boutique. When one is caught shoplifting by the store manager, the others rally to her support, and they collectively slaughter him—without any apparent forethought or added motive. The film chronicles their arrest by the police and their examination by a female court psychiatrist. Like *Violette*, the narrative is rendered in flashback, beginning with the women's incarceration and regressing to the day of the crime. Like *Violette*, the story also progresses to the women's trial. But the attitude expressed toward the female killer is very different in the Gorris film; the Dutch director refashions the murder-movie genre to create a "feminist thriller."[33]

In many respects, *A Question* counters established notions of the female offender that circulated in *Violette*. While most theorists have noted that women generally kill in domestic settings, *A Question* places the act in a quintessentially public space, a shopping mall. Furthermore, the victim is a total stranger to the women, not an intimate or a loved one. The extraordinary nature of their crime is underscored

[31] Meda Chesney Lind, "Re-Discovering Lilith: Misogyny and the 'New' Female Criminal," in Curt Taylor Griffiths and Margit Nance, *The Female Offender* (Burnaby, British Columbia: Criminology Research Center, Simon Fraser University, 1980), 1.
[32] Ibid.
[33] The term was used by Peter Stack in a review "Three Women Who Murder a Man on the Spot," *San Francisco Chronicle*, 21 October 1983.

by the words of criminologists who write: "Unlike male violent offenders, the victims of women rarely includ[e] store keepers . . . or
others slain or assaulted in the course of committing robberies and
burglaries."[34]

While theorists like Pollak had decried the "masked character of female crime," in *A Question* the transgressive act is overt. The three
women murder in the full light of day before witnesses—other patrons
of the shop. Furthermore, none of them denies the crime when pursued
by the police or questioned by the doctor. The psychiatrist, in fact, calls
one of the women "ruthlessly honest." Instead of employing the secretive tool of poison, the women use the obvious weapons at hand: plastic coat hangers, glass shelves, shopping carts. A male detective who
comments on the case clearly misunderstands their truthfulness. He
tells the psychiatrist: "It's an open and shut case; they didn't deny anything. They weren't very clever; if they'd wanted to get rid of someone
they should have done it professionally."

The circumstances of their crime also oppose the coveted notion that
masculine chivalry shields women from punishment. In *A Question*,
the male police officers, detectives, and lawyers, seem anxious to cap-
ture and convict the women. In this regard, one is reminded of an early
American primitive film, *Photographing a Female Crook* (1904), in
which several policemen drag a woman into a room for a mug shot
and brutally restrain her. As the camera tracks in, she sneers at the lens,
refusing to mask her hostility. It is this scenario that erupts decades
later in *A Question*—in both the men's violence and the women's rebellion. If any acts of chivalry are sustained in this narrative, they are
perpetrated by the *female* boutique customers, who refuse to be witnesses and remain silent about the crime during the trial. Their reticence makes them implied accomplices.

The characterization of the three women also defies established ideas
about the female criminal, who, as Monahan pointed out, is seen as
some "exciting creature." Here the criminals are quintessentially average people; the psychiatrist even tells her husband, at one point, that
she sees women like that every day: on the street, at work, or in the
butchershop. The law enforcers, however, still harbor stereotypes.
When the psychiatrist first visits the prison, a detective tells her that he
can spot this type of woman "a mile away."

[34] David A. Ward, Maurice Jackson, and Renee E. Ward, "Crimes of Violence by
Women," in Freda Adler and Rita James Simon, *The Criminology of Deviant Women*
(Boston: Houghton Mifflin, 1979), 137.

Female crime is often attributed to the psychic maladjustment of "deviant" women. As Jones has stated, lawyers often "put the blame on menstrual tension, hysterical . . . disease, [or] insanity."[35] While *Violette* conforms to this portrayal, *A Question* does not, and it offers a radical challenge to this position. One of the ways in which the two films differ is in their rendering of point of view. In *Violette*, many of the flashbacks are identified with the protagonist's consciousness (for example, her childhood recollections of her stepfather). The flashbacks in *A Question* do not generally carry this personal psychic sense; they are identified with an omniscient narrator. There is another distinction between the two works. In *Violette*, the process of evaluating the protagonist's mental health is done covertly, whereas in *A Question*, it is brought out into the open through the character of Dr. Janine Van den Bos (Cox Habema), the forensic psychiatrist. In fact, Gorris's interest lies not in whether the women are guilty of a crime but in whether they are sane or insane.

It is significant that Gorris's script calls for a *female* psychiatrist to judge the women's psychic state. In the classical cinema, a male therapist has been entrusted with the task (for example, in *The Dark Mirror* or *The Three Faces of Eve* [1957]). Mary Ann Doane has noted the use of physicians in melodrama to diagnose the female condition through employment of a "medical discourse," tainted with sexist values.[36] In *A Question*, no such psychoanalytic theories are utilized; Janine views her clients through her own eyes. As Linda Williams has noted, she acts as a reader of the women's life texts—and a skilled one she turns out to be.[37] There is even a moment when the film mocks traditional psychoanalytic theory. When Janine questions Andrea about her sex life, the latter sarcastically queries the doctor as to whether she and her husband "pray to Freud after fucking."

Janine understands the women because she refuses to narrow her focus solely to the question of individual dementia; rather, she sees the women within a social context—a perspective that has typically been denied the female offender. The spectator learns information about the women that places them within a larger cultural framework. These perceptions sometimes coincide with those unearthed by Janine, and

[35] Jones, 93.

[36] Mary Ann Doane, *The Desire to Desire: The Woman's Film of the 1940s* (Bloomington and Indianapolis: Indiana University Press, 1987), 38–69.

[37] Linda Williams, "A Jury of Their Peers: Questions of Silence, Speech and Judgment in Marleen Gorris' *A Question of Silence*," paper presented at the meeting of the Society for Cinema Studies, New York University, 1985.

sometimes they do not. (For example, flashbacks inform us what the women did after the crime—material of which Janine is unaware.) In portraying the women, Gorris employs what Mary Gentile has called a sociological "short-hand" to make clear that each of her protagonists stands for Everywoman.[38] The fact that Gorris focuses on *three* criminals (versus Chabrol's one) indicates the extended nature of her vision.

The first woman we meet is Christine (Edda Barends), a housewife. In the credit sequence, we see her in her living room: the camera pans from a baby in a playpen to Christine (in her robe) sitting on the couch eating chocolates. A television sound track blares from offscreen. Near the end of the shot, she moves toward the window and looks out vacantly. In this one brief scene, Gorris establishes Christine as a depressed homemaker, seemingly trapped in her apartment. Later, through flashback editing, we witness other moments in her life: an afternoon in her chaotic abode with toys strewn around; an early morning scene, in which her husband demands she get his briefcase. When Janine finally interviews him, he complains that what he wanted was "peace and quiet. Christine could have kept [the kids] quiet; . . . she had nothing to do all day." He asks: "How could she do this to me? She should have known I'm useless with kids." Through these vignettes, we perceive his insensitivity and refusal to acknowledge his wife's domestic chores as work. It is not surprising that Christine has become catatonic, refusing to converse with anyone. While the police assume that her silence is a psychotic reaction to the murder, Janine believes the condition predated the crime, locating its roots in the stressful circumstances of Christine's personal life.

The second woman we meet is Ann (Nelly Frijda), a waitress in a restaurant. During the credit sequence, we see her verbally sparring with male customers who chide her about being overweight. "A couple of steps wouldn't hurt your figure," one of them shouts, as he asks her to bring something to his table. Later, we hear the men exclude her from a discussion about money. "All women know about economics is how to open their hands on cash," one of them says. When the police come to arrest her at work, she brazenly tells her customers; "I killed someone; I sat on top of him." Through flashbacks of her home life and interviews with Janine, we learn that Ann is a divorced woman, living alone—seemingly happy to be without a man "to nag her." In one brief scene, we get a recollection of her family sitting in their living

[38] Mary Gentile, *Film Feminisms* (Westport, Conn., and London: Greenwood Press, 1985), 161.

room, transfixed before the television set—hardly a very positive portrayal of her marital arrangements. Ann is clearly a woman with no options; when the doctor asks her why she does not get another job, she laughs in her face. It would seem that her daughter is also trapped; Ann tells us that the girl has gotten pregnant to ensnare a man. Ann is not marketable within the heterosexual economy: she is not beautiful and violates the requirement of female passivity.

The third woman is Andrea (Henriette Tol), an executive secretary. We witness scenes of her life that attest to another genre of female oppression. Our first view takes place in her office. Her boss sits on one side of a desk, dictating a letter, and she sits on the other. The blocking bespeaks a hierarchy with broader implications, and the desk separates them in more than a spatial sense. In later flashbacks, we see her taking part in a business meeting—the only woman at a table of men. When she offers her evaluation of certain markets (a task well beyond that of a secretary), the men ignore her words. When a male colleague rephrases her statement, all applaud his perceptions. As she sits there, angrily and obsessively stirring her coffee, we understand her pent-up frustration. When Janine interviews Andrea's boss, he confesses that she was the "best worker [he] ever had." When the doctor inquires why he had never considered promoting her to the board of directors, he answers that she was a secretary, and that is all. Andrea has been pigeonholed, despite her abilities, and she is spiritually and economically cramped by her position. (As one critic has noted, her work history represents the "dark side of a film like 9 to 5" [1980]).[39] Over the course of the narrative, we learn a few other things about Andrea's life. As the doctor listens to a tape she has recorded, we hear Andrea discussing her mother's displeasure with her spinsterhood. She has been told that "an unmarried daughter is not respectable, not normal," that "men don't like old maids." Clearly, there have been pressures in Andrea's life beyond the work place, which reflect conventional figurations of woman.

These vignettes of the three murderesses provide capsule summaries of how women are contained and thwarted within contemporary Western culture. It is noteworthy that each of the women looks out a window at some point in the film: Christine in her living room, Andrea in prison, Ann in her apartment. This classic image seems to stand for the vacancy in each woman's life, for her desire to escape.

[39] Linda Gross, "*Question of Silence*: A Darker 9 TO 5," *Los Angeles Times*, 16 March 1984, 4.

287

Though the psychiatrist is not on trial, we (and she) begin to view her own life as parallel to those of her clients. Significantly, we witness scenes of her domestic existence during the credit sequence—when we are also introduced to the three criminals. In the first shot, Janine and her husband, who is trying to work, are lying on the sofa. The television blasts offscreen, as it does in the homes of Christine and Ann. As the camera pivots around the couple, Janine playfully begins seducing her husband, though he rebuffs her attempts and continues to read. Finally, she takes his pen and pretends to draw a line on his chest; he pounces on her and they begin to make love. As Gentile has pointed out, the doctor's whimsical act looks much like a stab—a gesture that echoes the murderous act of her patients.[40]

At first glance, the doctor's life seems antithetical to that of her clients: she is a professional woman, married to a lawyer who seems to accept her career. At one point, when she is at home working on the case, he tells her that dinner is ready, implying a certain equality in their marriage. But her patients' lives increasingly seem to permeate her own. Evening after evening, she sits in her study, hunched over her tape recorder, listening to the three women's testimony. In one sequence, she rewinds the tape to one of Ann's cynical remarks about marriage, and we sense Janine's suspicion that it applies to hers. In a later episode, when she and her husband are in bed, we see momentary flashes of the crime onscreen, obviously a representation of the doctor's mental point of view. In the following sequence, a montage of images of the women interrupts the couple's lovemaking. The scene concludes with the doctor awakening from a nightmare and getting out of bed, going down to her study to listen to more interviews. On the tape, she asks: "Do you wonder why Christine stopped talking?" This query now applies to her as well.

Toward the end of the film, the doctor experiences a more direct confrontation with her husband. She has testified at the trial that she believes the women are sane. Though the judge urges her to make this a "provisional diagnosis," she is not persuaded. The prosecutor is overtly hostile, insinuating that "she is speaking not only as a psychiatrist, but as a woman." Rather than deny his charge, she agrees. At the lunch recess, she and her husband meet in a restaurant and he criticizes her stance. He suggests that she "express herself less vehemently" and "back-pedal" on her position. When she accuses him of protecting his own reputation, he reveals that he does not wish to lose

[40] Gentile, 157.

clients "over this sordid affair." Even a modern marriage cannot withstand such female autonomy.

Although each woman's life is different, each experiences oppression in a man's world. As Janine begins to perceive the social problems faced by her clients, she becomes reluctant to explain their crime in terms of individualized psychic motives—or to interpret it as a fluke occurrence. She sees their act as what we might term a "social drama": women responding to persecution by men. Significantly, when she sits at her desk listening to tapes, she plays with a series of metal balls hanging in a frame: when she hits the first, the last one bounces up in response. This game symbolizes the process that has led to the women's crime. Pressures applied in one area of their lives erupted in another. The fact that the women had no contact prior to the crime shocks the police. When a detective first interviews the women, Ann complains that the man has not even introduced them. He responds in disbelief: "You mean, you didn't *know* each other?" This demonstrates that, despite their isolated lives, the women have shared a similar experience of patriarchy that has made them ready to participate in the murder. As Molly Haskell has written, one of the strengths of the film is that it shows us "the blood-curdling truth of a rage that can't be turned into a Problem for discussing and solving on 'The Phil Donahue Show,' a rage that we ignore at our peril."[41]

It is the character of Andrea who is the most perceptive about the teleology of the crime. When the doctor interviews her in prison and asks if the victim could have been a woman, Andrea replies: "No." When the doctor asks her why, Andrea answers: "Even though some women are so stupid you could kill them, we couldn't have then." The doctor queries: "But you've always worked with men?" To which Andrea responds: "*For* men." When the doctor asks if the men were all so "stupid," Andrea answers "Yes," staring boldly at the camera. Later in the courtroom, a similar issue causes the women to laugh hysterically, disrupting the trial. The prosecutor says: "I see no difference between this case and if they had killed a female shop owner or . . . if three men had killed the female owner of a shop." This thought is ridiculous to the women, who intuitively understand the symbolic nature of their crime and its premise of sexual difference. Significantly, the very first shot of the trial begins with a pan of the jury members, who are all male.

[41] Molly Haskell, "Some Films Men and Women Can't Talk About . . . and a Few They Can," *Ms.* (May 1984): 18.

During Janine's examination of her clients, she realizes the encoded nature of their act. When her husband asks why the women should have mutilated their victim, she asks whether he has ever seen photographs of war atrocities—drawing parallel between the women's struggles with patriarchy and a state of siege. And we, as spectators, must begin to regard this homicidal drama on a symbolic level if we are to respond empathetically.

Much has been made of the negative male reaction to the film, which chronicles (and could be seen to condone) the brutal murder of a man by a band of women. Ted Mahar, in the Portland *Oregonian*, writes: "It's hard to avoid the conclusion that [Gorris is] saying any woman is morally justified in killing any man."[42] Few women, feminists or not, would endorse such a tactic either. If viewed as a social drama, however, the events in *A Question* can be accepted for what they are: a theatrical, ritualistic enactment of cultural conflict.

Anthropologist Victor Turner has noted how societal tensions are often expressed in what seems to be a preestablished "scenario":

> A social drama is initiated when the peaceful tenor of regular, norm-governed social life is interrupted by the *breach* of a rule controlling one of its salient relationships. This leads swiftly or slowly to a state of *crisis*, which, if not soon sealed off, may split the community into contending factions and coalitions. To prevent this, *redressive* means are taken by those who consider themselves or are considered the most legitimate or authoritative representatives of the relevant community. Redress usually involves ritualized action, whether legal . . . religious . . . or military. . . . If the situation does not regress to *crisis* . . . the next phase of social drama comes into play, which involves alternative solutions to the problem. The first is *reconciliation* of the conflicting parties following the judicial, ritual or military processes; the second, *consensual recognition of irremediable breach*, usually followed by the spatial separation of the parties.

Turner notes that since social dramas interrupt the flow of everyday life, they "force a group to take cognizance of its own behavior in relation to its own values." Thus they "contain reflexive processes and generate cultural frames in which reflexivity can find a legitimate place."[43]

---

[42] Ted Mahar, "*A Question of Silence* Calculated to Confuse, Arouse Viewer," [Portland] *Oregonian*, 23 June 1984.

[43] All quotes from Victor Turner, *From Ritual to Theatre: The Human Seriousness of Play* (New York: Performing Arts Journal Publications, 1982), 92.

We would be hard-pressed to find a better "script" for the narrative enacted in *A Question* than Turner's delineation of social drama. In murdering the shopkeeper, the women radically "breach" the "peaceful tenor of regular, norm-governed social life." As a result, a "crisis" ensues in which the community is split into "contending factions and coalitions." "Redressive" measures are taken through the ritualized legal process. No reconciliation of the parties seems possible. Rather, there is "consensual recognition of irremediable breach." The film even literalizes the notion that a breach is marked by a "spatial separation." After the women have descended the steps from the courtroom, Janine emerges from the courthouse as her husband waits across the street. Near her, at the building entrance, are the women who witnessed the crime and remained silent, tacitly giving their support. The doctor stands in a geographical limbo, trying to decide with whom she is allied. In the closing moments of the film, she turns in the women's direction. Turner also noted how social dramas encourage reflexivity about cultural values. In *A Question*, this soul-searching is experienced by the psychiatrist, and by the audience as well.

While Turner emphasizes the theatrical aspects of social life, he also remarks on the social aspects of drama:

> In a complex culture it might be possible to regard the ensemble of performative and narrative genres . . . as a hall of mirrors . . . in which social problems, issues and crises . . . are reflected as diverse images, transformed, evaluated or diagnosed. . . . In this hall of mirror the reflections . . . provoke not merely thought, but also powerful feelings and the will to modify everyday matters in the minds of the gazers.[44]

If the fictional world of *A Question* delineates a social drama, the theatrical form of the film creates a "hall of mirrors" in which the spectator can see that social world reflected and refracted. There is even a literalization of this process within the text. During the prison scenes, Gorris's camera peers at video screens before which guards sit, scrutinizing the inmates—another variety of "mirror" in which the social world is "transformed, evaluated or diagnosed." The violent reaction to the film also makes clear Turner's belief that drama provokes "not merely thought" but also "powerful feelings." (A male film reviewer, for example, wrote: "It may be hard for some men to deal with the implications of this work. From a male perspective, it's easily the year's most startling horror film.")[45]

---

[44] Turner, 104–5.   [45] Stack.

We must bring a cultural perspective to *A Question* if we are to avoid misreading it. The murderous act at the narrative's core should not be seen as a realistic occurrence, despite the fact that it is based upon an actual event. Though Gorris had read about an Amsterdam housewife who bludgeoned a shop owner, she transforms that event in *A Question*.[46] What we have here is no document of a slaying but rather a ceremonial performance that encodes a broader social drama. Several critics have mentioned in passing the film's ritualistic qualities, but they have not examined them in sufficient depth.[47]

According to the *New Columbia Encyclopedia*, ritual or ceremony involves the "expression of shared feelings and attitudes through more or less formally ordered actions of an essentially symbolic nature performed on appropriate occasions." The ritualistic act itself entails "stereotyped bodily movements, often in relation to objects possessing symbolic meaning." Furthermore, "ceremonies express, perpetuate and transmit elements of the value and sentiment system and aim at preserving [them] . . . from doubt and opposition; moreover, they intensify the solidarity of the participants."[48]

The slaughter of the shopkeeper in *A Question* assumes ceremonial implications. Gorris takes pains to demonstrate that, for each participant, the murder is the culmination of years of oppression within patriarchy, and that the victim is merely a societal "scapegoat."[49] Thus I would suggest that we envision the narrative as (what Maya Deren would call) a "ritual in transfigured time."

Central to this portrayal is Gorris's depiction of the murder itself. Throughout the film, via its flashback structure, we see glimpses of it. Early on images of Christine and the psychiatrist in prison are intercut with shots of the housewife wheeling her baby carriage in the mall, approaching the boutique. This recollection goes as far as Christine's shoplifting, but no further; future flashbacks will progress to the instant of the crime. The fullest rendition of the murder comes as a flashback that follows a confrontation between Janine and her husband over their views on the case. We see the shopkeeper approach Christine, and then the other two women silently encircle him, as though

[46] Mentioned in Glenn Lovell, "Feminism Taken to the Limit," *San Jose [Calif.] Mercury*, 16 February 1984.
[47] Williams, 3; B. Ruby Rich, "Lady Killers: It's Only a Movie, Guys," *Village Voice*, 7 August 1984, 51.
[48] William H. Harris and Judith S. Levey, eds. *New Columbia Encyclopedia* (New York and London: Columbia University Press, 1975), 494.
[49] Williams, 3.

drawn by some magical spell. They ultimately assume a formalized triangular configuration, reminiscent of the blocking of a gunfight in a Sergio Leone western.⁵⁰ In a series of distended choreographed gestures, we see each woman strike the man: Christine punches and kicks him; Andrea hits him with a broken plastic coat hanger; Ann stabs him with a shattered glass shelf. The salesman, who has fallen to the ground, is below the frame line, completely out of view—like an offstage corpse in Shakespearean tragedy. The shop customers look on mutely, then leave the premises. The only sound we hear is the strange electronic music that functions as a score.

Gorris's stylized mode of rendering the murder emphasizes its ritualistic nature. It proceeds like a silent ceremonial performance—of "stereotyped bodily movements" utilizing "objects possessing symbolic meaning." The rite is performed on an "appropriate occasion," since shopping is a quintessential experience of tension and temptation for women. Early on, criminologist Cesare Lombroso had noted this, attributing the prevalence of female shoplifters to woman's "weak" sense of property and her "need" for fine clothing to attract men.⁵¹ As Linda Williams has noted, the shopkeeper can also be seen as a "scapegoat"—a man who stands for the sins of patriarchy. The mode in which the women mutilate his body makes the symbolism even clearer; as the coroner says, "[His] genitals [were] barely recognized as such."

The acts performed by the women after the murder also have a ritualistic tone. We learn of them only gradually, through flashbacks, since the women are reticent to discuss them with Janine. This is one of the few details they hide from her, as though aware that their acts had resonant implications. In one flashback, we see Christine and her child on a ferris wheel after the crime—a ceremonial act symbolizing the freedom she now feels, a liberty that runs counter to the constrained circumstances of her life. In another recollection, we see Ann eating a fancy and plentiful French meal that she has prepared for herself—a repast with symbolic overtones (like a Jewish seder). Gorris's cinematic means of rendering this event (a tracking shot around the table) is highly stylized, which adds to its ritualistic sense. Finally, another flashback depicts Andrea walking down the street after the murder. A car stops, and the male driver eyes her and asks: "How much?" Surprisingly, she quotes him a figure and goes off in his vehicle. We

---

⁵⁰ I am thinking, for example, of *The Good, the Bad, and the Ugly* (1967) or of *Once Upon a Time in the West* (1969).

⁵¹ Lombroso, in Leonard, 2.

later see her in his hotel room, having intercourse with him like a whore. Clearly, this act has ceremonial overtones for her. Andrea seeks to literalize what she has experienced as the grand metaphor of her female life: prostitution.

Other aspects of the film suggest a mythic interpretation. During the trial, when the prosecutor describes the condition of the victim's body, he states that it appeared as though a "high heeled army of Furies" had savaged it. This reference to the Greek legend is hardly accidental; as Williams has noted, *A Question* directly engages that fable.[52] The *New Columbia Encyclopedia* summarizes the tale as follows:

> Born from the blood of Uranus, their function was to punish wrongs committed against kindred blood regardless of the motive. They were usually represented as three ugly crones with bat's wings, dog's heads and snakes for hair. Their names were Megaera [envious], Tisiphone [blood avenger] and Alecto [unceasing, i.e., in pursuit]. When called upon to act, they hounded their victim until he died in torment. In the myth of Orestes, they appear as Clytemnestra's agents of revenge. After Athena absolves Orestes of guilt in the murder of his mother, the Furies accept her decision and become known as the Eumenides [kindly ones].[53]

The three women "punish wrongs committed against kindred blood," specifically against females. Unlike the legend, however, they are ordinary women, not "ugly crones with bat's wings, dog's heads and snakes for hair." As opposed to the myth, there is no reassuring denouement; the women exit the court in defiance, and we have no sense that they will ever become "the kindly ones." Rather than accept traditional myths (be they of the Furies or of the female offender), Gorris fashions new ones, reformulating established legends to suit her own purposes. For Williams, however, Gorris's revision is not a matter of facile opposition:

> Gorris has not simply changed the monstrous into the beautiful, the negatives into positives, the repressive ending into a liberatory one. In fact, the film does not so much revise the *Orestia* with a female defined happy ending as it re-opens all the questions supposedly solved by Athene's original judgment against women. . . . The language of such judgment, it suggests, does not yet exist.[54]

[52] Williams, 9–10.   [53] Harris and Levey, 1028.   [54] Williams, 10.

Williams also finds mythological implications in the women's court-room hysteria, which she compares to the "laugh of the Medusa," coined by Hélène Cixous.[55] To take these ancient references one step further, the boutique customers who witness the crime might be seen as the silent chorus of Greek drama.

If the women's murderous act resembles a ceremony more than a realistic occurrence, it is also highly theatrical—as though they had engaged in a group performance. Thus we might view the murder not as a real-life event but as a modernist drama, enacted outside the confines of the stage. In her book on the contemporary experimental theater, Margaret Croyden discusses how recent playwrights and directors annihilate the proscenium arch by producing "theatre in churches, garages, studios, cellars, cafes, streets, stadiums, gymnasiums, schools—or simply in any open space."[56] Perhaps the dramatic slaughter of the shopkeeper can be seen as extending that progression to a shopping mall. Furthermore, in Croyden's discussion of avant-garde performance, she stresses the influence of Antonin Artaud's "theater of cruelty," whose purpose is "to elicit the guilt of the audience, to make them feel as cruel as what they see portrayed on the stage . . . to make the audience leave the theatre in a state of . . . irritation and hostility."[57] Artaud also feels that "the audience should come face to face with [its] taste for crime . . . even [its] cannibalism."[58]

Artaud's ideas have profound implications for *A Question*. The murderous event that we witness within Gorris's fiction will either elicit "guilt" in us or "a taste for crime." The act also leaves us in a state of "irritation" rather than complacency. Within the narrative, characters discuss this issue in another context. One evening, when the Van den Boses are having company, they all mention how people are trained to ignore serious problems through stimulation of their pleasure. In *A Question*, Gorris frustrates such facile pleasure and makes us confront the demons of which Artaud spoke. Taking theatrical parallels one step further, one can also view the murder as a drama within a drama: the women seem to "perform" it before the attentive "audience" composed of boutique customers. Even the relentless silence of the sequence bespeaks contemporary drama's suspicion of language. As Croyden writes: "Words, equated with the mealy-mouthings of the power elite, were to be distrusted. . . . [Playwrights] repudiated theatre

[55] Ibid.
[56] Margaret Croyden, *Lunatics, Lovers and Poets—The Contemporary Experimental Theatre* (New York, San Francisco, and Toronto: McGraw-Hill, 1974), xviii.
[57] Artaud, quoted in Ibid., 62.   [58] Ibid., 63.

as literature and substituted in its place a non-verbal theatre, one of 'cruelty' and ritual."[59]

Beyond the question of theatrical technique, silence in the film has other meanings, which concern the position of women in traditional culture. In fact, the "sounds of silence" echo on various levels. There is, of course, Christine's catatonia, engendered by her frustrations as a mother and wife. Though the police link it to the commission of a crime, her husband confesses that she "never talked much." Her silence is positioned very differently from that of Elisabeth Vogler in *Persona*, who is seen to be a selfish fraud. In *A Question*, Christine's refusal to talk is represented as a valid response to an unresponsive world. Unlike Violette, she is not viewed as a vapid woman who has nothing to say.

Other women are silent in the film. When Andrea attends a meeting of her firm's board of directors, she mutely and angrily stirs her coffee when her insights are ignored. Her silence is not without content; it signifies a host of humiliations. We also have the silence of the customers who patronize the boutique on the fateful day. Their refusal to stop the murder, or to alert the police, bespeaks unspoken complicity and support.

Even the psychiatrist participates in the silence. When she first arrives at the prison, she is met by a male detective who proceeds to lecture her about the case without allowing her to get a word in edgewise: "There's no doubt about it, they're completely crazy. But I don't have to explain to you what you know professionally. . . . I assume you're usually assigned to women." The clear condescension in his voice, his assault of language, locks Janine into taciturn resentment. Later on, of course, when she asserts her opinion at the trial, the judge, the prosecutor, and her husband all attempt to make her "eat her words." The final aspect of the doctor's silence, however, has a more positive valence. Throughout the film, we see her at her desk playing the taped interviews with her clients. Here her silence has a classically "feminine" sense, for she is a good listener. Through her mute receptivity, the words of the women are finally heard and legitimized.

In delineating these various senses of silence, and in underscoring the topic in the film's title, Gorris emphasizes the problematic relationship of woman to language—an issue that has been addressed in several previous chapters. There is even an image in the film that encapsulates this phenomenon. When Janine first arrives at the prison, a

[59] Croyden, xvii.

matron takes down her name as she passes the front desk. As the psychiatrist proceeds through the halls, we see an automatic writing machine transferring information about her to a pad on another desk within the institution. Throughout the film, we feel this sense of woman being "written" by language instead of her having control of the discourse herself. Retrospectively, Janine's aggressive act of marking her husband's chest with his pen takes on broader implications, as does her act of wresting a book from his hands.

In line with this cultural reading of woman's silence, there is also the issue of her muteness under patriarchal law—the specific setting invoked in the film. As criminologist Freda Adler has written:

> *Monologue, not dialogue, has characterized the law's discourse with [woman].* The controversy between rule of law and rule of men was never relevant to women—because, along with juveniles, imbeciles, and other classes of legal nonpersons, they had no access to law except through men. The democratic interchange of public opinion, legislative act, and judicial interpretation that ensured the viability and responsiveness of the law for men was totally *silent* for women. They had no public opinion of record, *no voice* in the legislature, no standing in court.[60]

Gorris does not simply catalogue woman's linguistic absence; rather, she presents certain models of opposition. There are the psychiatrist's audiotapes—which retrieve the women's life texts—inaudible to everyone else. Furthermore, Janine encourages the silent Christine to communicate on another level by drawing pictures of her experience. Through Christine's visual imagery (recurrent drawings of a man, a woman, and a child within a frame), we comprehend the claustrophobic nature of her existence as a stereotypical middle-class wife and mother. She draws her first sketches on newspaper—a symbol of masculine/historical discourse; moreover, she draws *three* series of boxes, as though to generalize her situation to all of the women on trial. Christine's sketches may also function as a validation of woman's alleged "right-brain" orientation—for female semantic potential beyond the purely verbal.

Central to this issue is the character of Ann, who is the most garrulous of the lot. While Christine refuses to speak and Andrea converses in measured phrases, Ann is a compulsive talker. Beyond that, she uses

60 Freda Adler, *Sisters in Crime: The Rise of the New Female Criminal* (New York: McGraw-Hill, 1975), 203 (my italics).

her linguistic skills aggressively. When the men in the restaurant mock her, she responds with cynical wit; when Janine suggests that she get a better job, she ridicules her naiveté. Even the loud clicking of her knitting needles seems to have aggressive connotations, reminding us of the legendary ones of Madame Defarge. But it is Ann's *laughter* that is her most salient vocal trait, and it bespeaks a host of words. It is with laughter that she answers the doctor's question about whether her daughter will visit her in prison. It is with laughter that she responds to the doctor's query about whether she wishes to remarry. The power of Ann's laughter is felt by the doctor, who repeatedly listens to it on her tape recorder, rewinding to the spot where it erupts. Ultimately, Ann's laughter seems to infect her cohorts. During one interview with the doctor, Andrea giggles when asked why the victim could not have been female; and when the same issue arises at the trial, Christine begins to chuckle. The women's laughter eventually spreads to the doctor and to the store patrons who have attended the trial.

This laughter has broad implications beyond that of the Medusa. It plays on the notion of hysteria, which can mean (on a technical level) a neurotic display or (on a colloquial level) a fit of laughter. In a sense, through her portrayal of the raucous laughter of her female offenders, Gorris is finding hysterical the previous depictions of them as hysterics—witness the case of Violette. This notion of laughter has even further ramifications. During our first view of Ann in the restaurant, one of her male customers asks if she "doesn't have a sense of humor" when he cruelly taunts her about her weight. Though he doubts her comic sense, *we* do not, seeing her wry and bemused dismissal of patriarchy throughout the narrative. Ann's laughter is the revolutionary kind envisioned by Mary Daly in *Gyn/Ecology*:

> There is nothing like the sound of women really laughing. The roaring laughter of women is like the roaring of the eternal sea. Hags can cackle and roar at themselves but more and more, one hears them roaring at the reversal that is patriarchy, the monstrous jock's joke. . . . But this laughter is the one true hope, for as long as it is audible there is evidence that someone is seeing through the Dirty Joke.[61]

Ann's attitude, ultimately, exceeds the narrative and colors the very tone of the film, for Gorris seeds *A Question* with moments of "black" comedy. Even the murder scene exudes this tone. Although the wom-

[61] Mary Daly, *Gyn/Ecology* (Boston: Beacon Press, 1978), 17.

23. *A Question of Silence* (1981). It is the roar of laughter of the women (Nelly Frijda, Edda Barrends, and Henriette Tol), associated with the Medusa and Hags, that fills the deafening silence.

en's slaughter of a shopkeeper is terrible, it is also ludicrous: the motive is a pilfered sweater, the weapons a display shelf and a grocery shopping cart. When the coroner tells us the man's body showed wounds from "a broken plastic coat hanger wielded with great violence," we have to contain a smile at this mock heroism. Perhaps this is what Carrie Rickey meant when she referred to Gorris's "subversively original humor."[62] To those spectators who recoil in moral outrage at the macabre sight of the murder, we might ask the same question hurled at Ann: "Don't you have any comic sense?"

Thus it is the roar of laughter that fills the deafening silence in *A Question*—an insolent laughter associated with the Medusa or with Hags (see fig. 23). It makes a travesty of stereotypes of the female offender—the very ones that circulated in *Violette*. The laughter also warns us not to take what we see in the film as entirely "serious," but to view it as an ironical and symbolic drama rather than a slice of life. As Janine tells the judge at the trial: "It's really quite funny." Those who misread the film's sexual politics or are naively shocked by its

[62] Carrie Rickey, in Gentile, "Three Women Kill a Man—For No Reason." *San Francisco Sunday Examiner and Chronicle*, 11 November 1983, 32. B. Ruby Rich also uses the term "comedy" to discuss the film. See "Lady Killers: It's Only a Movie, Guys," *Village Voice*, 7 August 1984, 51–54.

ethical tone may find themselves the object of ridicule, the butt of Gorris's grand cinematic "joke." Interestingly, critic B. Ruby Rich describes certain screenings of *A Question* that produced a replication of the dynamics of laughter portrayed in the film: "At the New Directors preview in New York, the audience recapitulated the film's own ending: man after man rose to confront Gorris with hostile or garbled questions, only to encounter laughter from most women in the audience."[63] As Chantal Akerman had warned us, woman's violence is "not commercial."

One reason for male antagonism to Gorris's project is that she jests so mercilessly with man's stereotypical *fears* of the assertive woman. As Jones has noted, during periods of agitation for women's rights, people generally expect a rise in female violent crime, despite the fact that the rate has been relatively constant over time[64]: "Society is afraid of both the feminist and the murderer, for each of them, in her own way, tests society's established boundaries."[65]

Set in the 1980s, an era following one that advocated women's liberation, *A Question* (with its army of Furies) lambasts and incarnates such prejudices, mischievously making man's "worst fears come true." In doing so, the film tests "society's established boundaries," and the limits of cinema as well.

In her diaries, Anaïs Nin inquires whether the female artist must free the dark side of her nature to achieve her full potential. "Must I write with my demons?" she asks. It is just such spirits that Gorris unleashes in *A Question*, using creation (as Nin would have it) to "feed the monster."[66]

[63] Rich, 52.   [64] Jones, 4.   [65] Ibid., 13.

[66] Anaïs Nin, *The Diary of Anaïs Nin, Volume Two 1934–1939*, Gunther Stuhlman, ed. (New York: Swallow and Harcourt, Brace & World, 1967), 218.

10 The Dialogic Text: An Epilogue

Double-Voiced Discourse

> [A]ny concrete discourse (utterance) finds the object at which
> it was directed already . . . overlain with qualifications, open
> to dispute, charged with value, already enveloped in an
> obscuring mist—or . . . by the "light" of alien words that have
> already been spoken about it. —M. M. Bakhtin[1]

Throughout this book, I have argued that an intertextual
framework is a resonant one within which to examine
women's cinema, counterposing the work of feminist filmmakers with
documents from the patriarchal cinema. Each chapter has facilitated a
synthetic dialogue between texts, whether *Riddles of the Sphinx* and
The Lady from Shanghai or *Dames* and *The Eighties*. While my model
was devised to highlight referential connections between specific films
(such as *Lianna* and *Sotto, Sotto*), the intertextual impulse has frequently jumped my textual boundaries. While I planned for *Sisters, or
The Balance of Happiness* to address the Hollywood twin film, it engaged *Persona* as well, despite my attempts to contain it.

In previous sections, although we artificially "induced" a confrontation between disparate works, we also encountered women's films
that concretely invoke the dominant cinema. *Riddles of the Sphinx* exhibited an image of Greta Garbo; *Lianna* alluded to *The Magnificent
Ambersons*; *Sotto, Sotto* referred to *Notorious*, *Divorce Italian Style*,
and *Le Diable au Corps*. Even these films have kept direct quotation
to a minimum, engaging intertextuality on the broad generic level.

In this chapter, I consider a work of a different order: Yvonne Rainer's *The Man Who Envied Women* (1985). If the notion of a "dialogue" between feminist and mainstream cinema has previously been
an activating metaphor, that figure of speech is literalized within *The
Man*. For Rainer creates a work whose composition is based on quotation from the classical cinema, whose abstract "story" incorporates
film clips from *Un Chien Andalou* (1929), *Dangerous* (1935), *Double
Indemnity* (1944), and *Wavelength* (1966–1967), to name but a few.
Rainer's work thus expands and extends the notion of the feminist

[1] M. M. Bakhtin, *The Dialogic Imagination*, Michael Holquist, ed., trans. Caryl
Emerson and Michael Holquist (Austin and London: University of Texas Press, 1981),
276.

301

"remake"—a concept loosely applied to other films in this book. Not only does Rainer allude to and revise a particular patriarchal genre, she swallows the dominant cinema whole, including co-opting, appropriating, and recycling it for her own aesthetic/ideological purposes. Though Rainer's work is the most complex and sustained of its kind, other recent women's films utilize such a "cannibalistic" strategy. Stephanie Beroes's *The Dream Screen* (1986) juxtaposes a contemporary narrative with excerpts from G. W. Pabst's *Pandora's Box*; Connie Fields's documentary, *The Life and Times of Rosie The Riveter* (1978), interrupts its contemporary interviews with extracts from government films of the 1940s.[2] This type of film illustrates the *intratextual* relation identified by Michael Riffaterre, "where the intertext is partly encoded within the text and conflicts with it because of stylistic or semantic incompatibilities."[3]

I conclude with an examination of this mode of film because its very existence not only crystallizes but validates my fundamental argument: that an intertextual approach is a compelling means of figuring the feminist cinema. Furthermore, Rainer's film is so encyclopedic that it restates numerous issues already confronted: the question of sexual difference, the nature of film spectatorship, the mythification of woman, the figure of the femme fatale, the function of parody, the pitfalls of spectacle, the role of film criticism, the ideology of cinematic language. Hence, in analyzing *The Man*, we will not only reinvestigate the value of an intertextual stance but reiterate the major concepts that have animated this book, as well as the field of feminist cinema and scholarship.

In discussing theories of intertextuality, we have referred to such figures as Roland Barthes, Harold Bloom, and Gérard Genette. Here we will explore the work of yet another major critic: the Soviet writer Mikhail Bakhtin. In particular, we will draw on *The Dialogic Imagination* to fathom the complex structure of *The Man*. Although Bakhtin's work focuses exclusively on the novel, his formulation has broad application to film.

According to Bakhtin, when one speaks about a particular literary subject, one finds that topic already saturated with previous statements:

[2] Yvonne Rainer's earlier films have also alluded to the dominant cinema. *Lives Of Performers* . . . (1972), for example, ends with a series of "imitation stills" from G. W. Pabst's *Pandora's Box*. It also includes a set of stills from Alfred Hitchcock's *Psycho* (1960).
[3] Michael Riffaterre, "Syllepsis," *Critical Inquiry* 6, no. 4 (1980): 627.

302

> For the writer of artistic prose . . . the object reveals first of all precisely the socially heteroglot multiplicity of its names, definitions and value judgments. Instead of the virginal fullness and inexhaustibility of the object itself, the prose writer confronts a multitude of routes, roads and paths that have been laid down in the object by social consciousness.[4]

Thus when feminist filmmakers confront a particular screen issue (be it romance, violence, friendship, or theater), they invariably face myriad linguistic and cinematic "routes, roads and paths" established by their precursors. The director who consciously alludes is only literalizing a process inherent in *all* discourse, acknowledged or repressed. For Bakhtin, when the artist quotes, he/she speaks in a double-voiced discourse, utilizing *"another's speech in another's language."* Such discourse works "to express authorial intentions but in a refracted way. . . . It serves two speakers at the same time and expresses simultaneously two different intentions."[5]

More radical than Bakhtin's claim that artistic creation looks backward is his notion that it simultaneously looks forward—to its reception by readers and writers. He states: "The word in living conversation is directly, blatantly, oriented toward a future answer-word: it provokes an answer, anticipates it and structures itself in the answer's direction."[6] One could argue that, by "talking back" to the dominant discourse, feminist counter-cinema is merely activating a dynamic inherent in all living discourse—that of responding to queries posed by earlier texts. Thus we might say that *Fatima* "invites" a reaction from future filmmakers, as do *Violette* and *Rich and Famous*.

For Bakhtin, language is marked at each moment by a particular social/historical context and ideological point of view: "All words have the 'taste' of a profession, a genre, a tendency, a party, a particular work, a particular person, a generation, an age group, the day and hour."[7] Thus, in utilizing the iconography of the dominant cinema, women filmmakers employ tropes already saturated with the taint of patriarchal assumptions, of particular historical epochs.

Bakhtin sees the novel as organized internally by a complex structure of interrelated discourses: "The language of the novel is a *system* of languages that mutually and ideologically interanimate each other."[8] For him, the task of stylistic analysis is to lay bare this architecture in the overall composition of the work.[9] Through its focus on

[4] Bakhtin, 278.   [5] Ibid., 324–25.   [6] Ibid., 280.   [7] Ibid., 293.   [8] Ibid., 47.
[9] Ibid., 416.

303

discourse, the novel also offers up the very "image" of language as the self-reflexive subject of the text: "Language in the novel not only represents, but itself serves as the object of representation."[10] In confronting *The Man*, we will want to keep Bakhtin's theories in mind: to chart the film's network of discourses and to uncover the images of language that it yields.

Sexual/Textual Politics: *The Man Who Envied Women*

> *I started . . . [the film] with a character, but as in all my films I then looked for texts rather than writing scenes. . . . One of my ploys is to constantly transpose conventional modes of address. Speech couched in another form gives it a very skewed sense. —Yvonne Rainer*[11]

The Man Who Envied Women is a feature-length work that lasts some 125 minutes. In its format, however, it does not resemble a conventional dramatic piece. Rather, like *Riddles of the Sphinx*, it offers both an abstract narrative line and a montage of discursive segments. As *Riddles* presents us with the story of Louise, so *The Man* offers us the tale of Trisha (Trisha Brown), an artist who has just turned fifty and split up with her husband. Here is how one reviewer summarized the film's minimal "plot":

> The story goes essentially like this: a woman leaves her husband (she is seen only from behind in an early scene, then she disappears from sight, but not sound, taking on the role of an internal voice). The camera is trained upon her husband Jack, who pursues his various interests: He lectures his class, he (presumably) seduces a female student, he eavesdrops on the conversations of others, he and a woman meet in a corridor, where they speak lengthy, mutually exclusive monologs, he exercises, and he contemplates the artwork his wife has left behind. The disembodied woman goes through the film reflecting upon Jack, on various socio-political and feminist subjects, and upon her own sexual and gender identity.[12]

---

[10] Ibid., 49.

[11] Yvonne Rainer, in Calvin Ahlgren, "There's No Narrative to This Woman's Tale," *San Francisco Chronicle*. (This was part of a press packet for the film, and the review was undated.)

[12] Michael Nelson, "*The Man Who Envied Women*," *Experimental Film Coalition Newsletter* 2, no. 4 (October/November/December 1985): 6.

Having offered us a story, however, Rainer does everything in her power to subvert its conventional impact and to oppose the stylistic techniques by which it would traditionally be rendered. She has stated: "I can give a description of the film and make it sound like a Hollywood movie, but the story isn't the main thing. All my films deal with develop[ment] and destruction of the narrative."[13]

The lead character is almost never present on the screen; she appears only once, and then is seen from behind. Rainer has explained her use of this decentering strategy by reference to recent film criticism:

> There's been a lot of feminist . . . theory about how the female image is manipulated and sexually objectified in film. I took this writing at face value and decided that my main female character was not going to be there in the flesh at all.[14]

By taking such work "at face value," she eliminates the female face—and, with it, the voyeuristic/masochistic aspects of spectator involvement. If anyone is the object of the viewer's gaze, it is the male, Jack Deller, who is incessantly visible onscreen.[15]

Recent critical theory has also given attention to the import of the woman's voice in discourse, whether repressed or liberated by the text. In *The Man*, Rainer transforms her protagonist into pure vocal presence—into "the controlling commentator and narrator." In utilizing this method, she not only pays homage to *Riddles* but to other works that seek to recoup woman's language through use of the voice-off. The contrapuntal orchestration of Jack and Trisha's words also rearticulates the basic structure of this book: that of dialogic "shot/countershot." As Berenice Reynaud remarks, the alternation of their voices constitutes the first of a set of oppositions in the film.[16]

Trisha's bodily absence also makes viewer identification difficult, denying the spectator conventional empathy with the heroine of this "woman's picture." One need only recall Lisa Berndle's omnipresence in *Letter from an Unknown Woman* to imagine how this situation

---

[13] Rainer, in Ahlgren.

[14] Yvonne Rainer, "Beyond Mythologies," *Experimental Film Coalition Newsletter* 2, no. 4 (October/November/December 1985): 3.

[15] Patricia Mellencamp, "Images of Language and Indiscreet Dialogue: *The Man Who Envied Women*," *Screen* 28, no. 2 (Spring 1987): 95.

[16] Kaja Silverman, "Dis-Embodying the Female Voice," in Mary Ann Doane, Patricia Mellencamp, and Linda Williams, *Re-Vision: Essays in Feminist Film Criticism* (Frederick, Md.: American Film Institute and University Publications of America, 1984), 131–49; Berenice Reynaud, "Impossible Projections," *Screen* 28, no. 4 (Autumn 1987): 42.

would be handled in the Hollywood mode. Rainer also introduces other female personae, refusing to privilege any one of them.[17] In contrast, Jack Deller is perennially on camera. But viewer empathy is frustrated, because two different actors play the same role (William Raymond and Larry Loonin)—a technique utilized in Akerman's *The Eighties*. At one point, Rainer self-reflexively addresses this issue of audience involvement. A man on the street tells a woman: "You know emotions are produced; they don't just happen." And she responds: "You mean they're synthetic?" In Rainer's view, the Hollywood cinema manipulates spectator feeling (like a drug that affects somatic moods). While Jack and his thoughts occupy the superficial focus of the film, Rainer depicts him within a feminist framework (as what he represents to women). For a change, it is the male whose authority is subverted, who is someone else's "projection," who is merely the "pseudocenter of the filmic discourse."[18]

Beyond these rather subtle means of abstracting the drama, Rainer uses the more disjunctive strategy of interrupting the "story line" with diverse, extraneous, non-narrative material: documentary footage of artists organizing against American policy in Latin America, newsreels of housing hearings in New York City, snatches of conversation from men and women on the street, excerpts from canonical films. Even in scenes that fall within the diegesis (Jack teaching his class, Jack and Jackie [Jackie Raynal] talking in a hallway, people commenting on Trisha's artwork), Rainer transcends the narrative universe by having a lecture mode replace dramatic dialogue. Jack pontificates in class on the writings of Foucault and Lacan, and during a party he and Jackie discuss theories of language, power, and sexual difference. Hence, these segments exist on the borderline of the storied and unstoried world.

The Man, like Rainer's earlier work, partakes of a "collage" structure, or mode of "radical juxtaposition."[19] (Interestingly, Rainer played a character named Josephine de Collage in Ulriche Ottinger's *Madame X* [1977].) This format fractures the spatiotemporal conti-

[17] Rainer, "Beyond Mythologies," 4.

[18] Claire Johnston, "Myths of Women in the Cinema," in Karyn Kay and Gerald Peary, *Women and the Cinema: A Critical Anthology* (New York: Dutton, 1977), 411.

[19] Rainer states that her method is that of a "collagist," in Janet Bergstrom, Sandy Flitterman, Elisabeth Hart Lyon, and Constance Penley, "Yvonne Rainer: An Interview," *Camera Obscura* 1 (Fall 1976): 89–90; Michael Sragow in "Rainer's Shooting Gallery," *San Francisco Examiner* (in film's press packet), calls her film an "audio-visual collage." Noël Carroll mentions "radical juxtaposition" in "Yvonne Rainer: Mortal Questions," *Soho Weekly News*, 13 February 1980, 44.

nuities of traditional narrative and moves beyond the ambiguous se-
gues of the art film (e.g., Zetterling's *The Girls*). It also fundamentally
challenges cinematic verisimilitude. As Rainer has stated: "From the
time I started making art . . . I've tried to question all notions of reality
we assimilate from cinema, particularly Hollywood cinema."[20]

The most original aspect of Rainer's work is its hyperbolic *montage
of modes of discourse*—a process by which language (be it filmic or
verbal) is stripped bare of any modicum of transparency. As Rainer
states: "I would like to believe that I subject such discourses to pressures and tests, or dislocations, e.g. a removal from their ordinary contexts . . . to unexpected physical and psychic spaces."[21] In writing on
the process of reference in literature, Carmela Perri argues that "when
a poem's, play's or novel's governing technique is allusion, it should be
called an allusion-poem, allusion-play, or allusion-novel, just as we
call any of these kinds an 'allegory' when it is informed with that technique."[22] If ever there were an occasion to coin the term "allusion-
film," it is for *The Man*.

Perri also claims that referential texts require great cognitive labor
from their readers, who must answer the intellectual riddles of the discourse. Hence, it seems fitting that, in the opening shot of *The Man*,
Jack sits in front of a screen that says "Screen *Tests*." For Jane Desmond, Rainer's challenges offer the spectator the "pleasure of compe-
tency"—one "less directly linked to notions of sexual pleasure than
those mechanisms related to voyeurism."[23]

Because of its referential nature, Rainer's work profits from a Bakh-
tinian approach. In examining it, however, we cannot proceed in a linear manner because her quotations are multilayered and multivalent,
harking back to one another, as well as to systems outside the text.[24]
Our critical model will be one of three-dimensionality and simultane-
ity, of reversibility and circularity—like Bakhtin's characterization of

[20] Rainer, "Beyond Mythologies," 3.
[21] Yvonne Rainer, "Some Ruminations around Cinematic Antidotes to the Oedipal
Net(les) While Playing With De Lauraedipus Mulvey, or, He May Be Off Screen, But . . ."
The Independent 9, no. 3 (April 1986): 22.
[22] Carmela Perri, "On Alluding," *Poetics* 7, no. 3 (September 1978): 306.
[23] Jane Desmond, "Yvonne Rainer and the Practice of Theory," paper presented at the
meeting of the Society for Cinema Studies, Montreal, May 1987, 10.
[24] There is a brief mention of Bakhtin in relation to *The Man* in Peggy Phelan, "Spatial
Envy: Yvonne Rainer's *The Man Who Envied Women*," *Motion Picture* 1, no. 3 (Win-
ter/Spring 1987): 18. It is not, however, pursued. The theories of Bakhtin have been
applied to other texts in feminist cinema. See Janice Welsch, "Documentary Dialogue:
Feminism, Bakhtin, and *Rosie the Riveter*" (unpublished paper).

307

the trajectory of discourse, which "weaves in and out of complex interrelationships, merges with some, recoils from others, intersects with yet a third group."[25]

Central among the language systems that Rainer layers like phyllo dough, or (for Desmond) "shuffles . . . like a shell game," is the "discourse of cinema."[26] While some women filmmakers have alluded to the dominant mode (or have fashioned their works as oblique revisions of classical genres), Rainer engulfs the mainstream film within her text (like a directorial "devouring mother") through a complex system of references and quotations. Her work thereby demonstrates Bakhtin's notion that the artist's object "exists [in] an elastic environment of other alien words about the same object, the same theme."[27] Specifically, Rainer's "object" is male/female relations; her cinematic references highlight that topic's linguistic "environment" and surface the ubiquitous tropes that have named and contained it.

The film's title immediately sparks associations with two works: François Truffaut's and Blake Edwards's *The Man Who Loved Women* (1977/1983), stories of a Don Juan (in the tradition of Stefan Brand) (see fig. 24). Rainer clearly has the figure of the womanizer in mind: Jack Deller frequently brags about his prowess with women, and his marriage collapses as a result of his adulterous exploits. (At one point, he even claims to "be in love with all women.") In a classical film (like *Letter from an Unknown Woman*), the Don Juan's pathology is masked, while in feminist works like *Straight through the Heart* and *The Man*, it is spotlighted. Jack is seen on numerous occasions at his

[25] Bakhtin, 276.
[26] Desmond, 3; Patricia Mellencamp refers to the film as entailing an "archaeology of discourses" in "Images," 95.
[27] Bakhtin, 276.

24. *The Man Who Loved Women* (1977). The hero (Charles Denner) surveys one of his conquests.

308

psychiatrist's office (like the hero of Edwards's film), and much of Trisha's narration concerns the infirmity of male consciousness. Moments of *The Man* even seem to allude to the Truffaut/Edwards works. A lady on the street says: " 'You can always tell how a woman feels about herself just by looking at her legs.' Can you imagine anyone saying something like that? I could have killed him." In both versions of *The Man Who Loved Women*, the camera focuses on the legs of the hero's lovers, and relishes the calf-level shots. Similarly, in Rainer's film, Jack pontificates on the various "categories" of women he has known.

Within the film-historical world, the title *The Man Who Envied Women* also conjures up the phrase "the man you love to hate," which once was attached to actor/director Erich von Stroheim and the villainous roles he enacted. In *Foolish Wives* (1921) and *Blind Husbands* (1919), von Stroheim took the part of a European womanizer (like Stefan Brand) who preyed on unsuspecting American matrons. At one point in *The Man*, Rainer cites the von Stroheim epithet when Trisha reports that she does not want to make her male protagonist into "a man you love to hate." Beyond referring to the Austrian filmmaker, Rainer reveals the danger to women of fueling their dislikes, of constructing man as a cardboard enemy.

Rainer's title goes beyond the realm of film history to remind us of the concept of "penis envy."[28] By substituting man for the envious subject, Rainer (like Karen Horney or Bruno Bettelheim) turns the table on Freud and sees the male as haunted by a lack.[29] A fragment of conversation overheard in the film even posits a "menstruation envy." A man on the street says: "Christ was crucified so that male saints could have periodic bleeding—just like women—that's what those stigmata are all about." But there is another reference that circulates around the title, *The Man Who Envied Women*. Within the realm of literary and cinematic history, no male hero "envies" women more than Mary Wollstonecraft Shelley's Dr. Frankenstein, whose monster is a surrogate child, fashioned technologically instead of biologically. In creating his homunculus, Dr. Frankenstein seeks to reanimate dead tissue, bringing old organic material back to life. In a sense, this is what Rai-

[28] Rainer herself mentions the pun on "penis envy" in Katie Russell, "Yvonne Rainer Eats Her Cake," *Cinema Studies* 2, no. 3 (Fall 1986): 2 (newsletter of the Department of Cinema Studies, New York University).
[29] See Karen Horney, "The Flight from Womanhood," in Harold Kelman, ed., *Feminine Psychology* (New York: Norton, 1967), 133–46; Bruno Bettelheim, *Symbolic Wounds: Puberty Rites and the Envious Male* (New York: Collier, 1971), 109–10.

ner accomplishes in her experimental film by quoting the "deceased" dominant cinema and filling it with a new feminist spirit.

Some have seen *The Man* as an ironic remake of *An Unmarried Woman* (1978).[30] Both films concern a middle-aged woman whose marriage breaks up, and both take place in the SoHo art world. While the Paul Mazursky film glosses over the tensions of male-female relations (by rushing the heroine into the arms of a handsome, sensitive, wealthy artist), Rainer's protagonist comes to bleaker conclusions about her romantic future. Toward the end of the film, Trisha states:

> Lately, I've been thinking yet again: I can't live without men, but I can live without a man. I've had this thought before, but this time the idea is not colored by stigma or despair or finality. I know there will sometimes be excruciating sadness, but I also know something is different now.[31]

The world of lower Manhattan, so glamorous in *An Unmarried Woman*, is seen here as a site of political, sexual, and economic struggle.

Aside from cinematic allusion, Rainer makes use of direct quotation, and it is important to comprehend the context in which these excerpts arise. In most cases, Jack (shown in medium shot) is seated on a chair facing the camera. Behind him, on a screen, are projected clips from other films (see fig. 25). The nature of his monologues (which have a confessional tone) leads us to conclude that these are therapy sessions, in which he addresses some offscreen psychoanalyst.

The mise-en-scène of these sequences literalizes certain notions of intertextuality. Michael Riffaterre states that, in apprehending a work, we are involved in a double reading—"simultaneously decipher[ing] the text that is before our eyes and the one that comes back to our memory."[32] What better metaphor could exist for this process than the viewer's perception of Jack, who sits before other images projected on the movie screen? Jack's stance also contrasts sharply with the traditionally conceived position of the female spectator—gullible, emotive, absorbed by the movies she sees. Jack, however, turns his back on the

---

[30] Judy Stone, in "Offbeat Film on Sex and Power," *San Francisco Chronicle* (press packet), mentions *An Unmarried Woman*. Michael Sragow, in "Rainer's Shooting Gallery," *San Francisco Examiner*, calls Rainer "a radical Mazursky."

[31] This quote is from the writing of Monique Wittig. Rainer mentions it in the "Beyond Mythologies" interview, 4.

[32] Michael Riffaterre, *Text Production*, trans. Terese Lyons (New York: Columbia University Press, 1983), 250.

310

25. *The Man Who Envied Women* (1985). The film images seem to be part of Jack (William Raymond)'s consciousness, his mind screen.

films, as though they were irrelevant to his concerns—just so much "feminine" popular culture.

Despite his dismissal of the cinema, Jack's position also represents the film images as part of *his* consciousness, *his* psychoanalytic discourse, *his* mind screen. This sense (of the classical cinema as a male fantasy) is familiar and has informed our discussions of *The Lady from Shanghai*, *Cobra Woman*, *A Stolen Life*, *The Dark Mirror*, *Rich and Famous*, and *Letter from an Unknown Woman*. Jack's sessions also remind us of Bergman's *Persona* and of the little boy whose Oedipal desires are realized on the movie screen.

It is important to consider Rainer's choice of film extracts, and what motivates her selection. The first is the infamous sequence from *Un Chien Andalou* in which Luis Buñuel looks at the moon, sharpens a razor, and cuts a woman's eye. Buñuel is an important precursor for all avant-garde artists, and we might view this sequence as an affectionate homage. Rainer's use of two actors for the role of Jack Deller also mimics Buñuel's tactic in *That Obscure Object of Desire* (1977), where two women embody the heroine.[33] But if Buñuel is a forefather,

---

[33] Rainer specifically mentions *That Obscure Object of Desire* in Katie Russell, "Yvonne Rainer Eats Her Cake," 2.

311

he is also a patriarchal one, and Rainer's quote surfaces the problematic aspects of his position. Film criticism of the 1970s and 1980s has demonstrated the crucial role of vision in the film viewing process, especially as it pertains to the figure of woman. In particular, our discussions of *Dames*, *Fatima*, *Take Off*, and *Letter from an Unknown Woman* have surfaced the fear of the female body (her genital "lack") and the specular processes of voyeurism and fetishism that have psychologically compensated for it. Buñuel's shocking image (of a man slicing a woman's eye) collects all those issues in one trope: man's fear of looking at woman, her bodily "slit," the danger of woman looking back. Significantly, this clip occurs as Trisha invokes a "discourse of the female body." She talks of how she recently "bloodied up [her] white linen pants," and of how her "gynecologist went down in Korean Airlines Flight 007." She affectionately recalls how her physician "put booties on the stirrup," and [that] "his speculum was always warm."

The parallels between Luis Buñuel and Jack Deller are also conspicuous. As Buñuel smokes in the movie image, so does Jack in his psychoanalytic session. When Jack attempts to seduce a graduate student, the blocking is reminiscent of that of Buñuel and his unfortunate woman. During the seduction sequence, Trisha's narration emphasizes the parallels between the two men. She says: "To quote Luis Buñuel, it is possible to have the whole story of Oedipus playing in your head and still behave at the table."

Another film excerpted is *Dangerous* (1935), starring Bette Davis—a movie about an actress on the skids who is the ruination of men. Our discussions of *Persona*, *Torch Song*, *Indiscreet*, and other films have revealed the performer as a favored role for the melodramatic heroine, especially if she suffers some telling psychological flaw. Rainer chose the clip from *Dangerous* because it cast woman as dramatic spectacle. She notes how, in the American classical cinema, "the female character is often a nightclub entertainer, a totally eroticized person. My main character [Trisha] is also a kind of performer or artist, possibly someone who performs before an audience, but the irony here is you never see her."[34]

Rainer frequently orchestrates parallels between Jack's life and the film scenarios through a dialogic interaction of texts. In one counseling session, Jack disparagingly remarks that his first wife referred to herself as a "girl," even at the age of thirty-five. This is immediately fol-

34 Rainer, "Beyond Mythologies," 4.

lowed by a clip from *Dark Victory*, in which George Brent asks Bette Davis if she has "been a good girl." This montage implies that men encourage the infantilism of woman, despite Jack's claims to the contrary.

The term "good girl," of course, implicates its opposite—and reminds us of the dichotomies of *Cobra Woman*, *The Dark Mirror*, and *A Stolen Life* (also starring Bette Davis). The title *Dangerous* conjures up all the myths of woman as femme fatale, be it Elsa Bannister or Violette Nozière. (In one clip, Bette Davis tells Franchot Tone, "I'm bad for people.") Trisha's monologue eventually confronts this issue head-on. She says: "In our culture a woman is desirable only so long as she can inspire fear. For the heterosexual male, woman is dangerous." This statement occurs while another relevant movie is on the screen: *Gilda*, (1946) with Rita Hayworth. Here the star of *The Lady from Shanghai* embodies another vamp who is redeemed only by the film's hokey ending. Later in *The Man*, we will see a shot from *In a Lonely Place* (1950), also a *film noir*.

Rainer includes an excerpt from *Double Indemnity*, a crime film about a wicked woman who encourages her lover to kill her husband. This work is also significant because the book on which the film was based was written by James Cain (alluded to in *Rich and Famous*), and the film script was written by Raymond Chandler, king of the hardboiled school of detective fiction. Later in *The Man*, when Jack brags about his success with women, his words are lifted from Chandler's diaries. Jack boasts, for example, that "the most puritanical woman I met went to bed with me a week after I met her." During the clip from *Double Indemnity*, Rainer also asserts its connections to Jack's consciousness. Just after he talks of how women must be treated with tenderness, Barbara Stanwyck implores her man to "hold her close."

One of the longest extracts in *The Man* is from George Romero's *Night of the Living Dead* (1968). While it plays, Trisha has an offscreen telephone conversation with friends. On several occasions, she refers to the issue of domestic life: "what passed for a family" in her existence. She also discusses Jean Eustache's *The Mother and the Whore* (1973), whose title invokes a similar theme. (In discussing that work in a 1976 interview, Rainer exclaimed: "What other film has so explicitly dealt with the child-man's expectations of women?"[35]) At one point, Trisha even relates adult male behavior to infantile scenar-

[35] Bergstrom, Flitterman, Lyon, and Penley, 81. Rainer makes additional references to the film on pages 81–84.

313

ios: "Men spend their lives alternating between punishing and seeking mothering from women, and carry their rage and terror out of the family realm and into the public." Given this context, the clip from Romero's film (of a zombie-like daughter stabbing her mother, and a brother murdering his sister) seems an ironic portrait of the brutal dynamics of the family. Critics like Robin Wood have often read the horror film in this vein.[36]

Alternately, the excerpt can be seen to exemplify masculine notions of "entertainment," inextricably interwoven with blood and guts. As the excerpt unwinds, Trisha explains why she called her hero Jack Deller (and not Jack Teller), noting that the latter name was "too close to the father of the hydrogen bomb." Despite her disclaimers, we sense the links between the horror film and nuclear violence, and fear that the legacy of male necrophilia may be "*years* of the living dead." By alluding to this broader context, Rainer (like Zetterling) expands her concerns beyond the microcosm of interpersonal relations to the macrocosm of international politics.

The Romero extract is presented in a different fashion than the others. On this occasion, we see an audience that looks at the film (but ignores Jack sitting onstage). Eventually, the spectators break out in a fight that rivals the carnage pictured onscreen. One critic noted that the viewers "stand in" for the missing psychiatrist—a notion that equates movie spectatorship with patient analysis.

At one point, an excerpt appears from Max Ophuls's *Caught* (1949), a work of the gothic cinema in which a young girl marries a millionaire and then tries to escape her fate. The title reminds us of other moments in Rainer's film, particularly the segment in which Jack and Jackie (who are ex-lovers) talk in a corridor during a party. Rainer's description of the sequence makes clear its connection to the notion of being "caught":

> The scene in the corridor is about seduction and repulsion, the old song and dance. . . . The corridor might be seen as a metaphor for the man's state. [Jack's] wife has left him and he's obsessed with women. . . . The corridor is a sort of physical metaphor for this kind of entrapment.[37]

Significantly, Jackie is dressed like a vamp, and, as Rainer states, she "seems to fit the stereotype of the 'dangerous' woman. She's dressed in

36 Robin Wood, *Hollywood from Vietnam to Reagan* (New York: Columbia University Press, 1986), 70–94.
37 Rainer, "Beyond Mythologies" 3.

314

a very low-cut gown and is doing some rather seductive things—the classic Hollywood image."[38] There are even more subtle links between the corridor scene and the extract of *Caught*, as Rainer notes in her discussion of the interrelationships of modes of discourse:

> Jackie Raynal is in the corridor talking about feminism and the new demands it has made on women. Her text contains images like going to a costume ball. . . . Now it cuts to a full frame of Barbara Bel Geddes and James Mason [in *Caught*] going onto the dance floor.[39]

Aside from quoting the mainstream cinema, Rainer excerpts films from the avant-garde (as well as dedicating *The Man* to Hollis Frampton). At one point, we see an image from Michael Snow's *Wavelength*, a film that eschewed the human figure along with narrative structure. Significantly, the shot from *Wavelength* depicts a loft space—the film's entire mise-en-scène. The hermetic seal around that loft is broken in Rainer's refusal to stay within a fine-arts context. Documentary footage presents New York City Council hearings on whether artists or the disadvantaged should be given low-rent spaces, and we are made to feel the problematic context in which avant-garde film gets made. As Trisha states: "I allied myself with others of my class, and we met the enemy and it was *us*." Rainer eventually supersedes the confines of the American art world to position her text within a discourse on patriarchy, colonialism, and global violence.

Rainer also refers to certain female colleagues or precursors within the avant-garde. At one point, a dance film clip appears in which Trisha Brown performs. The shot is from *Water Motor* (1978) by Babette Mangolte, the cinematographer of other Rainer films. Jackie Raynal (who plays Jackie) is also a cinéaste, having made such works as *Deux Fois* (1970).[40] The voice of artist Martha Rosler is heard on the soundtrack as well.

In its montage of cinematic discourses, *The Man* not only quotes from, or alludes to, specific works, it presents a smorgasbord of filmic modes. Many of the clips are from the classical cinema, and Rainer's

---

[38] Ibid.   [39] Ibid.

[40] For an analysis of *Deux Fois*, see Janet Bergstrom, Sandy Flitterman, Elisbeth Hart Lyon, and Constance Penley, "An Interrogation of the Cinematic Sign: Woman as Sexual Signifier: Jackie Raynal's *Deux Fois*," *Camera Obscura* 1 (Fall 1976): 11–26. See also "*Deux Fois*: Shot Commentary," 27–52. It is interesting that this premier issue of *Camera Obscura* also contains two sections devoted to Rainer's work: "Yvonne Rainer: An Introduction," 53–75; and "Yvonne Rainer: Interview," 76–96.

basic story (about the travails of Trisha and Jack) follows the model for conventional romance. Other excerpts, however, come from the experimental realm, and *The Man* itself fits within this broad category. Furthermore, the film incorporates documentary style through footage of City Council hearings and artist demonstrations, making it a virtual encyclopedia of cinematic languages.[41]

Through her use of film references, Rainer speaks in a "double-voiced discourse." Rather than present her views on sexual politics directly, she does so by quoting others, simultaneously displacing those discourses and refracting her own ideas.[42] She thus turns the language of the canonical cinema into an *image*, representing it (rather than allowing it simply to represent). In the process, she reveals that discourse is always ideological—a fact apparent in the excerpts of dangerous women, carnivorous families, or good and bad girls. She also demonstrates how the context for allusions is crucial: that the film extracts issue from Jack's neurotic male mind gives them a decidedly ironic cast.[43]

Beyond irony, Rainer draws heavily on the trope of parody in her inflection of cinematic excerpts. As Linda Hutcheon has remarked, this "is one of the ways in which modern artists have managed to come to terms with the weight of the past."[44] We have come across this mode before: Gunvor Nelson burlesques the filmic striptease; Doris Dörrie mocks gothic fiction and the fairy tale; Stephanie Beroes travesties romantic prose; Chantal Akerman sends up the musical; John Sayles ridicules film scholarship. Rainer, however, harnesses parody in two distinct ways.

After showing a clip from *Un Chien Andalou*, a pioneering surrealist work that replicates the dream, Rainer lauches her own oneiric fantasy—but in a comical mode. In this episode, Rainer is situated in a domestic environment doing absurd culinary tasks (throwing dishes on the floor, removing a decoy duck from the refrigerator). William Raymond then appears and maneuvers her into a "tango kiss." The couple retires to bed. Meanwhile, Rainer's voice is heard offscreen commenting on the reverie, casting it in decidedly Freudian terms:

> Hey! What's this? . . . There's my mother and she's only 48 years old. . . . My God, what's *Jack* doing in here? . . . That's

---

[41] Jane Desmond discusses the various modes of filmic discourse in her article.

[42] Bakhtin, 333.   [43] Ibid., 358.

[44] Linda Hutcheon, *A Theory of Parody* (New York and London: Methuen, 1985), 29.

me in the bed. He and *I* shouldn't be making love. Jack and *Mama* are supposed to be married in this dream, not Jack and me.

Clearly, the "tango kiss" relates this sequence to the Buñuel work, parts of which were evidently accompanied by Latin dance music. But the dream also constitutes a parody of the Electral dilemma, which was configured quite seriously in a film like *Violette*.

In other segments, rather than construct an original jest, Rainer forces the classical cinema to mock (or parody) itself merely by framing it in a devious manner. For Hutcheon, parody is based on the theme of difference, on "an opposition or contrast between texts."[45] By embedding the dominant cinema within her experimental film, Rainer makes that antithesis clear—both on a formal and an ideological level.

Ultimately, Rainer's orchestration of the "discourse of cinema" must be seen within the setting of other languages with which it coexists. These systems also confront the issue of male/female relations and extend the critique launched through filmic references. There is the "discourse of common wisdom" (similar to Roland Barthes's cultural code).[46] Repeatedly, we hear snatches of conversation between men and women on the street, whose words echo and parody conventional stereotypes and misconceptions. A woman says: "I don't want a man who's my equal. I want a man who knows more than me." A man claims that "only gays and women get emotionally involved in love." We often hear one person quote someone else in a manner that reveals patriarchal beliefs. On one occasion, a man stands in the corridor with Jack and Jackie, talking about a guy he knows who does not see the "fuss" about rape, who thinks that "the vagina is only an orifice like any other." When Jack becomes enraged and starts to attack the man, the latter defends himself by shouting: "Hey, *I* didn't say it!" What this shows is how clichés are circulated, how "in real life people talk most of all about what others talk about."[47] Rainer complicates this situation by having her film's protagonists mouth the words of famous writers. As she states, language is "uttered but not possessed by my performers as they operate within the filmic frame."[48] Jack is a ventriloquist for Raymond Chandler, Trisha for Monique Wittig, and Jackie for Meaghan Morris. This sense of the appropriation of language is extended by Jack's practice of eavesdropping on people. He walks

[45] Ibid., 32.
[46] Roland Barthes, *S/Z*, trans. Richard Miller (New York: Hill and Wang, 1974), 20.
[47] Bakhtin, 338.   [48] Rainer, quoted in Phelan, 17.

317

around town wearing large headphones that are perhaps feeding him some prerecorded text. But he also seems to listen surreptitiously to other people's language—a virtual "auditeur."

Along with the "discourse of common wisdom" is the "language of humor"—a symbolic system that reflects the social tensions of its day. In *The Man*, several people on the street crack jokes loaded with cynical meaning. One woman asks another a Sphinx-like riddle, "What is the best way to a man's heart?" and responds, "Through his chest." This gag draws on the difference between metaphorical and literal meaning (between man's heart as a figurative synecdoche and as a bodily organ). But it also brings to the fore a shift in feminine consciousness from submission to revolt, and represents the gallows humor so apparent in *A Question of Silence*. Later in the film, another woman mocks the language of the comic aphorism by stating: "A feminist is a man who's found a new way to meet broads." Implicit in this witticism is the notion that woman's discourse can be co-opted by the male. *The Man* is replete with such significant comical moments. Peggy Phelan states that Rainer's metaphysics "can't go too long without a joke."[49] And Mary Russo finds in Rainer's satire "the conflictual laughter of social subjects in a classist, racist, ageist, sexist society."[50] Given Rainer's penchant for both humor and quotation, it is intriguing that theorists have perceived similarities in the two processes. Perri writes that "it is useful to compare alluding with joking, as the latter is described by Freud. . . . It is no diachronic accident that [the] etymological origin of 'allusion' is the Latin *alludere,* to joke, jest, mock, or play with."[51]

Rainer also invokes the "discourse of mythology"—a system we found integral to *The Lady from Shanghai*. In one of Trisha's monologues, she examines the legend of the dangerous woman, linking it to archetypal fears of the female body: "For the heterosexual male, woman is dangerous because she menstruates. The mystery and power of the menses evoke in him the fear of castration." On another occasion, a man on the street recounts an American Indian tale in which a fellow uses a big stick to plug up a "devouring vagina." He adds: "But . . . the bottom line is women really *do* want to devour men." Finally, even Trisha's discussion of the mother/whore dichotomy brings up Si-

---

[49] Phelan, ibid.

[50] Mary Russo, quoted in Mellencamp, "Images," 101. From "Female Grotesques: Carnival and Theory," in Teresa de Lauretis, ed., *Feminist Studies/ Critical Studies* (Bloomington: Indiana University Press, 1986), 213–29.

[51] Perri, 301.

mone de Beauvoir's notion that for every female myth, there is one that takes the opposite position.[52]

Among the "discourses of everyday life" that Rainer considers is the "first-person confessional." Trisha's initial monologue complains:

> It was a hard week. I split up with my husband and moved into my studio. The hot water heater broke and flooded the textile merchant downstairs.

Sometimes her reflections veer into a "discourse of the unconscious," and her narration (like that of Louise in *Riddles*) borders on stream of consciousness. Early in the film, she muses:

> Oh, oh, oh the biting man; the man who looks; the man who offers the little girl candy in return for. . . . They were all there in full regalia.

Here we have the flip side of the male dread of woman. But while masculine anxieties are based on such fantasies as the *vagina dentata*, female fears (of voyeurs and sexual molesters) are unfortunately more real.

On certain occasions, Trisha's monologues bespeak the "discourse of sociology." In delineating how young women are favored in our society, she states:

> The currency of this view in Western culture with its frequent accompaniment of despair is upheld and offset by privileges associated with being a fertile young woman. But these privileges . . . are paid for with the agreement that they will be lost at the coming of menopause.

Juxtaposed with this is the "discourse of male bravado," which has been honed to a fine art by Jack (and Raymond Chandler). On one occasion, Jack states condescendingly:

> I knew so little about women then; I know almost too much now. And yet I have for a moment failed to realize that they face hazards in life which a man does not face and therefore should be given a special tenderness and consideration.

Segments of "political discourse" invoke problems beyond the women's movement. Once, when considering the artist/indigent conflict, Trisha states:

[52] Simone de Beauvoir, *The Second Sex*, trans. H. M. Parshley (New York: Random House, 1974), 223.

In Guatemala the war against Communism is, in actuality, a war against the poor. Here, in America, the war against the poor does not yet have to be masked as a war against Communism.

Sometimes Trisha mocks Jack's political discourse as a way of retaliating. In discussing his infidelities, she parodies the manner in which he would justify the situation:

> He was a mass of contradictions and what else could one expect under Capitalism? "Consistency is the hypocrisy of repressed bourgeois liberals," he would say.

She then launches another attack, mimicking and appropriating his mode of analysis, hoisting him on his own petard:

> Sometimes, fresh from reading Fredric Jameson or Russell Jacoby I could play his game at equal cross purposes. "Consumption of goods in the economic sphere runs parallel with sexual consumption in the personal. The womanizer needs a 'new model' to replace the old. The new model, though shoddier than the old, diverts attention from one's boredom, or emptiness, or terror."

Rainer not only mocks male political discourse but also satirizes the clichés of feminism, making a facile binary opposition impossible. (She says that she is just as interested in "bad guys making progressive political sense" as in "good girls shooting off their big toe and mouth.")[53] At one point, Jack finds a message on his answering machine (spoken by Rainer): "I just had lunch with a woman who once had an affair with you, a while back, who's now a lesbian and a black belt in karate." Similarly, in creating female protagonists for her films, Rainer refuses to concoct some homogenized ideal:

> I have no more investment in triumphant woman than I have in sex-object woman. I can only reflect the reality of my own experience, which continues to be about loving, hating, acting stupid, "waking up," trying to "sleep," being in despair, being courageous, being terrified, getting excited, getting outraged, laughing. A story about a woman who is only courageous is not enough for me.[54]

[53] Rainer, "Some Ruminations," 25.
[54] Rainer, in Bergstrom, Flitterman, Lyon, and Penley, 96.

Hearing this, we suspect that Rainer would have patience for a character like Anna Blume in *Straight through the Heart*—a woman who refuses to be "triumphant" or "courageous," like Lisa Berndle.

Just as political language is frequently used to woman's disadvantage, so is "medical discourse"—a system encountered in the 1940s twin films and in *Violette*. On numerous occasions, Rainer invokes the institution of psychoanalysis to reveal its misogyny. One woman on the street states:

> So, his shrink says to him, "If you're going to fool around with other women, you'd better learn to become a better liar"; and goddamn it, he did!

In the 1940s melodrama, the heroine's mind/body were often envisioned as a topography of symptoms to be decoded by the astute male physician. A critique of this position occurs on several occasions in Rainer's work. When someone asks Trisha how she is, she morbidly replies:

> How am I? Well, considering my . . . cystic breasts, my uterine fibroids, my absorption problems . . . my varicose veins, and my deteriorating cervical disk, I guess I'm doing okay.

But it is through an analysis of the "language of advertising" that Rainer accomplishes her major attack on the medical establishment. Trisha has left a tableau of images tacked to the wall in Jack's apartment.[55] One of them is an advertisement from a professional journal hawking a hormonal product prescribed for menopausal women. A middle-aged female is depicted, in medium close-up, who shows the unmistakable signs of mental distress. An offscreen voice (Martha Rosler) analyzes the advertisement, noting that the matron is "portrayed as nothing but an inner life—a disorder," that the text is addressed to the male physician, and that the product, ironically, is named "*conjugated* estrogen." She also contrasts the advertisement to another in Trisha's collage aimed at the man who "owns his first million [and] knows what it takes to make it in this world."

The "language of advertising," however, is only part of the larger "discourse of journalism" that Rainer lambasts in the film. Next to the advertisements, Trisha has tacked an "About Men" column from the *New York Times*, authored by a priest. When the column is first seen,

---

[55] Interestingly, Rainer has mentioned that she pins up such "collages" on her own wall as sketches for works in progress. See Bergstrom, Flitterman, Lyon, and Penley, 86.

Rainer complains that the essays give voice to "male sensitivity" recently liberated from masculine stoicism. She states (from offscreen):

> It's the . . . wimpiest version of why men should change. It's again that they themselves will benefit as opposed to how the rest of us *suffer* from the way men are. This column's all about how the *man* suffers.

She also notes that "About Men" appeared at that time in the prestigious Sunday magazine, while its counterpart, "Hers," came out in the Thursday "Home" section, along with advertisements for furnishings. Later, Rosler says that "About Men" is pernicious because it implies that women "have gotten ahead of the game," that journalism "must redress the balance." Relating it to the advertisement for female hormones, she remarks: "it seems that what men want is an ability to feel without the necessity of the hormones that are imposed on us poor victim women."

Within Trisha's tableau (which Rainer terms "a gallery of contemporary issues"[56]), two other textual artifacts appear: a photograph of decapitated heads (from *Mother Jones*), taken in San Salvador, and an article from the *New York Times Magazine* written by an agent of the KGB. Again, the connections with earlier documents are resonant: the KGB agent's discourse opposes that of the priest in "About Men"; the bloodied head (a classic symbol of castration) reminds us of the problematic female body—dreaded in myth and cinema, as well as in medical advertisement. In a sense, Trisha's tableau is a microcosm of Rainer's filmic style, which places disparate texts in radical juxtaposition.

Other journalistic references impinge on male/female relations. Jack picks up an issue of *Playboy*, which has arrived with his left-wing mail: his liberal consciousness finds no contradiction in his conservative sexual politics. As he gazes at the centerfold, Rainer herself crawls before the camera, shouting: "Will all menstruating women please leave the theater!" Not only does her action fracture the diegetic illusion, it asserts the presence of the female body repressed in the sanitized, erotic pinup. Finally, it reengages the notion of female sexuality as dangerous—as necessitating the radical act of banishment.

If men have their girlie magazines, women have their self-help columns. In a parody of this mode, a woman's voice asks:

> Dear Abby: I've found *Playboy* magazine in my boyfriend's apartment. . . . Shouldn't sex with me be enough for him? — Available

56 Rainer, "Beyond Mythologies," 4.

Abby responds: "Don't question men's desires, and stay available."

Lest we assume that voyeurism is confined to the stratum of pornography, Rainer plants another image that directs the same charge at traditional art. As though to illustrate the theories of John Berger, we are shown a classic painting of a naked woman (Manet's *Déjeuner sur l'herbe*), as Trisha's stream-of-consciousness monologue intones: "I, the nude on the grass."

Beyond references to the pictorial arts, Rainer also orchestrates the "discourse of literature" to advance her feminist arguments, particularly that of masculine rhetoric. As Sandra M. Gilbert has written:

> To give revisionary answers to ... questions about literary women is also to ask and answer questions about literary men, about the dynamics of male-female relations in the world of letters, about the nexus of genre and gender, about the secret intersections of sexuality and textuality.[57]

We have already mentioned Raymond Chandler, and there are references to Ralph Ellison as well. In discussing male immaturity, Trisha also mentions various Anglo-Saxon nursery rhymes, all of which focus on the masculine position: "The house that Jack built, Jack Sprat could eat no fat, Little Jack Horner, Jack and Jill went up the hill, Jack be nimble, Jack be quick." But within the literary dimension, it is the "language of critical theory" that Rainer stresses.

The commentaries on Trisha's tableau are prototypical of art criticism, which excavates a work's meaning and significance. It is important that Jack Deller is a college professor, and that in one lengthy scene he lectures his class, mentioning such thinkers as Freud, Lacan, Derrida, and Saussure. (In her script for the film, Rainer even writes in a part for Peter Wollen to analyze the newspaper collage.) On some level, Rainer takes these theoretical ideas quite seriously, since Jack's talk touches on topics integral to her film: the constitution of language, the varieties of speech, cinema theory, sexual difference, psychoanalysis, etc. Sometimes, in fact, his words seem eminently appropriate to a discussion of the film he is *in*. During his lecture he mentions the function of irony, clearly a central strategy of *The Man*. He also points out that when difference is repressed, it is often seen as opposition—a concept that explains the male fears of women cataloged by Rainer.

Despite this, his lecture is parodied as a discourse to hold in question. At one point, Jack mentions having recently met with Foucault

[57] Sandra M. Gilbert, "What Do Feminist Critics Want?" in Elaine Showalter, ed., *The New Feminist Criticism* (New York: Pantheon, 1985), 35.

for "just a personal conversation." He promises to tell the students an anecdote about it someday. Here we have the sense of a good-old-boy network, of Deller name-dropping prominent theorists. Implicit in the mimicking of critical discourse is the sense that it is inherently a male terrain, that while it may be useful for women (as it is for Rainer herself), total allegiance to it can become yet another form of oppression. As Trisha says: "If a girl takes her eyes off Lacan and Derrida long enough to look, she may discover she is the invisible man." Significantly, at another point, Trisha informs someone that Jack's last name is meant to signify "Tell Her"—just what we presume men (like Freud, Lacan, and others) are always doing to women.

While warning of the dangers of masculine discourse, Rainer cites the work of certain female thinkers. In one conversation, Trisha suggests that her friends read Dorothy Dinnerstein and Nancy Chodorow.[58] Rainer also quotes from women's writing. When Jackie converses with Jack in the hallway, she uses the words of Meaghan Morris; when Trisha talks about her relations with men, she "borrows" her words from Monique Wittig:

> I know there will sometimes be excruciating sadness, but I also know something is different now—something in the direction of unwomanliness—not a new woman, or non-woman or misanthropist, or anti-woman and not non-practicing lesbian—maybe unwoman is also the wrong term—a-woman is closer—a-womanly—a-womanliness.

If the classical cinema speaks of *A Man and a Woman*, Rainer's film envisions *A Man and A-woman*.[59]

Dark Victory: Toward A-Cinema

[F]ilms can only be rerun or remade. —Stanley Cavell[60]

As Trisha (and Wittig) struggle for a way to be women (without actualizing male stereotypes or opposing them in a simplistic fashion),

---

[58] Dorothy Dinnerstein, *The Mermaid and the Minotaur* (New York, Hagerstown, Md., San Francisco, and London: Harper & Row, 1976); Nancy Chodorow, *The Reproduction of Mothering* (Berkeley, Los Angeles, and London: University of California Press, 1978).

[59] *A Man and a Woman* (1966) is a French film made by Claude Lelouch.

[60] Stanley Cavell, *Pursuits of Happiness: The Hollywood Comedy of Remarriage* (Cambridge, Mass., and London: Harvard University Press, 1981), 52.

so Rainer and the other feminist filmmakers we have encountered struggle for what we might term "a-cinema."

While filmmakers like Mulvey/Wollen, Beroes, von Trotta, Dörrie, and Zetterling implicitly critique the dominant film in their work, Rainer does so explicitly by incorporating excerpts of the classics into her screen collage. She thereby brings to the surface the intertextuality submerged in previous feminist cinema. In fact, her work is so "derivative" that it bears comparison to the literary *cento* as described by Bakhtin—a "patchwork" genre that is "a poetic compilation . . . of passages selected from the work of great poets of the past."[61]

Furthermore, many of Rainer's clips have direct relevance to films we have previously critiqued. Rita Hayworth, of *The Lady from Shanghai*, reappears in *The Man* as Gilda; the femme fatale, examined in *Violette* and *A Question of Silence*, returns as the heroine of *Double Indemnity*. The actress, analyzed in *Persona* and *The Girls*, recurs in a clip from *Dangerous*.

Many of the issues confronted in the book are echoed in Rainer's film: the mythification of woman (discussed in *The Lady from Shanghai* and *Riddles of the Sphinx*), the medical discourse (examined in the twin films and *Violette*), voyeurism and fetishism (noted in *Dames*, *Fatima*, and *Take Off*), parody (analyzed in *The Eighties* and *Straight through the Heart*). Beyond this, Rainer even tackles the metacritical task of examining the theories that explain her art. She quotes Freud, Lacan, Derrida, Foucault, Dinnerstein, and Chodorow—a pantheon of thinkers who have influenced recent film practice and scholarship.

Finally, Rainer takes on the problem of the female spectator (what does she "want"?)—an issue that has wended its way through this book. According to one critical faction, the classical cinema has failed woman by giving her either no pleasure at all or the false promises of objectification and masochism. (Like Judy in *Dance, Girl, Dance*, woman is merely this cinema's "Stooge.") Another group has attempted to unearth the submerged feminine voice in such films (their textual saving graces), arguing that female viewers are not as naive or self-punitive as we had supposed. In *The Women Who Knew Too Much*, for example, Tania Modleski takes a revisionist stance on the work of Alfred Hitchcock, which feminists have frequently maligned.[62] A third position has formed around the avant-garde cinema—seen to

[61] Bakhtin, 69. (This term occurs within a footnote.)

[62] Tania Modleski, *The Women Who Knew Too Much: Hitchcock and Feminist Theory* (New York: Methuen, 1988).

be the female viewer's only salvation—allowing her to be (like Bubbles in *Dance, Girl, Dance*) "lily white." Judith Mayne characterizes this problem in an overview of feminist film criticism. She describes how contemporary theory

> posits a monolithic object, the classical Hollywood cinema, in relation to which the female spectator can occupy only an alienated, and ultimately impossible, position. Hence, much feminist criticism has been concerned *to open up* the dualities of the classical cinema, whether in the name of female spectatorship or in the name of a new kind of cinematic practice.[63]

This question of female spectatorship has surfaced numerous times in the book, both inside and outside the filmic diegeses. In our discussion of *Letter from an Unknown Woman*, we likened Lisa Berndle to a film fan, and her lover to a matinee idol. In our examination of *Violette*, we noted the murderess's fascination with screen stars—her pinups of Bette Davis and Lillian Gish. In *Sotto, Sotto*, Ester's "perversion" is tied to her fanatical film fixation. By contrast, in the oppositional works, woman's spectator status is imagined quite differently. Lianna Massey refuses to go to the cinema and, only in her most despondent moments, succumbs to the lure of daytime TV. In *Riddles of the Sphinx*, the only film mentioned is a feminist one: Mary Kelly's *Post Partum Document*. Finally, in *The Bad Sister*, our heroine is a *critic*, making woman's defensive viewing posture all the more clear.

In my analysis of various films, I have occupied the different "positions" of the female spectator. In discussing *Rich and Famous*, for example, I found myself largely barred from the text, while in *Dames* I found reassuring elements of "critique." In dealing with feminist "theory film," I enacted the third stance, moving on more rarefied and purist ground.

In *The Man*, Rainer embraces all the possibilities and contradictions of female spectatorship and accepts the fact that we cannot yet sort them out. Thus she affectionately includes myriad classical movie clips—nostalgic cinematic moments that she refuses to relinquish, that return, though repressed. (They are the images she clearly "loves to hate.") Here Rainer allows herself a certain ambivalence and remains suspicious of prescriptions to be cinematically (or politically) "correct." As she notes:

[63] Judith Mayne, "Feminist Film Theory and Women at the Movies," *Profession 87* (New York: Modern Language Association), 15 (my italics).

> Just as I can't manipulate my position in the scheme of things to match the ideal of the person I ought to be, neither can I bring myself to try creating an exemplary woman through my films. . . . my women will probably continue to vacillate between being fools, heroines, and—yes—victims. Victims of their own expectations no less than those of the opposite sex, or of the prevailing social mores.[64]

The same might be said of the female audience.

But Rainer does more in *The Man* than monumentalize the woman viewer's confusion; she opens up (as Mayne suggests) a space for her to inhabit the text. While the character of Trisha is ostensibly a persona within the narrative (who simply is unrepresented on screen), her status as a voice-off (seen once from the rear) makes her seem an *extra-textual* presence, not only beyond the filmic frame but outside its diegesis. In fact, she seems to stand in for the female spectator who (along with her) observes Rainer's film.

At certain points, Trisha's status as viewer is given prominence. At one moment, she discusses with friends her experience of *The Mother and the Whore*; at another, she comments (as though a member of the audience) on the wall collage projected on the screen; in an obvious instance, she anticipates the lines of a film clip: during a passage from *Clash by Night*, she notes, "This is where he says: 'A man is nothing without a woman.'" If Trisha is a surrogate for the female spectator, her invisibility configures this viewer as unfathomable—an "*unknown woman*" to film scholarship and to herself. In Rainer's invocation of this and all other theoretical issues, her film constitutes a virtual catalogue of the major tendencies in feminist cinema and criticism of the 1970s and 1980s.

The Man also provides us with a final opportunity to comprehend the value of an intertextual approach. If some are displeased with the notion of women's films as "remakes" of the mainstream cinema, it should be understood that such a process is not limited to women's art but is a condition of all discourse. Bakhtin writes: "Every age re-accentuates in its own way the works of its most immediate past. The historical life of classic works is in fact the uninterrupted process of their social and ideological re-accentuation."[65] What Rainer and other filmmakers do is precisely to "re-accentuate" the classical cinema—and through this displacement, make it speak in a different voice. This condition neither distinguishes women's cinema nor demeans it; rather, it

[64] Rainer, in Bergstrom et al., 95.   [65] Bakhtin, 420–21.

situates that work within the dynamic interplay of film history. Edward Said has commented on the irrelevance of "originality" to modern art: today, "[t]he writer thinks less of writing originally, and more of rewriting."[66] Similarly, Roland Barthes has instructed us that the subject approaching the text is never a unique presence but is "already itself a plurality of other texts."[67]

Beyond constituting a mode of revision, reaccentuation is also a means of reclaiming. For Bakhtin, this process allows works to "continue to grow and develop even after the moment of their creation."[68] Thus reaccentuation can offer the female viewer an out from feminist "puritanism" by allowing her the guilty pleasures of the dominant film. She can have her cake and eat it too, can claim a (dark) victory.[69]

Bakhtin makes a final point that helps us formulate the legacy of an intertextual approach. In discussing how discourse solicits an answer, he says: "To some extent, primacy belongs to the response, as the activating principle: it creates the ground for understanding. . . . *Understanding comes to fruition only in the response.*"[70] In creating a counter-cinema reactive to the classical mode, feminist filmmakers are not only opposing that model but *understanding* it—grappling with it and their placement in its universe. Thus the process of addressing mainstream film is not one of stasis (as some might fear) but one of movement; not one of passivity but one of activity; not one of entrapment but one of growth.

As filmmakers struggle to comprehend sexual difference and the cinema, so do the spectators of their films. Intertextual works require enormous energy from their readers, who are also "active co-creators."[71] The feminist counter-cinema rewards the efforts of the spectator. If it requires her to recall and reframe the history of film, it also allows her "to *re-imagine*" it, as Rainer would say.[72]

Rainer dedicates *The Man* to Hollis Frampton, whose thoughts are relevant here. Although Frampton was not interested in conventional film chronology, he was intrigued by what he called its "metahistory":

> The historian of cinema faces an appalling problem. Seeing in his subject some principle of intelligibility, he is obliged to make

---

[66] Edward Said, *The World, The Text, and The Critic* (Cambridge: Harvard University Press, 1983), 135.

[67] Barthes, 10.   [68] Bakhtin, 422.

[69] See Janet Bergstrom, "Enunciation and Sexual Difference," *Camera Obscura* 3–4 (1979): 58–59; David Rodowick, "The Difficulty of Difference," *Wide Angle* 5 (1982): 4–15; Laura Mulvey, "Afterthoughts on 'Visual Pleasure and Narrative Cinema' Inspired by *Duel in the Sun* (King Vidor, 1946)," *Framework*, nos. 15–17 (1981): 12–15.

[70] Bakhtin, 282 (my italics).   [71] Hutcheon, 93.   [72] Rainer, in Ahlgren.

himself responsible for every frame of film in existence. . . . The metahistorian of cinema, on the other hand, is occupied with inventing a *tradition*, that is, a coherent wieldy set of discrete monuments, meant to inseminate resonant consistency into the growing body of his art. . . . Such works may not exist, and then it is his duty to make them.[73]

In excerpting films in *The Man*, Rainer has functioned as a "metahistorian," reimagining and rearranging film history (as I have done in this book) to reveal a particular pattern. In creating *The Man*, she also activates Frampton's final option—of fashioning the works that must be realized in order to give film history its "proper" shape.

As feminist directors have responded to the canonical cinema, so I have reacted to their work and thereby attempted to fathom the question of women and film. In *The Man*, Rainer allows the character of Trisha to "stand in" for the female spectator as well as for *her*: both are middle-aged artists living in New York. As Trisha is an alter ego for Rainer, so Rainer is a "double" for me, since her film performs an act of criticism and metahistory similar to my own. If Trisha's wall tableau mirrors the structure of Rainer's film, both echo the collagist mode of this book, which seeks to juxtapose cinematic discourses, to rearrange its monuments, to comprehend the patriarchal and feminist film, to engage the theories that have explained and contained them.

[73] Hollis Frampton, "For a Metahistory of Film: Commonplace Notes and Hypotheses," *Artforum* (September 1971): 31–35.

Special thanks to Tania Modleski for suggesting that I look at *The Man*, and to Dana Polan for suggesting its use in an epilogue.

329

Appendix
List of Additional Films and Topics for Teaching

If one were to teach a course on women and film that utilized this book, one could obviously program the specific films that I have discussed. On the other hand, one might want (a) to treat the same subjects but choose alternate films; or (b) to treat different subjects and other films. The following list is offered as variations on the theme.

I have taught many of the films suggested below and know that they work well within the context I have established. My mention of others is based on more distant and casual recollection. I do not mean to imply that each pair of films selected will include neat patriarchal and feminist poles; many works fall somewhere in-between.

I have not provided rental information for the titles mentioned because it changes so frequently and varies for the United States and Europe. Also, the proliferation of videotape in recent years has meant that schools can frequently more economically purchase (than rent) particular films. Therefore, I have provided only the dates and directors of the films in question.

Alternate Films on the Topics Covered

CHAPTER 1/THE SHOWGIRL. For other feature films about the showgirl, consider using Howard Hawks's *Gentlemen Prefer Blondes* (1953), Charles Vidor's *Cover Girl* (1944), or Josef von Sternberg's *The Blue Angel* (1929). For the counter-cinema one could also discuss Dorothy Arzner's *Dance, Girl, Dance* (1940)—as opposed to viewing it primarily as a musical, as I do in Chapter 5. One might also consider *I'm No Angel* (1933). Although Mae West did not, technically, direct her films, she tends to be considered their "auteur." *I'm No Angel* is based on one of her stories.

CHAPTER 2/MYTHIC DISCOURSE. One might use G. W. Pabst's *Pandora's Box* (1928) and compare it with Stephanie Beroes's *The Dream Screen* (1986), which utilizes clips from the Pabst film and invokes the legend. Another interesting classical film that draws on mythology is Jacques Tourneur's *The Cat People* (1942). Laura Mulvey and Peter Wollen's film *Penthesilea* (1974) also critiques traditional myths.

CHAPTER 3/THE ACTRESS. From the mainstream cinema, one could focus on any of the films I mention in passing (e.g., *Torch Song*

[1953], *All About Eve* [1950], *Indiscreet* [1958], or one could choose other films about the actress, like *Imitation of Life* [1934/1959]). For the feminist counterresponse, one could examine Jeanne Moreau's *Lumière* (1976) or Yvonne Rainer's *The Lives of Performers* (1972).

CHAPTER 4/HETEROSEXUAL ROMANCE. For a traditional work on the topic, one could show Ken Russell's *Women in Love* (1970). Other women's films on the subject include: Maria Luisa Bemberg's *Camila* (1984), Helke Sanders's *The Trouble with Love* (1984), and Humberto Solas's *Lucia*/Part 1 (1972). The latter is directed by a man, hence illustrating once more that a feminist filmmaker can be male.

CHAPTER 5/GENRE. Instead of focusing on the musical and its revision, one could approach another genre. For example, one could counterpose a female gothic film (like Robert Siodmak's *The Spiral Staircase* [1946]) with an avant-garde variation on the form (Maya Deren's *Meshes of the Afternoon* [1943]). Or one could counterpose a pirate film with Ulriche Ottinger's *Madame X* (1977). One could also contrast a standard melodrama like D. W. Griffith's *Way Down East* (1920) with a reconstruction of that form, Sally Potter's *The Gold Diggers* (1983). One might also examine "screwball comedy," counterposing a traditional film like Howard Hawks's *His Girl Friday* (1940) with Susan Seidelman's *Desperately Seeking Susan* (1985).

CHAPTER 6/THE DOUBLE. An interesting set of alternate films to compare would be Federico Fellini's *Juliet of the Spirits* (1965) and Susan Seidelman's *Desperately Seeking Susan* (1985). They do not deal with twins but do concern the female doppelgänger. (I have written about the films in *Close Viewings* [Florida State University Press], edited by Peter Lehman.) Brian De Palma's *Sisters* (1973) could also be used as a contemporary update of the 1940s Hollywood twin film.

CHAPTER 7/FRIENDSHIP. Instead of *Rich and Famous*, one might use George Cukor's earlier film *The Women* (1939). For recent women's films about friendship, one might consider Agnes Varda's *One Sings, The Other Doesn't* (1977) or Diane Kurys's *Entre Nous* (1983).

CHAPTER 8/LESBIANISM. For other sympathetic portrayals of lesbianism (in films directed by women), one might consider Diane Kurys's *Entre Nous* (1983), Donna Deitch's *Desert Hearts* (1985), or Leontine Sagan's *Maedchen in Uniform* (1932). One might also consider using Franco Brusati's *To Forget Venice* (1980), in which both male and female homosexuality are empathetically treated.

331

CHAPTER 9/THE MURDERESS. For another feminist view of a murderess, one might show Chantal Akerman's *Jeanne Dielman, 23 Quai du Commerce, 1080 Bruxelles* (1975).

Additional Topics and Films

MOTHERS AND DAUGHTERS. Albert and David Maysles's *Grey Gardens* (1976) compared with Su Friedrich's *The Ties that Bind* (1984)—two documentaries on the topic. One might also compare classical films like Michael Curtiz's *Mildred Pierce* (1945) or John Stahl's *Imitation of Life* (1934) (remade by Douglas Sirk in 1959) with experimental works of the counter-cinema like Chantal Akerman's *News from Home* (1977) or Michelle Citron's *Daughter Rite* (1978).

CHILDBIRTH. Stan Brakhage's *Window Water Baby Moving* (1959) compared with Marjorie Keller's *Misconceptions* (1973–1977).

THE AGING WOMAN. Billy Wilder's *Sunset Boulevard* (1950) compared with Lee Grant's *Tell Me a Riddle* (1980).

THE FEMALE ADOLESCENT. Jaromil Jires's *Valerie and Her Week of Wonders* (1971) or Brian De Palma's *Carrie* (1976) compared with Nelly Kaplan's *Nea* (1978) or Diane Kurys's *Peppermint Soda* (1978).

WOMEN AND NON-TRADITIONAL WORK. A mainstream wartime film like *Rosie the Riveter* (1944) juxtaposed with Connie Fields's *The Life and Times of Rosie the Riveter* (1978).

WOMEN AND PORNOGRAPHY. A commercial film like Paul Schrader's *Hardcore* (1979) compared with Bette Gordon's experimental *Variety* (1984).

THE FEMALE PHOTOGRAPHER. Irvin Kershner's *The Eyes of Laura Mars* (1978) compared with Valie Export's *Invisible Adversaries* (1976).

THE MARRIED WOMAN. Two silent films—Erich von Stroheim's *Foolish Wives* (1922) compared with Germaine Dulac's *The Smiling Madame Beudet* (1922).

THE UGLY DUCKLING. Irving Rapper's *Now, Voyager* (1942) compared with Suzana Amaral's *The Hour of the Star* (1986).

ANIMATION. Traditional animated films involving female characters (Betty Boop or Minnie Mouse) compared with Vera Neubauer's *Animation for Live Action* (1979).

332

FEMINIST REVOLUTION. Federico Fellini's *City of Women* (1980) compared with Lizzie Borden's *Born in Flames* (1983).

PROSTITUTION. Alan Pakula's *Klute* (1971) compared with Lizzie Borden's *Working Girls* (1986) or Chantal Akerman's *Jeanne Dielman, 23 Quai du Commerce, 1080 Bruxelles* (1975).

MAGIC. The films of Georges Méliès compared with those of Diana Barrie (e.g., *My Version of the Fall* [1978] and *Magic Explained* [1980]). Gunvor Nelson's *Take Off* (1973) can also be seen as a revision of the trick film.

DOMESTIC SPACE. Vincent Sherman's *Harriet Craig* (1950) compared with Dorothy Arzner's *Craig's Wife* (1936).

RAPE. William Dieterle's *The Accused* (1948) compared with Yannick Bellon's *Rape of Love* (1979).

WOMAN ARTIST. Compton Bennett's *The Seventh Veil* (1945)—about a woman pianist—or Curtis Bernhardt's *Devotion* (1946)—about the Brontë sisters—compared with Judy Collins and Jill Godmilow's *Antonia, A Portrait of the Woman* (1974)—about orchestra conductor Antonia Brico—or with Gillian Armstrong's *My Brilliant Career* (1980), about a writer.

Index

masochism, 58; and romance, 129; in *Sisters, or The Balance of Happiness*, 210–11, 213; woman as victim of, 163–64; woman and, 28, 101, 112, 117, 131. *See also* sisters, as masochist; woman, as masochist

Mason, James, 315

maternity. *See* mother; motherhood

matricide. *See* Electral complex

Mayne, Judith: on patriarchal cinema, 19; on interior monologue, 55; on self-reflexivity, 133; on screen metaphor, 160–61; on female spectator, 326

Mayron, Melanie, 233, 246

maze, 59, 61–62, 107; in *The Lady from Shanghai*, 45, 46–48; in *Riddles of the Sphinx*, 61, 62. *See also* Welles, Orson

Mazursky, Paul, 310

Medusa, 29–30, 44, 127, 144*n*23, 295, 298–99

Mellen, Joan, 250–51

Mellencamp, Patricia, 11

melodrama, 16, 162, 163–67, 174, 321

men: authority of, 306; and chauvinism, 262, 267; and destruction, 84–85, 211, 314; fears of, about women, 281–82; as hysteric, 102–3; immaturity of, 41–43, 46, 313–14, 323; and male discourse, 8, 41; and male passage, 46; as myth, 45–46; and power, 96, 121, 139, 211–12; and science and technology, 212–13, 214; and sexuality, 124; stereotypes of friendships of, 217, 219; and twins, 187; as violent, 284. *See also* machismo; patriarchy

menopause, 321

menstruation, 70, 88, 270, 309, 318, 322

Metropolis (1926), 192, 212

Metzger, Radley, 250

Midnight Cowboy (1969), 216

A Midsummer Night's Dream, 256

Mildred Pierce (1945), 56, 225, 228

Miller, J. Hillis, 14

Millett, Kate, 3

mirrors, 34, 147, 160, 183, 207, 274

The Mirror-Image of Dorian Gray in the Yellow Press (1984), 17

mirroring: in *Dames*, 138, 141; and mirror phase, 45, 76–77; and myth, 172; in *Persona*, 76–77, 79, 80; in *A Question of Silence*, 291; in *Riddles of the Sphinx*, 57–58; and twins, 187, 191; *Violette*, 274, 279. *See also* doppelgänger; double; doubling; mirrors; self-reflexivity

Misconception (1977), 12

Mitten ins Herz. See Straight through the Heart

Modleski, Tania, 3, 325; and castration, 106; and hysteria, 102, 104; and woman's desire, 96, 100; on sexual violence, 258; on *Swept Away*, 252

Moers, Ellen, 4

Monahan, Florence, 273, 284

Monroe, Marilyn, 133

montage, 23, 306–7, 315–16; in lesbian film, 265, 267; in *The Man Who Envied Women*, 304, 313; in *Persona*, 71; in *Riddles of the Sphinx*, 51, 52, 55, 62; in *A Question of Silence*, 288

Montesano, Enrico, 253, 257

Montez, Maria, 177

Moreau, Gustave, 51

Morning Bath (1896), 24

Morris, Meaghan, 317, 324

Morrisey, Paul, 250

mother: as actress, 80, 118; attachment of male to, 115–16, 120–21, 184; and career, 55, 60, 81–82; as dangerous, 43–44, 75–76; fixation with, 116; in *The Lady from Shanghai*, 42–43; as lover, 105–6; as martyr, 118; and mother/whore dichotomy, 193, 318–19; as mystery, 51; as myth, 46; single, 56, 58, 96, 101, 225; as Sphinx, 199; separation from, 54; as substitute, 107; woman as, 43, 62, 75–76, 127. *See also* motherhood

motherhood: depicted in film, 78–79, 88; discourse of, 59; dual nature of, 193; as depicted in *Letter from an Unknown Woman*, 101, 105; and mother/child relationship, 54, 70, 76, 120–21, 190, 201, 228–29; as depicted in *Persona*, 73–74, 75, 77; as depicted in *Riddles of the Sphinx*, 51, 54, 55, 58–60, 62. *See also* Oedipal complex; Oedipal tale

The Mother and the Whore (1973), 313, 327

Mulvey, Laura: and *The Bad Sister*, 194–200, 202–5; and experimental film, 11, 14; films of, 13, 16, 217; and the fe-

male spectator, 242; and *Riddles of the
Sphinx*, 49–53, 56–58, 60–62
Munch, Edvard, 206
murder, 278, 292–94. *See also* murderess
murderess: in *The Bad Sister*, 195–96; effect of patriarchy on, 287, 289–90,
292; as insane, 278; in *The Lady from
Shanghai*, 39; "masculine" tendencies
of, 269, 271; and menstruation, 270–
71, 285; as mystery, 274; and patriarchy, 282, 293, 300; in *Persona*, 73; as
"perverse," 269; and promiscuity, 276,
278; punishment for, 280, 282; and rebellion, 283–84; and relationship with
mother, 276, 278; sanity of, 285; as
scapegoat, 292; sisters as, 181–82;
stereotypes of, 271–72, 284–85; in
Straight through the Heart, 113; as
subject in film, 66, 176–77, 269–300.
See also The Bad Sister; criminal; murder; *A Question of Silence*; *Straight
through the Heart*; *Violette*
musical: and the American Dream, 159,
164–65; avant-garde, 14, 132; as comedy, 138, 143; as genre, 22; and the
love triangle, 162; mainstream, 17;
melodrama and, 163–64, 167; parody
of, 168–70; and patriarchy, 134, 164;
rejection of male discourse in, 154–55;
and sexual differences, 133; and the
spectator, 157–58; stereotype of
women in, 135–37; woman and, 132–
71. *See also Dames*
Music in the Dark (1974), 81
myth: discourse of, 32–62; in *The Lady
from Shanghai*, 32–49; in mother as,
46; *A Question of Silence*, 282–83; in
Riddles of the Sphinx, 49–62; woman
as, 16, 19, 32, 37, 49–50. *See also* discourse, of mythology; fairy tales; Oedipal complex; Oedipal tale; Sphinx

Nanook of the North (1920–1921), 268
narcissism, 43, 47–48, 97. *See also* Freud,
Sigmund
narrative: development of, 305; in *Riddles of the Sphinx*, 57, 60–62; stream-
of-consciousness, 54, 61, 212, 319,
323; structure of, 46, 244–45; wom-
en's, 97–98. *See also* language
Nelson, Gunvor, 26–31, 242, 316

Ness, Ellion, 27
Newman, Paul, 250
Night of the Living Dead (1968), 313–14
Nin, Anaïs, 57, 300
9 to 5 (1980), 287
Nochlin, Linda, 4, 7
Norwood, Robin, 93, 94, 101
Notorious (1946), 17, 254–55
Now, Voyager (1942), 3
Nowell-Smith, Geoffrey, 110
Nozière, Violette, 272, 274, 278, 381
nude, female, 25–26, 28, 247, 323

That Obscure Object of Desire (1977),
311–12
The Odd Couple (1968), 216
Odyssey, 37–39
Oedipal complex: in film, 22, 87; in *The
Lady from Shanghai*, 70; in *Letter
from an Unknown Woman*, 97, 104,
106, 107; and male canon, 9; in *Per-
sona*, 74, 76–77, 79–80; in *Straight
through the Heart*, 118; in *Violette*, 78,
277–78, 279; and *The Bad Sister*, 199.
See also Oedipal tale
Oedipal tale: and *The Lady from Shang-
hai*, 39–44, 46, 50, 51; and *Riddles of
the Sphinx*, 57, 61. *See also* Oedipal
complex
O'Hara, Maureen, 148
Old Acquaintance (1943), 217, 223, 233
Olympia (Manet), 28
Ophuls, Max: and *Caught*, 314–15; film
techniques of, 218; and *Letter from an
Unknown Woman*, 16, 89–90, 107,
111, 114, 125, 127
*The Other Half of the Sky: A China
Memoir*, 243
Ottinger, Ulriche, 17, 306
Our Betters (1933), 224
Our Relations (1936), 179
Ouspenskaya, Maria, 148
Oxenberg, Jan, 251

Pabst, G. W., 204, 302
Pandora's Box (1929), 204, 302
Paris, 120, 248
parody: of classical cinema, 317; of critical discourse, 323–24; in *The Man
Who Envied Women*, 316, 325; of musicals, 144, 146, 166, 168–70; of polit-